SOCIAL PRINCIPLES
AND
ECONOMIC LIFE

REV. JOHN F. CRONIN, S.S., Ph.D.

ASSISTANT DIRECTOR, DEPARTMENT OF SOCIAL ACTION
NATIONAL CATHOLIC WELFARE CONFERENCE

[REVISED EDITION]

**THE BRUCE PUBLISHING COMPANY
MILWAUKEE**

NIHIL OBSTAT:

VERY REV. MONSIGNOR VINCENT A. YZERMANS
Censor deputatus

IMPRIMATUR:

✠ PATRICK A. O'BOYLE
Archbishop of Washington
May 19, 1966

Library of Congress Catalog Card Number: 66–24254

(5/66)

TO THE MEMORY OF MY MOTHER

PREFACE

THIS book offers to its readers a studied explanation of Catholic social principles in the light of American economic life. The social teaching of the Church is basically a mixture of ethics, moral theology, and prudent judgment as applied to the field of social economics. It is called Catholic because of its immediate source. But its principles are so founded in human nature that men of all creeds can readily see its truth and wisdom. While it has been presented authoritatively by various statements of recent popes, its roots go back to the inspired words of Holy Writ.

The primary sources used are the social writings and addresses of recent popes. These statements crystallize and apply to modern conditions social principles developed from scriptural teachings and natural law. In presenting Catholic social teaching, textual excerpts from authoritative sources are reprinted in each chapter. This practice gives the reader convenient opportunity to study the documents which are being explained and applied. Each set of excerpts is then explained in the light of general ethical and moral principles. Where useful, background material is supplied. This is sometimes necessary where the full meaning of writings destined for the entire world may not be immediately evident in terms of our language and customs. Moreover, there are many important points where the encyclicals are either silent or not conclusive. In these cases moralists often differ in their views. On controversial questions, different points of view are presented and references given for further study. Moreover, the best available experts have been consulted. In this way, a distinction is made between what is clear or generally agreed upon and what is still the subject of serious discussion.

The ethical commentary is accompanied by an application of principles to current American economic conditions. Economic application is especially needed as a service to the great body of Catholics, clergy and laity, who are already familiar with the broad principles of social ethics. Unfortunately, these principles are not easily applied in the complex world of economic life. In many cases, it is even difficult to learn the facts to which principles pertain. Even when the facts are known, there may be disputes as to the relevant economic laws governing the situation. Yet, unless moral norms are applied properly, they remain abstract and indefinite. We have not hesitated in other fields, such as medical ethics, to face delicate issues in applying principles. There is even greater need in the social field for concrete application, since the popes, dealing with world-wide problems, must necessarily speak in general terms. But time and again they have urged Catholic social scientists to apply principles to the problems of their day and age.

Practical application is likewise needed if our teachings are to be honored by the non-Catholic world. Too often Catholics are secretly apologetic about their social teachings. They act as if they were an *arcana disciplina*, truths too sacred to be bandied about. Such diffidence is largely unwarranted. On the contrary, when our principles are presented in language and context familiar to Americans, they usually meet with enthusiastic acceptance.

In presenting our social ethics, the order of treatment involves a progression from general principles to fields of more limited application. There are three main parts to the present book. In the first, the social problem is outlined in relation to the broad bases of human nature. The general social teachings of the Church are given. Judgment is passed upon other social philosophies prevalent in the modern world. In the second part, the focus is narrowed to special fields, such as capital, labor, wages, family, property problems, and the state. Finally, in the third part, there are considered other vital social institutions and problems, such as international economic life, race problems, and rural life. The concluding chapter relates social principles to social action.

Two types of bibliographical aids are offered. Each chapter is followed by a select reading list, usually confined to standard works generally available in libraries. In addition, a more comprehensive annotated series of lists is offered as an Appendix to the book.

It is hoped that this book will appeal to clergy and laity concerned with the urgent social problems of our time and anxious to understand the teaching of the Church on these issues. The present study is also designed for textbook use in our seminaries, colleges, and universities.

In a time of inner renewal in the Church and ferment in the world, there is need for careful, systematic study of the social teachings of our popes and bishops. Thus we shall be solidly grounded for our crusade to restore all things in Christ, that our society may be inspired by justice and charity.

REV. JOHN F. CRONIN, S.S.

PREFACE TO THE REVISED EDITION

WHEN the first edition of this book was published in 1959, both the author and the publisher had reason to expect that no major changes would be needed for at least a decade. They reckoned without Pope John XXIII and his *aggiornamento*. The publication of *Mater et Magistra* and *Pacem in Terris* and the new winds coursing through the open window of the Church made substantial revisions imperative.

Primary among the changes are the inclusion in most chapters of excerpts from these two encyclicals, with corresponding deletions of less timely earlier material. To the author's surprise, date of publication was no guide in determining what was timely. The great social encyclicals of Popes Leo XIII and Pius XI were hardly touched in the pruning. In the writings of Pope Pius XII, it was noted that the more carefully prepared solemn addresses and broadcasts to the world survived better than occasional talks to pilgrims.

When the material quoted from Popes John XXIII and Paul VI involved a notable advance in Catholic social thinking, it was necessary to comment on these developments in the appropriate chapters. This was particularly true in regard to socialization, democracy, communism, Christian social order, labor-management relations, property, international problems, agriculture, and Catholic action.

Apart from new encyclical commentary, there was need to face up to radical changes in certain problems treated in the first edition of this book. Communism, poverty, and race are examples of issues calling for new treatment. Finally, the opportunity to make major changes permitted a tightening up of arguments that seemed too extensive for current needs. Sections on profits, the living wage, and concrete steps for social reform were rewritten in a tightened and more direct fashion.

JOHN F. CRONIN, S.S.

ACKNOWLEDGMENTS

THIS present edition would not have been possible without the gracious willingness of authorities at the National Catholic Welfare Conference to release the author temporarily from office duties. In particular, the Most Reverend Patrick A. O'Boyle, Chairman of the Administrative Board of N.C.W.C., was most solicitous that the author have the time and privacy necessary for this task. Thanks are also due to Monsignors Paul Tanner, General Secretary of N.C.W.C., and George G. Higgins, Director of the Department of Social Action, who not only agreed to this decision, but also generously offered to assume many of the duties assigned to the author. Likewise, many other colleagues in N.C.W.C., the National Council of Churches, and the Synagogue Council of America were most understanding in carrying a larger share of the burden of interreligious, interracial work.

The editors of *The Pope Speaks* graciously allowed quotations from their valuable periodical. Eugene Willging, late director of the Mullen Library at Catholic University, extended full use of the facilities of the Library.

Miss Mira F. Luy offered valuable assistance in editing the manuscript and proofreading printed copy.

To all, the author expresses a heartfelt "Thank You."

AUTHORITATIVE REFERENCES

THE following list names the major documents used as authoritative sources in the text. They are listed in chronological order in each main heading. After each document, a key is given which indicates the source used for the text cited. Where possible, English translations or originals were used. Where there was a discrepancy in dates between the translation and the original in *Discorsi e Radiomessagi*, the date given in the original was used. Numbers in parentheses after each reference indicate the chapters in which the document was cited. If citations are found in practically every chapter, this is noted by the use of *passim* instead of chapter numbers.

Pope Leo XIII

Immortale Dei, November 1, 1885 (Husslein) (IV, XIII)
Rerum Novarum, May 15, 1891 (N.C.W.C.) (*passim*)
Graves de Communi, January 18, 1901 (Husslein) (II, VIII, XVII)
Letter to Italian Bishops, December 8, 1902 (A.S.S.) (XVII)

St. Pius X

Il Fermo Proposito, June 11, 1905 (P.Pe.) (P.P.) (XVII)

Pope Benedict XV

Letter to Bishop of Bergamo, March 11, 1920 (C.L.) (XVII)

Pope Pius XI

Ubi Arcano, December 23, 1922 (Husslein) (XIV)
Casti Connubii, December 31, 1930 (Husslein) (X, XI)
Quadragesimo Anno, May 15, 1931 (N.C.W.C.) (*passim*)
Non Abbiamo Bisogno, June 29, 1931 (Husslein) (V)
Caritate Christi Compulsi, May 3, 1932 (Husslein) (I, III, XVII)
Ad Catholici Sacerdotii, December 20, 1935 (Husslein) (XVII)
Mit Brennender Sorge, March 14, 1937 (Husslein) (III)
Atheistic Communism, March 19, 1937 (N.C.W.C.) (*passim*)

Pope Pius XII
1939–1948

Summi Pontificatus, October 20, 1939 (P.P.) (IV, V, XIV, XVII)
Sertum Laetitiae, November 1, 1939 (P.P. and N.C.) (IX)
La Solennità della Pentecoste, June 1, 1941 (P.P.) (II, III, IV)
Nell' Alba, December 24, 1941 (P.P.) (I, III, XIV)
Christmas Broadcast, 1942 (P.P.) (III, IX, XII)
To Italian Workers, June 13, 1943 (C.M.) (XI)
Mystici Corporis, June 29, 1943 (N.C.) (XV)
Radio Address, September 1, 1944 (C.M.) (I, III, XII)
Christmas Message, 1944 (XIII)
To Italian Workers, March 11, 1945 (C.M.) (VII)
To College of Cardinals, June 2, 1945 (C.M.) (V)
To the Holy Roman Rota, Oct. 2, 1945 (D.R.) (XIII)
On Women's Duties, October 21, 1945 (C.M.) (I, V, XI)
To Negro Publishers, May 27, 1946 (Osservatore Romano) (XV)
To Sacred College of Cardinals, June 2, 1947 (C.M.) (II)
Letter to Semaines Sociales, July 18, 1947 (C.M.) (VII)
To Sacred College of Cardinals, June 2, 1948 (C.M.) (XVII)
To Christian Association of Italian Workers, June 29, 1948 (C.M.) (IX)
To Young Men, September 12, 1948 (C.M.) (II)
To Representatives of Fiat Automobile Plant, October 31, 1948 (C.M.) (III)

1949–1955

To Catholic Employers, May 7, 1949 (C.M.) (IV, VII, VIII, XIII)
To Women of Italian Catholic Action, July 24, 1949 (C.M.) (XI)
Letter to Semaines Sociales, July, 1949 (N.C.) (II)
To International Union of Family Organizations, September 20, 1949 (D.R.)
   (X)
Address to International Congresses for Social Study and Social Action, June
   3, 1950 (C.M.) (VIII, XIII)
Humani Generis, August 12, 1950 (N.C.) (II)
Christmas Message, 1950 (N.C.) (XI)
To Spanish Employers and Workers, March 11, 1951 (D.R.) (XII)
To Delegates of Italian Catholic Action, July 16, 1952 (N.C.) (XV)
To Members of Pax Christi, September 13, 1952 (N.C.) (XVII)
To Austrian Catholics, September 14, 1952 (C.M.) (I, VIII)
Christmas Message, 1952 (C.M.) (I, VIII, IX, X, XI)
On Centenary of St. Thomas the Apostle, December 31, 1952 (D.R.) (IV)
To Italian Catholic Workers Association, May 14, 1953 (N.C.) (XVII)
To Autonomous Institute of Popular Housing, November 21, 1953 (N.C.)
   (XI)
To Italian Catholic Jurists, December 6, 1953 (N.C.) (XIV)
To Cardinals, Archbishops, and Bishops of Rome, November 2, 1954 (T.P.S.)
   (II)
To Railroad Workers of Rome, June 26, 1955 (T.P.S.) (IX)
Christmas Message, 1955 (T.P.S.) (IX)

1956–1958

To the Italian Federation of Commerce, February 17, 1956 (T.P.S.) (V, VIII, XI)

To Members of the Vatican Diplomatic Corps, March 4, 1956 (T.P.S.) (III)

To the Society for the Construction of Waterworks, April 13, 1956 (T.P.S.) (XIII)

To Spanish Social Week, May, 1956 (A.A.S.) (IV)

To the Apostolate of the Sea, September 7, 1956 (D.R.) (XV)

To the International Association of Economists, September 9, 1956 (T.P.S.) (X)

Radio Address to International Congress of Catholic Doctors, September 11, 1956 (T.P.S.) (III)

To International Association for Financial and Fiscal Law, October 2, 1956 (T.P.S.) (XII)

Radio Address to the Federation of Italian Women, October 14, 1956 (T.P.S.) (XI)

To Pilgrimage of Working People from the City of Terni, November 18, 1956 (T.P.S.) (II)

Christmas Message, 1956 (T.P.S.) (II, III)

To Christian Union of Executives and Businessmen, March 7, 1957 (T.P.S.) (X)

To Assembly of the International Movement of Catholic Intellectuals, April 27, 1957 (T.P.S.) (II)

To "Stations de Plein Air" Movement, May 3, 1957 (T.P.S.) (XI)

To Christian Associations of Italian Workers, June 7, 1957 (T.P.S.) (IX, X)

To World Union of Catholic Women's Organizations, September 29, 1957 (T.P.S.) (XVII)

Aspects of Automation, October 23, 1957 (T.P.S.) (X)

To Directors of Chemical Products Organizations, January 10, 1958 (T.P.S.) (IX)

To Italian Workers, May 1, 1958 (N.C.) (IV)

To Italian Federation of Middlemen and Business Agents, June 22, 1958 (N.C.) (II)

To Delegates of the Hematological Congress, September 5, 1958 (T.P.S.) (XV)

Pope John XXIII

To Members of U.N. Housing Committee, November 14, 1958 (N.C.) (XI)

To Italian Catholic Jurists, December 11, 1958 (N.C.) (XIII)

To Christian Association of Industrialists and Managers, January 30, 1959 (T.P.S.) (VII)

Mater et Magistra, May 15, 1961 (T.P.S.) (passim)

Cardinal Cicognani to Canadian Social Week, October 16, 1961 (N.C.) (X)

Pacem in Terris, April 11, 1963 (T.P.S.) (passim)

Pope Paul VI

Address to President Kennedy, July 2, 1963 (N.C.) (XV)

Address to Secretary General Thant, July 11, 1963 (N.C.) (XIV)

Papal Secretariat of State, to French Social Week, July, 1963 (N.C.) (XII)
Cardinal Cicognani, Letter to Canadian Social Week, August 16, 1963 (N.C.)
(IX)
To Pastoral Study Week, September 6, 1963 (N.C.) (VI)
Ecclesiam Suam, August 6, 1964 (N.C.) (VI)

Vatican Council II

Message to Humanity, October 20, 1962 (N.C.) (XV)
Constitution on the Church, November 21, 1964 (T.P.S.) (XV, XVII)
Declaration on the Relation of the Church to Non-Christian Religions, October
28, 1965 (N.C.) (XV)
Decree on the Apostolate of the Laity, November 18, 1965 (N.C.C.M.)
(IV, XVII)
Constitution on the Church in the Modern World, December 7, 1965 (Guild
Press) (II, III, IV, VI, IX, XII, XV)

American Hierarchy

Pastoral Letter, 1919 (H) (VII)
Discrimination and the Christian Conscience, 1958 (N.C.) (XV)
Racial Justice and Harmony, 1963 (N.C.) (XV)

Other Authorities

Summa Theologiae, St. Thomas Aquinas (IV)
Peace in Industry, Australian Hierarchy, 1947 (A.N.S.C.A.), (IX)
Socialization, Australian Hierarchy, 1948 (C.M.) (XII)
Pastoral Letter, French Cardinals, September 8, 1949 (C.M.) (V)
Pastoral Letter, Hierarchy of Quebec, February, 1950 (S.E.) (IX, X)
Morality in Public Life, Australian Hierarchy, 1950 (C.M.) (II)
Standard of Living, Australian Hierarchy, 1954 (C.M.) (X)
The Church in the Modern World, French Hierarchy, June, 1954 (N.C.)
(VI)
On Right-to-Work Law, Bishops of State of Ohio, March 20, 1958 (N.C.)
(IX)
Code of Social Principles, 1952 English translation of 1948 French revision
(Oxford: Catholic Social Guild) (II, III, IV, VII)

Key

A.A.S.: Acta Apostolicae Sedis (Rome: Typographia Vaticana, 1909–)
A.S.S.: Acta Sanctae Sedis (Rome: Typographia Vaticana, 1878–1908)
A.N.S.C.A.: Australian National Secretariat of Catholic Action (Melbourne,
Australia)
C.L.: Ryan, J. A., and Husslein, J., The Church and Labor (New York: Mac-
millan, 1920)
C.M.: Catholic Mind
D.R.: Discorsi e Radiomessagi di sua Santità Pio XII (Rome: Tipographia
Poliglotta Vaticana, 1939–1959)
Guild Press: The Documents of Vatican II (New York: Guild Press, 1966)
H.: Huebner, R. M., Our Bishops Speak (Milwaukee: Bruce, 1952)

Husslein: Husslein, J. (ed.), *Social Wellsprings* (Milwaukee: Bruce, 1940–1942)

N.C.: National Catholic Welfare Conference

N.C.C.M.: National Council of Catholic Men

P.P.: Koenig, H. (ed.), *Principles for Peace* (Milwaukee: Bruce, 1943)

P.Pe.: *The Pope and the People* (London: Catholic Truth Society, 1937)

S.E.: *Service extérieur d'éducation sociale*, Quebec

T.P.S.: *The Pope Speaks* (3622 12th Street, N.E., Washington, D. C. 20017)

See also Sister M. Claudia Carlen, I.H.M., *A Guide to the Encyclicals of the Roman Pontiffs* (New York: H. W. Wilson, 1939), *Guide to the Documents of Pius XII* (Westminster, Md.: Newman, 1951), and *Dictionary of Papal Pronouncements* (New York: Kenedy, 1958). These books list original sources, translations, and important commentaries in connection with major pontifical documents.

N.B.: When paragraph numbers are used in the excerpts cited throughout the book, they correspond to those followed in the editions listed under the Authoritative References noted above.

CONTENTS

PART I. THE CHRISTIAN SOCIAL ORDER

Part I

THE CHRISTIAN SOCIAL ORDER

Chapter I

THE SOCIAL QUESTION

SOCIAL AND ECONOMIC EXPLOITATION

John XXIII, Mater et Magistra

10. Leo XIII spoke in a time of social and economic upheaval, of heightening tensions and actual revolt. Against this dark background, the brilliance of his teaching stands out in clear relief.

11. As is well known, the outlook that prevailed on economic matters was for the most part a purely naturalistic one, which denied any correlation between economics and morality. Personal gain was considered the only valid motive for economic activity. In business the main operative principle was that of free and unrestricted competition. Interest on capital, prices — whether of goods or of services — profits and wages, were to be determined by the purely mechanical application of the laws of the market place. Every precaution was to be taken to prevent the civil authority from intervening in any way in economic matters. The status of trade unions varied in different countries. They were either forbidden, tolerated, or recognized as having private legal personality only.

12. In an economic world of this character, it was the might of the strongest which not only arrogated to itself the force of law, but also dominated the ordinary business relationships between individuals, and thereby undermined the whole economic structure.

13. Enormous riches accumulated in the hands of a few, while large numbers of workingmen found themselves in conditions of ever increasing hardship. Wages were insufficient even to the point of reaching starvation level, and working conditions were often of such a nature as to be injurious alike to health, morality, and religious faith. Especially inhuman were the working conditions to which women and children were sometimes subjected. There was also the constant specter of unemployment and the progressive disruption of family life.

14. The natural consequence of all this was a spirit of indignation and open protest on the part of the workingman, and a widespread tendency to subscribe to extremist theories far worse in their effects than the evils they purported to remedy.

Pius XI, Quadragesimo Anno

3. For toward the close of the nineteenth century, the new kind of economic life that had arisen and the new developments of industry had gone to the point in most countries that human society was clearly becoming divided more and more into two classes. One class, very small in number, was enjoying almost all the advantages which modern inventions so abundantly provided; the other, embracing the huge multitude of

working people, oppressed by wretched poverty, was vainly seeking escape from the straits wherein it stood.

54. Property, that is, "capital," has undoubtedly long been able to appropriate too much to itself. Whatever was produced, whatever returns accrued, capital claimed for itself, hardly leaving to the worker enough to restore and renew his strength. For the doctrine was preached that all accumulation of capital falls by an absolutely insuperable economic law to the rich, and that by the same law the workers are given over and bound to perpetual want, to the scantiest of livelihoods. It is true, indeed, that things have not always and everywhere corresponded with this sort of teaching of the so-called Manchesterian Liberals; yet it cannot be denied that economic-social institutions have moved steadily in that direction. That these false ideas, these erroneous suppositions, have been vigorously assailed, and not by those alone who through them were being deprived of their innate right to obtain better conditions, will surprise no one.

59. But since manufacturing and industry have so rapidly pervaded and occupied countless regions, not only in the countries called new, but also in the realms of the Far East that have been civilized from antiquity, the number of the nonowning working poor has increased enormously and their groans cry to God from the earth. Added to them is the huge army of rural wage workers, pushed to the lowest level of existence and deprived of all hope of ever acquiring "some property in land," and, therefore, permanently bound to the status of nonowning worker unless suitable and effective remedies are applied.

60. Yet while it is true that the status of nonowning worker is to be carefully distinguished from pauper-

ism, nevertheless the immense multitude of the nonowning workers on the one hand and the enormous riches of certain very wealthy men on the other establish an unanswerable argument that the riches which are so abundantly produced in our age of "industrialism," as it is called, are not rightly distributed and equitably made available to the various classes of the people.

62. All these things which Our Predecessor has not only suggested but clearly and openly proclaimed, We emphasize with renewed insistence in Our present Encyclical; and unless utmost efforts are made without delay to put them into effect, let no one persuade himself that public order, peace, and the tranquillity of human society can be effectively defended against agitators of revolution.

105. . . . it is obvious that not only is wealth concentrated in our times but an immense power and despotic economic dictatorship is consolidated in the hands of a few, who often are not owners but only the trustees and managing directors of invested funds which they administer according to their own arbitrary will and pleasure.

109. Free competition has destroyed itself; economic dictatorship has supplanted the free market; unbridled ambition for power has likewise succeeded greed for gain; all economic life has become tragically hard, inexorable, and cruel. To these are to be added the grave evils that have resulted from an intermingling and shameful confusion of the functions and duties of public authority with those of the economic sphere — such as, one of the worst, the virtual degradation of the majesty of the state, which, although it ought to sit on high like a queen and supreme arbitress, free from all partiality and

intent upon the one common good and justice, is become a slave, surrendered and delivered to the passions and greed of men.

132. Hence arises that unquenchable thirst for riches and temporal goods, which has at all times impelled men to break God's laws and trample upon the rights of their neighbors, but which, on account of the present system of economic life, is laying far more snares for human frailty. Since the instability of economic life, and especially of its structure, exacts of those engaged in it most intense and unceasing effort, some have become so hardened to the stings of conscience as to hold that they are allowed, in any manner whatsoever, to increase their profits and use means, fair or foul, to protect their hard-won wealth against sudden changes of fortune. The easy gains that a market unregulated by law opens to everybody attracts large numbers to buying and selling goods, and they, their one aim being to make quick profits with the least expenditure of work, raise or lower prices by their uncontrolled business dealings so rapidly according to their own caprice and greed that they nullify the wisest forecasts of producers. The laws passed to promote corporate business, while dividing and limiting the risk of business, have given occasion to the most sordid license. For We observe that consciences are little affected by this reduced obligation of accountability; that furthermore, by hiding under the shelter of a joint name, the worst of injustices and frauds are perpetuated; and that, too, directors of business companies, forgetful of their trust, betray the rights of those whose savings they have undertaken to administer. Lastly, We must not omit to mention those crafty men who, wholly unconcerned about any honest usefulness of their work, do not scruple to stimulate the baser human desires and, when they are aroused, use them for their own profit.

135. With the rulers of economic life abandoning the right road, it was easy for the rank and file of workers everywhere to rush headlong also into the same chasm; and all the more so, because very many managements treated their workers like mere tools, with no concern at all for their souls, without indeed even the least thought of spiritual things. Truly the mind shudders at the thought of the grave dangers to which the morals of workers (particularly younger workers) and the modesty of girls and women are exposed in modern factories; when we recall how often the present economic scheme, and particularly the shameful housing conditions, create obstacles to the family bond and normal family life; when we remember how many obstacles are put in the way of the proper observance of Sundays and Holy Days; and when we reflect upon the universal weakening of that truly Christian sense through which even rude and unlettered men were wont to value higher things, and upon its substitution by the single preoccupation of getting in any way whatsoever one's daily bread. And thus bodily labor, which Divine Providence decreed to be performed, even after original sin, for the good at once of man's body and soul, is being everywhere changed into an instrument of perversion; for dead matter comes forth from the factory ennobled, while men there are corrupted and degraded.

Pius XI, On Atheistic Communism

47. But when on the one hand we see thousands of the needy, victims of real misery for various reasons beyond their control, and on the other so many round them who spend huge sums of money on useless things and frivolous amusement, We cannot fail to remark with sorrow not only that justice is poorly observed, but that the precept of charity also is not sufficiently appreciated, is not a vital thing in daily life.

Pius XI, Caritate Christi Compulsi

3. From greed arises mutual distrust, that casts a blight on all human dealings; from greed arises hateful envy, which makes a man consider the advantages of another as losses to himself; from greed arises narrow individualism, which orders and subordinates everything to its own advantages without taking account of others, on the contrary cruelly trampling underfoot all rights of others. Hence the disorder and inequality from which result the accumulation of the wealth of nations in the hands of a small group of individuals who manipulate the market of the world at their own caprice, to the immense harm of the masses. . . .

28. In place of moral laws, which disappear together with the loss of faith in God, brute force is imposed, tramping on every right. Old-time fidelity and honesty of conduct and mutual relations, extolled so much even by the orators and poets of paganism, now give place to speculation in one's own affairs, as in those of others, without reference to conscience.

Pius XII, Nell' Alba, Christmas, 1941

1748. For the human spirit, overwhelmed in the confusion of this moral abyss, by its alienation from God and Christian practices, no other course remained but that of turning all its thoughts, purposes, and enterprises and every evaluation of men's possessions, actions, and labor and directing them to the material world, striving and sweating with might and main to spread out in space, to surpass all previous accomplishments in the attainment of riches and power, to engage in a competition of speed, to produce in greater quantity and quality everything that material advancement and progress seemed to require. These very symptoms appear in politics as an unlimited demand for expansion and political influence without regard to moral standards. In economic life they are represented by the predominance of mammoth concerns and trusts. In the social sphere it is the agglomeration of huge populations in cities and in the districts dominated by industry and trade, an agglomeration that is accompanied by the complete uprooting of the masses who have lost their standards of life, home, work, love, and hatred. By this new conception of thought and life, all ideas of social life have been impregnated with a purely mechanico-materialistic character.

1749. With the increasing lack of restraint, outward compulsion and domination founded purely on power seemed to prevail over the forces of order, which established the relations of law and charity in their natural and supernatural foundations as they had been laid down by God. To the detriment of human dignity and personality as well as society, the conception makes headway that it is might which creates right. Thus private property is being abused on the one hand as a means of exploitation; on the other hand, as a reason for envy, revolt, and hatred. The situation ensuing therefrom is being exploited by a struggle of interests which is being waged without any restraint.

Pius XII, Radio Address, September 1, 1944

We see the small and medium holdings diminish and lose their value in human society, and constrained to join in a conflict ever more difficult and without hope of success.

On the one side, We see immense riches dominating public and private economic life and often even civil life; on the other, the countless number of those who, deprived of every direct or indirect security of their own livelihood, take no further interest in the true and higher values of the spirit, abandon their aspiration to genuine freedom and throw themselves at the feet of any political party, slaves to whoever promises them in some way bread and security; and experience shows of what tyranny, under such circumstances, human nature is capable even in our times.

Pius XII, On Women's Duties, October 21, 1945

. . . can a woman . . . hope for her real well-being from a regime dominated by capitalism? . . . You know its characteristic signs and you yourselves are bearing its burden: excessive concentration of population in cities; the constant, all-absorbing increase of big industries; the difficult and precarious state of others, notably those of artisans and agricultural workers; and the disturbing increase in unemployment.

THE SOCIAL PROBLEM TODAY

Pius XII, To Austrian Catholics, September 14, 1952

Today the Church looks back upon the first phase of modern social dispute. At its center stood the problem of the workingman: the distress of the proletariat and the task of lifting this class of society, exposed defenselessly to the caprices of economic ups and downs, to a status of dignity equal to that enjoyed by the other classes, and of endowing it with clearly defined rights. This task has been solved — at any rate in its essentials — and the Catholic world has honestly and effectively contributed to its solution. Even if in certain groups of countries the realization of this problem and action came very late at the eleventh hour, the social principles and directives stated by the successors of St. Peter during the past sixty years have, on the whole, become common property of Catholic thought and action.

If the signs of the times are not misleading, then the questions and task coming to the fore in the second phase of the social dispute, which we have probably already entered, are of a different nature. We shall now point out two of them:

The overcoming of the class struggle through an organic co-ordination of employer and employee, for class struggle can never be a goal of Catholic social ethics. The Church is always aware of its duties toward all classes and layers of the people.

In the second place, the protection of the individual and of the family against the vortex which threatens to draw them into an all-embracing socialization, at the end of which looms the very real nightmare of "Leviathan." The Church will conduct this fight to the utmost, because the highest things are at stake: human dignity and the salvation of the soul.

Pius XII, Christmas Message, 1952

Modern industry has unquestionably had beneficial results, but the problem which arises today is this: will a world in which the only economic form to find acceptance is a vast productive system be equally fitted to exert a happy influence upon society in general and upon the three fundamental institutions of society in particular?

We must answer that the impersonal character of such a world is contrary to the fundamentally personal nature of those institutions which the Creator has given to human society. In fact, marriage and the family, the state, and private property tend of their very nature to form man as a person, to protect and render him capable of contributing through his own voluntary co-operation and personal responsibility to the similarly personal life and development of human relations. The creative wisdom of God is therefore alien to that system of impersonal unity which strikes at the human person, who is origin and end of society, and in the depths of His being an image of his God.

      *   *   *

Here may be recognized the origin and source of that phenomenon which is submerging modern man under its tide of anguish: his "depersonalization." In large measure his identity and name have been taken from him; in many of the more important activities of life he has been reduced to a mere material object of society, while society itself has been transformed into an impersonal system and into a cold organization of force.

John XXIII, Mater et Magistra

46. In the twenty years which have elapsed since the changing economic climate noted at that time by Pius XII the economic scene has undergone a radical transformation, both in the internal structure of the various states and in their relations with one another.

47. In the field of science, technology, and economics we have the discovery of nuclear energy, and its application first to the purposes of war and later, increasingly, to peaceful ends; the practically limitless possibilities of chemistry in the production of synthetic materials; the growth of automation in industry and public services; the modernization of agriculture; the easing of communications, especially by radio and television; faster transportation and the initial conquest of interplanetary space.

The social and political fields

48. In the social field we have the development of social insurance and,

in the more economically advanced communities, the introduction of social security systems. Men in labor unions are showing a more responsible awareness of major social and economic problems. There is a progressive improvement in basic education, a wider distribution of essential commodities, greater opportunities for advancement in industry and the consequent breaking down of class barriers, and a keener interest in world affairs shown by people of average education.

At the same time, however, this assessment of the increased efficiency of social and economic systems in a growing number of communities serves also to bring to light certain glaring discrepancies. There is, in the first place, a progressive lack of balance between agriculture on the one hand, and industry and public services on the other. Secondly, there are areas of varying economic prosperity within the same political communities. Finally — to take a world view — one observes a marked disparity in the economic wealth possessed by different countries.

49. To turn to the political field, We observe many changes. In a number of countries all classes of citizens are taking a part in public life, and public authorities are injecting themselves more each day into social and economic matters. We are witnessing the break-away from colonialism and the attainment of political independence by the peoples of Asia and Africa. Drawn together by their common needs nations are becoming daily more interdependent. There is, moreover, an ever extending network of societies and organizations which set their sights beyond the aims and interests of individual countries and concentrate on the economic, social, cultural, and political welfare of all nations throughout the world.

Millions in dire straits

68. We are filled with an overwhelming sadness when We contemplate the sorry spectacle of millions of workers in many lands and entire continents condemned through the inadequacy of their wages to live with their families in utterly subhuman conditions. This is probably due to the fact that the process of industrialization in these countries is only in its initial stages, or is still not sufficiently developed.

69. Nevertheless, in some of these lands the enormous wealth, the unbridled luxury, of the privileged few stands in violent, offensive contrast to the utter poverty of the vast majority. In some parts of the world men are being subjected to inhuman privations so that the output of the national economy can be increased at a rate of acceleration beyond what would be possible if regard were had to social justice and equity. And in other countries a notable percentage of income is absorbed in building up an ill-conceived national prestige, and vast sums are spent on armaments.

70. In economically developed countries, relatively unimportant services, and services of doubtful value, frequently carry a disproportionately high rate of remuneration, while the diligent and profitable work of whole classes of honest, hard-working men gets scant reward. Their rate of pay is quite inadequate to meet the basic needs of life. It in no way corresponds to the contribution they make to the good of the community, to the profits of the company for which they work, and to the general national economy.

260. This era in which we live is in the grip of deadly errors; it is torn by deep disorders. But it is also an era which offers to those who work with the Church immense possibilities in the field of the apostolate. And therein lies our hope.

John XXIII, Pacem in Terris

156. What has so far been achieved is insufficient compared with what needs to be done; all men must realize that. Every day provides a more important, a more fitting enterprise to which they must turn their hands — industry, trade unions, professional organizations, insurance, cultural institutions, the law, politics, medical and recreational facilities, and other such activities. The age in which we live needs all these things. It is an age in which men, having discovered the atom and achieved the break-through into outer space, are now exploring other avenues, leading to almost limitless horizons.

YOUNGER readers of the preceding quotations may be astonished at the strength and even violence of papal language in condemning social and economic abuses. Fortunately, most of such readers have had no direct experience of the extreme evils cited. Nonetheless, there are two valid reasons for citing these passages and for beginning with a study of what is called the "social question." The first reason is the old adage that history is man's greatest teacher. When we understand the historical reasons for certain laws and institutions, we can better realize their purpose in modern society.

A second reason for careful reading of the strong indictments of social abuses is the tragic fact that many still persist in various parts of the world today. A Roman Jesuit, one of the world's great social scientists, remarked in a private conversation: "It is most difficult for the Holy Father to address the world on social and economic problems. He confronts a world that lives partly in the times of Pope Leo XIII, partly in the times of Pope Pius XI, and yet a world that has seen the exuberant prosperity of such nations as the United States and West Germany."

Many areas of Asia, Africa, and Latin America are indeed blighted by the evils cited by Pope Leo XIII. Extreme poverty lives almost side by side with fabulous wealth. By contrast the Common Market appears to be leading Europe to unprecedented prosperity. Within the communist world, divergences and strains are beginning to appear, with some nations progressing and others either stagnant or regressive.

Even to understand American economic society, and its place in world affairs, it is useful and even necessary to seek a wider historical perspective. With this in mind, we begin by discussing a civilization that in many ways reflected Christian morality. We refer to medieval society, so often favorably commented upon by the popes. Next we study the breakdown of this society and the advent of modern industrialism, with its many social problems. Finally, we try to pinpoint the social problem in the United States today.

A Christian Social Order. Medieval society in Europe is important to the Christian social scientist mainly because religious ideals permeated the *institutions* of that society. There is a substantial difference between moral principles as accepted by individuals, and these same principles embedded in social institutions. Individual moral conduct reflects the opportunities and moral strength of the persons concerned. But when right principles are enmeshed in the very fiber of society, through its laws, customs, and institutions, those who are morally weak or even evil face powerful compulsions to conform to accepted standards.

The term institutions might well be explained here, since it recurs frequently in the chapters to follow. An institution is a stable and deep-rooted pattern of human conduct. It is stronger and more fundamental than custom. The family, private property, and the prevailing code of business ethics can be described as institutions. By contrast, the practice of teen-age single dating would rather be called a custom, since fortunately it is not yet entrenched as a permanent feature of our society.

It is important that social institutions direct men toward goals consonant with the moral law. Otherwise it becomes extraordinarily difficult for men of good will to fight the pressures engendered by faulty social institutions. Catholics who feel that the social problem can be solved in the confessional alone, or in religion classes, or by pious practices, or by good personal leadership are misreading the lessons of history and sociology.

Insofar as the social question springs from human greed and avarice, from pride of life and lust for power, it will always be with us. Man, hurt in intellect and weakened in will, is prone to evil as well as good. There will always be selfish men, ambitious for power and material success, whatever the means used to accomplish their ends. But men do not act in a social vacuum. The sanctions of society have a strong impact upon the wills of individuals. Hence it is of compelling importance to study how social climate helps or hinders the influence of Christian principles upon economic life.

In medieval times, as today, the Church formulated a moral code for social life. But the influence of the Church upon society was far greater in the Middle Ages. Its teachings about justice, political life, property, the social virtues, avarice, and usury were often as effective in the marketplace as would be a Supreme Court decision in the United States today.

Good men were encouraged and evil men constrained by the body of principles laid down by theologians and canonists.

Church influence is best seen in such institutions as feudalism and the guild system, and in its teachings on the just price, usury, and property.

Feudalism is often treated in modern writings as the equivalent of slavery. But contemporary documents emphasize the fact that the serf, while in a status of dependence, had rights as well as duties. He was bound to the land, but he could not be expelled from it. There was effective machinery to protect his rights. In contrast to the anarchy of the Dark Ages, feudal society represented an advance toward the ideal of full freedom and human dignity. "All powerful custom determined every man's rights and obligations. This fact alone was enough to prevent the pitiless severity to which the free exercise of economic supremacy gives rise under the spur of profit."[1]

Medieval guilds were legally recognized organizations that both represented and regulated industrial and commercial activity. They aimed to protect the rights of both workers and employers, while safeguarding the consumer. To do this, they established standards of quality, training of apprentices, and fair prices. These guilds deteriorated starting with the fourteenth century. They became monopolistic and oppressive. But at their best periods they did apply moral concepts to economic society.

The ethical norm determining the conduct of the guilds was the common good, an expression of which was the just price. Basically this involved equality in exchange. The price of an article must conform to its true value, as determined by public authority or common estimate. It would be immoral for either a buyer or seller to exploit a monopoly position in order to lower or raise the price. The price should not be so low as to impoverish workers, artisans, or merchants; nor should it be so high as to deprive the poor of the necessities of life. The significant point is that this ethical norm was accepted by the commercial and industrial community and institutionalized in the guilds.[2]

Ethics also entered into the sphere of finance. The condemnation of

---

[1] H. Pirenne, *Economic and Social History of Medieval Europe* (New York: Harcourt, 1937), p. 64. Many historians hold that the power of law and custom, involving the consent of the governed, made medieval society democratic in a real sense. For an extensive documentation from non-Catholic sources, see R. W. and A. J. Carlyle, *A History of Medieval Political Teaching in the West* (New York: Putnam, 1903–1936). See also R. H. Tawney, *Religion and the Rise of Capitalism* (New York: Harcourt, 1926), and A. Fanfani, *Catholicism, Protestantism, and Capitalism* (New York: Sheed, 1936).

[2] The best English treatment of medieval ethical ideas is contained in G. A. O'Brien, *Essay on Mediaeval Economic Teaching* (New York: Longmans, 1920).

usury was bound to affect economic life. While a return from rent and partnership was permitted, pure interest was considered an unjust exaction. Many of the considerations which enter into the modern interest rate, such as a charge for the risk of loss, were allowed, but a fee for the use of money as such was outlawed. The basic reason for this was that money, in contrast to real property, was considered unproductive. Hence a charge for its use was an exploitation of another's needs, not a participation in a productive venture. The influence of Church teaching on usury was so great that, even in the late Middle Ages, the powerful Antwerp Bourse and the House of Fugger sent couriers to Rome for moral rulings on their transactions.

Above all these particular practices was a concept of property. Private ownership was considered to be in accord with the nature of man. Private property is a normal expression of man's right of ownership. But property should be used in such a way as to promote the common interest of all. Right laws and customs would lead to such a happy situation that the advantages of both private and common ownership would be preserved. Moreover, actual ownership would be diffused, since possession of property is an important distinction between the slave and the free man. The property owner has resources which minister to his freedom. Moreover, the social virtues, such as liberality, should guide the individual in the use of his property.[3]

Thus there emerges a picture of a theocentric society, with economic life governed by moral obligations embodied in social institutions. At its peak, this society combined a large measure of justice with economic stability. Yet it was not adverse to progress, as is testified by the great growth of commerce and industry during the medieval period. Such a society offers a striking contrast to modern notions, in that economic life was then strictly subordinate to cultural, moral, and religious considerations.

THE RISE OF THE SOCIAL PROBLEM

The system was to fail, although not from any inherent weakness in the approach. A combination of events served to sharpen man's acquisitive instincts, at the very time that a decline in religious fervor and observance was taking place. The fearful catastrophe of the Black Death (1347) in itself would have been sufficient to disrupt even the most stable of societies. Not only did it depopulate much of Europe, but its impact was hardest upon the leaders of society who ministered to the sick and dying.

[3] See W. J. McDonald, *The Social Value of Property According to Saint Thomas Aquinas* (Washington: Catholic University, 1939).

Religious fervor declined for other reasons as well. Many abuses grew within the Church. Schisms and heresies became more common. Even the papacy itself had unworthy members, while the period of exile at Avignon (1309–1377) was weakening and disruptive. These trends culminated in the Protestant Revolt. The influence of the Church upon society declined as it engaged in a terrific struggle for internal reform and the return of its lost members. It could be said that, from the sixteenth until the mid-nineteenth century, the Church was preoccupied with the hard core of doctrinal orthodoxy and moral reform.

The newly formed Protestant churches, after an uncertain beginning, were to turn away from the ideal of organized social morality. Both Luther and Calvin accepted much of the economic morality of the Church. But the branches springing from Lutheranism were to carry religious individualism to its logical conclusion. With religious belief left largely to personal conscience and private interpretation of Scripture, there was little chance for a widely accepted social morality to be imposed on the institutions of society. At the same time, the Calvinist root of Protestantism was to develop the concept of "calling." The sign of predestination to heaven was God's blessing upon one's "vocation." In the minds of many, this led to an equation of material success and divine approval.[4]

As the influence of religious and moral sanctions lessened, other factors were to offer positive stimulus to business enterprise. Among these was the revival of commerce which began with the Crusades. Commerce expanded until the quest for supplies and markets led to the discoveries of New-World colonial opportunities in the fifteenth and sixteenth centuries. The growth of merchant power in turn brought about a clash between the medieval city and the feudal nobility. This struggle gradually developed into the broader contests which led to modern nationalism. An alliance between merchant groups and ambitious lords favored the consolidation of national power, particularly in France and England. These new states then used every means to stimulate economic growth as an instrument for political power. By the seventeenth century, France under Louis XIV was even to impose a form of statism upon business, in order to regulate it in the interest of national strength.

---

[4] This point is treated in detail by Tawney and Fanfani, cited earlier. See also E. Troeltsch, *The Social Teaching of the Christian Churches* (London: Allen & Unwin, 1949). For current Protestant views, see E. Duff, *The Social Thought of the World Council of Churches* (New York: Association Press, 1956).

While commerce expanded, both of its own momentum and as a result of state encouragement, businessmen were growing restive under government controls. They turned eagerly to the theories formulated by the great pioneer economists of the eighteenth century. These theories are now known as *laissez-faire* individualism. It was held that economic life was regulated by its own natural laws, which should not be subject to interference by the state or any other group. These laws are based on the human desire to maximize pleasure and minimize pain. Man is considered basically selfish in his economic pursuits. But, by the benevolent designs of Providence, man's selfishness actually leads to the greatest common good. In the struggle for survival, each man produces to the best of his ability. The sum of such efforts is maximum production at the highest quality possible. Hence, the good of all is served. Any interference with this process, through state or private intervention, only leads to decreased production and increased misery. Free competition must be the sole guiding rule of economic life.

Transition to Modern Times. By the eighteenth century, the social institutions of earlier ages, embodying a moral and religious code in their practices, were largely gone. Their ideological base was destroyed as a result of the factors noted above. Moreover, the very process of commercial and industrial growth and change was important in breaking up social organizations founded under different conditions. Great movements of population, the subdivision of labor as a result of new processes, and the enlargement of the market necessarily outmoded the guilds and their customs. Even if society had not changed in its moral and ethical framework, economic developments would have called for profound modification of existing institutions. By the eighteenth century, however, the temper of society was such that earlier organizations were destroyed without being replaced. As a result, the masses of workers in the newly expanded cities became a proletariat, a formless group without internal coherence, security, or direction in economic life.

The policy of freedom was to lead to an enormous expansion of commerce and industry. But the price paid in terms of human suffering was indeed great. Speculative orgies led to periodic depressions that caused prolonged unemployment and intensive suffering. Poor families sent children to work even at such early ages as five or six. A seventeen-hour day was not uncommon. In English coal mines, women were harnessed to the carts to pull up coal, since the tunnels were too narrow to permit the use of animals. During the early part of the nineteenth century, Negro slaves in the agricultural United States were often better treated than "free" workers in the great industrial and commercial nations.

Conditions in the United States never reached the levels of degradation that were all too common in Europe. The safety valve of the frontier, with its vista of virgin lands and unlimited opportunity, prevented the worst forms of exploitation. Yet, during the nineteenth century, we too were plagued with panics and unemployment, slums, long hours of work, child labor, exploitation of workers and savage repression of unions, the victimization of the farmer, and sharp contrasts between wealth and poverty. These conditions persisted into the present century, although living standards gradually improved. The worst evils of exploitation were slowly disappearing as a result of legislation and unionization. Nevertheless, comprehensive social reform here was not achieved until the 1929 depression led to the New Deal legislation of 1933–1938.[5]

The rise of the social problem produced strong reactions, especially in Europe. Two patterns particularly were to emerge. One was a socialist trend that reached its ideological peak with the writings of Karl Marx and Nicolai Lenin and its practical expression in the communist movement that flowed from the Russian revolution of 1917. The other current was the movement toward Christian social reform, starting in Germany and France early in the nineteenth century and culminating in the great social writings of Leo XIII, Pius XI, Pius XII, and John XXIII. These writings deeply influenced the Christian Democratic parties that governed much of Western Europe after World War II.

The citing of socialist and Christian movements should not detract from the achievements of many, not formally connected with either camp, who sponsored labor organization and social legislation during the past century. Yet socialism and Christianity were the leading ideological forces of the time. Those who acted independently of such movements were nevertheless powerfully influenced by the ferment of thought they engendered.[6]

These reactions to the social evils attendant upon the Industrial Revolution brought about far-reaching reforms. In the United States,

[5] For reference material, see M. Josephson, The Robber Barons (New York: Harcourt. 1934). and F. L. Allen, The Lords of Creation (New York: Harper. 1935).

[6] See P. T. Moon, The Labor Problem and the Social Catholic Movement in France (New York: Macmillan, 1921), M. P. Fogarty, Christian Democracy in Western Europe, 1820–1953 (Notre Dame: University of Notre Dame Press, 1957), and J. F. Cronin and H. W. Flannery, Labor and the Church (New York: Hawthorn, 1965.) In the present century, the persistent effort of socialists to secure legislation benefiting the worker explains the political strength of this movement in Western Europe. Catholics were less active in this regard before World War II.

at least, the crude exploitation of earlier days is now exceptional, directed largely against Negroes and the Spanish-speaking, who are still unable to achieve their full rights. Such measures as fiscal and monetary reforms, unemployment compensation, guaranteed wages, farm price supports, and heavy government spending have lessened the likelihood that a severe and prolonged depression may occur. Living standards have climbed to historic highs. As a result of these and other changes, the question arises: Does the United States have a social problem in the form outlined in papal writings? Can we rightly say that papal strictures upon economic society do not apply to current conditions here? To answer these questions, it may be useful to examine our contemporary economic life in the light of Christian teachings.

THE SOCIAL PROBLEM TODAY

Since the present chapter has stressed so strongly the philosophy and moral principles behind a given period of history, it is only logical to begin our inquiry at this level. The New Deal reforms of the 1930's were, in general, imposed by law upon an unwilling business community. In the interval the viewpoint of the business world has changed considerably. Thus, regulation of the securities' markets and the banking community is now regarded as inevitable in the light of the abuses of earlier years. Social security is not now questioned; indeed, it is often supplemented by industrial pensions and other "fringe benefits" in labor-union contracts. Government aid to farmers seems to be accepted in principle, although there are disputes over particular programs. Labor's right to organize is generally recognized, even when it is denied in practice in some areas.

It is difficult to generalize about a nation as large and diverse as the United States. Yet the preponderance of evidence indicates that most Americans now accept the idea that government has the right and duty to prevent economic abuses, on the part of either business or labor, that detract from the general welfare. Businessmen, with a minority in opposition, feel that they have definite obligations toward the community, their workers, stockholders, and customers. The idea that profit is the only motivating force in business does not seem to prevail today. In other words, the competitive individualism of the postmedieval period is no longer the dominant factor in our society.

The question often arises, however, as to the depth of the change. Many contend that individualism persists in a different form. They cite as examples the alleged group individualism that is said to manifest itself in great concentrations aiming at economic and political power and at influencing public opinion. To give concrete examples: business has been charged with price-fixing in an effort to secure unreasonable profits; organized labor is said to secure high wages for its members at the expense of other elements in the community; and farmers are blamed for demanding price-support programs that pile up ever increasing surpluses of unneeded commodities. All these groups are alleged to be seeking to dominate government, particularly the federal government, so as to secure special favors for their members.

Closely related to the charges just made is the claim that there is an excessive concentration of power in modern society. Individuals and small groups are losing out. Giant aggregations in industry, commerce, finance, labor, and farming are becoming ever more powerful. Political power is being increasingly centralized in Washington, in spite of professed efforts to reverse the trend. As a result, many contend, the organization is everything, the individual is nothing.

In this connection, the student should read carefully the papal Christmas message of 1952, or at least the excerpt cited at the head of this chapter. Pope Pius XII was worried over the "depersonalization" of modern society, its excessively mechanical character. We seem to have lost the ability to distinguish between ends and means, seeking ever increasing supplies of goods and gadgets — more than we need — as ends good in themselves, not merely as means to secure higher goals. We lose sight of the individual and the family, and private property as their economic supports, as the real goals of social and economic achievement.[7]

While general living standards in the United States have increased sharply, particularly since 1945, problems still persist. It is not certain that we can control inflation without slowing economic growth and causing deflation and unemployment. Moreover, prosperity is uneven. Many men are practicing "moonlighting," or the holding of two jobs, in the effort to keep afloat. The number of married women workers, including mothers of young children, has mounted at an appalling rate. Thousands of families receive incomes inadequate by any reasonable standard. In all probability, the bulk of these families are members of minority groups or are marginal farmers. At the other extreme, many feel that the cult of constantly increasing living standards is making our society too materialistic and pleasure mad.

---

[7] See J. K. Galbraith, *The Affluent Society* (Boston: Houghton Mifflin, 1958) for an economic analysis often parallel to papal pronouncements on this subject.

More specific evils may be found in some segments of our society. Some business firms turn out shoddy goods or offer poor services. A particular complaint is the high cost of servicing complicated products, such as an automobile or television set, and the conviction that some service firms are exploiting the public by gross overcharges. Another abuse that often affects the poorer groups is the charging of high interest rates on installment sales. Some contracts are written in such a way as to keep the unwary in debt, even after an article has been repossessed. False and deceptive advertising, particularly over the radio, often misleads those who can least afford the loss. One hidden factor in costs is the rather prevalent practice of commercial bribery and corruption.

Many families still cannot afford housing suitable for their needs. Slums and urban blight plague many areas, in spite of many excellent redevelopment programs. Race discrimination is often involved here, and in business hiring policies as well. Another hiring practice that causes severe hardship is unwillingness to hire workers over forty.

Organized labor is no longer a weakling needing every help it can get. It has become rich and powerful. An important part of the labor movement has been plagued with corruption, racketeering, and autocracy. Less publicized, but possibly more dangerous in the long run, is the immense economic power achieved by some unions. A union monopoly of transportation, for example, can paralyze a nation almost overnight.

Three points have become particularly clear in the mid-1960's, namely, the persistence of poverty in certain areas, the increasing challenge of automation, and the stubborn fact of unemployment.

It is now clear that in many parts of our nation poverty is endemic. There are depressed areas, exploited groups such as migrant workers, and disadvantaged classes including aged persons, members of minority groups, and those suffering physical or emotional handicaps. The tragedy here is that poverty persists, often over several generations, in spite of ever-growing general prosperity.

Automation likewise is seen to be a far more serious problem than was first realized. Technological change not only affects our farms and factories, but it is becoming an increasing factor in white-collar operations. Displacement of workers has reached such a level that it is extremely difficult to come up with workable solutions for the plight of these idled workers.

Closely akin to the first two problems is the fact that our economy can be apparently prosperous and stable, and yet leave about five percent of the work force unemployed. While a million or more new jobs are created each year, a similar number of workers are being displaced by new and more efficient processes. Furthermore, the maturing of the postwar "baby crop" means that a much larger number of new workers will be seeking jobs.

These points are noted, not in any way to belittle the great achievements of the American economy, but only to point out that the work of social reform is a continuing task. Our living standards are unquestionably high. The pattern of income distribution has greatly improved. The percentage of the extremely rich or extremely poor has been declining, as more and more Americans move into the "middle class."

But the ultimate test of a society is not its distribution of wealth, important as that may be. The real test is the prevalence of justice and charity in relationships among men. We must ask: Does a given social pattern contribute to family life and minister to human dignity? Poverty, fraud, and injustice point up the urgency of reforming society according to Christian principles. But the absence or the minimizing of these abuses does not mean that we can become complacent and feel that the social teaching of the Church has no relevance in our country.

In 1959, Nikita Khrushchev boasted that Soviet living standards would soon excel those of the United States. If his boast were to be fulfilled, it would still be unimportant. So long as communism persisted in the U.S.S.R., its people would still be slaves, even if well-fed and well-housed slaves. Material prosperity is not the ultimate goal of society. It can be a good, and its absence can be an evil, but it is not the highest good even in the temporal order. This thought should serve as a necessary background to any discussion of Christian social principles.

READINGS*

J. F. Cronin and H. W. Flannery, *The Church and the Workingman*, Chaps. 7–12.
A. Fanfani, *Catholicism, Protestantism, and Capitalism*.
H. Johnston, *Business Ethics*, Chap. 6.
B. L. Masse, *Justice for All*, Chap. 2.
J. Messner, *Social Ethics* (rev. ed.), pp. 353–393.
G. A. O'Brien, *Essay on Mediaeval Economic Teaching*.
R. H. Tawney, *Religion and the Rise of Capitalism*.
E. Troeltsch, *The Social Teaching of the Christian Churches*.

---

* For further readings, see List No. 1 in the Appendix. Publishers, dates of publication, and descriptive data on books listed above may also be found in the Appendix.

Chapter II

THE CHURCH AND THE SOCIAL PROBLEM

Leo XIII, Graves de Communi

10. For it is the opinion of some, which is caught up by the masses, that the social question, as they call it, is merely economic. The precise opposite is the truth. It is first of all moral and religious, and for that reason its solution is to be expected mainly from the moral law and the pronouncements of religion.

Leo XIII, Rerum Novarum

24. We approach the subject with confidence and surely by Our right, for the question under consideration is certainly one for which no satisfactory solution will be found unless religion and the Church have been called upon to aid.

25. Assuredly, a question as formidable as this requires the attention and effort of others as well, namely, the heads of the state, employers and the rich, and finally, those in whose behalf efforts are being made, the workers themselves. Yet without hesitation We affirm that if the Church is disregarded, human striving will be in vain. Manifestly, it is the Church which draws from the Gospel the teachings through which the struggle can be composed entirely or, after its bitterness is removed, can certainly become more tempered.

42. But it must not be supposed that the Church so concentrates her energies on caring for souls as to overlook the things which pertain to mortal and earthly life. As regards the nonowning workers specifically, she desires and strives that they rise from their most wretched state and enjoy better conditions.

Pius XI, Quadragesimo Anno

41. Yet before proceeding to explain these matters, that principle which Leo XIII so clearly established must be laid down at the outset here, namely, that there resides in Us the right and duty to pronounce with supreme authority upon social and economic matters. Certainly the Church was not given the commission to guide men to an only fleeting and perishable happiness but to that which is eternal. Indeed "the Church holds that it is unlawful for her to mix without cause in these temporal concerns"; however, she can in no wise renounce the duty God entrusted to her to interpose her authority, not of course in matters of technique for which she is neither suitably equipped nor endowed by office, but in all

things that are connected with the moral law. For as to these, the deposit of truth that God committed to Us and the grave duty of disseminating and interpreting the whole moral law, and of urging it in season and out of season, bring under and subject to Our supreme jurisdiction not only the social order but economic activities themselves.

42. Even though economics and moral science employ each its own principles in its own sphere, it is, nevertheless, an error to say that the economic and moral orders are so distinct from and alien to each other that the former depends in no way on the latter. Certainly the laws of economics, as they are termed, being based on the very nature of material things and on the capacities of the human body and mind, determine the limits of what productive human effort cannot, and of what it can attain in the economic field and by what means. Yet it is reason itself that clearly shows, on the basis of the individual and social nature of things and of men, the purpose which God ordained for all economic life.

43. But it is only the moral law

which, just as it commands us to seek our supreme and last end in the whole scheme of our activity, so likewise commands us to seek directly in each kind of activity those purposes which we know that nature, or rather God the Author of nature, established for that kind of action, and in orderly relationship to subordinate such immediate purposes to our supreme and last end. If we faithfully observe this law, then it will follow that the particular purposes, both individual and social, that are sought in the economic field will fall in their proper place in the universal order of purposes, and We, in ascending through them, as it were by steps, shall attain the final end of all things, that is God, to Himself and to us, the supreme and inexhaustible Good.

130. Yet it is not rash by any means to say that the whole scheme of social and economic life is now such as to put in the way of vast numbers of mankind most serious obstacles which prevent them from caring for the one thing necessary; namely, their eternal salvation.

Pius XI, On Atheistic Communism

34. The Church does not separate a proper regard for temporal welfare from solicitude for the eternal. If she subordinates the former to the latter according to the words of her divine Founder, "Seek ye first the Kingdom of God and His justice, and all these things shall be added unto you," she is nevertheless so far from being unconcerned with human affairs, so far from hindering civil progress and material advancement, that she actually fosters and promotes them in the

most sensible and efficacious manner. Thus even in the sphere of social economics, although the Church has never proposed a definite technical system, since this is not her field, she has nevertheless clearly outlined the guiding principles which, while susceptible of varied concrete applications according to the diversified conditions of times and places and peoples, indicate the safe way of securing the happy progress of society.

Pius XII, La Solennità della Pentecoste, June 1, 1941

1676. It is . . . the indisputable competence of the Church, on that

side of the social order where it meets and enters into contact with the moral order, to decide whether the bases of a given social system are in accord with the unchangeable order which God, our Creator and Redeemer, has shown us through the natural law and Revelation . . . the Church, guardian of the supernatural Christian Order in which nature and grace converge, must form the consciences even of those who are called upon to find solutions for the problems and the duties imposed by social life. Upon the form given to society, whether conforming or not to the divine law, depends and emerges the good or ill of souls, depends the decision whether men, all called to be revived by the grace of Christ, do actually in the detailed course of their life breathe the healthy vivifying atmosphere of truth and moral virtue or the disease-laden and often fatal air of error and corruption. Before such a thought and such an anticipation, how could the Church, loving Mother that she is, solicitous for the welfare of her children, remain an indifferent onlooker in their danger, remain silent or feign not to see or take cognizance of social conditions which, whether one wills it or not, make difficult or practically impossible a Christian life? . . .

Pius XII, To Sacred College of Cardinals, June 2, 1947

By disposition of Divine Providence, the Catholic Church has formulated and promulgated its social doctrine. She points out the path to be followed, and no hope of achieving temporal gain, or fear of losing possessions, or of appearing less in harmony with modern civilization, or less national or social, could authorize true Christians to deviate even a hair's breadth from this path.

Pius XII, To Young Men, September 12, 1948

The social question, beloved sons, is undoubtedly an economic question also, but even more than that it is a question which concerns the ordered regulation of human society. And, in its deepest sense, it is a moral and therefore a religious question. As such, it may be summed up thus: have men — from the individual to the people, and right through to the community of peoples — the moral strength to create such public conditions that in the life of society there will not be any individuals or any peoples who are merely objects, that is to say, deprived of all right and exposed to exploitation by others, but all instead will be subjects, that is, having a legitimate share in the formation of the social order and able, according to their art or profession, to live happily and tranquilly with sufficient means of support, protected effectively against the violence of an egoistic economy, in freedom defined by the general welfare, and with full human dignity, each respecting his neighbor as he respects himself? Will humanity be capable of generating and possessing the moral strength to realize such a social order?

Pius XII, Letter to Semaines Sociales, 1949

There can be no incompatibility between a realism, healthfully nourished by facts, statistics, and economic laws, and a social order quite legitimately imbued with aspirations for more justice and humanity. These two aspects of the same problem are complementary; to them can be applied the words of the Gospel, *Haec oportuit facere et illa non omittere.*

Pius XII, Humani Generis, August 12, 1950

20. Nor must it be thought that what is expounded in Encyclical Letters does not of itself demand consent, since in writing such Letters the Popes do not exercise the supreme power of their Teaching Authority. For these matters are taught with the ordinary teaching authority, of which it is true to say: "He who heareth you, heareth me"; and generally what is expounded and inculcated in Encyclical Letters already for other reasons appertains to Catholic doctrine. But if the Supreme Pontiffs in their official documents purposely pass judgment on a matter up to that time under dispute, it is obvious that that matter, according to the mind and will of the same Pontiffs, cannot be any longer considered a question open to discussion among theologians.

Pius XII, To Cardinals, Archbishops, and Bishops of Rome, November 2, 1954

Therefore, when it is a question of instructions and propositions which the properly constituted shepherds (i.e., the Roman Pontiff for the whole Church, and the Bishops for the faithful entrusted to them) publish on matters within the natural law, the faithful must not invoke that saying (which is wont to be employed with respect to opinions of individuals): "the strength of the authority is no more than the strength of the arguments." Hence, even though to someone, certain declarations of the Church may not seem proved by the arguments put forward, his obligation to obey still remains.

Pius XII, To a Pilgrimage of Working People From the City of Terni, November 18, 1956

Meanwhile We remind all whom it concerns that even though . . . economic problems must be met and solved in accordance with the laws of production, distribution, circulation, and consumption of goods in their relation to the social order, it is equally certain that these same laws can be formulated and applied with human understanding and Christian charity. We must not lose sight of the fact that, by introducing the principles of ethics into our investigation of economic facts, we do no violence to the economy, but rather contribute effectively to the correct solution of the problems that it poses and confronts.

Pius XII, Christmas Message, 1956

Efforts at correction have been made through large-scale institutional reforms, often too broad in scope or based on false principles; but the reform of institution is not as urgent as that of conduct.

Pius XII, To Assembly of the International Movement of Catholic Intellectuals, April 25, 1957

Without by any means forgetting that his goal is to contribute to his neighbor's salvation, the Christian must be ever mindful that the establishment of God's Kingdom in men's hearts and in social institutions very often requires a minimum of human development, a simple demand of reason to which a man normally assents even if he does not have the grace of faith.

For this reason, the Christian will always be ready to work for the relief of every material distress and for the development of some common basis of knowledge. In a word, he will be diligent to achieve the betterment of the poor and the disinherited. And in this way he will be certain of fulfilling a great obligation placed on him by collective charity, that of clearing the way to a worthy life for many men and of thereby making their co-operation in common effort easier. All this will lead men to a better state of life, enabling them to look higher, to welcome the Light and embrace the only Truth which can make them free (John 8, 32).

Pius XII, To Italian Federation of Middlemen and Business Agents, June 22, 1958

When, for instance, one says "business is business," a norm is adopted which, if considered as an absolute and universal principle, must be included among the maxims that no Christian conscience could accept, for that which applies to every human activity equally applies to economic operations. They must be subject to divine, natural, and positive laws.

John XXIII, Mater et Magistra

2. Christianity is the meeting point of earth and heaven. It lays claim to the whole man, body and soul, intellect and will, inducing him to raise his mind above the changing conditions of this earthly existence and reach upward for the eternal life of heaven, where one day he will find his unfailing happiness and peace.

3. Hence, though the Church's first care must be for souls, how she can sanctify them and make them share in the gifts of heaven, she concerns herself too with the exigencies of man's daily life, with his livelihood and education, and his general, temporal welfare and prosperity.

179. Now, in bringing people to Christ, the Church has invariably, both now and in the past, brought them many social and economic advantages. For true Christians cannot help feeling obliged to improve their own temporal institutions and environment. They do all they can to prevent these institutions from doing violence to human dignity. They encourage whatever is conducive to decency and virtue, and strive to eliminate every obstacle to the attainment of this aim.

180. Moreover, in becoming as it were the lifeblood of these people, the Church is not, nor does she consider herself to be, a foreign body in their midst. Her presence brings about the rebirth, the resurrection, of each individual in Christ; and the man who is reborn and rises again in Christ never feels himself constrained

from without. He feels himself free in the very depth of his being, and freely raised up to God. And thus he affirms and develops that side of his nature which is noblest and best.

218. The permanent validity of the Catholic Church's social teaching admits of no doubt.

222. . . . We must reaffirm most strongly that this Catholic social doctrine is an integral part of the Christian conception of life.

226. . . . the Church's social doctrine, the light of which is truth, justice its objective, and love its driving force.

Vatican Council II, The Church in the Modern World

43. Often enough the Christian view of things will itself suggest some specific solution in certain circumstances. Yet it happens rather frequently, and legitimately so, that with equal sincerity some of the faithful will disagree with others on a given matter. Even against the intentions of their proponents, however, solutions proposed on one side or another may be easily confused by

many people with the gospel message. Hence it is necessary for people to remember that no one is allowed in the aforementioned situations to appropriate the Church's authority for his opinion. They should always try to enlighten one another through honest discussion, preserving mutual charity and caring above all for the common good.

The Australian Hierarchy, Morality in Public Life, September, 1950

The power of organized bodies in the modern world is so immense that there is no man or woman whose personal life is not intimately affected by the policies they formulate.

Organizations, in themselves, are inanimate. Dead things do not make policies. Policies are made by men, the men who lead the organizations, the men who elect them or who passively allow them to lead.

With such immense consequences following upon their policies and their actions, it is intolerable that members should permit their organizations to base their policies on lying, on dishonesty, on fraud, on greed, or on the lust for power.

Above all, it is intolerable that those Christians who, in either capac-

ity, compose these organizations, should follow two moral codes — one, in their personal life, which does not permit lying or dishonesty or fraud or greed, and another, in their public life, which regards all of these things as lawful instruments of policy.

For the Christian, sin is sin whether it is committed in the course of private or public life. And although the gravity of the sin committed in the formulation of many public policies will vary with the degree of knowledge, with the position of responsibility and with the motives of the person concerned, and also with the effects of his wrongdoing, no sin is ever palliated by the consideration that it is committed not for private gain, but for public policy.

Code of Social Principles

89. Economic laws relate to human acts. These laws are discovered through the study of psychology and

history and the observation of facts. Economic laws can produce certain evil or unjust consequences according to the conditions under which they are allowed to operate. A surplus of goods or services, for instance, results in their depreciation.

91. Since economic phenomena relate to human affairs, the interpretation which is put upon them calls for an exact knowledge of human nature and of imponderable factors in the psychological and moral order which react upon human activities; it depends upon a multitude of other than statistical data. Into this work of interpretation necessarily enter metaphysical ideas regarding human nature, its origin, its destiny, the relative values of men, and their mutual relations.

The Catholic economist must seek these ideas in Christian philosophy, if he wishes to remain logical with himself.

92. Besides, the Church herself has here both the competence and the right to intervene, certainly not in the technical sphere, but in all that touches the moral law. For, if it is true that the Church has received the mission to lead mankind to eternal happiness, she can never forget that economic activity must be subject to the moral law and that the temporal end is subordinate to the eternal.

POPE PIUS XI made clear that "the body of truth that God committed to Us, and the grave duty of disseminating and interpreting the whole moral law . . . bring under and subject to Our supreme jurisdiction not only the social order but economic activities themselves."[1] This assertion of authority over economic life has astonished many persons, including some within the Catholic Church. This is the more true because the divorce of religion from social life, noted in the preceding chapter, has often been taken for granted in modern times. To correct any misconceptions on this point, it is important to state clearly why the Church speaks on social and economic matters, the authority of this teaching, how it should be interpreted, and how moral pronouncements are to be applied to everyday life.

RIGHT AND DUTY TO INTERVENE

The Church stresses two areas in which moral law affects economic life. The first concerns the consciences of individuals as they participate daily in their chosen fields of activity. This we may term personal morality. The second area involves the moral effects of social conditions: the implications of the laws, customs, and institutions of economic life. These affect individuals because they are members of various groups, such as labor unions, corporations, or trade associations. It also affects them in their capacity as citizens. We may call this social morality.

---

[1] Quadragesimo Anno, No. 41.

Among good men, there are likely to be few who question the right of
the Church to pronounce on matters of *personal morals*. They accept the
idea that justice, charity, and similar obligations apply universally. Theft
in the course of business is just as much a violation of justice as it is
in the case of a thief who steals a purse. Of course, there are businessmen
who have double standards. They accept such axioms as: "Let the buyer
beware" or "All's fair in business." But it is doubtful that really sincere
merchants stifle their consciences with such axioms.

Social morality is another matter. Persons who may be eminently fair
in their direct dealings with others may act quite differently as members of a corporation, a labor union, or a political party. Even when
they may not sanction sins of commission by such groups, they may be
blind to sins of omission. Group individualism, mentioned earlier, seems
to justify indifference toward their social responsibilities. Because of this
confused state of many consciences, it is advisable to spell out in more
detail the morality of human actions in the economic sphere.

Personal Morality. Theologians note three factors that influence the
morality of our actions: the object sought, the motives of the doer, and
the circumstances under which we act. Each of these factors should be
considered in any economic decision.

Certain economic problems involve a purely objective morality. Thus, a
promotion venture which is permeated with fraud is dishonest of its
very nature. The same is true if economic force is used to compel another
to do something wrong. Abuse of a monopoly position by the charging
of clearly exploitive prices is contrary to the virtue of justice. Stealing
does not become right, merely because it is accomplished in the course
of large-scale business transactions. On the other side of the picture,
certain business practices can be called morally good by their nature.
Thus the inventor who markets a new process that will create useful
employment renders a service to society. The industrialist who gives an
example of fine human relations in his plant is acting according to
sound ethics.

In other cases, motives will influence the morality of a transaction.
While good motives will never make right out of wrong, it is possible to
do something morally good or neutral for unsound motives. It is not
wrong in itself to amass wealth, but greed and avarice are sinful. The
acquisition of economic power may be a normal result of shrewd and
successful business operations, but it may also be the product of pride
and disordered ambition. A labor leader may often be morally justified in

calling a strike, yet it is not inconceivable that personal pique or like unworthy motives may enter into his decision. Thus, he could be guilty through unethical motives.

Finally, circumstances and especially the impact upon others enter into the morality of business operations. Actions may not be judged in isolation. A factory which gives out obnoxious fumes might legitimately be constructed in a remote region. If the same factory were constructed in a residential neighborhood, it would lower property values and make homes useless for living purposes. Again, factory waste dumped into a river could ruin its drinking and recreational values. An industrial process that would poison the workers in the plant would be wrong. A pace of operations that would burn out a worker's energy in a few years would do him an injustice. Thus, the moral nature of a transaction may not be judged in the abstract. The total picture must be considered, particularly the social effect of a given operation.

The fact that morally wrong practices often prevail in the economic world indicates that not everyone has a right conscience about such matters, or that many fail to live up to their known obligations. The production and sale of shoddy goods, cheating in the servicing of appliances, or the failure of workers to do a good job even when well paid, all are too common to allow us to be complacent. So far as Catholics are concerned, there is room for more sermons on these topics, better religious teaching in the schools, and more realistic texts in ethics and moral theology.

Social Morality. The religious teaching that we are "our brother's keeper" applies in a much broader area than personal contacts with workers, employers, or customers. It extends also to the social effects of decisions made by impersonal economic groups. Actions by labor unions, corporations, political pressure groups or legislatures must be judged by their impact upon the general welfare. It is wrong to seek group interests when this causes grave harm to the community as a whole. The common good of all must be the supreme norm to be used in judging the social effects of individual and group decisions. Undoubtedly most religious persons accept this principle as a general statement. Yet, it is often evaded through self-deception, omission, or sheer inertia.

One method of flouting the general welfare is the practice of clothing selfish actions in the guise of disinterested public service. To illustrate, corporations rarely complain that their own profits are excessive. Unions may demand substantial wage increases in times of inflation so as to keep up with living costs. When conditions are reversed, they want additional increases in order to stimulate business by means of increased purchasing power. Likewise, farm groups and political parties seem to find a parallel between their desires and the general good. It is difficult to avoid the conclusion that many public appeals to the common good are mere rationalizations of decisions adopted primarily for group interests.

Again, few conscientious persons escape the stings of conscience when they participate, however remotely, in really selfish and antisocial actions. But many fail through omission, even though they might balk at directly committing an unjust or selfish deed. An example would be indifference toward the root causes of such problems as poverty or racial discrimination in a community. People who contribute to charity drives, in order to take care of some of the effects of destitution, slum living, or discrimination against minorities, may never dream that they have an obligation to seek the prevention or the radical cure of such evils. Many who are concerned about poverty at home remain indifferent to the sufferings of millions in remoter areas of the world.

Custom and inertia also explain slowness in seeking basic reforms. The fact that conditions have prevailed over centuries make many accept them as inevitable or even natural. They fail to realize that certain evils tend to be self-perpetuating, unless outside help is given. Thus, malnutrition and disease cause low living standards in many areas of the world. Low standards in turn make it impossible to secure needed food and medicines. Again, when a minority group is denied equal opportunity in education, housing, and job prospects, it is bound to be culturally submerged. These very cultural differences are then used as an excuse for further discrimination.

Why the Church Intervenes. From the viewpoint of the Church, there is a double obligation, affecting both the material and the spiritual welfare of our neighbors, that applies in these cases. First, there is the direct duty to seek the material welfare of our fellow man. We are obliged to feed the hungry and clothe the naked. And the best form of help, as Moses Maimonides once said, is helping people to help themselves. Second, there is the fact that, so far as we know, adverse social conditions contribute to the loss of souls. Pope Pius XII said that some conditions make "difficult or practically impossible a Christian life."[2] These are strong words, but hundreds of serious thinkers, from Aristotle to the present-day moralists, have stated that there is a form of poverty

---

[2] *Supra*, p. 23.

that hinders the practice of virtue. The Gospel ideal of poverty involves detachment from material things. But the grinding destitution of many persons causes them to be almost exclusively preoccupied with the material.

One does not need to be a materialist or a determinist to hold that external conditions often affect human behavior. Children in slums, for example, are less likely than middle-class children to have a good home life. In the former situation, both parents may be working and hence unable to give adequate time to the guidance of their children. Housing may be so poor that the streets are more attractive than home for play and relaxation. Yet, on the streets children not only meet bad companions, but they also suffer many rebuffs that can engender in them antisocial attitudes. These facts may explain the high correlation between slum living and delinquency.

Nor is the Church indifferent to the broader consequences of social injustice. Much of the appeal of communism throughout the world is based on its program to cure social ills. We grant that this program is deceptive. But the embracing of communism by a nation is a process not easily reversed. Once its adherents have taken power, they use force to maintain themselves.

The bitter fact is that, when given the choice between freedom and bread, many will sacrifice freedom. Political freedom is often an empty phrase to the man on the park bench, without a job or assurance that he will eat. Desperate men can always convince themselves that things will be different in their country, just as today French or Italian communists (in the lower ranks) try to reconcile communism with love of country and of Church. In the face of such a menace, can anyone say that the Church should confine itself to worship and keep out of the market place? Under these conditions, indifference to the social problem would be inviting a persecution so drastic that millions may apostatize rather than face it. Nor should it be said that we must fight this evil with spiritual weapons only. Not only is the social question a moral question, and hence a problem for the Church, but the exclusively spiritual approach to any material problem is of doubtful doctrinal orthodoxy. We do not seek to cure epidemics by prayer alone; we use our God-given intelligence to discover causes and remedies. We should be no less zealous in facing the social problem.

To summarize, the Church has the right to discuss social problems because they are at the same time moral problems. It has the duty to enter this field, because its teaching mission includes the moral law as well as dogmas of faith. This duty is reinforced by the urgency of modern problems. Failure to solve them may lead to the loss of souls, the more so if it brings about the totalitarian state. This much established, it is important to define the precise scope and nature of intervention by the Church.

HOW SOCIAL TEACHINGS APPLY TO ECONOMIC LIFE

Moral Law and Economic Life. When the Church teaches on social questions, it deals with moral, not technical issues. It is not the function of the Church, as such, to choose, for example, between Keynesian and classical economics. It does not usually pronounce upon interest theories or techniques for computing national income. It may incidentally raise these issues, if moral factors intervene. But normally the Church treats of direct moral considerations such as those affecting man, the family, the state, property, and God's purpose in economic life.

The fact that ethical and value judgments are interposed in economic matters does not mean that the Church questions the validity of economic law. On the contrary, there is no disposition to deny the soundness of physical and economic laws. If a poor country is afflicted with a famine, no amount of preaching about proper living standards will prevent hardship, unless aid from without is forthcoming. Should incomes be increased in a nation that cannot increase production, then inflation is a necessary result, barring unusual fiscal or control measures. The laws implied in these examples are based on either the nature of material things or valid generalizations about human behavior.

But human foresight can change the conditions under which physical and economic laws operate. Famine can often be prevented by good irrigation systems. It can be alleviated by generous contributions from wealthier nations. Inflation can be forestalled either by preventing an increase of a nation's money supply or by provisions to expand production. In such ways, laws, policies, and programs do affect the working of economic law.

In applying moral principles to economic life, we must avoid two extremes. One is the determinism of those who claim that economic laws are so absolute that any interference with them is fatal. Modern nations have shown considerable ability to control their economies. Even nations dedicated to a relatively free economy, such as Germany and the United States, employ fiscal and monetary controls to prevent inflation and deflation. In reality, there is no such thing as a purely economic system.

All economic theories involve certain assumptions about human nature. Some are merely more explicit than others in stating these assumptions.

The other extreme is the voluntarism that states, in effect, that what is morally desirable can be easily achieved by men of good will. The fallacy of this approach can be proved by many examples. One instance is the phenomenon of serious business depressions. A major depression is a serious matter. No one can be sure of profiting from it; most people lose heavily as a result. But only in recent years have we had much success in controlling such tragic events. Even now there is not complete agreement as to the causes of a depression or the means to prevent or cure a slump. The fact that a slump is tragic for all is no guarantee that we can find proper remedies for it. Hence when the Church teaches the moral desirability of certain objectives, such as a family living wage, it has raised a problem, not solved it. It is up to men of good will, using proper economic means, to achieve the end pointed out by moral teaching.

How Church Teaching Is Determined. Before we discuss problems connected with the application of moral law, it is well to understand clearly just how one knows the moral teaching of the Church on economic matters. Clearly, as in all other matters of faith, the first source is the See of St. Peter. The popes have the right and duty to teach with authority on matters of faith or morals. Even when they are not pronouncing infallibly, they speak with clear authority. Catholics must give their assent, at the very least in terms of religious obedience, to the Vicar of Christ. Bishops likewise teach with authority in their own dioceses. Clergy and faithful must obey them, unless the Holy See directs otherwise in special cases. In addition, the common teaching of the Fathers and theologians of the Church must be accepted, unless higher authority decides differently.

In accepting the teaching authority of the Church, we must be careful to interpret correctly what is taught and how it is taught. For example, a papal encyclical might exhort the faithful to follow a given practice as most useful. Such is the case, for example, when Pope Pius XI advocated profit-sharing.[3] It is obvious from the context that this is neither a doctrinal teaching nor a disciplinary command. It is an exhortation demanding prudent and filial consideration, but it is not meant to command the faithful. But in other matters, such as the condemnation of communism, the pope is peremptory and decisive. No Catholic could disregard this position and advocate communism as defined by the pope.

---

[3] *Quadragesimo Anno*, No. 65.

Again, any papal document must be interpreted in accord with the customary norms used by theologians. They use the context to determine the solemnity and universality of any teaching. This is an intricate process, since the external form of certain pronouncements may offer no indication of their universality. Solemn encyclicals may contain passages that are merely counsels, not commands. Occasional discourses to pilgrims, particularly in the pontificate of Pope Pius XII, often contain broad doctrinal declarations. By contrast, some of his world-wide discourses, such as Christmas or Easter messages, dealt extensively with localized problems, as for example, the European Common Market.

There may be changes of emphasis as conditions warrant. Thus, in the citations given in this chapter are passages stressing both institutional and moral reforms. Either, cited out of context, could be used to favor an excessive stress upon one or another approach to social reform. Actually, papal teaching insists upon both aspects, although there is an understandable tendency to stress the method that at any given time may be neglected in broad areas.

The context used in judging papal documents must also take account of the full historical situation that prompted the document. Many political statements of Pope Leo XIII relate to nineteenth-century problems. He was concerned with certain abuses in newly formed democratic regimes. But his successors would be far more likely to emphasize the virtues of democracy and the evils of centralized power, especially when it is totalitarian. Again, Pope Pius XI excoriated the economic system of his day for many evils. To apply every word literally to the present economic situation of the United States or West Germany would be a stultifying misapplication of the pope's meaning. On the other hand, there are areas of Europe, Latin America, Asia, and Africa, in which the strong language of *Quadragesimo Anno* is literally applicable today.

Two points must be kept in mind at all times. The first is that, as Pope John XXIII reiterated, the social teaching of the Church is a part of doctrine and not merely pious exhortation.[4] Second, we must be scrupulous in presenting Catholic social teaching in its entirety. In many important areas the Church takes a position of moderation between two extremes. A good example is its teaching on the function of government — a middle road between pure individualism and statism. In the effort to keep this balance, individual popes have made statements which, taken out of textual and historical context, could be used to distort Catholic

---

[4] See *Mater et Magistra*, Nos. 218, 222, cited *supra*, p. 26.

teaching. There is both unity and progression in papal social doctrine and any careful effort to interpret and apply principles must take these facts into account.

All these observations are but aids in the direction of one goal: understanding what the popes taught and how they taught it. Thus we distinguish between matters of faith and those statements that are pastoral counsels. We differentiate between eternal truths based on revelation or natural law and judgments tied to specific changing historical events. With intelligence, sincerity, and good faith, it should not be too difficult to obtain a clear and consistent idea of the Church's teaching on great social matters. It is true that there have been controversies among Catholics as to both the content and the application of Catholic social teaching. Many of these controversies, however, need never have occurred. They were often the product of strongly partisan disputes, in which one side or another sought to use some papal statement to vindicate its position. Too often the statement in question was used out of context, or at least without reference to its historical background. By contrast, those who humbly seek to learn the entirety of the Church's social teaching should at least attain reasonable certainty and clarity in regard to the content of such teaching. Problems of application, of course, are more difficult, as will be noted presently.

Application of Moral Principles. Once it is clear what the popes teach and how they teach it — as a matter of divine faith, or natural law, or merely a prudential recommendation — the next step is to apply it to practical economic life. We repeat here that the Church teaches morals, not economics. Yet this moral teaching, to be fruitful, must be applied. It cannot be left in the abstract. Like other moral teachings of the Church, its application is often difficult. We cannot merely tell the faithful: "This is the law," any more than we can assume that the Ten Commandments can be readily applied in utmost detail by anyone of good will. Volumes of moral theology have been written to guide pastors of souls in applying these commandments. Centuries of thought have gone into these applications. We need equal diligence in developing the full implications of Catholic social teaching.

A common fallacy to be avoided is the confusion between the moral teaching of the Church and an individual writer's application of this doctrine to concrete affairs. The writer may understand perfectly the teaching of the Church. But he could be wholly wrong in application because of a faulty understanding of economic life. For example, a theologian might advocate compulsory arbitration of all labor disputes, on the grounds that the Church is opposed to class strife. The fallacy here lies in the choice of means to prevent disputes from developing into strikes. Experience has shown that arbitration of differences about wages and other economic issues involves a degree of outside control of a firm that, in effect, leads to socialism. Socialism, of course, is likewise condemned by the Church. This example shows the necessity of economic insight, as well as theological competence, by those who would make moral pronouncements on current social issues.

Consequently, it is best, when applying Church teaching to a concrete problem, explicitly to separate moral principles from historical and economic presuppositions used in making the final prudential judgment. Thus listeners or readers will not confuse the authoritative teaching of the Church with the fallible, even though expert, judgments of the specialist who is applying such truths. Thus, the writer could state why a controversial question is a moral problem and what moral principles apply. He could then give a factual analysis of the relevant economic and social factors. Finally, he could present his conclusion as to the proper policy in a given set of circumstances.

These points should not deter the laity, or the clergy who are not specialists, from endeavoring to apply justice and charity to everyday problems. Ideally such persons should seek advice from those expert in both economics and Church social teaching. Should this prove to be impractical at any time, it is better to act according to the spirit of the Church, as understood at the time, than to be guided by secularist axioms. God's blessing will not be denied to such men of good will.

Finally, it is well to remember that the bulk of Church social teaching is based on natural law rather than on divine revelation. This means that, in an overwhelming number of cases, these truths can be defended on the basis of human reason alone, without appeal to authority. This point is particularly relevant when one is discussing social morality with non-Catholics. If they are willing to accept natural-law teachings on man and society, they should not quarrel with the social teaching of the Church. Actually a large number of distinguished non-Catholic scholars, both in Europe and the United States, have openly professed their admiration for papal social teachings. Thus, the Catholic in business, labor, or politics need not feel that he will be considered rash when he promotes policies based on Christian social principles. On the contrary, many men of good will may rally to his cause and support well-considered applications of universally acknowledged truths.

READINGS*

J. Y. Calvez and J. Perrin, *The Church and Social Justice*, Chaps. 1–4.
J. F. Cronin and H. W. Flannery, *The Church and the Workingman*, Chap. 1.
B. W. Dempsey, *The Functional Economy*, Chaps. 1, 4, 23.
J. C. Ford and G. Kelly, *Contemporary Moral Theology*, Vol. I, Chaps. 1–3.
B. L. Masse, *Justice for All*, Chap. 1.
J. Messner, *Social Ethics* (rev. ed.), pp. 747–947.
F. H. Mueller, "The Church and the Social Question," in J. N. Moody and J. G. Lawler (eds.), *The Challenge of Mater et Magistra*.
O. von Nell-Breuning, *Reorganization of Social Economy*, pp. 79–89.
G. Wills, *Politics and Catholic Freedom*.

---

* For further readings, consult List No. 2 in the Appendix.

Chapter III

MAN AND ECONOMIC LIFE

THE NATURE OF MAN

Leo XIII, Rerum Novarum

57. No one may with impunity outrage the dignity of man, which God Himself treats with great reverence, nor impede his course to that level of perfection which accords with eternal life in heaven. Nay, more, in this connection a man cannot even by his own free choice allow himself to be treated in a way inconsistent with his nature, and suffer his soul to be enslaved; for there is no question here of rights belonging to man, but of duties owed to God, which are to be religiously observed.

Pius XI, On Atheistic Communism

27. Man has a spiritual and immortal soul. He is a person, marvelously endowed by his Creator with gifts of body and mind. He is a true "microcosm," as the ancients said, a world in miniature, with a value far surpassing that of the vast inanimate cosmos. God alone is his last end, in this life and the next. By sanctifying grace he is raised to the dignity of a son of God, and incorporated into the Kingdom of God in the Mystical Body of Christ. In consequence he has been endowed by God with many and varied prerogatives: the right to life, to bodily integrity, to the necessary means of existence; the right to tend toward his ultimate goal in the path marked out for him by God; the right of association and the right to possess and use property.

Pius XII, Christmas Broadcast, 1942

1831. The origin and the primary scope of social life is the conservation, development, and perfection of the human person, helping him to realize accurately the demands and values of religion and culture set by the Creator for every man and for all mankind, both as a whole and in its natural ramifications. A social teaching or a social reconstruction program which denies or prescinds from this internal essential relation to God of everything that regards man, is on a false course; and while it builds up with one hand, it prepares with the other the materials which sooner or later will undermine and destroy the whole fabric. And when it disregards the respect due to the human person and to the life which is proper to that person, and gives no thought to it in its organization, in legislative and executive activity, then instead of serving society, it harms it; instead of encouraging and stimulating social thought, instead of realizing its hopes and expectations, it strips it of all real value and reduces it to an utilitarian formula which is openly rejected by constantly increasing groups.

1832. If social life implies intrinsic unity, it does not, at the same time, exclude differences which are founded in fact and nature. When we hold fast to God, the Supreme Controller of all that relates to man, then the similarities no less than the differences of men find their allotted place in the fixed order of being, of values, and hence also of morality.

1844. First: He who would have the star of peace shine out and stand over society should co-operate, for his part, in giving back to the human person the dignity given to it by God from the very beginning; should oppose the excessive herding of men, as if they were a mass without a soul; their economic, social, political, in-

tellectual, and moral inconsistency; their dearth of solid principles and strong convictions, their surfeit of instinctive sensible excitement and their fickleness.

1845. He should favor, by every lawful means, in every sphere of life, social institutions in which a full personal responsibility is assured and guaranteed both in the earthly and the eternal order of things.

1847. Second: He who would have the star of peace shine out and stand over society should reject every form of materialism which sees in the people only a herd of individuals who, divided and without any internal cohesion, are considered as a mass to be lorded over and treated arbitrarily; he should strive to understand society as an intrinsic unity, which has grown up and matured under the guidance of Providence, a unity which — within the bounds assigned to it and according to its own peculiar gifts — tends, with the collaboration of the various classes and professions, toward the eternal and ever new aims of culture and religion.

John XXIII, Pacem in Terris

9. Any well-regulated and productive association of men in society demands the acceptance of one fundamental principle: that each individual man is truly a person. His is a nature, that is, endowed with intelligence and free will. As such he has rights and duties, which together flow as a direct consequence from his nature. These rights and duties are universal and inviolable, and therefore altogether inalienable.

11. But first We must speak of man's rights. Man has the right to live. He has the right to bodily integrity and to the means necessary for the proper development of life, particularly food, clothing, shelter,

medical care, rest, and, finally, the necessary social services. In consequence, he has the right to be looked after in the event of ill-health; disability stemming from his work; widowhood; old age; enforced unemployment; or whenever through no fault of his own he is deprived of the means of livelihood.

13. He has the natural right to share in the benefits of culture, and hence to receive a good general education, and a technical or professional training consistent with the degree of educational development in his own country. Furthermore, a system must be devised for affording gifted members of society the opportunity of en-

gaging in more advanced studies, with a view to their occupying, as far as possible, positions of responsibility in society in keeping with their natural talent and acquired skill.

30. Once this is admitted, it follows that in human society one man's natural right gives rise to a corresponding duty in other men; the duty, that is, of recognizing and respecting that right. Every basic human right draws its authoritative force from the natural law, which confers it and attaches to it its respective duty. Hence, to claim one's rights and ignore one's

duties, or only half fulfill them, is like building a house with one hand and tearing it down with the other.

87. As we know from experience, men frequently differ widely in knowledge, virtue, intelligence and wealth, but that is no valid argument in favor of a system whereby those who are in a position of superiority impose their will arbitrarily on others. On the contrary, such men have a greater share in the common responsibility to help others to reach perfection by their mutual efforts.

Pius XII, Address to Representatives of Fiat Automotive Plant, October 31, 1948

The Church does not promise that absolute equality which others are proclaiming because she knows that life in human society always and of necessity produces a whole range of degrees and differences in physical and mental traits, in inward dispositions and inclinations, in occupations and in responsibilities. But at the same time

she assures you full equality in human dignity, as also in the Heart of Him who calls unto Himself all those who labor and are heavily burdened, and invites them to take upon themselves His yoke and find peace and rest for their souls; for His yoke is sweet and His burden light (cf. Matt. 11, 28–30).

Leo XIII, Rerum Novarum

26. There are truly very great and very many natural differences among men. Neither the talents, nor the skill, nor the health, nor the capacities

of all are the same, and unequal fortune follows of itself upon necessary inequality in respect to these endowments.

Vatican Council II, The Church in the Modern World

29. Therefore, although rightful differences exist between men, the equal dignity of persons demands that a more humane and a just condition of life be brought about. For excessive economic and social differences

between the members of the one human family or population groups cause scandal, and militate against social justice, equity, the dignity of the human person, as well as social and international peace.

Code of Social Principles

4. In the legal order, individualism betrays itself in a radical subjectivism

which attributes absolute independence to the human person and unconditional value to individual rights. The political constitutions of the nineteenth century have fallen more than once into this extreme.

MAN IN SOCIETY

Vatican Council II, The Church in the Modern World

25. Man's social nature makes it evident that the progress of the human person and the advance of society itself hinge on each other. For the beginning, the subject and the goal of all social institutions is and must be the human person, which for its part and by its very nature stands completely in need of social life. This social life is not something added on to man. Hence he develops through his dealings with others, through reciprocal duties, and through fraternal dialogue all his gifts and is able to rise to his destiny.

Pius XI, Mit Brennender Sorge

35. Real common good ultimately takes its measure from man's nature, which balances personal rights and social obligations, and from the purpose of society, established for the benefit of human nature. Society was intended by the Creator for the full development of individual possibilities, and for the social benefits which, by a give-and-take process, everyone can claim for his own sake and that of others. Higher and more general values, which the collectivity alone can provide, also derive from the Creator for the good of man, and for his full development, natural and supernatural, and the realization of his perfection. To neglect this order is to shake the pillars on which society rests, and to compromise social tranquillity, security, and existence.

Pius XI, On Atheistic Communism

29. But God has likewise destined man for civil society according to the dictates of his very nature. In the plan of the Creator, society is a natural means which man can and must use to reach his destined end. Society is for man and not vice versa. This must not be understood in the sense of liberalistic individualism, which subordinates society to the selfish use of the individual; but only in the sense that by means of an organic union with society and by mutual collaboration the attainment of earthly happiness is placed within the reach of all. In a further sense it is society which affords the opportunities for the development of all the individual and social gifts bestowed on human nature.

34. Thus authority is reconciled with liberty, the dignity of the individual with that of the state, the human personality of the subject with the divine delegation of the superior; and in this way a balance is struck between the due dependence and well-ordered love of a man for himself, his family and country, and his love of other families and other peoples, founded on the love of God, the Father of all, their first principle and last end.

Pius XII, Radio Address to International Congress of Catholic Doctors, September 11, 1956

The individual is not only anterior to society by reason of his origin; he is superior to it in virtue of his destiny as well. Society, to the formation and development of which individuals are ordered, is merely the universal means intended by nature to bring people into contact with one another.

The relation here of part to whole is entirely different from that which exists in the physical body. When man is born into society, he is already provided with independent rights by the Creator; he carries on his activity by giving and receiving, and through his collaboration with other men he creates values and obtains results which, by himself, he could not effect nor even, as an individual, transmit. These new values show that society has its own pre-eminence and dignity; but this does not bring about a change in the relation We pointed out above because these higher values (society itself, for instance), are in their turn put in relation by nature to the individual and to people in general.

Pius XII, Christmas Message, 1956

On the contrary, religion and the reality of the past teach that the social structures, such as matrimony and family, the community and professional groups, social union in personal property, are essential cells which secure man's freedom and, along with it, his function in history. Hence they cannot be tampered with, and their essence cannot be the subject of arbitrary revision.

John XXIII, Mater et Magistra

219. Individual human beings are the foundation, the cause, and the end of every social institution. That is necessarily so, for men are by nature social beings. This fact must be recognized, as also the fact that they are raised in the plan of Providence to an order of reality which is above nature.

220. On this basic principle, which guarantees the sacred dignity of the individual, the Church constructs her social teaching.

John XXIII, Pacem in Terris

16. The family, founded upon marriage freely contracted, one and indissoluble, must be regarded as the natural, primary cell of human society. The interests of the family, therefore, must be taken very specially into consideration in social and economic affairs, as well as in the spheres of faith and morals. For all of these have to do with strengthening the family and assisting it in the fulfilment of its mission.

31. Since men are social by nature, they must live together and consult each other's interests. That men should recognize and perform their respective rights and duties is imperative to a well ordered society. But the result will be that each individual will make his whole-hearted contribution to the creation of a civic order in which rights and duties are ever more diligently and more effectively observed.

Leo XIII, Rerum Novarum

71. The end of civil society concerns absolutely all members of this society, since the end of civil society is centered in the common good, in which latter, one and all in due proportion have a right to participate. Wherefore, this society is called public because through it "men share with one another in establishing a commonwealth." On the other hand, societies which are formed, so to speak, within its bosom are considered private and are such because their immediate object is private advantage appertaining to those alone who are thus associated together. "Now a private society is one which is formed to carry out some private business, as when two or three enter into association for the purpose of engaging together in trade."

72. Although private societies exist within the state and are, as it were, so many parts of it, still it is not within the authority of the state universally and per se to forbid them to exist as such. For man is permitted by a right of nature to form private societies; the state, on the other hand, has been instituted to protect and not to destroy natural right, and if it should forbid its citizens to enter into associations, it would clearly do something contradictory to itself, because both the state itself and private associations are begotten of one and the same principle, namely, that men are by nature inclined to associate.

SOCIALIZATION

Mater et Magistra

59. Certainly one of the principal characteristics which seem to be typical of our age is an increase in social relationships, in those mutual ties, that is, which grow daily more numerous and which have led to the introduction of many and varied forms of associations in the lives and activities of citizens, and to their acceptance within our legal framework. Scientific and technical progress, greater productive efficiency, and a higher standard of living are among the many present-day factors which would seem to have contributed to this trend.

60. This development in the social life of man is at once a symptom and a cause of the growing intervention of the state, even in matters which are of intimate concern to the individual, hence of great importance and not devoid of risk. We might cite as examples such matters as health and education, the choice of a career,

and the care and rehabilitation of the physically and mentally handicapped.

It is also partly the result, partly the expression of a natural, well-nigh irresistible urge in man to combine with his fellows for the attainment of aims and objectives which are beyond the means or the capabilities of single individuals. In recent times this tendency has given rise to the formation everywhere of both national and international movements, associations and institutions with economic, cultural, social, sporting, recreational, professional, and political ends.

Advantages and disadvantages

61. Clearly, this sort of development in social relationships brings many advantages in its train. It makes it possible for the individual to exercise many of his personal rights, especially those which we call economic and social and which pertain to the

necessities of life, health care, education on a more extensive and improved basis, a more thorough professional training, housing, work, and suitable leisure and recreation. Furthermore, the progressive perfection of modern methods of thought-diffusion — the press, cinema, radio, television — makes it possible for everyone to participate in human events the world over.

62. At the same time, however, this multiplication and daily extension of forms of association brings with it a multiplicity of restrictive laws and regulations in many departments of human life. As a consequence, it narrows the sphere of a person's freedom of action. The means often used, the methods followed, the atmosphere created, all conspire to make it difficult for a person to think independently of outside influences, to act on his own initiative, exercise his responsibility, and express and fulfill his own personality. What then? Must we conclude that these increased social relationships necessarily reduce men to the condition of being mere automatons? By no means.

Creation of free men

63. For actually this growth in the social life of man is not a product of natural forces working, as it were, by blind impulse. It is, as we saw, the creation of men who are free and autonomous by nature — though they must, of course, recognize and, in a sense, obey the laws of economic development and social progress, and

cannot altogether escape from the pressure of environment.

64. The development of these social relationships, therefore, can and ought to be realized in a way best calculated to promote its inherent advantages and to preclude, or at least diminish, its attendant disadvantages.

65. To this end, a sane view of the common good must be present and operative in men invested with public authority. They must take account of all those social conditions which favor the full development of human personality. Moreover, We consider it altogether vital that the numerous intermediary bodies and corporate enterprises — which are, so to say, the main vehicle of this social growth — be really autonomous, and loyally collaborate in pursuit of their own specific interests and those of the common good. For these groups must themselves necessarily present the form and substance of a true community, and this will only be the case if they treat their individual members as human persons and encourage them to take an active part in the ordering of their lives.

66. As these mutual ties binding the men of our age one to the other grow and develop, governments will the more easily achieve a right order the more they succeed in striking a balance between the autonomous and active collaboration of individuals and groups, and the timely co-ordination and encouragement by the state of these private undertakings.

THE PURPOSE OF ECONOMIC LIFE

Pius XI, Caritate Christi Compulsi

30. No leader in public economy, no power of organization will ever be able to bring social conditions to a peaceful solution, unless first in the

very field of economics there triumphs moral law based on God and conscience. This is the underlying value of every value in the political life as well as in the economic life of nations; this is the soundest "rate of exchange." If it is kept steady, all the rest will be stable, being guaranteed by the immutable and eternal law of God.

Pius XI, Quadragesimo Anno*

75. The various occupations will combine and coalesce into, as it were, a single body and like members of the body mutually aid and complete one another. For then only will the social economy be rightly established and attain its purposes when all and each are supplied with all the goods that the wealth and resources of nature, technical achievement, and the social organization of economic life can furnish. And these goods ought indeed to be enough both to meet the demands of necessity and decent comfort and to advance people to that happier and fuller condition of life which, when it is wisely cared for, is not only no hindrance to virtue but helps it greatly.

110. Since the present system of economy is founded chiefly upon ownership and labor, the principles of right reason, that is, of Christian social philosophy, must be kept in mind regarding ownership and labor and their association together, and must be put into actual practice. First, so as to avoid the reefs of individualism and collectivism, the twofold character, that is individual and social, both of capital or ownership and of work or labor must be given due and rightful weight. Relations of one to the other must be made to conform to the laws of strictest justice — commutative justice as it is called — with the support, however, of Christian charity. Free competition, kept within definite and due limits, and still more economic dictatorship, must be effectively brought under public authority in these matters which pertain to the latter's function.

Pius XII, La Solennità della Pentecoste, June 1, 1941

1685. Likewise the national economy, as it is the product of the men who work together in the community of the state, has no other end than to secure without interruption the material conditions in which the individual life of the citizens may fully develop. Where this is secured in a permanent way, a people will be, in a true sense, economically rich because the general well-being, and consequently the personal right of all to the use of worldly goods, is thus actuated in conformity with the purpose willed by the Creator.

1686. From this, beloved children, it will be easy for you to conclude that the economic riches of a people do not properly consist in the abundance of goods, measured according to a purely and solely material calculation of their worth, but in the fact that such an abundance represents and offers really and effectively the material basis sufficient for the proper personal development of its members.

Pius XII, Nell' Alba, Christmas, 1941

1751. Nobody should think that by indicting the materialism of the nineteenth and twentieth centuries We intend to blame technical progress. No. We do not indict what fundamentally is a gift of God; for, as the

* See also Nos. 42–43 cited in Chapter II, p. 22.

Lord God makes wheat to grow from earth and soil, thus, when He created the world, He hid for us in the depth of the earth treasures, metals and precious stones, so that they may be mined by man for his needs, for his works, and for his progress. The Church, the mother of so many European universities, attracts today, as she always did, the most prominent scientists; but she is well aware that man can use every good entrusted to him, even the freedom of will, either for good or for evil. Thus the spirit and the direction in which technical progress has been used has now resulted in science having to expiate its own errors. Science has been misused for destruction, and, in fact, today it destroys the very buildings that it yesterday proudly erected.

Pius XII, Christmas Broadcast, 1942

1851. Those who are familiar with the great Encyclicals of Our Predecessors and Our Own previous messages know well that the Church does not hesitate to draw the practical conclusions which are derived from the moral nobility of work, and to give them all the support of her authority. These exigencies include, besides a just wage which covers the needs of the worker and his family, the conservation and perfection of a social order which will make possible an assured, even if modest, private property for all classes of society, which will promote higher education for the children of the working class who are especially endowed with intelligence and good will, will promote the care and the practice of the social spirit in one's immediate neighborhood, in the district, the province, the people, and the nation, a spirit which, by smoothing over friction arising from privileges or class interests, removes from the workers the sense of isolation through the assuring experience of a genuinely human, and fraternally Christian, solidarity.

Pius XII, Radio Address, September 1, 1944

Technical progress does not determine economic life as a fatal and necessary factor. It has indeed too often yielded timidly to the demands of rapacious, selfish plans calculated to accumulate capital indefinitely; why should it not then yield also to the necessity of maintaining and ensuring private property for all, that cornerstone of social order? Even technical progress, as a social factor, should not prevail over the general good, but should rather be directed and subordinated to it.

John XXIII, Mater et Magistra

73. In view of the rapid expansion of national economies, particularly since the war, there is one very important social principle to which We would draw your attention. It is this: Economic progress must be accompanied by a corresponding social progress, so that all classes of citizens can participate in the increased productivity. The utmost vigilance and effort is needed to ensure that social inequalities, so far from increasing, are reduced to a minimum.

74. From this it follows that the economic prosperity of a nation is not so much its total assets in terms of wealth and property, as the equitable division and distribution of this

wealth. This it is which guarantees the personal development of the members of society, which is the true goal of a nation's economy.

246. Certainly, the Church teaches — and has always taught — that scientific and technical progress and the resultant material well-being are good things and mark an important phase in human civilization. But the Church teaches, too, that goods of this kind must be valued according to their true nature: as instruments used by man for the better attainment of his end. They help to make him a better man, both in the natural and the supernatural order.

SINCE the Church considers the social question to be also a moral question, and since it reacts to this challenge by detailed moral teachings, it is pertinent to consider now the basic moral principles that affect economic life. The present chapter treats of the nature of man, society, and economic life. These realities, subject to the scrutiny of right reason, give us the fundamental basis for an economic ethic. In the following chapter the same problem is examined in terms of human conduct: the virtues that impel us to live morally and rationally in economic society. From these two processes of inquiry, the reader acquires the bedrock principles used in later chapters as we pass judgments first upon the major economic philosophies of our day (Chapters V–VII) and then the controlling institutions of American society (Chapters VIII–XVII).

THE NATURE OF MAN

Under God, man is the center of the universe. Man has an inner dignity, based on his nature, origin, and destiny, which all must respect. This nature is the immediate source of rights and duties. It confers upon man an aura of sacredness which is not shared by the animals of the field or by purely material things.

But man does not live alone. To realize fully his powers and aspirations, he must live in the society of his fellow man. This fact, to a degree, modifies the rights and duties which spring from the nature of the individual. It also adds new rights and duties.

Such in a nutshell is the foundation of Catholic social theory. The detailed spelling out of man's prerogatives and obligations is but an amplifying of these fundamental principles. Time and again, the great encyclicals of recent popes have come back to this bedrock upon which a sound social order must rest.

The Dignity of Man. The dignity of man springs from his nature. It is not conferred by society, nor is it merely a product of law or custom. Certain rights are inalienable. They may not be abridged or taken away by any man. Long before the Christian era, sound philosophers reached this conclusion, however imperfectly. Man has a soul. He has reason and free will. This spiritual nature raises him above the animal kingdom, and even higher above lifeless matter. Man is thus lord of the universe. Lesser things are made to serve his needs. He may use them in accordance with the law of his nature and nature's God.

In addition, Christian revelation teaches us of an even higher status of man. We know that man is destined, provided he is worthy, for an immortal life with God. Even in this world, the Christian in the state of grace shares in the life of God. He is "an adopted son of God," "a temple of the Holy Spirit," "a brother of Christ," and may be "a member of the mystical body of Christ." This special and gratuitous solicitude of God toward the creature made in His image and likeness confers a unique dignity upon every man. Christ teaches that what is done to the least of the little ones is done to Him.

Even among those who do not accept the full Christian revelation, there is often a traditional respect for the dignity of man. In most of the world, human life is held to be sacred. The taking of life, or even the doing of violence to the human person, is considered a crime. Men will risk their own lives to avoid even the involuntary killing of another. Thus, when an automobile driver sees a child dart into the street in front of him, he applies the brakes and swerves at the risk of fatal injury to himself. When a person falls overboard from a ship, an effort is made to rescue him, though this may involve great danger to the seamen concerned. In such circumstances, there is no calculation of cost or of the relative talents and achievements of the individuals in danger.

A great portion of Christian social ethics could be derived from this one principle of man's worth. It could be the basis of a philosophy of labor. The right to work at a decent wage, the right to fair and just treatment, and many similar rights follow from the dignity of man. Man is more than a machine or a commodity.

Because of man's nature, the great modern heresy of statism stands condemned. Any system which holds that man's rights are conferred by the state, and that they may be modified or taken away at the whim of a despot, is unnatural and grossly immoral. Communism is wrong, not primarily because of its economic tenets, but because it makes men slaves of the state. National socialism and fascism were wrong, not in the first place because of their wars of aggression, but because they made man a tool in the hands of a dictator. Wherever the state arrogates to itself supreme power, disregarding the law of God and man's inalienable rights, it is a monstrosity contrary to all reason.

The evil roots of statism are many. But in the United States, we should particularly note the influence of Auguste Comte and his philosophy of positivism. His sociology holds that the state is antecedent to man and is the source of man's rights. We are fortunate indeed to have escaped the full implications of this theory. But we should not ignore the fact that this system is taught and accepted in many American universities. It has infected our intellectual world with an empiricism and experimentalism which denies the idea of natural rights and basic moral principles. This fact undoubtedly explains in part the sympathy of some intellectuals toward collectivism and communism. With others, it leads to secularism and pragmatism. Thus, we have a rapidly shifting society, based on expediency, not principle.

A sound social philosophy also repudiates materialism. Man has a spiritual soul, and this is the source of human nobility. A concentration upon material achievement, to the detriment of the spiritual, is a perversion of right order. The material world is to be the servant of man, not his master. Economic life is not an end in itself; it must be subordinated to higher and nobler laws. Here again, we Americans must be vigilant in regard to our values. We have achieved such wonders of material progress that we are prone to exaggerate its importance. The cultivation of the mind and the soul is, after all, man's greatest boast.

More controversial is the assertion made by some that modern industrialism, with its assembly-line techniques, does violence to the dignity of man. It is held that repetitive labor is degrading, whereas creative and responsible labor is ennobling. But this type of work has always existed. The hoe-and-stick form of agriculture is certainly as monotonous as the assembly line. We should try, however, to make the surroundings of work help, rather than hinder, the development of man's personality.

The Rights of Man. Upon man's nature there are founded certain inalienable rights. A right is generally defined as an inviolable moral power which a person has to do something, or to have, acquire, or dispose of something. A duty is a moral obligation of doing or not doing something. Rights and duties are interconnected. One man's right imposes upon another the duty of respecting his prerogatives. Nevertheless, rights and duties may conflict in practice. Hence there is vital need for classifying rights and determining their relative priorities.

One method of evaluating rights is in terms of their origin. Thus, some rights spring directly from nature, whereas others are conferred by law or by man. The rights to live and to marry are natural; the right to a government job may derive from law; and the right to use another's house may come from a contract made between men. These examples also illustrate the priority of rights. Those rooted directly in human nature are fundamental and may not be abrogated by law or by agreement among men. On the other hand, just laws, enacted in the interest of the common welfare, take precedence over private contracts. Divine law is higher than the law of man. Of man's natural rights, those involving directly the spiritual side of his nature would be more vital than those connected with his physical well-being. Hence it would not be sound to treat all rights equally, not distinguishing between the higher and the lower.

A second basis for evaluation is the relative necessity of rights for their intended purpose. Thus, the right to possess property is closely connected with the natural right to live. But not all property ministers equally to the right to live. The meager stock of food and clothing of the very poor is more necessary for them than the millions possessed by a wealthy man. In the one case, the goods described are needed for the welfare of the human person. In the second instance, many of the possessions are superfluous in terms of survival. The urgency of a right deepens as it goes closer to its source and justification.

A final classification pertinent here concerns the relative priority of community rights in contrast to individual rights. Here Catholic thinking takes a turn which may surprise many. The common good has precedence over individual rights *in the same sphere*. Even with the most fundamental rights, this is true. An illustration of this point is war, in which individuals risk their lives for the welfare of the nation and the lives and liberties of others. At first glance, this point might seem to be a concession to statism. However, when the term "common good" is correctly defined, the apparent conflict will vanish. The more detailed explanations given in subsequent chapters will make this point clear.

Confusion in regard to rights and duties can be avoided when the universe is considered in relation to the master plan of the Creator. There are two profound philosophical truths in particular which should not be overlooked in discussing the foundations of social ethics. First, the world is purposive. All nature strives toward determined ends. Man, however, seeks the ends of his being consciously and freely. Second, reality is pluralistic, with gradations of being and consequently of value. Spiritual being is of a higher nature than material; living being is "more real" than nonliving being. While every grade of being tends to seek its own ends, it is at the same time subordinate to higher forms of reality. Thus, animals serve man and nonliving matter is assimilated and often transformed by living beings. In man the needs of the body are subsidiary to those of the soul.

When metaphysics is applied to the field of ethics, we have a sound basis for a distinction among various types of rights. Thus, rights essential for the basic ends of man's existence are more important than and have priority over nonessential rights, even of a higher order. For example, a man should not risk his life to protect a work of art from vandals. His right to one type of cultural perfection, though higher in nature than the right to bodily survival, is relatively nonessential, whereas the latter is essential. On the other hand, among rights equally necessary for the ends of man's nature, the higher would take precedence over the lower. In times of persecution, men rightly die rather than apostatize from their religious faith. Essential values of the spirit are more important than bodily survival.

In line with this reasoning, the economic order exists to minister to the human person. When economic institutions become perverted, so that essential ends of man's nature are not adequately realized, a change in economic life is morally justified. This point is fundamental to the present study.

These general principles will take on life and vigor when they are applied to concrete problems. Indeed, most of the field of social ethics is concerned with the classifying of relative rights and duties. Delicate balances must be struck between conflicting rights in the same sphere and in different spheres. The basic dignity of the individual must be interpreted in the light of his duties to society. Then a clear picture will emerge of a social order, conformable to man's nature, as seen in terms of sound reason and divine revelation. At the same time, it is necessary to sound a warning that the application of general principles to concrete problems is not always easy. While the principles are unchanging, shifting and differing analyses of contingent facts lead to differences and disputes. Thus it happens that many, who accept without reservation the social teaching of the Church, may differ in matters of application and policy.

Fundamental Rights. Recent encyclicals have enumerated nearly a score of basic rights, but those connected with socioeconomic problems are apposite here.[1] In this sphere, the right to live is most fundamental. This conforms with the deep-rooted instinct of self-preservation, which is so clearly a part of man's nature. Negatively, this right is expressed in the commandment "Thou shalt not kill." Positively, it involves the right to the necessary means for existence. This means not only a minimum of food, clothing, and shelter, but the obtaining of this minimum in a manner conforming with human dignity. It demands a socioeconomic order which affords men the opportunity to live as human beings. Mere animal survival is not living in a human sense.

Family rights are closely connected with the right to live. The physical, emotional, and spiritual needs of man are normally satisfied only in a family environment. The instinct to propagate the race is deep-rooted in our nature. Furthermore, we know from divine revelation, reason, and experience that monogamous family life is the only acceptable way for preserving the human race. Accordingly, a sound social order must minister to the needs of family life.

The right to possess property is also fundamental. Individual and family living in a human way would not ordinarily be possible otherwise. If all goods were in common, we would face an intolerable choice between two evils. On the one hand, there could be a disorderly struggle for immediate needs. Organized economic life would be impossible, and strife and contention the normal course of events. On the other hand, the community could control all wealth. But this would place in the hands of the collective group, and its ruler, absolute power over the individual and the family. Neither way of life meets the demands of human nature.

The right of association likewise springs from man's nature. We are social creatures, intimately dependent upon one another. The full powers of the individual are realized only in conjunction with others. In the economic sphere, organization is normally necessary for efficient and orderly production. So universal is this instinct for association that it can be called a basic human trait. Hence man has the natural right to form groups or teams for lawful ends.

Finally, the social order should be so organized that higher rights, not enumerated here, should be protected. Man has spiritual and cultural needs in addition to the physical. Rights in this sphere are generally of a

---

[1] For a lengthy enumeration, with many quotations from the popes, see Robert Kothen, *L'Enseignement social de l'Église*, pp. 166–214. J. A. Messner, in his volume *Social Ethics* (St. Louis: Herder, 1949), pp. 222–226, lists fourteen basic rights. Other listings may be found in the *Code of Social Principles*. Pope John XXIII's Encyclical *Pacem in Terris* has an unusually complete presentation of fundamental human rights.

higher order than those connected with bodily needs. The lower should minister to the higher; certainly it should not impede or conflict with nobler ends.

The Equality of Man.   On the basis of man's nature and fundamental rights, we can say that "all men were created equal." Men are equal in origin, nature, and destiny. All are created alike by God. All possess the same basic human qualities of reason and free will. All have immortal souls destined to eternal life. All are called to the higher destiny revealed in the teachings of Christ.

While men have a moral equality, at the same time they have individual differences which may not be ignored. Not all have the same talents or dispositions. There are varying degrees of intelligence among individuals. Characters differ, as do tastes and aptitudes. In addition to inborn variations, circumstances and environment affect people deeply. Family care, the degree of education, and economic status are bound to make a difference.

As a result, it would be contrary to human nature to expect or to demand absolute equality among men. There is nothing inherently wrong in the distinction between leaders and followers, the well-to-do, and those less endowed with material goods, the educated and the uneducated. These distinctions could be wrong, however, if their source were vitiated or their unnecessary continuance were contrary to the common good. Leadership based on force and violence could be unjust. Unequal distribution of wealth could proceed to extremes which would be harmful to society.

An intriguing question concerns political equality. The Church has been traditionally reluctant to pronounce judgment upon forms of government. Its concern has rather been that governments be just, that they rule under law, and that this be in conformity with the law of God. Because of the inequalities of men, some Churchmen have even been hesitant in past centuries to espouse the idea of popular sovereignty. In this light, it is interesting to note the approach of Pope John XXIII in *Pacem in Terris.* The ideal type of government advocated in this encyclical is for all practical purposes representative and democratic in spirit.

On the same line of reasoning, there are current demands for greater industrial democracy. Granted the inequalities among men, it is still true that modern economic life is so pervasive in its influence and so exacting in its demands, that those partaking in it should have a greater voice in directing its course. In earlier societies, life was so organized that men could keep a basic independence, even though economically subject to another. There was more opportunity to shift from one job to another, to become an independent craftsman or to own a small enterprise. Today even the directors of huge factories are often subordinate officials, taking orders from a central office or from financial groups who control the company. It may well be questioned whether all inequalities existing today spring from unequal ability, or whether some come from a form of social organization which is encroaching upon the basic rights of the individual.

A problem of inequality which, while not strictly economic, has important social and economic overtones involves racial discrimination, particularly against Negroes. There is hardly any need to elaborate upon the un-Christian nature of such practices. A conception of life which would deny basic rights to a whole race merely because of the accident of color is essentially barbaric. By contrast, a true Christian social order calls for the harmonious integration of all groups into the social body. It does not reject the fact of diversity, but it achieves an organic union of various groups within the body politic and economic.

While the principles enunciated here are by their nature universal, it is useful to state explicitly that justice and right must be given to minority groups. Indeed, many of our social problems exist in heightened form among exploited peoples. Thus, Negroes, Mexicans, and Puerto Ricans suffer more than others from poverty, inadequate housing, insufficient facilities for medical care and education, and poor working conditions. Hence the obligations outlined in these pages apply especially where the abuses are greater. This is particularly true of the need for *organized* social action, as demanded by the virtue of social justice. Education, laws, and other forms of community influence and pressure should be used to counter these evils. Indeed, broad programs for social reform are not likely to be successful, if one group can be exploited with impunity. The competitive pressure from such underpaid workers would lower standards for all.

It is shameful that the most vocal proponents of racial justice have been the American communists. It speaks well for the basic good sense of minorities that communists have found so few recruits from their midst. Nevertheless, there is no assurance that Negroes and others will always remain unresponsive to the pleas of agitators. Moreover, in the present world struggle Americans would be indeed shortsighted were they to overlook the propaganda value for the Soviet Union derived from American discrimination. The great peoples of the Orient, especially, feel bitter about racial slurs. It would be tragic were our domestic prejudices to drive them into the Soviet or Communist Chinese orbit, while we were spending billions for an anticommunist foreign policy. These points will be developed in Chapter XV.

MAN IN SOCIETY

The discussion of rights thus far has centered primarily upon the individual and only incidentally upon society. In a sense, this emphasis is correct. Society exists for the individual, and not the reverse. But in another sense the approach just taken needs completion. Man is a social animal, as well as a person with rights and duties based upon his individual nature. Indeed, social living is essential to the full development of the human personality. Moreover, it is an aspect which needs stress in the United States, since our traditions have been heavily individualistic. Only recently has our Catholic educational system begun to emphasize the requirements of social living. Again, we have the reputation of being a nation of many laws, but yet restive under law and occasionally defiant of law. Our frontier tradition of resourcefulness and individual initiative has persisted long after the frontier has been closed, and has been felt in fields where social co-operation is also needed.

The Social Nature of Man. Man's physical and psychological being shows that he is social. Physically, man is helpless without society. At birth, he is weak and puny. He needs the fostering care of the family to survive. He matures slowly, in contrast to the animal kingdom, where the young are rarely dependent for more than a few months or a year. In the struggle for survival, man does not have the physical resources to meet the challenge of savage nature. He has not the strength of the lion or tiger, the fleetness of the antelope, the cunning and sensitiveness of the fox, the natural defenses of the porcupine, the protective coloration of the rabbit, the agility of the squirrel, or other of the qualities, refined senses, or instincts which nature gives to animals for their self-protection. Without society, the child would freeze in the winter, starve for lack of food, or be the easy prey of any predatory animal.

Psychologically, man needs society. In contrast to the animal, we are born with few instincts. We do not sense dangers, nor do we realize what natural foods are good and what poisonous. We only learn from others in these vital matters. Moreover, our rational nature develops only in society. Men who live isolated lives rarely achieve fully balanced personalities, and often lose their sanity. Even the family is too small a unit for the full development of personality. Introverted, ingrown families are not adapted for living in this complex world. The overprotected and excessively sheltered child becomes a problem. Our minds, wills, and characters grow and become strong only in the give and take of social living.

Man has strong aspirations for social living. He seeks the company and values the esteem of his fellow man. The desire to love and to share in the love of others is among the deepest traits of our nature. Hence it is only to be expected that a rich social life characterizes human existence. Even our relationships to lower orders of being tend to be social. Thus, man the worker exercises dominion over the world. He performs, as it were, a task of creation in changing and ennobling lesser goods. But he has found that work must be performed as part of a harmonious pattern of social life, if it is to be fully effective.

Society is almost essential for economic life and the physical survival of the race. It may be just possible for a single family in a suitable environment to meet its economic needs. By heavy and unceasing toil, it could obtain the bare minimum of food, clothing, and shelter necessary to survive. Only a few families could be maintained under such conditions. Even the primitive farming, hunting, grazing, and nomadic societies afforded a living to but a relatively few. For the large population of modern times, social organization is essential.

In economic life, organization permits needed forms of specialization, division of labor, and large-scale production, with consequent multiplication of skill and efficiency. When men specialize, they acquire great skills in their particular fields. By division of labor, a large operation can be broken down into many simple tasks, which each worker can perform more efficiently. As individual tasks become simpler, they are subject to mechanization, whereby human skills can be multiplied greatly. The machine takes over the skill of the individual worker, and power resources concentrate in a small factory energies which could be supplied only by thousands of workers. Thus, the essentials of living can be obtained for large populations with relatively small effort, and time is made available for luxuries, cultural living, social relationships, and other characteristically human occupations.

Man's Social Rights and Obligations. Since social living is part of man's nature, this fact is bound to modify our concept of rights and duties based on the individual person. Not only are individual rights qualified by the impact of equal or even superior rights of others, but specific rights and duties arise from the fact of social living.

Among the more fundamental rights is the right of association mentioned earlier. What man's nature impels him to do is clearly a right provided it is exercised within the bounds of reason. The associations of interest here are those connected with the economic order. They include business partnerships and corporations, labor unions, various forms of co-operatives, industrial councils, and similar natural groupings. The functioning of these societies should, of course, be governed by the laws of justice and the common good. Within these bounds, they have a right to exist peaceably. Any effort by a more powerful society to destroy them is morally wrong. Such would be the case in a totalitarian state, which permits only organs under its absolute control to survive. Again, if a corporation were to use its economic power to dissolve a labor union desired by its workers, it would be acting unjustly.

Basic among the social duties of man is the obligation to contribute, according to his position, to the common good. Since society is natural to man, he must share the responsibilities as well as the privileges of social living. Of course, not all societies are equally necessary. Some, such as the state or the family, flow from nature itself. Others, such as choral groups or bridge clubs, are purely matters of taste and convenience. There is a third group which occupies an intermediate position which is difficult to classify today. This comprises associations which are virtually indispensable to achieve some necessary good. Thus, some argue that in modern society the labor union is a practical necessity in order to achieve some basic rights of man. This point will be discussed subsequently, but it illustrates the complex nature of the common good. However, the principle is clear: when a society is necessary to achieve some basic end springing from man's nature, we are not privileged to be neutral.

While society exists to serve man, it is also necessary for his welfare. By using society for the welfare of all, each individual secures his own well-being. This means that a proper balance must be struck between individual rights and social responsibility. The working out of this formula in detailed problems is not easy, but it is a task which may not be shirked. In facing this problem, the principles given earlier in regard to the priority of rights will enable us to secure results fully consonant with human nature.

SOCIALIZATION

When *Mater et Magistra* was released, its qualified advocacy of socialization caused a minor tempest. The term was used in the unofficial modern-language translations issued by the Vatican, but it was replaced by various circumlocutions in the official Latin text. Much of the controversy, however, was the result of hasty reporting and headline writing. Socialization, as used by the Vatican translators, simply reflects the fact that modern life is becoming more social. Men are increasingly interdependent. The trend toward growing governmental controls over business is but one phase of this development. Actually the appraisal of this trend by Pope John was not substantially different from those of his predecessors.

There was some difference, and this fact is important in assessing the function of papal social encyclicals. A social encyclical is not written in a vacuum. It is the application of timeless truths, derived from natural law and Scripture and developed by theologians, to the problems of a given moment of history. Since social conditions change, concrete papal judgments and warnings may also change, even when they are based on the same enduring moral principles.

It can be said that the papacy has a tendency to "lean against the wind." Knowing that human nature appears to go to extremes, the papacy is often forced to warn against existing trends. Thus, Popes Leo XIII and Pius XI emphasized the need for strong government intervention in economic life, because supine governments in their day permitted grievous exploitation of workers and the politically helpless. As the pendulum swung toward the other extreme, Pope Pius XII warned against unnecessary nationalization of industry and extreme concentration of political power. Faced with a still different set of conditions, it was to be expected that Pope John would come up with answers somewhat at variance with those of his predecessors.

The increasing complexity of social life is a fact. It stems from many factors, such as man's social nature, the growth in population, greater ease of communication, rising living standards, scientific and technical progress, and the ever mounting demands upon the modern state. One need only read about the simpler life of the eighteenth century to realize how all-pervasive is the change today.

Some of this simpler life persisted well into the twentieth century, and the yearning for it shows through in several of the earlier social encyclicals. By contrast, *Mater et Magistra* faces up to modern changes as largely irreversible facts. They have potentialities for good, such as higher living standards, better education, and increased participation in public life. They have their dangers, and the encyclical reflects an awareness of the literature about the organization man, the image makers, and the status seekers. It notes the charge that men are becoming automatons as a result of the pressures of society upon the individual.

But it rejects this charge! What man creates man can control morally. The Pope challenges leaders of government to decentralize power whenever feasible. This is best done by strengthening intermediate groups in society. In terms of our nation, this means revitalizing state and local governments. It calls for giving more power to socially responsible corporations and labor unions. Neighborhood associations should be encouraged to make cities better places in which to live.

This plea for a balance of power, as is clear from the context of both encyclicals, is not the sloganeering "states' rights" of some extremists. These groups oppose federal controls over the economy, but offer no compensating sense of social responsibility on the part of states, corporations, and individuals. Yet government must promote the common good, the general welfare, and it may not remain supinely impotent or inactive when basic human rights are being violated.

THE PURPOSE OF ECONOMIC LIFE

The type of society most germane to the present study is the economic order, with all its ramifications among other social institutions. One of the major problems of modern times is the reorientation of economic life, so that it may conform to God's purpose in creating material things.

Goals Sought. Of first importance is the realization that economic life is subordinate to higher values. It deals with the material order, and this by its nature is inferior to matters cultural and spiritual. The lower should minister to the higher. Hence the basic purpose of economic life is to provide man with the necessities for survival, and the foundations for cultural and spiritual life. It will achieve this when every willing and able worker can earn at least a stable decent wage for himself and his family. This wage will provide necessities, a minimum opportunity for comfort and leisure, and some chance to realize nonmaterial aspirations according to the interests and talents of the individual.

Economic life should furnish, insofar as possible, opportunity for individuals to develop and utilize their personal talents. It should be the material foundation of an educational system which will bring out abilities and skills. For those whose aptitudes are mechanical, this would mean at least adequate vocational training. Where abilities tend toward the intellectual or the professional spheres, there should be sufficient opportunities for advanced study. In general, the trend should be toward an increase in leisure, so that man can be freed from excessive preoccupation with material things.

An important step toward this goal would be the wider distribution of wealth, particularly the actual ownership of property. In this way, individuals would have greater independence. They would be able to exercise personal choice as to the use of their resources for themselves and their families. There would also result a greater stability in economic life, to the extent that a smaller proportion of individuals would depend upon giant economic organizations. In principle, this method of securing cultural benefits is preferable to organized efforts by the state to provide for many of the needs of its citizens. Of course, we should not condemn social insurance, grants-in-aid for education, or civic recreational and cultural developments. In modern times these are necessary. But it is still desirable that individuals have the greatest possible freedom to direct their own lives in these fields. A more equitable distribution of resources would help bring this about.

A phrase that recurs throughout both encyclicals of Pope John XXIII is "Economic progress must be accompanied by a corresponding social progress." The Pope rejects the "trickle-down" theory of economic life, which holds that as the economy prospers and accumulates great wealth, much of this will seep down to the poor. This did happen to a degree in some industrial nations, but in others wealth accumulated to the few and destitution remained with the many.

Neither does Pope John accept the Spartan concept, held by most communist nations and some developing countries, that one or two generations must remain in penury while capital is accumulated so that future generations can prosper. Whatever history says about the success of such tactics, the cost in terms of human sacrifice is too great. Economic progress must be matched by increase in social services: education, medical care, good housing, and social insurance. Wealth should be distributed equitably and social inequalities kept to a minimum.

While *Mater et Magistra* does not specify any single method for achieving these goals, it assumes in discussing agriculture that there will be taxation according to ability to pay, social insurance, and government provision for essential social services. The Pope writes in the context of European economies and may be using these examples as illustrations of one method, without indicating that this is necessarily the only feasible way of realizing these ends. The essential point is a fair distribution of national income, eliminating gross disparities between the rich and the poor.

Although widespread diffusion of ownership is the most desirable foundation for individual freedom and economic stability, it is nevertheless a fact that many will remain in the status of wage earners. Under these circumstances, a goal of social policy must be the preservation and enhancement of human dignity under conditions of economic dependence. The wage earner must at the minimum be accorded his basic rights and treated as befits a human being. Above this level of essential rights there are opportunities for giving the worker greater participation in the economic process. He could be given a more definite voice in matters which greatly affect his welfare. In this way, to use the language of Pope Pius XII, he would no longer be a mere object — a passive factor in the economic planning of others — but he would be a subject, a person exercising some control over his own destiny. Society would not be mechanical — a mass held together by external force — but it would be organic, based on the intelligent co-operation of free men and independent but collaborating social groups.

In attaining material wealth, technical progress can be a substantial help. The popes have insisted that, in condemning certain abuses in the socio-economic sphere, they were not minimizing the value of modern technology. Wisely used, these processes can bring about the abolition of want. They can make food, clothing, and housing abundant for the needs of all. Moreover, they can provide leisure and comfort for many, and ultimately for all. Such goals are in themselves desirable from the viewpoint of Christian virtue. Excessive poverty brings a preoccupation with material things which injures the dignity of human nature and is contrary to the law of God. Of course, this wrongful solicitude about material things can come from an opposite extreme, when men seek wealth for its own sake and become preoccupied with amassing riches. Greed, vanity, and lust for power are also contrary to the law of God.

Most important today is the need for stability in economic life. Alternations between inflation and deflation are upsetting to higher values. Family life is strained. Men cannot make reasonable plans for the future. They are unhappy in good times for the fear of what is to come. Stability is mainly a problem of organization. It is obvious that we have the natural resources, technical skill, power, machines, labor supply, and managerial talent to abolish want and produce a high standard of living. It is equally

obvious that we have not so organized these factors that we are able to
utilize them fully. This is the problem and challenge of our age. Organization in turn is a social problem. It involves the harmonious working
together of individuals and groups. The many organizations and institutions
needed to effectuate policy will vary in different times and places. Economic science, prudential judgment based on experience, and social ethics
will work together in bringing about the desired result. This would be the
Christian social order, the restoring of all things in Christ.

Reform of Institutions. The first steps toward this goal will be the
infusion of Christian principles of justice and charity into the various
classes of society. Four great groups are important in this connection:
capital, labor, the farming community, and government. By capital is
meant, not merely finance, but the ownership of all productive property.
This would include industry, business, and the service trades. The aim
would be the spread of social justice and charity among each of the four
groups so that each would seek the common welfare as well as individual
goals. This would not be primarily a matter of forming a Christian conscience among individuals, important as this is. Rather it would involve a
reform of the *institutions* of society. If the institutions of society tend
toward wrong ends, the efforts inspired by personal good will are likely to
be nullified. On the other hand, if the institutions of society are sound,
they will contain and constrain men of ill will, preventing them from
doing serious harm.

The work of reform is committed to all classes of society. In one sense,
the state, as the supreme social group, should take the lead in seeking to
reform social institutions. The common good is its very reason of being.
But at the same time, the state itself may often be in need of reform. In
modern times, it has reacted from a *laissez-faire* individualism, where it
stood by impotently in the face of great injustice, to some approximation
of statism, where it absorbed powers which should be committed to lesser
groups. The state best seeks social justice by aiding subordinate groups to
perfect institutions which bring about harmonious and prosperous economic life. Other groups in turn, inspired by Christian principles, should
endeavor to correct evils in their spheres of action, and to direct their aims
in the light of justice and charity. Thus we would achieve a basic reorientation of society.

Clearly this is an immense task. But it is made easier by the fact that
other alternatives are being rejected. In much of the world, the old order
has been cast aside. But some of the newer forms, such as communism,

are worse than those which they supplanted. As extremes are shown to be unsound, men are bound to respect the moderation and sanity of the Christian social ethic. If we can formulate it in detail, and show its applicability to a complex society, it may well be received as were the first good tidings of the Gospel.

READINGS*

J. Y. Calvez, *Social Thought of John XXIII*, Chap. 1.
J. Y. Calvez and J. Perrin, *The Church and Social Justice*, Chaps. 5, 8.
J. F. Cronin, *Christianity and Social Progress*, Chaps. 3–5, 30.
H. Johnston, *Business Ethics*, Chaps. 3, 6.
J. Messner, *Social Ethics* (rev. ed.), pp. 1–122, 324–330, 928–930.
P. Riga, *Peace on Earth*, Part I.

* For further readings, see List No. 3 in the Appendix.

Chapter IV

THE SOCIAL VIRTUES

JUSTICE

Commutative Justice

Pius XI, Quadragesimo Anno

47. That justice called commutative commands sacred respect for the division of possessions and forbids invasion of others' rights through the exceeding of the limits of one's own property; but the duty of owners to use their property only in a right way does not come under this type of justice, but under other virtues, obligations of which "cannot be enforced by legal action."

110. . . . the twofold character, that is individual and social, both of capital or ownership and of work or labor must be given due and rightful weight. Relations of one to the other must be made to conform to the laws of strictest justice — commutative justice, as it is called, with the support, however, of Christian charity.

Distributive Justice

Leo XIII, Rerum Novarum

49. Consequently, among the numerous and weighty duties of rulers who would serve their people well, this is first and foremost, namely, that they protect equitably each and every class of citizens, maintaining inviolate that justice especially which is called distributive.

Pius XI, Quadragesimo Anno

25. The function of the rulers of the state, moreover, is to watch over the community and its parts; but in protecting private individuals in their rights, chief consideration ought to be given to the weak and the poor.

Pius XII, Address to Catholic Employers, May 7, 1949

It would be just as untrue to assert that every particular business is of its nature a society, with its personal relationships determined by the norms of distributive justice to the point where all without distinction — owners or not of the means of production — would be entitled to their share in the property, or at the very least in the profits, of the enterprise.

Such a conception stems from the assumption that every business belongs naturally within the sphere of public law. The assumption is inexact. Whether the business is organized in the form of a corporation or an association of all the workmen as part owners, or whether it is the private property of an individual who signs a wage contract with all his employees, in the one case as in the other it falls within the competence of the private-law discipline of economic life.

Social Justice

Leo XIII, Immortale Dei

22. Nevertheless, as We have laid down, to take no share in public matters would be equally as wrong (We speak in general) as not to have concern for, or not to bestow labor upon, the common good.

Leo XIII, Rerum Novarum

14. . . . however the earth may be apportioned among private owners, it does not cease to serve the common good of all. . . .

48. For the state is bound by the very law of its office to serve the common interest.

50. . . . all citizens, without exception, are obliged to contribute some-thing to the sum-total common good.

52. It is not right, as We have said, for either the citizen or the family to be absorbed by the state; it is proper that the individual and the family should be permitted to retain their freedom of action so far as this is possible without jeopardizing the common good and without injuring anyone.

Pius XI, Quadragesimo Anno

49. It follows from what We have termed the individual and at the same time social character of ownership, that men must consider in this matter not only their own advantage but also the common good.

57. Therefore, the riches that economic-social developments constantly increase ought to be so distributed among individual persons and classes that the common advantage of all, which Leo XIII had praised, will be safeguarded; in other words that the common good of all society will be kept inviolate. By this law of social justice, one class is forbidden to exclude the other from sharing in the benefits.

71. Every effort must therefore be made that fathers of families receive a wage large enough to meet ordinary family needs adequately. But if this cannot always be done under existing circumstances, social justice demands that changes be introduced as soon as possible whereby such a wage will be assured to every adult workingman.

74. Hence it is contrary to social justice when, for the sake of personal gain and without regard for the common good, wages and salaries are excessively lowered or raised; and this same social justice demands that wages and salaries be so managed, through agreement of plans and wills, insofar as can be done, as to offer to

the greatest possible number the opportunity of getting work and obtaining suitable means of livelihood.

85. The most important among these interests is to promote the cooperation in the highest degree of each industry and profession for the sake of the common good of the country.

88. Loftier and nobler principles — social justice and social charity — must, therefore, be sought whereby this dictatorship may be governed firmly and fully. Hence, the institutions themselves of peoples and, particularly, those of all social life, ought to be penetrated with this justice, and it is most necessary that it be truly effective, that is, establish a juridical and social order which will, as it were, give form and shape to all economic life.

101. But it does violate right order when capital hires workers, that is the nonowning class, with a view to and under such terms that it directs business and even the whole economic system according to its own will and advantage, scorning the human dignity of the workers, the social character of economic activity and social justice itself, and the common good.

110. The public institutions themselves, of peoples, moreover, ought to make all human society conform to the needs of the common good; that is, to the norm of social justice.

Pius XI, On Atheistic Communism

51. In reality, besides commutative justice, there is also social justice with its own set obligations, from which neither employers nor workingmen can escape. Now it is of the very essence of social justice to demand from each individual all that is necessary for the common good. But just as in the living organism it is impossible to provide for the good of the whole unless each single part and each individual member is given what it needs for the exercise of its proper functions, so it is impossible to care for the social organism and the good of society as a unit unless each single part and each individual member — that is to say, each individual man in the dignity of his human personality — is supplied with all that is necessary for the exercise of his social functions. If social justice be satisfied, the result will be an intense activity in economic life as a whole, pursued in tranquillity and order.

53. It happens all too frequently, however, under the salary system, that individual employers are helpless to insure justice unless, with a view to its practice, they organize institutions the object of which is to prevent competition incompatible with fair treatment for the workers. Where this is true, it is the duty of contractors and employers to support and promote such necessary organizations as normal instruments enabling them to fulfill their obligations of justice.

Pius XII, La Solennità della Pentecoste, June 1, 1941

1685. Hence, it follows that the care of such a common good does not imply a power so extensive over the members of the community that in virtue of it the public authority can interfere with the evolution of that individual activity which We have just described, decide directly on the beginning or — excepting the case of legitimate capital punishment — the ending of human life, determine at will the manner of his physical, spiritual, religious, and moral movements in opposition to the personal duties or rights of man, and to this end abolish or deprive of efficacy his natural rights to material goods. To deduce such extension of power from the care of the common good would be equivalent to overthrowing the very meaning of the word common good, and falling into the error that the proper scope of man on earth is society, that society is an end in itself, that man has no other life which awaits him beyond that which ends here below.

Pius XII, Message on Centenary of St. Thomas the Apostle, December 31, 1952

. . . the social teaching of the Church . . . is based on social justice, on the duty of each to the community, and of the community to each; its goal is peace in the social order, a composing of conflicting interests, so that the humblest in a nation may have at least what is sufficient; its strength is in its uncompromising reverence for the honor and natural rights of every human being.

Pius XII, To Spanish Social Week, May, 1956

A social sense teaches individuals precisely the contrary. It makes them conscious of their social duties, it urges them to take into account in all their activities their membership in a community, to be preoccupied with the welfare of their neighbors and with the common good of society. It works on the social conscience of men and, as a *habitus*, it disposes them to reach the purposes which God and society expect from them. This is, therefore, the sense of general or legal justice of which scholastic philosophers speak and which the pontifical documents often call social justice.

John XXIII, Pacem in Terris

53. Men, both as individuals and as intermediate groups, are required to make their own specific contributions to the general welfare. The main consequence of this is that they must harmonize their own interests with the needs of others, and offer their goods and services as their rulers shall direct — assuming, of course, that justice is maintained and the authorities are acting within the limits of their competence. Those who have authority in the State must exercise that authority in a way which is not only morally irreproachable, but also best calculated to ensure or promote the State's welfare.

54. The attainment of the common good is the sole reason for the existence of civil authorities. In working for the common good, therefore, the authorities must obviously respect its nature, and at the same time adjust their legislation to meet the requirements of the given situation.

55. Among the essential elements of the common good one must certainly include the various characteristics distinctive of each individual people. But these by no means constitute the whole of it. For the common good, since it is intimately bound up with human nature, can

never exist fully and completely unless the human person is taken into account at all times. Thus, attention must be paid to the basic nature of the common good and what it is that brings it about.

56. We must add, therefore, that it is in the nature of the common good that every single citizen has the right to share in it — although in different ways, depending on his tasks, merits and circumstances. Hence every civil authority must strive to promote the common good in the interest of all, without favoring any individual citizen or category of citizen.*

Code of Social Principles

175. Economic life is dependent on justice and charity.

Along with commutative justice, which governs contracts, and distributive justice, which regulates social burdens and benefits, due place must be given to social or legal justice, which relates to the common good, of which authority has the care and which each individual member of the social body is bound to serve and enrich. The individual, as the beneficiary of this common good, is in some measure its guardian, although it is the rulers who are primarily responsible for it.

Social justice should permeate the institutions and the entire life of the people. Its efficacy should be especially manifest in the creation of a juridical and social order which informs the whole economic life.

St. Thomas Aquinas, Summa Theologiae

The common good is the end of each individual member of a community, just as the good of the whole is the end of each part (II, II, 58, 9, ad 3).

The good of the individual is subordinate to the good of the many (II, II, 47, 11, ad 3).

The common good . . . and the particular good of the individual differ not only in respect of the many and the few, but also under a formal aspect (II, II, 58, 7, ad 2).

The common good takes precedence over the private good if it be of the same genus (II, II, 152, 4, ad 3; see also, I, II, 113, 9, ad 2).

Every law is directed toward the common good . . . any command toward a particular object does not have legal effect, except insofar as it is directed toward the common good (I, II, 90, 2).

The common good is to be preferred to private good (II, II, 32, 6).

Right reason . . . judges that the common good is better than the good of an individual (II, II, 47, 10).

He who seeks the common good of the many consequently seeks his own good as well . . . private good cannot exist without the common good of the family, or the city, or the state (ibid., ad 2).

Among human goods, the public good is pre-eminent over private good (II, II, 117, 6).

SOCIAL CHARITY

Pius XI, Quadragesimo Anno

4. Quite agreeable, of course, was this state of things to those who thought it in their abundant riches the result of inevitable economic laws and accordingly, as if it were for charity to veil the violation of justice

---

* See also M. M. Nos. 78–80, infra, pp. 197–198, 299.

which lawmakers not only tolerated but at times sanctioned, wanted the whole care of supporting the poor committed to charity alone.

88. Social charity, moreover, ought to be as the soul of this order, an order which public authority ought to be ever ready effectively to protect and defend.

137. But in effecting all this, the law of charity, "which is the bond of perfection," must always take a leading role. How completely deceived, therefore, are those rash reformers who concern themselves with the enforcement of justice alone — and this, commutative justice — and in their pride reject the assistance of Charity! Admittedly, no vicarious charity can substitute for justice which is due as an obligation and is wrongfully denied. Yet even supposing that everyone should finally receive all that is due him, the widest field for charity will always remain open. For justice alone can, if faithfully observed, remove the causes of social conflict but can never bring about union of minds and hearts. Indeed all the institutions for the establishment of peace and the promotion of mutual help among men, however perfect these may seem, have the principal foundation of their stability in the mutual bond of minds and hearts whereby the members are united with one another. If this bond is lacking, the best of regulations come to naught, as we have learned by too frequent experience. And so, then only will true co-operation be possible for a single common good when the constituent parts of society deeply feel themselves members of one great family and children of the same Heavenly Father; nay, that they are one body in Christ, "but severally members one of another," so that "if one member suffers anything, all the members suffer with it." For then the rich and others in positions of power will change their former indifference toward their poorer brothers into a solicitous and active love, listen with kindliness to their just demands, and freely forgive their possible mistakes and faults. And the workers, sincerely putting aside every feeling of hatred or envy which the promoters of social conflict so cunningly exploit, will not only accept without rancor the place in human society assigned them by Divine Providence, but rather will hold it in esteem, knowing well that everyone according to his function and duty is toiling usefully and honorably for the common good and is following closely in the footsteps of Him, who, being in the form of God, willed to be a carpenter among men and be known as the son of a carpenter.

Pius XI, On Atheistic Communism

46. Still more important as a remedy for the evil we are considering, or certainly more directly calculated to cure it, is the precept of charity. We have in mind that Christian charity, "patient and kind," which avoids all semblance of demeaning paternalism, and all ostentation; that charity which from the very beginning of Christianity won to Christ the poorest of the poor, the slaves. And We are grateful to all those members of charitable associations, from the conferences of St. Vincent de Paul to the recent great relief organizations, which are perseveringly practicing the spiritual and corporal works of mercy. The more the workingman and the poor realize what the spirit of love animated by the virtue of Christ is doing for them, the more readily will they

abandon the false persuasion that Christianity has lost its efficacy and that the Church stands on the side of the exploiters of their labor.

47. But when on the one hand We see thousands of the needy, victims of real misery for various reasons beyond their control, and on the other so many round about them who spend huge sums of money on useless things and frivolous amusement, We cannot fail to remark with sorrow not only that justice is poorly observed, but that the precept of charity also is not sufficiently appreciated, is not a vital thing in daily life.

48. . . . There is a divine regenerating force in this "new precept" (as Christ called it) of Christian charity. Its faithful observance will pour into the heart an inner peace which the world knows not, and will firmly cure the ills which oppress humanity.

49. But charity will never be true charity unless it takes justice into constant account. A "charity" which deprives the workingman of the salary to which he has a strict title in justice, is not charity at all, but only its empty name and hollow semblance. The wage earner is not to receive as alms what is his due in justice. And let no one attempt with trifling charitable donations to exempt himself from the great duties imposed by justice. Both justice and charity often dictate obligations touching on the same subject matter, but under different aspects; and the very dignity of the workingman makes him justly and acutely sensitive to the duties of others in his regard.

Pius XII, Summi Pontificatus, October 20, 1939

1437. . . . the re-education of mankind must be, above all things, spiritual and religious. Hence, it must proceed from Christ as from its indispensable foundation; must be actuated by justice and crowned by charity.

Pius XII, To Italian Workers, May 1, 1958

Let other workers' associations say "justice is enough for us!" as though the virtues of justice and charity were enemies of one another. The contrary is certainly true. There is in fact no genuine justice which is not preceded and prepared by the warmth of charity.*

Vatican Council II, The Church in the Modern World

30. It becomes increasingly true that the obligations of justice and love are fulfilled only if each person, contributing to the common good, according to his own abilities and the needs of others, also promotes and assists the public and private institutions dedicated to bettering the conditions of human life.

Code of Social Principles

176. But justice is far from exhausting the whole of one's duty towards others. Over and above its requirements, there is a limitless field

* See M. M., No. 120, infra, p. 244.

for that brotherly love which men owe to each other as sons of the same Heavenly Father and descendants of the same first parents; a field of initiative, service and personal sacrifice for the common good. Charity thus finds a most important part to play in economic life. . . .

As to social charity, it ought to be the soul of that juridical and social order, which is the care of the public authorities and which ought to inform the entire economic life, as has been said above.

SUBSIDIARY VIRTUES

Pius XI, Quadragesimo Anno

47. . . . the duty of owners to use their property only in a right way does not come under this type of justice [commutative], but under other virtues, obligations of which "cannot be enforced by legal action."

50. The Sacred Scriptures and the Fathers of the Church constantly declare in the most explicit language that the rich are bound by a very grave precept to practice almsgiving, beneficence, and munificence.

IN ORDER to secure the proper organization of economic life, as briefly outlined in the preceding chapter, three requirements must be met. First, men must have a proper view of man and society, particularly economic society. This may be called an informed Christian conscience. Next, they must develop habits of acting in accord with these truths. These habits are the social virtues which are treated in the present chapter. They help us live up to the demands of both personal and social morality, explained in Chapter II. Finally, the personal virtue of men of good will must take institutional form in the laws, customs, and organizations of society. In this way right conduct will be given a pervasive and permanent influence. Selfish and evil actions will be prevented or counteracted.

Of the social virtues, justice is commonly considered the most important. It deals with rights and duties and hence fixes precisely the obligations of all persons participating in economic society. But justice is complemented by the bonds of charity and by certain subsidiary virtues related to charity.

JUSTICE

Kinds of Justice. Justice is defined as a constant habit or intention of giving each person his due. Persons in this definition include moral persons, such as corporations or government bodies. They too have rights and duties. When we speak of rights, we refer to the moral power to possess or obtain something. The idea of right involves a definite and clear obligation, not merely proprieties. Contracts, for example, involve rights and duties. By contrast, the laws of etiquette, generally speaking, express proprieties. They oblige in terms of considerateness and gentility, not justice.

We ordinarily speak of three kinds of justice. The first is general or legal justice, which calls for giving society its due. Under this virtue we are bound to consider the common good as well as our particular aims in all our actions. Some writers do not consider legal justice as a strict virtue, in the sense that it commands us to do certain acts which are proper to it alone. Rather, according to their point of view, it gives an overtone and direction to other virtues, directing their exercise in the light of the general welfare. Thus, almsgiving is commanded under the virtue of charity, but in helping the unfortunate legal justice binds us to consider the common good. Legal justice would incline us to one form of charity in preference to another. Other authors, however, do speak of specific actions commanded by legal justice in its own right. This is particularly true of the aspect of legal justice which is called social justice. Whichever view is held, legal justice involves the duties of the individual in regard to the community. He is obliged to seek the common good.

In contrast to general justice are the more particular forms of this virtue, called distributive and commutative justice. Distributive justice deals with the obligations of the community and its leaders toward the individual members. It calls for an equitable and proportional distribution of benefits and burdens to the members of society. Thus, legislators must be fair in giving out benefits (such as social insurance) or burdens (such as taxes). A father must be equitable in treating his children. Equity in such cases does not necessarily mean equality, since the needs of one may be greater than those of another. The socialist maxim: "From each according to his ability, to each according to his needs," is a fair approximation of distributive justice. If we could use mechanical terms to apply to virtues, we might say that the direction of flow is reversed when one compares legal and distributive justice. The one involves the individual's duty to society; the other, the rights of the person in connection with a given society. Hence some authors call social justice "contributive justice."

Finally, there is commutative justice, often called strict justice or exchange justice. Commutative justice differs from the other forms, in that the rights or duties concerned are specific, definite, and clearcut. Contributive and distributive justice create real obligations, but it is often difficult to pinpoint their precise implications. Men of good will could differ as to what is a fair tax rate or upon the citizen's obligation to vote in any given election. By contrast, the right to possess or obtain something, such as a specified piece of property, is quite definite. This right usually originates through exchange, such as the purchase of goods or services or a contract specifying wages to be paid for a certain amount of work.

Each of these three forms of justice is important for social life. This point will be elaborated upon in the treatment to follow.

Commutative Justice. Commutative justice normally applies in two ways: the right to possess and the right to obtain. We have the right to possess property, including intangible wealth such as good will or reputation, that truly belongs to us. Our original title to the object in question may have derived from purchase, contract, or discovery. It may be conferred or made specific by law, as in the case of copyrights or patents. If we do not already have the object, we may have the right to obtain it. For example, a fire-insurance contract permits us to claim compensation for covered damages in case of fire. When we make a loan, we have the right to recover at a specified time.

The practice of strict justice is essential for our economy. Indeed it is questionable that organized economic society could exist, if most men were not honest. Yet dishonesty is one of the plagues of our society. It creates or intensifies many social problems. A few examples will make this clear.

When we buy some product in a store, we expect to get our money's worth. We look for the equality of exchange called for by commutative justice. If the object we purchase does not work well, breaks down frequently, or soon wears out, we normally feel that we have been cheated. Here we meet a frequent source of injustice in our present economic system. Too often the consumer has no way of knowing the worth of his purchase. This is particularly true of complex products, such as household appliances, television sets, automobiles, and even clothing. There is no excuse for manufacturing or selling worthless goods. Equally blameworthy is any misrepresentation of quality so substantial that the buyer is deceived into purchasing a given item. Such actions are violations of strict justice. The buyer is given something essentially different from what he expected.

Justice also applies to the price of goods and services. Even when the quality is adequate, the price may involve exploitation of the consumer. When medieval moralists spoke of a just price, they meant a price that would return a reasonable profit to the seller. If a higher price is secured through exploitation of the need or ignorance of the buyer, this action is unjust. Unfortunately, the worst offenders in this regard are stores which cater to the poorer elements of the community. They often sell shoddy goods at high prices, using the lure of allegedly cheap credit. Most of the time this credit is also very high priced.

Related to these two abuses is the practice of fraudulent advertising. It is understood in our society that an advertiser will exaggerate the worth of his product. He may concentrate upon nonessential qualities that have a certain glamour appeal. Our courts have held that "puffing" and one-sided praise of a product do not constitute misrepresentation. Moralists may accept this judgment. But the files of any Better Business Bureau are usually filled with cases that go far beyond the bounds of conventional exaggeration. Once again, the very poor are often the victims of these exploiters. They are eager for bargains, yet often unable to distinguish the real quality of goods. Hence they fall prey to those who have no scruples in their advertising practices.

Injustice can also be committed by the worker who fails to give a reasonable amount of work in return for his pay. The proper pace of work is a rate that does not undermine the health of the worker over the span of his working life. It would be unfair to determine work norms on the basis of the maximum possible output of a young man. Obviously he cannot keep up this pace until he retires. Yet it is equally unfair to restrict output because of laziness. Normally it is not sound to slow down in a job, so as to stretch out work and cut down unemployment. Lower productivity weakens an economic system. More basic solutions than stretchouts or shorter work weeks must be found for the problem of unemployment.

These examples show the impact of strict justice in economic life. Yet it would be a mistake to ignore the social factors that may partially explain objectively unjust actions. A merchant, facing the policies of unscrupulous competitors, may feel compelled to adopt some of them in order to stay in business. He may even argue that, if he did not do so, the field would be monopolized by the least desirable business firms. Again, a worker is often under extreme social pressure to conform to the norms set by his fellows. It is no solution of these problems to say: "Let justice be done, though the heavens fall." The real solution is to prevent the economic pressures that force men to choose between dishonesty and bankruptcy. This can be done only by community action. For this reason, commutative justice needs to be supplemented by distributive and social justice.

Distributive Justice. In the traditional usage, the term "distributive justice" is applied to rulers of states. It obliges them to secure for each citizen his due and proportionate share of both the advantages and the burdens involved in the conduct of civil society. The older theologians talked of the fair distribution of public offices, on the one hand, and of taxes on the other. A more modern example is social legislation or public subsidies. Benefits thus distributed are not given on a basis of arithmetical equality, but rather in consideration of need and other special circumstances. Thus, a federal subsidy for education which would be based only on the tax contributions of the states would be self-defeating. The states which were able to pay the most taxes would be least in need of subsidies. In this regard, Pope Leo XIII stated that governments should look out especially for the needs of the poor, since the rich can often take care of themselves. Benefits distributed by the state can be very important in modern economic life. Examples of this are subsidies for low-cost housing; subsidies for farmers or high-cost producers of needed goods; justified tariffs; distribution of social-insurance benefits in view of needs as well as contributions; contributions for public hospitals in rural areas; and grants to special groups, such as reasonable pensions for soldiers. The same observation applies to the sharing of burdens. On the basis of distributive justice, it is fair that the wealthy should pay proportionately higher taxes than the poor. Taxes on luxuries are more equitable than taxes on necessities.

Two points in the social teaching of Pope John XXIII are pertinent to this study of distributive justice. The Pope insisted that economic progress be accompanied by corresponding social progress. And he held that taxation can be an important factor in redistributing income as one phase of this process. These concepts recur frequently in his encyclicals (see M.M., Nos. 73, 131–132).

Older moralists often applied the principles of distributive justice to private industry. They argued, for example, that the needs of workers are often greater than those of stockholders. Hence, they concluded, a living wage must be paid, even though as a result no profits were available. The flaw in this reasoning stems from the fact that business property is not community property. It is not in the same category as civic or family possessions. For this reason, Pope Pius XII stated, using European legal terminology, that the business firm is in the private-law rather than the public-law category in respect to its property and profits.[1] It may be affected

---

[1] The reference to private law reflects the European practice of legal enforcement of certain regulations drawn up by private associations. The closest parallel here would be enforcement of medical- or bar-association rules.

by distributive justice because it is subject to the state. But its relations with its employees are governed by commutative and social justice, not distributive.

Indeed, it is well to remember that, even in government itself, policies suggested by distributive justice are not absolutes. Should they conflict with the common good, with the demands of social justice, they must yield to the higher claims of the public welfare. For example, progressive taxation, based on ability to pay, is a sound policy. But if the rates are set so high for the wealthy that they discourage private enterprise and prevent investment for industrial expansion, the common good suffers. Under these circumstances, social justice requires a rate that permits new investment, with consequent increase in employment and living standards. Only when we understand fully the demands of social justice can we determine accurately the proper spheres of commutative and distributive justice.

Social Justice.   We noted above that moralists do not agree completely upon all phases of legal and social justice. In view of this fact, it is best not to begin with a definition of social justice. Instead we shall proceed inductively from the writings of Pope Pius XI and note how he viewed the nature and function of this virtue.

In the first place, the Pope often contrasts organized effort with individual effort, social morality with personal morality. Many times he notes the helplessness of the individual when confronted with a difficult social problem, such as ruthless competition. His remedy in each case is organized effort to cure the evil. What employers and workers cannot do as individuals, they can often accomplish as citizens or as members of economic groups. In each case, the Pope insists that social justice compels them to act in an organized fashion. This is their duty, inasmuch as they are bound to contribute to the common good.

This point is particularly important in evaluating programs of social reform that emphasize personal leadership and example. Such programs are good, so far as they go. But often they do not go far enough. Leadership can be an important first step in a program of organized effort. But if it does not lead to group action, it is often of little value in rooting out entrenched social evils.

Another point to remember is that not all social ills spring from individual malice. An economic society comprised only of virtuous members could suffer from many ills because of faulty organization. It could, for example, be plagued with economic depressions because it lacked a sound monetary and fiscal system. Another illustration is the employer who says that he does not need unions because he treats his workers fairly. He may indeed be endeavoring to pay good wages and to offer the best of working conditions. Yet he may lack the talent needed to set up a sound personnel policy. As a result, there may be countless frictions and grievances that lead to bad morale among his workers. His good will is not implemented by proper organization of his plant.

A second point emphasized by the Pope is the need for imbedding moral principles in the very fabric of society. He calls for the customs, institutions, and laws of a society to reflect God's demand upon the economic order. A reform of institutions, no less than a reform of morals, is a prime necessity. It is not enough to organize for a better society. The results of social action must be permanent. This means that the rules governing stable social patterns must be sound. Competition, for example, should be controlled so that it promotes the common good. This may be done by law. Or it may be accomplished by enforceable codes of business and labor ethics.

A good example in point is the reform attempt of organized labor during the years 1957–1958. Certain standards of ethics were drawn up by the A.F.L.-C.I.O. An Ethical Practices Committee was formed to police these standards. Penalty for violation was expulsion from the federation. These steps can be classified as organized action for the common good. But to make these principles an institutional part of organized labor, further steps are needed. One would be to revise the constitutions of the member unions, when necessary, so that the code of ethical practices and rules designed to protect union democracy would be part of the basic law of each union. In addition, outside policing power — either in the federation or in government — should prevent usurpation of power or summary disregard of constitutional standards.

It is naïve to imagine that sound customs, laws, and institutions will prevent all economic evils. Civil law does not prevent all crime. But the deterrent effect of good social patterns is great. Even when they are flouted, it is easier to correct the evil than it would be in the absence of such standards. This is particularly the case with American society, if certain sociological analyses are correct. It is asserted that Americans are, in the language of Riesman, "other-directed," in contrast to peoples who are "inner-directed" or "tradition-directed." In effect, this means that the influence of community opinion is more decisive than it is in societies whose members are more influenced by inner convictions or by accepted traditions.

If it is true that the average American wants to conform to group standards, to be liked and accepted by his fellows, it is most important that such standards conform to moral laws and the demands of the common good. The informal ethics of a business community, the customs developed by a body of workers, the rules of a profession, all may be highly influential in determining the moral tone of a community.

The third point emphasized by the Sovereign Pontiff is that our efforts be directed toward securing the common good. This common good may be described as conditions of social life that favor the proper ends of a society and its individual members. In the economic sphere, it means arrangements that lead to abundant production and equitable distribution of goods and services needed for the individual and the family. Any society, public or private, works toward the common good when its actions enhance the welfare of its individual members and society as a whole. It may be compared to a general condition of health in a living body that in turns aids the healthy functioning of individual organs of the body.

It is necessary to remember that the common good of society is judged by the effects any given program may have upon its members. For this reason, it would be wrong to consider any society as an end in itself to the detriment of the rights of its constituents. Statism, for example, is evil because it seeks to enhance the power of the state as such, even to the point of denying essential rights of citizens. Socialism is wrong because it emphasizes the material element in society, to the exclusion of more important values. An overcentralized state arrogates to itself functions that can and will be performed properly by lower bodies. This violates the principle of subsidiarity, which holds that power and responsibility should be decentralized as far as the general welfare permits.

On the other hand, the common good is more than the sum of individual goods. If everyone were to act merely for his own interest, we would have anarchy, not society. Organized effort and proper codes of conduct are needed to avoid certain evils and to promote prosperity and social harmony. While society exists to serve the individual and the family, it has its own rights which must be acknowledged if it is to function. Thus we steer a middle course between the twin evils of statism and unregulated individualism.

These abstract statements will take on more point and effectiveness when they are applied to particular problems in later chapters. But, even at this stage, it is clear that American life does not meet the ideal outlined here. Many of our economic societies are mere pressure groups, aiming to gain the most for their own members, whether or not the common good is obtained. There are even cases — racketeers in a few labor unions are an example — when they do not even seek the interests of their members. Because of this basic disorganization of economic life, there is terrific pressure for the state to force justice and morality upon the social order. While the state is doing its duty in meeting this need, the situation is not ideal. Excessive state intervention curbs initiative and destroys freedom. Social justice envisions a hierarchy of societies, each sensitive to the needs of the common good, with the state directing, stimulating, guiding, and co-ordinating such activities to the extent that the public interest demands.

Social justice may now be defined as a virtue which inclines the individual to seek the common good, and particularly directs him to seek in an organized fashion to achieve an economic society whose laws, customs, and institutions are directed toward the promotion of the common good.

Close reading of the encyclicals of Pope John XXIII reveals the fact that this pontiff was sparing in the use of the term social justice. He preferred such phrases as "justice and equity" and "justice and humanity." The concept is the same, but the various controversies over the meaning of social justice are avoided by using the older terminology.

SOCIAL CHARITY

Social charity seeks many of the ends of social justice, but its motivation is different. The emphasis is upon love of neighbor, not upon rights and duties. Justice cannot bring about the complete union and harmony that will make society a smoothly functioning body. It cannot procure the generosity, patience, and tolerance needed in the slow years of transition between a disorganized society and one that is united in the interest of the common welfare. In fact, because of the frailty of human nature, it often happens that the vigorous quest for justice may actually drive men asunder. In theory, we can condemn injustice and yet not pass judgment on the motives of those who perpetrate injustice. In practice, we do not always separate the man from his deeds. Hence, were we content to limit ourselves to denouncing social injustice, we might actually divide society into warring classes. Thus, if organized labor were to attack some business practices, the effect might be to produce a united front of one group against the other. Even those who do not condone injustice might feel a sense of solidarity with their group which is being attacked. We might have a form of the class struggle occasioned by the pursuit of justice.

From this, of course, one should not conclude that the fight for justice should be slackened. Rather, it must be completed by the kindly bonds of charity. This is the more true since much social injustice is not necessarily a product of individual malice. Where the institutions of society are unsound, it is possible for well-meaning individuals to be caught in the snares of a bad system. Conventions, customs, and institutions lead them to practices which they may deplore, but feel helpless to remedy by themselves. Unless we take the pessimistic attitude that most men are evil, we should be willing to appeal to the better instincts even of those who are enmeshed in objective evil. Without such attitudes, it is difficult to see how we can achieve the co-operation and organization postulated by social justice.

Social charity fits in well with the demands deriving from the dignity of the human person. Many of these obligations, it is true, hold in terms of justice. But the recognition of a man's individual worth also calls for a certain good will toward him as a person. He does not then feel that he is submerged in a large group, whether this be civil society, a labor union, or a factory working force. Rather he senses the bonds of human relationship between himself and others, whether they be his fellow workers or his employer. Indeed, the prolific literature currently produced on human relations as a key to industrial labor relations is mainly an effort to implement the Christian virtue of charity. Personnel experts speak of the need for communication, participation, and teamwork in the factory. They stress individualized treatment of a worker's problems in the plant and elsewhere. Such techniques are said to be the key to the building of a happy and efficient working force. Yet we do not exaggerate in saying that these human-relations programs could well be implementations of the commandment second only to the law of love for God.

Just as human-relations programs are the employer's expression of charity, so also we might call union-management harmony efforts the union's way of living up to this virtue. When a union seeks to meet with the employer on terms of co-operation rather than enmity, it is acting in a Christian fashion. The idea of essential class struggle is Marxist, not Christian. There is no inherent conflict between a worker's loyalty to his union and his loyalty to his company. Even granting the historical fact that many unions were formed to remedy injustice and hence often grew up in an atmosphere of bitterness, it is not necessary to perpetuate such attitudes. With intelligence and good will on both sides, relations of genuine friendliness are possible. Indeed, they are more common in American industry than is generally realized. Furthermore, personal contacts between union officials and industrial leaders, particularly in solving common problems, can bring about a mutual respect which is the prelude for deep co-operation. Such a phenomenon was observed in various joint government committees during World War II, such as the War Labor Board or the War Production Board.

In the socioeconomic field, co-operation is often facilitated by referring to issues as problems, which they often are, rather than immediately denouncing them as injustices. A problem offers a challenge to the participants to reach a solution. Discussions may be had as to feasible methods of meeting the issue. After much give-and-take, it is often possible to reach a sound conclusion. By contrast, denunciations and the proposal of ready-made solutions often stir up resentments. A man who is condemned for practicing injustice often feels bound to defend his position and yields only reluctantly and with poor grace. But if the same man is asked to co-operate in meeting a problem, even though it is mainly of his own making, he often shows more good will. Furthermore, he can thus save face without difficulty.

Social charity is particularly useful in dealing with problems that involve explosive emotional overtones. An example is the race situation in the United States. Racial discrimination is unjust and we must never retreat on this point. But the actual working out of a program of racial betterment calls for immense amounts of good will on both sides. This was proved by the uneven pattern of results in the United States during the mid-1960's. Carefully prepared and quiet programs of racial integration succeeded. Ill-conceived and poorly prepared plans in the same area failed. It is easy to demand and denounce, while it is often most difficult to get a meeting of minds on complex evils rooted in long traditions. The former is the approach of justice alone, the latter involves justice tempered by charity. Lasting social reform usually needs the healing touch of social charity. This point is beautifully expressed in Vatican Council II's *Declaration on the Apostolate of the Laity* (No. 8):

Our charitable activity today can and ought to include every single member of the human family, and all his needs. Wherever people are poorly fed, clothed, housed, lack medical care, employment, education and the facilities for living a genuinely human life, wherever they are tormented by hardship or illness, wherever they suffer exile and imprisonment, there precisely should Christian charity be present, seeking them out and finding them in order to comfort them with its deep concern and support them with the help it offers. This obligation rests primarily on those individuals, and nations, who are themselves prosperous.

So that no one may be excluded from this kind of love, and that its universality be sharply evident, let us see in our neighbor the likeness of God, to whose image he has been created, and the person of Christ the Lord, to whom in reality is offered whatever is given to the needy; let us respect with the greatest gentleness the personal dignity and freedom of those we help; let the purity of our intention be unsoiled by any seeking for our own advantage, or any search for power; let us first satisfy the demands of justice and not offer as the outpouring of charity what is already owed under the claim of justice; let us eliminate the causes of distress, not merely its symptoms; and let us so manage our assistance that those who receive it will gradually be freed from dependence on others and become capable of helping themselves.

Subsidiary Virtues. Social charity is sometimes aided by certain subsidiary virtues often mentioned in connection with social problems. Among these are almsgiving, liberality, and munificence.

Almsgiving is compassionate giving to the needy, motivated by love of God and neighbor. Social reforms may never remove all forms of poverty and need. Even if we do have social institutions to take care of most problems, there is still a place for personal giving and kindness. Moreover, there are many projects that may be useful for the community, yet unsuitable for government or other organized aid. Private donations in substantial amounts have done much good in this borderline field.

Liberality is the right use of external goods, a mean between prodigality and avarice. It involves a proper type of indifference to worldly wealth. Pope Pius XI indicates as a special function of this virtue the investing of superfluous wealth in productive enterprise. Thus community wealth is increased and new jobs are made available. Today a wealthy man might use his funds to aid promising new projects, instead of seeking the safe haven of tax-exempt bonds.

A special form of liberality is munificence, or the parting with great sums of money. This indicates a great freedom of spirit in regard to possession of external goods and a notable devotion to the common welfare. A common form of this virtue is the establishing of foundations with large fortunes as their bases. Many worthwhile community enterprises have been fostered in this manner. Substantial donations to hospitals, schools, and universities, works of charity, and religious enterprises belong in this category. An interesting example with socioeconomic implications is the setting aside of a fund to promote new enterprises involving unusual financial risk but holding great promise for the community. A wealthy

American family is currently supporting such a project. Another illustration is a giant limited-dividend and relatively low-cost housing program sponsored by a large insurance company. Such use of wealth can promote social goals and mitigate the evils which might otherwise be expected from large concentrations of funds and of economic power.

The tendency toward equalization of incomes, and tax laws that make it difficult to accumulate large fortunes, will diminish opportunities to exercise the virtue of munificence. Indeed, the traditional sources of supply for university and other endowment funds have been drying up. Future donations for such causes may of necessity come from hitherto untapped sources, such as corporations, labor unions, or service clubs. New methods may be devised for securing help from the large number of persons who, although not wealthy, are in comfortable circumstances. In this way, many worthwhile activities may survive without the dangers involved in seeking government aid.

Finally, we may list among the virtues pertinent to the solution of the social problem the virtue of prudence. Prudence is often misunderstood as a virtue that inclines a person to move with restraint so as not "to upset the boat." Actually, prudence dictates the right choice of means in seeking an end. At times, when the end sought is urgent, prudence may well counsel vigorous and forthright action. Reasonable means to an end do not necessarily involve a timorous course of conduct.

In all matters concerned with the exercise of practical reason, prudence calls for careful study of problems and principles, the weighing of alternative courses of action, and the final selection of a course that seems most likely to produce the best results. Of itself, it leads neither to caution nor boldness. It may best be phrased: "Think before you act, and then act reasonably."

READINGS*

St. Thomas Aquinas, *Summa Theologiae*, II, II, q. 31, 32, 58, 61, 78, 117, 134.
J. Y. Calvez and J. Perrin, *The Church and Social Justice*, Chaps. 6–7.
J. F. Cronin, *Christianity and Social Progress*, Chap. 5.
B. W. Dempsey, *The Functional Economy*, Chaps. 8, 11, 19.
H. Johnston, *Business Ethics*, Chaps. 4–5.
W. J. McDonald, *The Social Value of Property According to St. Thomas Aquinas*, Chap. 2.
J. Messner, *Social Ethics* (rev. ed.), pp. 123–150, 314–341.
J. A. Ryan, *Distributive Justice*.

* For further readings, consult List No. 3 in the Appendix.

Chapter V

CURRENT AND RECENT SOCIAL PHILOSOPHIES

INDIVIDUALISM

Pius XI, Quadragesimo Anno

10. He [Leo XIII] sought no help from either Liberalism or socialism, for the one had proved that it was utterly unable to solve the social problem aright, and the other, proposing a remedy far worse than the evil itself, would have plunged human society into greater dangers.

25. With regard to civil authority, Leo XIII, boldly breaking through the confines imposed by Liberalism, fearlessly taught that government must not be thought a mere guardian of law and of good order, but rather must put forth every effort so that "through the entire scheme of laws and institutions . . . both public and individual well-being may develop spontaneously out of the very structure and administration of the state."

78. Things have come to such a pass through the evil of what we have termed "individualism," that, following upon the overthrow and near extinction of that rich social life which was once highly developed through associations of various kinds, there remain virtually only individuals and the state.

133. Strict and watchful moral restraint enforced vigorously by governmental authority could have banished these enormous evils and even forestalled them; this restraint, however, has too often been sadly lacking. For since the seeds of a new form of economy were bursting forth just when the principles of rationalism had been implanted and rooted in many minds, there quickly developed a body of economic teaching far removed from the true moral law, and, as a result, completely free reign was given to human passions.

Pius XI, On Atheistic Communism

38. There would be today neither socialism nor communism if the rulers of the nations had not scorned the teachings and maternal warnings of the Church. On the bases of Liberalism and laicism they wished to build other social edifices which, powerful and imposing as they seemed at first, all too soon revealed the weakness of their foundations, and today are crumbling one after another before our eyes, as everything must crumble that is not grounded on the one cornerstone which is Christ Jesus.

Pius XI, Quadragesimo Anno

88. Just as the unity of human society cannot be founded on an opposition of classes, so also the right ordering of economic life cannot be left to a free competition of forces. For from this source, as from a poisoned spring, have originated and spread all the errors of individualistic economic teaching. Destroying through forgetfulness or ignorance the social and moral character of economic life, it held that economic life must be considered and treated as altogether free from and independent of public authority, because in the market, i.e., in the free struggle of competitors, it would have a principle of self-direction which governs it much more perfectly than would the intervention of any created intellect. But free competition, while justified and certainly useful provided it is kept within certain limits, clearly cannot direct economic life — a truth which the outcome of the application in practice of the tenets of this evil individualistic spirit has more than sufficiently demonstrated. Therefore, it is most necessary that economic life be again subjected to and governed by a true and effective directing principle. This function is one that the economic dictatorship which has recently displaced free competition can still less perform, since it is a headstrong power and violent energy that, to benefit people, needs to be strongly curbed and wisely ruled. But it cannot curb and rule itself.

107. This concentration of power and might, the characteristic mark, as it were, of contemporary economic life, is the fruit that the unlimited freedom of struggle among competitors has of its own nature produced, and which lets only the strongest survive; and this is often the same as

saying, those who fight the most violently, those who give least heed to their conscience.

108. This accumulation of might and of power generates in turn three kinds of conflict. First, there is the struggle for economic supremacy itself; then there is the bitter fight to gain supremacy over the state in order to use in economic struggles its resources and authority; finally there is conflict between states themselves, not only because countries employ their power and shape their policies to promote every economic advantage of their citizens, but also because they seek to decide political controversies that arise among nations through the use of their economic supremacy and strength.

109. The ultimate consequences of the individualist spirit in economic life are those which you yourselves, Venerable Brethren and Beloved Children, see and deplore: free competition has destroyed itself; economic dictatorship has supplanted the free market; unbridled ambition for power has likewise succeeded greed for gain; all economic life has become tragically hard, inexorable, and cruel. To these are to be added the grave evils that have resulted from an intermingling and shameful confusion of the functions and duties of public authority with those of the economic sphere — such as, one of the worst, the virtual degradation of the majesty of the state, which although it ought to sit on high like a queen and supreme arbitress, free from all partiality and intent upon the one common good and justice, is become a slave, surrendered and delivered to the passions and greed of men. And as to international relations, two different streams have issued from the one fountainhead: on the one hand, eco-

nomic nationalism or even economic imperialism; on the other a no less deadly and accursed internationalism of finance or international imperialism whose country is where profit is.

THE SYSTEM OF CAPITALISM

Leo XIII, Rerum Novarum

26. Therefore, let it be laid down in the first place that a condition of human existence must be borne with, namely, that in civil society the lowest cannot be made equal with the highest. Socialists, of course, agitate the contrary, but all struggling against nature is vain. There are truly very great and very many natural differences among men. Neither the talents, nor the skill, nor the health, nor the capacities of all are the same, and unequal fortune follows of itself upon necessary inequality in respect to these endowments. And clearly this condition of things is adapted to benefit both individuals and the community; for to carry on its affairs community life requires varied aptitudes and diverse services, and to perform these diverse services men are impelled most by differences in individual property holdings.

Pius XI, Quadragesimo Anno

101. With all his energy Leo XIII sought to adjust this economic system according to the norms of right order; hence, it is evident that this system is not to be condemned in itself. And surely it is not of its own nature vicious. But it does violate right order when capital hires workers, that is, the nonowning working class, with a view to and under such terms that it directs business and even the whole economic system according to its own will and advantage, scorning the human dignity of the workers, the social character of economic activity, and social justice itself and the common good.

103. But, with the diffusion of modern industry throughout the whole world, the "capitalist" economic regime has spread everywhere to such a degree, particularly since the publication of Leo XIII's Encyclical, that it has invaded and pervaded the economic and social life of even those outside its orbit and is unquestioningly impressing on it its advantages, disadvantages, and vices, and, in a sense, is giving it its own shape and form.

Pius XII, On Women's Duties, October 21, 1945

On the other hand, can a woman, perhaps, hope for her real well-being from a regime dominated by capitalism? We do not need to describe to you now the economic and social results that issue from it. You know its characteristic signs, and you yourselves are bearing its burden: excessive concentration of population in cities, the constant all-absorbing increase of big industries, the difficult and precarious state of others, notably those of artisans and agricultural workers, and the disturbing increase of unemployment.

*   *   *

Pius XII, To the Italian Federation of Commerce, February 17, 1956

Freedom of economic activity cannot be justified and maintained except on condition that it serves a higher freedom, and has the ability, when need arises, to renounce a part of itself, in order not to fall short of the moral imperative. Otherwise, it will be difficult to restrain the ever-growing tendency towards a type of society whose economic and political organization constitutes the very negation of any sort of freedom.

John XXIII, Mater et Magistra

51. It should be stated at the outset that in the economic order first place must be given to the personal initiative of private citizens working either as individuals or in association with each other in various ways for the furtherance of common interests.

52. But — for reasons explained by Our predecessors — the civil power must also have a hand in the economy. It has to promote production in a way best calculated to achieve social progress and the well-being of all citizens.

53. And in this work of directing, stimulating, co-ordinating, supplying and integrating, its guiding principle must be the "principle of subsidiary function" formulated by Pius XI in Quadragesimo Anno.

57. Experience has shown that where personal initiative is lacking, political tyranny ensues and, in addition, economic stagnation in the production of a wide range of consumer goods and of services of the material and spiritual order — those, namely, which are in a great measure dependent upon the exercise and stimulus of individual creative talent.

58. Where, on the other hand, the good offices of the state are lacking or deficient, incurable disorder ensues: in particular, the unscrupulous exploitation of the weak by the strong. For men of this stamp are always in evidence, and, like cockle among the wheat, thrive in every land.

Pastoral Letter, French Cardinals, September 8, 1949

By condemning the actions of communist parties, the Church does not support the capitalist regime. It is most necessary that it be realized that in the very essence of capitalism — that is to say, in the absolute value that it gives to property without reference to the common good or to the dignity of labor — there is a materialism rejected by Christian teaching.

SOCIALISM

Leo XIII, Rerum Novarum

7. To cure this evil, the Socialists, exciting the envy of the poor toward the rich, contend that it is necessary to do away with private possession of goods and in its place to make the goods of individuals common to all, and that the men who preside over a municipality or who direct the entire state should act as administrators of these goods. They hold that, by such a transfer of private goods from private individuals to the com-

munity, they can cure the present evil through dividing wealth and benefits equally among the citizens.

8. But their program is so unsuited for terminating the conflict that it actually injures the workers them-selves. Moreover, it is highly unjust, because it violates the rights of lawful owners, perverts the functions of the state, and throws governments into utter confusion.

Pius XI, Quadragesimo Anno

113. [Present-day] socialism, is surely more moderate. It not only professes the rejection of violence but modifies and tempers to some degree, if it does not reject entirely, the class struggle and the abolition of private ownership. One might say that, terrified by its own principles and by the conclusions drawn therefrom by communism, socialism inclines toward and in a certain measure approaches the truths which Christian tradition has always held sacred; for it cannot be denied that its demands at times come very near those that Christian reformers of society justly insist upon.

114. If the foregoing happens, it can come even to the point that imperceptibly these ideas of the more moderate socialism will no longer differ from the desires and demands of those who are striving to remold human society on the basis of Christian principles. . . .

116. Yet let no one think that all the socialist groups or factions that are not communist have, without exception, recovered their senses to this extent either in fact or in name. For the most part they do not reject the class struggle or the abolition of ownership, but only in some degree modify them. Now if these false principles are modified and to some extent erased from the program, the question arises, or rather is raised without warrant by some, whether the principles of Christian truth cannot perhaps be also modified to some degree and be tempered so as to meet socialism halfway and, as it were, by a middle course, come to agreement with it. . . .

117. But what if socialism has really been so tempered and modified as to the class struggle and private ownership that there is in it no longer anything to be censured on these points? Has it thereby renounced its contradictory nature to the Christian religion? . . . Whether considered as a doctrine, or an historical fact, or a movement, socialism, if it remains truly socialism, even after it has yielded to truth and justice on the points which we have mentioned, cannot be reconciled with the teachings of the Catholic Church because its concept of society itself is utterly foreign to Christian truth.

119. Because of the fact that goods are produced more efficiently by a suitable division of labor than by the scattered efforts of individuals, Socialists infer that economic activity, only the material ends of which enter into their thinking, ought of necessity to be carried on socially. Because of this necessity, they hold that men are obliged, with respect to the producing of goods, to surrender and subject themselves entirely to society. Indeed, possession of the greatest possible supply of things that serve the advantages of this life is considered of such great importance that the higher goods of man, liberty not excepted, must take a secondary place and even be sacrificed to the demands of the most efficient production of goods. This damage to human dignity, undergone in the "socialized" process of production, will be easily offset, they say, by the abundance of socially produced goods which will pour out in pro-

fusion to individuals to be used freely at their pleasure for comforts and cultural development. Society, therefore, as socialism conceives it, can on the one hand neither exist nor be thought of without an obviously excessive use of force; on the other hand, it fosters a liberty no less false, since there is no place in it for true social authority, which rests not on temporal and material advantages but descends from God alone, the Creator and last end of all things.

120. If socialism, like all errors, contains some truth (which, moreover, the Supreme Pontiffs have never denied), it is based nevertheless on a theory of human society peculiar to itself and irreconcilable with true Christianity. Religious socialism, Christian socialism, are contradictory terms; no one can be at the same time a good Catholic and a true Socialist.

NONCOMMUNIST STATISM

Pius XI, Non Abbiamo Bisogno

49. And here We find Ourselves confronted by a mass of authentic affirmations and no less authentic facts which reveal beyond the slightest possibility of doubt the resolve (already in great measure actually put into effect) to monopolize completely the young, from their tenderest years up to manhood and womanhood, for the exclusive advantage of a party and of a regime based on an ideology which clearly resolves itself into a true, a real pagan worship of the state — the "statolatry" which is no less in contrast with the natural rights of the family than it is in contradiction with the supernatural rights of the Church.

57. A conception of the state which makes the rising generations belong to it entirely, without any exception, from the tenderest years up to adult life, cannot be reconciled by a Catholic either with Catholic doctrine or with the natural rights of the family.

Pius XII, Summi Pontificatus, October 20, 1939

1420. To consider the state as something ultimate to which everything else should be subordinated and directed, cannot fail to harm the true and lasting prosperity of nations. This can happen either when unrestricted dominion comes to be conferred on the state as having a mandate from the nation, people, or even a social class, or when the state arrogates such dominion to itself as absolute master, despotically, without any mandate whatsoever. If, in fact, the state lays claim to and directs private enterprises, these, ruled as they are by delicate and complicated internal principles which guarantee and assure the realization of their special aims, may be damaged to the detriment of the public good, by being wrenched from their natural surroundings, that is, from responsible private action.

1429. The idea which credits the state with unlimited authority is not simply an error harmful to the internal life of nations, to their prosperity, and to the larger and well-ordered increase in their well-being, but likewise it injures the relations between peoples, for it breaks the unity of supranational society, robs the law of nations of its foundation and vigor, leads to violation of others' rights, and impedes agreement and peaceful intercourse.

* See also *Quadragesimo Anno*, Nos. 91–96, for a guarded appraisal of the fascist economic and social system.

Pius XII, Address to Sacred College of Cardinals, June 2, 1945

He [Pope Pius XI] proclaimed to the world on Passion Sunday, 1937, in his encyclical *Mit Brennender Sorge* what National Socialism really was: the arrogant apostasy from Jesus Christ, the denial of His doctrine and of His work of redemption, the cult of violence, the idolatry of race and blood, the overthrow of human liberty and dignity.

THE preceding chapters explained some fundamentals of a Christian social order and also alluded to evils poisoning economic life. It is now timely to examine in a systematic fashion the roots of these evils. The first topic treated, individualism, is the philosophy that contributed to the overthrow of the medieval social system and led in great part to the growth of our modern economic order. While it inspired many great commercial and industrial achievements, it also spawned appalling abuses. Capitalism is historically connected with this spirit of individualism, although in many areas it has changed in the direction of accepting social responsibility.

In reaction to individualism the social and political pendulum often swung to the other extreme of statism. Statism in modern times has taken two main forms. When the emphasis was primarily economic, it appeared in the guise of socialism. By contrast, where the problem was mainly political, the overcentralized state took the form of political dictatorship, fascism or national socialism. In these latter cases, patterns of ownership were not usually changed, but the owners were subjected to extreme political control.

Communism, of course, belongs among these systems. Ideologically, it is a branch of socialism. In its actual development since it took root in Russia in 1917, it has consistently exhibited a totalitarian pattern of government. It may be said to combine the bad features of socialist economic life and totalitarian political life. For this reason it is treated separately, rather than as a branch of socialism. Because of its obvious impact upon the modern world, it is the subject of a separate chapter.

INDIVIDUALISM

Individualism, called Liberalism by Pope Pius XI and most European writers, is considered the primary source of the social evils described in the encyclicals. As a system, it is roughly described in the phrase "every man for himself." It has developed in two forms, corresponding to different historical stages. In its earlier form, it exhibited these characteristics: morally and philosophically, it held that man was a law unto himself and that self-seeking is the prime rule of life; economically, it manifested itself in the form of unregulated free competition; and politically, it maintained that the state should hold aloof from economic life, except when it was protecting property rights.

The later form of individualism was conditioned by the economic changes resulting from its earlier form. Extreme competition was modified by the development of large firms; the absorption of competitors; trends toward monopoly; economic dictatorship made possible by centralized financial controls; and the effort of the business community to win control of the state, so that its power could be used to the advantage of this group. Consequently, individual selfishness yielded to group individualism; free competition was modified and sometimes replaced by monopoly; and the state became a partisan prize whose control was sought by competing groups, rather than the aloof policeman of *laissez-faire* days.

The historical roots of individualism were outlined briefly in Chapter I. It was a reaction to the religious and moral controls of the medieval period, and the political controls of eighteenth-century nationalism in France and England. Philosophers such as Jean Jacques Rousseau and Thomas Hobbes contributed its ideological basis, arguing that man was good (Rousseau) or hopelessly predatory (Hobbes). If man is good, then he does not need state control to do what is right. If he is completely bad, one cannot stop ruthless competition. These philosophical views were often reinforced by certain religious trends in Lutheranism and Calvinism, as well as by the Jansenist heresy within the Catholic Church.

At the same time, the classical economists, particularly Adam Smith, David Ricardo, and John Stuart Mill, contributed an economic justification of the trend. They argued that unlimited competition forces every man to work his hardest. It leads to the best possible goods at the cheapest prices. Thus maximum production and optimum distribution are obtained. The encyclicals refer to these writers as the Manchester School.

It is obvious from what has been said in preceding chapters that these arguments spring from a faulty view of human nature. Man is neither wholly good nor wholly bad by nature. He is wounded by original sin, but he is capable of natural virtue and of even greater achievements when he has the guidance, inspiration, and divine help obtained through acceptance of religious faith. He needs society, not because he is evil, but because God created man for social living. Even if unlimited selfishness were capable of creating the material benefits promised by the Manchester School, it would have to be rejected as contrary to man's nature and hence God's law. Actually, history records that a *laissez-faire* economic system produced great social evils and limited economic benefits.

From a strictly economic viewpoint, it is significant that many business-men constantly strive to soften the impact of competition. Trends toward consolidation, monopoly, fair-trade laws, price fixing, and sharing of markets show that unlimited competition is not always accepted by the business community. Its consequences in the form of exploitation of labor, waste of natural resources, and the social waste caused by periodic depressions led to a constantly growing body of social legislation.

Hardly anyone in the United States today, except a few theoretical writers, seems willing to face in practice the rigors of unlimited competition. This does not mean that the theory has been abandoned in social polemics. On the contrary, business groups are often willing to apply it to farmers, farmers to organized labor, and labor to business. But each group wants to hold on to the benefits it has obtained from favorable legislation. Business would remove farm price supports, but fights for the protective tariff. Labor would punish business monopoly, but it rejects the application of antitrust laws to its own actions. Thus, as was noted before, atomistic individualism has been replaced by group individualism.

For these reasons, it is pointless to discuss in detail the ill effects of eighteenth-, nineteenth-, or early twentieth-century individualism. So far as we can see, there has been an irrevocable decision against either the atomistic competition of earlier days or the more recent economic dictatorship. What we have today is a society still partially infected by the philosophy of individualism, but subject to strong political and social controls. Powerful economic groups try to swing the state in directions they favor. However, as their power becomes excessive, countervailing forces arise and check them.[1] None of these clashing forces seems likely to achieve permanent domination over the others.

The current impact of individualism is twofold. First, as a philosophy that stresses selfishness and rejects the common good, it pushes society in a direction contrary to Christian social teaching. Obviously it cannot be reconciled with the principles outlined in Chapters III and IV. Second, the reaction to individualism has its own dangers. Present-day American economic life is obviously sounder than the earlier forms that provoked

---

[1] See J. K. Galbraith, *American Capitalism: The Concept of Countervailing Power* (Boston: Houghton Mifflin, 1952).

the demand for social controls. But the trend toward centralization is disturbing. Politically, it has led to enormous enhancement of the power of the federal government. In economic society, it has made more difficult the survival of smaller units in business, farming, and labor. The result is the phenomenon of increasingly centralized power, remote from the individual, the family, and small, easily controlled groups. This threatens a loss of liberty and a diminution of the status of individual members of the political and economic communities. These are the problems that Americans must solve if economic life is to be infused with Christian principles.

CAPITALISM

In many areas of the world, the spirit of individualism just described is considered as identical with capitalism. We in the United States, however, think that our form of capitalism is different. In general American usage, capitalism may be described as an economic system characterized by private ownership of the means of production, substantial freedom of enterprise to determine the main economic conditions of production, stress on the profit motive, and the use of funds invested in land, resources, buildings, and machines in a notable portion of enterprises. Succinctly, private ownership, free enterprise, the profit motive, and the use of invested funds are the main elements of our capitalistic system.

Few Americans seriously dispute the value of private capitalism. We take our system for granted, almost as much as we do the air around us. Hence it comes as a shock to many to read European condemnations of capitalism, especially when these come from Catholic circles and even from the papacy itself. This would be less of a problem, were we to examine the ideas behind the term used. In Europe, capitalism is often used as synonymous with excessive concentration of wealth, exploitation of workers, and an antisocial mentality among employers. Many who condemn capitalism in Europe admire the American system. This applies even to doctrinaire socialists.

The specific elements which characterize our economic system are not at variance with Catholic social teaching. The Church favors private property and free enterprise, always with the proviso that there are social obligations as well as rights attached to these institutions. Nor is there anything immoral in seeking a profit or using saved funds to build new physical capital. It is true that American business has at times abused its power. But we speak of such abuses as deviations from moral norms in a system that is not intrinsically wrong.

The Wage Contract. Historically, one of the notable features of capitalism has been the wage system, whereby one or more workers contribute skill and energy, using the property of another, to produce goods or services. The products of such activity are sold by the owner of the property, who pays the workers for their contribution and retains a part as payment for his own share in the process, namely, the use of his property. Such a system, says Pope Pius XI, "is not to be condemned." "It is not of its own nature vicious." But it is a grave abuse when capital uses its power in such a way that it scorns "the human dignity of the workers, the social character of economic activity, and social justice itself and the common good." Accordingly, the hiring of workers by an employer is an acceptable mode of economic life, provided the social aspect of the process is not ignored.

In the modern world, it would be almost impossible to have any other system. World population has expanded to such a degree that the use of machines and mass-production methods seems essential if we are to maintain even a minimum standard of living. Increases in living standards almost invariably involve an increase in invested capital. Thus, in the United States, it can be shown that real wages per worker have gone up in direct proportion to increased capital investment. Today the typical American worker has at his disposal over fifteen thousand dollars' worth of tools, buildings, and resources. These multiply his skill and efficiency to such a degree that he can work only half as long as was customary fifty years ago, and yet receive three times as much real income. Such is the contribution of physical capital, which may be defined as the machines and resources bought with money capital. Even socialism and communism acknowledge the value of physical capital, although under these systems it is generally owned by the state. Socialist enterprises hire workers in much the same way as do their capitalist competitors.

An even more fundamental reason for the owner-worker distinction was noted by Pope Leo XIII, namely, human inequality. Men differ in skills, abilities, character, zeal, energy, and like qualities. Some are timid and retiring; others are forthright and resolute. There are men who are conservative and cautious, whereas their fellows may be daring and even reckless. With such major diversities in human nature, it is not surprising that men should be divided into the skilled and the unskilled and into leaders and followers. Nor is it remarkable that unequal talents are among the factors leading to inequality in wealth. In some cases individuals saved from their income, at times through several generations, to build up a great enterprise. In other instances, promoters used the money of others, obtained by borrowing or the sale of shares of ownership, to create some firm. Within an enterprise, men of exceptional ability are given the positions of responsibility. On lower levels, workers are classified according to their skills.

Of course, not all economic inequality is traceable to differences in ability. Elements of luck, ruthlessness, favoritism, and similar factors not connected with genuine ability have been important factors in many well-known success stories. But, at least there are enough variations in human qualities that inequality is not necessarily a result of exploitation. In general, this thesis need not be argued in America. Few in our midst accept the Marxian idea that capital is essentially predatory, stealing a surplus value which really belongs to the workers. Nor do we object to inequality of fortune or position, provided it is based on evident ability and not dishonest means. The average worker does not begrudge the manager of an enterprise his salary, nor the owner his profits provided they are "fair." But this element of fairness requires considerable definition and clarification, as will be further explained in Chapter VIII.

SOCIALISM

The Theory of Socialism.   In contrast to individualism, socialism exalts the state in the economic sphere. Socialism has taken so many forms within the past century that it is difficult to specify its exact meaning today. Generally speaking, socialism calls for community ownership of the means of production. On the theory that private property in productive goods is the basis of economic exploitation, and the premise that free enterprise varies between wasteful competition and antisocial monopoly, it is held that drastic remedies are needed. Nothing less than community ownership of productive property will permit planned production without exploitation.

The degree of proposed socialization varies among the several schools of socialists. The system has moderated somewhat from an earlier position which would take over all forms of productive property. Some socialists would exempt small business firms and land held by small farmers. They would concentrate upon large, dominant enterprises. Likewise, there is variety in the type of control advocated. Some would have direct state ownership. Others would favor independent state corporations. Finally, there is a school which would have smaller groups, such as guilds of workers, taking over enterprises.

Most modern socialism holds for democratic methods of seizure, with fair compensation for the former owners. Likewise, it professes that control of the seized property should be democratic, at least through popular participation in a socialist government. In some cases the tendency toward class warfare has been mitigated. Socialists attack the inefficiency of present owners rather than their alleged exploitation of workers. These moderating trends were noted in *Quadragesimo Anno*.

A formal distinction must be made between socialism and nationalization. It is possible to achieve socialism through progressive nationalization of enterprises, but it is also feasible to have considerable state ownership without socialism. A similar distinction can be made between socialism and economic planning, although not all would admit this. In theory, it is possible to have private enterprise with a substantial degree of state control. Some writers would contend that such a situation would inevitably lead to socialism or worse. This, however, is a debatable point.

Finally, we must distinguish between socialism based on ideology — often chosen in reaction to abuses in the capitalist world — and socialism as a tribal custom. In many parts of Africa, for example, property has for generations been held by the tribe, not by individuals. When nations having such customs adopt modern technology, they often retain the earlier pattern of ownership.

A Critique of Socialism. Pope Pius XI observed the great changes which have come about in socialism. He even stated that many of its concrete proposals do not differ greatly from the just demands of Christian social reformers. He noted with approval its recession from positions regarding the class war and revolutionary violence. Nevertheless, he stated that true socialism, based on its historical principles, is incompatible with Christian teaching.

One basic objection to socialism is its inherent materialism. It organizes social life exclusively in the interests of economic efficiency. With greater and greater production the main aim of society, it is evident that higher values are sacrificed for the sake of material goods. It may be objected that capitalism is likewise materialistic. But capitalism is not identical with civil society. Moreover, it is hardly a reform of capitalism to take over and intensify one of its less desirable features.

Socialism likewise endangers human liberties. If all economic power is concentrated in the hands of the state, such a state has absolute power.

Even if it is organized along democratic lines, there are great pressures toward absolutism. Here is a concentration of power much more extensive than under the most dictatorial forms of capitalism. Such centralization is inherently dangerous, no matter what safeguards against abuse are established. Moreover, there are persuasive arguments that central control of economic life is possible only by totalitarian methods. When other incentives are removed, compulsion remains as a last resort. It is not unlikely that a socialist government must either put down resistance by workers or lapse into anarchy. But if it acts against the group that gives it political support, it must either yield power to the opposition or consolidate it by dictatorial methods. There is no easy escape from this dilemma.

There are also strong economic reasons against the practicability of socialism. The idea that a planned economy is more efficient than a well-functioning free economy is a fallacy. Central planning imposes the decisions of the few upon the many. Under a free economy each consumer through his purchases participates in planning. Businessmen through their investments likewise plan. Their activities are co-ordinated in the market through the price mechanism. In this way the quantity and quality of goods, the distribution of labor and capital, and the rewards to producers are calculated in terms of consumer needs and available resources. It is true that defects exist in the actual functioning of our market economy, as was noted earlier in this chapter. But the remedy is a free economy working for sound social ends, not a controlled economy which squanders the initiative and planning of the many only to replace it with the plans of the few. Quite apart from the elements of compulsion inherent in socialism and central planning, it is quite doubtful that centralism can use human and material resources as efficiently as a free economy. To repeat, the issue is not between planning and anarchy, but between the planning of the few and the decisions of the many.[2]

It is for these reasons that the Pontiff states that no Catholic may be a socialist. He calls the term "Christian Socialism" a contradiction. However, this stricture applies only to socialism in the literal sense of the term. Too often, in the United States, the term socialism is loosely applied to any proposed reform measure which would extend government authority in the economic field. Thus, health-insurance measures are sometimes mislabeled socialism or socialized medicine. Obviously, social-

---

[2] For a succinct treatment of this problem, see J. Messner, *Social Ethics*, pp. 818–823, and L. von Mises, *Human Action* (New Haven: Yale University Press, 1949), Chap. 26.

ism in the technical sense has a very definite meaning. Even extensive nationalization is not of necessity socialism, although it may be undesirable for other reasons. Only if such measures are part of a pattern leading to complete state ownership of industry or control over services can we call them socialist.

NONCOMMUNIST STATISM

While socialism is the antithesis of individualism by virtue of state ownership of productive property, there are other forms of statism where control rather than ownership is the distinguishing feature. Thus, national socialism and fascism did not take over private industry, but they subjected economic life to strict state control. The system of ownership was undisturbed, but the owners were by no means their own masters in running their businesses. Prices were often regulated, production quotas set, and rigid patterns of working conditions imposed. The owners were allowed to receive profits, but they were often told how these must be invested in terms of economic expansion. Like every other phase of life in a totalitarian economy, business was forced to accept state dictatorship.

In discussing these varieties of statism, a sharp distinction must be made between state control of economic life and totalitarian control of all phases of life. This distinction is vital in appraising many modern government systems. Totalitarianism is essentially evil. By its very nature, it embodies a false concept of society. It denies basic rights to individuals. The total state intrudes in fields where government has no normal authority to enter. It probes deeply into family relationships, ignores parental authority in education, suppresses vital individual freedoms, and thus makes the citizen the slave of the state. It is unnecessary to elaborate in detail how all this perverts the notions of individual dignity, the function of society, and the true nature of the common good.

By contrast, the absence of popular democratic control is a relative rather than an absolute evil. Historically, monarchy, tribal rule, and forms of dictatorship have been, until recent centuries, the prevailing political forms among most of mankind. While it is well to emphasize the virtues of democracy, it is the part of realism to note also its preconditions. It is difficult to have true democratic rule without a minimum of popular general education, adequate means of communication, the existence of a middle class, and some economic security for the poorer classes of society.

For this reason, it is difficult to form valid generalizations about dictatorships in contemporary political society. In older states, such as Spain and Portugal, dictatorships entered when democratic government had broken down. In Spain, the reason was civil war. In Portugal, it was corruption and inefficiency, which bankrupted the government. In Latin America, the problem is often one of the absence of a middle class and the wide gulf between rich and poor. There is still another problem with nations, particularly in Asia and Africa, newly emerged from colonialism. Here we may find that the preceding colonial rule had not prepared an adequate civil service, so that the new nations find severe and often impossible handicaps to the practice of democracy.

For these reasons, we may accept the fact that some dictatorships are unavoidable. The indictment against this form of rule is based, not necessarily upon its beginnings in a nation, but upon its desire to perpetuate itself. When a ruler fails to use his power to prepare a nation for a viable democracy, he is betraying the best interests of his people.

CONCLUSION

In theory, as we shall note in Chapter XIII, it is not the form of government that matters, but the justice of its rule. But the power of the modern state is so absolute that the citizen rarely has recourse against injustice. For this reason it is safe to say that any condition that tends to overcentralize political power is dangerous. Individualism may produce such a result through reaction to the problems it creates. Socialism and statism directly enhance the power of the state. They must all be rejected as inadequate in terms of the needs of mankind.

The ultimate test of any society is its total impact on man and the family. If it promotes conditions consonant with man's dignity and rights, it is seeking the true common good. When its emphasis is distorted and man suffers, then it is lacking, no matter what material or political benefits it may obtain. Man lives in society, but society exists to help the individual and the family.

READINGS*

On Individualism and Socialism:
C. Clune, Christian Social Reconstruction, Chap. 6.
J. Messner, Social Ethics (rev. ed.), pp. 604–629, 716–719, 936–947.
O. von Nell-Breuning, Reorganization of Social Economy, Chaps. 14–15.
On Statism:
C. Dawson, Religion and the Modern State.
H. Johnston, Business Ethics, Chap. 12.
J. Messner, Social Ethics, pp. 566–579.
H. A. Rommen, The State in Catholic Thought.

* For further readings, see List No. 4 in the Appendix.

Chapter VI

COMMUNISM

Pius XI, Quadragesimo Anno

112. Communism teaches and seeks two objectives: unrelenting class warfare and absolute extermination of private ownership. Not secretly or by hidden methods does it do this, but publicly, openly, and by employing every and all means, even the most violent. To achieve these objectives there is nothing which it does not dare, nothing for which it has respect or reverence; and when it has come to power, it is incredible and portentlike in its cruelty and inhumanity. The horrible slaughter and destruction through which it has laid waste vast regions of eastern Europe and Asia are the evidence; how much an enemy and how openly hostile it is to Holy Church and to God Himself is, alas, too well proved by facts and fully known to all. Although We, therefore, deem it superfluous to warn upright and faithful children of the Church regarding the impious and iniquitous character of communism, yet We cannot without deep sorrow contemplate the heedlessness of those who apparently make light of these impending dangers, and with sluggish inertia allow the widespread propagation of doctrine which seeks by violence and slaughter to destroy society altogether. All the more gravely to be condemned is the folly of those who neglect to remove or change the conditions that inflame the minds of peoples and pave the way for the overthrow and destruction of society.

Pius XI, On Atheistic Communism

8. The communism of today, more emphatically than similar movements in the past, conceals in itself a false messianic idea. A pseudo-ideal of justice, of equality and fraternity in labor impregnates all its doctrine and activity with a deceptive mysticism, which communicates a zealous and contagious enthusiasm to the multitudes entrapped by delusive promises. This is especially true in an age like ours, when unusual misery has resulted from the unequal distribution of the goods of this world. This pseudo-ideal is even boastfully advanced as if it were responsible for a certain economic progress. As a matter of fact, when such progress is at all real, its true causes are quite different, as for instance the intensification of industrialism in countries which were formerly almost without it, the exploitation of immense natural resources, and the use of the most brutal methods to insure the achievement of gigantic projects with a minimum of expense.

9. The doctrine of modern com-

munism, which is often concealed under the most seductive trappings, is in substance based on the principles of dialectical and historical materialism previously advocated by Marx, of which the theoreticians of Bolshevism claim to possess the only genuine interpretation. According to this doctrine there is in the world only one reality, matter, the blind forces of which evolve into plant, animal, and man. Even human society is nothing but a phenomenon and form of matter, evolving in the same way. By a law of inexorable necessity and through a perpetual conflict of forces, matter moves toward the final synthesis of a classless society. In such a doctrine, as is evident, there is no room for the idea of God; there is no difference between matter and spirit, between soul and body; there is neither survival of the soul after death nor any hope in a future life. Insisting on the dialectical aspect of their materialism, the Communists claim that the conflict which carries the world toward its final synthesis can be accelerated by man. Hence they endeavor to sharpen the antagonisms which arise between the various classes of society. Thus the class struggle with its consequent violent hate and destruction takes on the aspect of a crusade for the progress of humanity. On the other hand, all other forces whatever, as long as they resist such systematic violence, must be annihilated as hostile to the human race.

10. Communism, moreover, strips man of his liberty, robs human personality of all its dignity, and removes all the moral restraints that check the eruptions of blind impulse. There is no recognition of any right of the individual in his relations to the collectivity; no natural right is accorded to human personality, which is a mere cogwheel in the communist system. In man's relations with other individuals, besides, Communists hold the principle of absolute equality, rejecting all hierarchy and divinely constituted authority, including the authority of parents. What men call authority and subordination is derived from the community as its first and only font. Nor is the individual granted any property rights over material goods or the means of production for, inasmuch as these are the source of further wealth, their possession would give one man power over another. Precisely on this score, all forms of private property must be eradicated, for they are at the origin of all economic enslavement.

12. What would be the condition of a human society based on such materialistic tenets? It would be a collectivity with no other hierarchy than that of the economic system. It would have only one mission: the production of material things by means of collective labor, so that the goods of this world might be enjoyed in a paradise where each would "give according to his powers" and would "receive according to his needs." Communism recognizes in the collectivity the right, or rather, unlimited discretion, to draft individuals for the labor of the collectivity with no regard for their personal welfare; so that even violence could be legitimately exercised to dragoon the recalcitrant against their wills. In the communistic commonwealth morality and law would be nothing but a derivation of the existing economic order, purely earthly in origin and unstable in character. In a word, the Communists claim to inaugurate a new era and a new civilization which is the result of blind evolutionary forces culminating in a humanity without God.

14. Such, Venerable Brethren, is the new gospel which Bolshevistic and atheistic communism offers the world

as the glad tidings of deliverance and salvation! It is a system full of errors and sophisms. It is in opposition both to reason and to divine revelation. It subverts the social order, because it means the destruction of its foundations; because it ignores the true origin and purpose of the state; because it denies the rights, dignity, and liberty of human personality.

15. How is it possible that such a system, long since rejected scientifically and now proved erroneous by experience, how is it, We ask, that such a system could spread so rapidly in all parts of the world? The explanation lies in the fact that too few have been able to grasp the nature of communism. The majority instead succumb to its deception, skillfully concealed by the most extravagant promises. By pretending to desire only the betterment of the condition of the working classes, by urging the removal of the very real abuses chargeable to the liberalistic economic order, and by demanding a more equitable distribution of this world's goods (objects entirely and undoubtedly legitimate), the Communist takes advantage of the present world-wide economic crisis to draw into the sphere of his influence even those sections of the populace which on principle reject all forms of materialism and terrorism. And as every error contains its element of truth, the partial truths to which we have referred are astutely presented according to the needs of time and place, to conceal, when convenient, the repulsive crudity and inhumanity of communistic principles and tactics. Thus the communist ideal wins over many of the better-minded members of the community. These in turn become the apostles of the movement among the younger intelligentsia who are still too immature to recognize the intrinsic errors of the system. The preachers of communism are also pro-

ficient in exploiting racial antagonisms and political divisions and oppositions. They take advantage of the lack of orientation characteristic of modern agnostic science in order to burrow into the universities where they bolster up the principles of their doctrine with pseudoscientific arguments.

17. There is another explanation for the rapid diffusion of the communistic ideas now seeping into every nation, great and small, advanced and backward, so that no corner of the earth is free from them. This explanation is to be found in a propaganda so truly diabolical that the world has perhaps never witnessed its like before. It is directed from one common center. It is shrewdly adapted to the varying conditions of diverse peoples. It has at its disposal great financial resources, gigantic organizations, international congresses, and countless trained workers. It makes use of pamphlets and reviews, of cinema, theater, and radio, of schools and even universities. Little by little it penetrates into all classes of the people and even reaches the better-minded groups of the community with the result that few are aware of the poison which increasingly pervades their minds and hearts.

22. For the first time in history we are witnessing a struggle, cold blooded in purpose and mapped out to the least detail, between man and "all that is called God." Communism is by its nature antireligious. It considers religion as the "opiate of the people" because the principles of religion which speak of a life beyond the grave dissuade the proletariat from the dream of a Soviet paradise which is of this world.

23. But the law of nature and its Author cannot be flouted with impunity. Communism has not been able, and will not be able, to achieve

its objectives even in the merely economic sphere. It is true that in Russia it has been a contributing factor in rousing men and materials from the inertia of centuries, and in obtaining by all manner of means, often without scruple, some measure of material success. Nevertheless we know from reliable and even very recent testimony that not even there, in spite of slavery imposed on millions of men, has communism reached its promised goal. After all, even the sphere of economics needs some morality, some moral sense of responsibility, which can find no place in a system so thoroughly materialistic as communism. Terrorism is the only possible substitute, and it is terrorism that reigns today in Russia, where former comrades in revolution are exterminating each other. Terrorism, having failed despite all to stem the tide of moral corruption, cannot even prevent the dissolution of society itself.

57. In the beginning communism showed itself for what it was in all its perversity; but very soon it realized that it was thus alienating the people. It has therefore changed its tactics, and strives to entice the multitudes by trickery of various forms, hiding its real designs behind ideas that in themselves are good and attractive. Thus, aware of the universal desire for peace, the leaders of communism pretend to be the most zealous promoters and propagandists in the movement for world amity. Yet at the same time they stir up a class warfare which causes rivers of blood to flow, and, realizing that their system offers no internal guarantee of peace, they have recourse to unlimited armaments. Under various names which do not suggest communism, they establish organizations and periodicals with the sole purpose of carrying their ideas into quarters otherwise inaccessible. They try perfidiously to worm their way even into professedly Catholic and religious organizations. Again, without receding an inch from their subversive principles, they invite Catholics to collaborate with them in the realm of so-called humanitarianism and charity; and at times even make proposals that are in perfect harmony with the Christian spirit and the doctrine of the Church. Elsewhere they carry their hypocrisy so far as to encourage the belief that communism, in countries where faith and culture are more strongly entrenched, will assume another and much milder form. It will not interfere with the practice of religion. It will respect liberty of conscience. There are some even who refer to certain changes recently introduced into Soviet legislation as a proof that communism is about to abandon its program of war against God.

58. See to it, Venerable Brethren, that the Faithful do not allow themselves to be deceived! Communism is intrinsically wrong, and no one who would save Christian civilization may collaborate with it in any undertaking whatsoever. Those who permit themselves to be deceived into lending their aid toward the triumph of communism in their own country, will be the first to fall victims of their error. And the greater the antiquity and grandeur of the Christian civilization in the regions where communism successfully penetrates, so much more devastating will be the hatred displayed by the godless.

Congregation of the Holy Office, July 13, 1949

The Supreme Sacred Congregation of the Holy Office has been asked: (1) Whether it is lawful to enlist in or show favor to the communist party? (2) Whether it is lawful to publish, read, or disseminate books, newspapers, periodicals, or leaflets in support of communist doctrine and practice or write any articles in them? (3) Whether Catholics who knowingly and freely perform actions as specified in Nos. 1 and 2 above may be admitted to the sacraments? (4) Whether Catholics, who profess and particularly those who defend and spread, the materialistic and anti-Christian doctrine of the Communists, ipso facto, as apostates from the Catholic faith, incur excommunication reserved especially to the Holy See?

The most eminent and reverend fathers, charged with the defense of matters pertaining to faith and morals, after having previously heard the opinion of the consultors at a plenary session held on Tuesday, the 28th day of June, 1949, decreed that the above-mentioned questions be answered as follows:

To No. 1 — In the negative, for communism is materialistic and anti-Christian. Besides, communist leaders, although they sometimes verbally assert that they are not opposed to religion, show themselves nevertheless, both by doctrine and by action, to be in reality enemies of God, of the true religion, and of the Church of Christ.

To No. 2 — In the negative, inasmuch as this is prohibited by law itself (of Canon 1399, Corpus Juris Canonici).

To No. 3 — In the negative, in accordance with the common principles governing refusal of the sacraments to those not having proper dispositions.

To No. 4 — In the affirmative.

And on the following Thursday, the 30th of the same month and year, His Holiness Pope Pius XII, when informed of the decision in the usual audience granted to His Excellency, the Most Reverend Assessor, approved and ordered to be published the above answers in the Acta Apostolicae Sedis.

John XXIII, Pacem in Terris

34. Man's personal dignity requires besides that he enjoy freedom and be able to make up his own mind when he acts. In his association with his fellows, therefore, there is every reason why his recognition of rights, observance of duties, and many-sided collaboration with other men, should be primarily a matter of his own personal decision. Each man should act on his own initiative, conviction, and sense of responsibility, not under the constant pressure of external coercion or enticement. There is nothing human about a society that is welded together by force. Far from encouraging, as it should, the attainment of man's progress and perfection, it is merely an obstacle to his freedom.

48. Hence, a regime which governs solely or mainly by means of threats and intimidation or promises of reward, provides men with no effective incentive to work for the common good. And even if it did, it would certainly be offensive to the dignity of free and rational human beings. Authority is before all else a moral force. For this reason the appeal of rulers should be to the individual conscience, to the duty which every man has of voluntarily contributing

to the common good. But since all men are equal in natural dignity, no man has the capacity to force internal compliance on another. Only God can do that, for He alone scrutinizes and judges the secret counsels of the heart.

127. We grant indeed that this conviction [that disputes between nations be resolved through negotiations, not wars] is chiefly based on the terrible destructive force of modern weapons and a fear of the calamities and frightful destruction which such weapons would cause. Therefore, in an age such as ours which prides itself on its atomic energy it is contrary to reason to hold that war is now a suitable way to restore rights which have been violated.

159. Again it is perfectly legitimate to make a clear distinction between a false philosophy of the nature, origin and purpose of men and the world, and economic, social, cultural, and political undertakings, even when such undertakings draw their origin and inspiration from that philosophy. True, the philosophic formula does not change once it has been set down in precise terms, but the undertakings clearly cannot avoid being influenced to a certain extent by the changing conditions in which they have to operate. Besides, who can deny the possible existence of good and commendable elements in these undertakings, elements which do indeed conform

to the dictates of right reason, and are an expression of man's lawful aspirations?

160. It may sometimes happen, therefore, that meetings arranged for some practical end — though hitherto they were thought to be altogether useless — may in fact be fruitful at the present time, or at least offer prospects of success.

But whether or not the moment for such co-operation has arrived, and the manner and degree of such co-operation in the attainment of economic, social, cultural and political advantages — these are matters for prudence to decide; prudence, the queen of all the virtues which rule the lives of men both as individuals and in society.

As far as Catholics are concerned, the decision rests primarily with those who take a leading part in the life of the community, and in these specific fields. They must, however, act in accordance with the principles of the natural law, and observe the Church's social teaching and the directives of ecclesiastical authority. For it must not be forgotten that the Church has the right and duty not only to safeguard her teaching on faith and morals, but also to exercise her authority over her sons by intervening in their external affairs whenever a judgment has to be made concerning the practical application of this teaching.

Paul VI, to Pastoral Study Week, September 6, 1963

Let no one believe that this pastoral solicitude which the Church underlines in its program today, which absorbs its attention and requires its care — let no one believe that this signifies a change of judgment regarding the errors spread in our society and already condemned by the Church, such as atheistic marxism for example. To seek to apply careful

and healing remedies to a contagious and lethal disease does not mean that one changes his opinion about it. It means rather that he seeks to combat it, not only theoretically but also practically. It means that he follows diagnosis with therapy, that he applies healing charity to doctrinal condemnation.

Paul VI, Ecclesiam Suam

These are the reasons which compel Us, as they compelled Our Predecessors and, with them, everyone who has religious values at heart, to condemn the ideological systems which deny God and oppress the Church, systems which are often identified with economic, social and political regimes, among which atheistic communism is the chief. It could be said that it is not so much that We condemn these systems and regimes as that they express their radical opposition to Us in thought and deed. Our regret is, in reality, more sorrow for a victim than the sentence of a judge.

Dialogue in such conditions is very difficult, not to say impossible, although, even today, We have no preconceived intention of excluding the persons who profess these systems and belong to these regimes. For the lover of truth discussion is always possible. The difficulties are enormously increased by obstacles of the moral order: by the absence of sufficient freedom of thought and action and by the perversion of discussion so that the latter is not made use of to seek and express objective truth but to serve predetermined utilitarian ends. This is what puts an end to dia-

logue. The Church of Silence, for example, speaks only by her sufferings, and with her speaks also the suffering of an oppressed and degraded society, in which the rights of the spirit are crushed by those who control its fate. If we begin to speak in such a state of affairs, how can we offer dialogue, when we cannot be anything more than a "voice crying in the wilderness" (Mark 1:3)? Silence, groaning, patience and always love, in such conditions, are the witness that the Church can still offer, and not even death can silence it.

*   *   *

Accordingly, bearing in mind the words of Our Predecessor of venerable memory, Pope John XXIII, in his Encyclical "Pacem in terris" to the effect that the doctrines of such movements once elaborated and defined, remain always the same, whereas the movements themselves cannot help but evolve and undergo changes, even of a profound nature (cf. n. 54), We do not despair that they may one day be able to enter into a more positive dialogue with the Church than the present one which We now of necessity deplore and lament.

French Hierarchy, The Church in the Modern World, June, 1954

The Church has always refused to be associated with a political anti-communism that denies the existence of social injustice, which is, nevertheless, the real cause of communism. She reminds us that "all error contains an element of truth." To seek

to improve the lot of the working classes, to suppress the very real abuses caused by the liberal economy, and to bring about an equitable distribution of wealth are undoubtedly perfectly legitimate objectives.

THE analysis of communism made in 1931 and 1937 by Pope Pius XI is, to say the least, a remarkable example of historical insight. To the Catholic, it is a tangible indication of divine guidance of the Church. Little that is written there needs to be changed to apply to the powerful communist empire of the late 1960's. Yet, at the time it was written, the world's keenest statesmen and political analysts considered the Soviet Union as a backward power, repulsive in its cruelty, but in no sense a menace to world peace and freedom. In view of what subsequently happened, the insight and foresight of the Pope were truly unique.

Now we judge communism in the light of astounding scientific and military achievements, sharp political victories, amazing success in subversion and psychological warfare, and notable gains achieved through economic penetration of developing nations. There is no need today to argue its power or emphasize the danger it poses to Christian civilization. Our need, rather, is to understand the movement and to see its strength as well as its weakness. Such understanding can be a first step toward safeguarding human freedom, and ultimately restoring freedom to the hundreds of millions under communist control. To achieve this understanding, we must first know communist theory, tactics, and practice.

The Theory of Communism. Communism is a system of dialectical materialism. It is based on the premise that matter is the only reality, with God, the soul, and spiritual values but fictions. Material forces dominate the evolution of the world. Most important of these are economic forces, since they determine man's ability to survive. In any society, the organized methods of production are the absolute determinants of that culture. Civil government, the family, the Church, and other social groups are merely by-products of economic organization.

This materialism is dialectical in the sense worked out by the German philosopher, Hegel. History is seen as a dynamic process, whereby groups of forces dominate a given period of time. But every action leads to an equal and opposite reaction. Applying dialectical materialism to the nineteenth-century world, Marx considered capitalism to be the dominant economic system which determined contemporary history. The heart of capitalism is the institution of private property, which enables a few persons to secure control of economic life. Property, of course, is fundamental, since it furnishes the means of existence for man. When property is in private hands, its owners thereby control the lives of other men, who are nonowners. They can force others to work for them at whatever wages the owners may choose. That such wages would be the minimum needed for subsistence was argued by the capitalist economist, Ricardo. Hence private property is essentially a means of exploitation. Economic value is created only by work, but the owners return to the workers only a fraction of what they produce. The remainder, the surplus value, is retained for the immense profits of the capitalists.

To safeguard this system of exploitation, owners have developed two institutions for repressing the proletariat, the non-owning workers. The first is the state, which through its various powers protects the property owner. Most important of these powers is the police force which cows the workers. The courts, law, and such institutions are but elaborate developments of police and military power. Moreover schools, the bourgeois press, and other opinion-forming agencies are tools of the capitalists. Even the family, in its present form, embodies the capitalist mentality. Monogamy and parental control of children are but extensions of the ownership principle. Hence civil society is but a protective integument for monopolistic owners.

The second institution created to defend property is organized religion, the opiate of the people. Religion is an anodyne which deadens the frustrations of the workers by promising them justice in another world. In the crude language of the Industrial Workers of the World (I.W.W. — Wobblies), it offers "pie in the sky, instead of pie on earth." Religion sanctions property ownership in its command: Thou shalt not steal. It teaches to its votaries meekness and submission. The other-world mentality robs them of the ambition to remedy abuses here and now. It is an ideal tool for the capitalists.

Nevertheless, the dialectical forces of history may not be denied. The process of exploitation creates the weapons whereby it will ultimately be abolished. First, it arouses in the workers an ever increasing sense of anger and resentment. They become embittered at their lot, the more so when they contrast it with the wealth and luxury secured by others with the fruits of their labor. The next step naturally follows. The workers are "disciplined, united, organized, by the very mechanism of the process of capitalist production itself." These workers, given solidarity by their oppressors, unite in a revolutionary upsurge. "Centralization of the means of production and socialization of labor at last reach a point where they become incompatible with their capitalist integument. This integument is burst asunder. The knell of capitalist private property sounds. The expropriators are expropriated."[1]

The communist party exists to aid in the class struggle and thereby accelerate processes of history. It must educate the workers to realize their oppression and the means of deliverance. It must take advantage of poverty and exploitation, but especially it must capitalize on the recurring depres-

---

[1] Karl Marx, quoted in H. Laski, *Communism* (New York: Holt, 1927), p. 108.

sions and imperialist wars which are inevitable in the existing system. The unemployed offer a fertile field for recruits. In pursuing this aim, the communists must not be deviated by the prospects of short-term reforms. While they may agitate for reforms, so as to win the allegiance of the workers, their demands must be insatiable, so that issues will always remain. This point is vital. Proletarian reform groups which would be satisfied with anything less than total revolution are traitors to the working class. They are more dangerous enemies than the capitalists themselves. The class struggle must be intensified, not mitigated.[2]

Since the struggle is world wide, communist organization must be international. From the beginning, communism took the form of various international movements. The best known was the Third International, also called the Comintern, which closely ruled various communist parties throughout the world. This movement was dissolved, at least ostensibly, during World War II. It was not replaced by any comparable organization of world communists. On the contrary, the Sino-Soviet split, the trend toward polycentrism among communist parties in the free world, and even the increasing independence of satellite states tended to fragment and dissipate communist unity.

Communist Tactics. The main function of international communism is to win over the oppressed workers and peasants and to prepare for a series of proletarian revolutions. Communist dictatorships are to be set up in order to liquidate the enemies of the people. This is an interim process, according to Marx. Once true socialism is achieved, the state will wither away, since there will be no need for it. Instead, the workers' soviets will rule, with each person contributing according to his ability, and receiving according to his need.

While Marxism as a theory enjoyed some successes throughout the world, it did not become a potent force until Vladimir Lenin perfected the tactics for revolutionary seizure of power. It is difficult to overstate the diabolical brilliance of Lenin. The world-wide success of his tactics is proof of their remarkable flexibility and appeal.

The center of all activity is the communist party. This is organized upon secret and conspiratorial lines, partly to avoid government repression,

[2] This element of communist theory is of vital importance for understanding communist tactics. Communists want issues, not reforms. American labor leaders and liberal legislators can cite scores of instances where our native communists killed reforms by making impossible demands or through propaganda which alienated middle-of-the-road groups. Noncommunist leftist movements, such as Social Democracy, understand this tactic and are far more bitter enemies of communists than are liberals or even conservative capitalists.

but also in part voluntarily. Secrecy aids subversion. At the same time it helps the party to obtain complete control over its members, since they are not subject to outside pressures. Internal organization of the party is dictatorial. Under its "democratic centralism" discussion is permitted prior to decisions, but once the ruling forces issue a command, it is absolute. Deviationists are summarily dismissed. Even drastic and contradictory changes in the party line must be accepted without questioning.

Under such strict control, recruiting is naturally a slow and careful process. There is no one type which could be called characteristic material for communism. Most of its recruits, however, fall into one of three groups: the seriously disgruntled, misled idealists, or ambitious opportunists. The first type is obvious material for a revolutionary movement. It includes victims of economic, racial, national, and religious or cultural discrimination. Many workers who become communists do so because of crass exploitation or bitter class-struggle experiences in trying to better economic conditions. In the United States, recruitment for this reason alone has not been too successful. The American party has achieved better results among middle-class and even occasional well-to-do persons who are victims of racial, religious, or cultural discrimination. Certain foreign-language groups are considered good prospects. Of the average seven thousand American communists, about 80 per cent belong in minority groups of one type or other.

The idealists who become communists are often intellectuals. Their interest may be either negative, revulsion against oppression; or positive, attraction for a planned society or some features of Soviet communism. Published material in Canadian and American espionage cases indicates that misguided idealists play an important part in communist plans. The initial appeal is made in terms of social justice, freedom of science, peace, or some other exalted consideration. The victim is gradually led to believe that his ideals can be realized only under communism. This explains, in part, why high-paid and respected scientists and other intellectuals joined the Soviet espionage apparatus in England, Canada, and the United States.

A third class of recruits includes ambitious persons who feel that the communist party is a source of advancement or protection. Obvious examples are the former nazis, fascists, and collaborators in Europe who quickly joined their respective communist parties to gain immunity and power. In Latin America and India, many intellectuals find little opportunity to use their talents. Some embrace communism as the best hope for their future. When communist infiltration into government and labor in the United States was at its peak, many found a party card a real opportunity for advancement. The same was true, at certain times, in the literary and entertainment fields.

When a subject is brought into the party, he is given a thorough indoctrination in the principles of Marx and Lenin. What is even more important, he is hermetically isolated from the capitalist world. He is led to distrust all bourgeois sources of information and to cut off friendly contacts with noncommunists. With such complete dependence upon the party, even for his thoughts, he soon becomes a fanatic. This explains in part the zeal which provokes admiration even from the enemies of communism. Another explanation of communist fanaticism is in terms of Darwinian selection: only zealots are attracted to such an extreme system and survive its rigorous demands upon its members.

Much of the secret of communist success lies in its strict organization and iron discipline. It is axiomatic that an organized, disciplined minority can usually outmaneuver a disorganized majority. In addition, communists use the weapon of massive deceit, the principle of the "big lie." By constantly calling their opponents warmongers and aggressors, and by appropriating to themselves the banners of peace and democracy, they have been able to confuse a large portion of the world.

The small communist party multiplies its influence by many tried and proved devices. It acts openly in the "united-front" approach, whereby it joins with other organizations for common action for a special objective. It is hoped that in such campaigns the party will be able to take over the movement and thus lead the larger groups. As a minimum result, it can gain good will, contacts, and respectability. Moreover, it is then in a position to press for ever higher demands, precluding real reform but embittering other participants in the process.

A second approach is the method called "boring-from-within." In these cases, secret communists secure places in influential organizations, such as government, labor unions, representatives of minorities, and organs for propaganda, such as press, radio, the screen, publishers, and book-review publications. Here the minimum aim is influencing policy along communist lines. The maximum objective is capture and control of such groups.

A third tactic is the formation of "front organizations," or groups apparently noncommunist but secretly organized and controlled by the party, which aim at ostensibly sound objectives. The method used here involves the determining of a high-sounding aim, such as peace, democracy, or some social reform. Then a core of names of prominent but naïve persons is secured as the organizing committee. On this basis, more names are obtained and fund-raising is started. With funds and names, it is possible to secure publicity, pressure upon government, and like objectives. The success of this tactic is amazing. While it has been exposed time and again, and individuals involved have realized their error in particular cases, it remains a reliable device for multiplying communist effectiveness. There seems to be an inexhaustible fund of prominent persons, who feel that they must be on record in favor of every worthy cause, but too busy to look into the real control of the group or to take any active part in the administration of the movement.

In addition to these broad programs, special approaches are developed for various interest groups, such as labor, Negroes, youth, women, consumers, tenants, the unemployed, pacifists, religious organizations, scientists, lawyers, doctors, teachers, social workers, librarians, book readers, and even businessmen. Thousands of such organizations have been listed by American investigative agencies. The amount of time, energy, and money which goes into such work is unbelievable in relation to the small size of the Communist Party, U.S.A.

Communist tactics have achieved results which are almost beyond belief. In scores of nations they have reached positions of real power. They can influence public opinion and government policy, even when they are a small minority. Often they achieve political success through balance-of-power tactics, siding with the group which offers them the most promises. More remarkable is their tenacious hold upon their spheres of influence, even after public opinion has been revolted by Soviet expansionist tactics. Their power of adaptation and deception is unique.

Soviet Communism. Communist theory was put into practice, for the first time on a large scale, in Russia. In 1917, the Russia of the Tsars gave way to a democratic government, which was then overthrown by the Union of Soviet Socialist Republics. At its very beginning, the communists put into effect their theories both of violent revolution and of contempt for moderate or even mildly radical reform. The actual communist revolt was not against the Tsars, but against the moderate Social Democratic government of Kerensky, which had earlier replaced the monarchy. The well-disciplined communist forces under Lenin instigated the second or "October" revolution.

Soviet conduct may be viewed under three aspects: economic organization, internal political life, and foreign policy. In each of these three spheres the general principles of Marx have been observed, but with strategic and tactical modifications by his successors. The path toward their ultimate goal has at times been brutally direct, but at other times devious and roundabout, with many diversions and even retreats.

In the economic sphere, after uncertain beginnings, certain definite policies began to emerge. Agriculture was forcibly collectivized, partly in the hope of more efficient production, but mainly to liquidate the last segments of private ownership. Industrial activity was controlled by a series of five-year plans, with primary emphasis upon heavy industry and scientific research. This concentration provided an excellent base for military power, but it left little for the Soviet consumer. Housing, clothing, and food have been consistently inadequate.

Production generally operates under centralized control, although some local autonomy has been promised. A centralized planning agency works out production quotas and prices. State banks finance individual factories in accord with the master plan. Thus far the factory managers have had little discretion in their operations, but they are rewarded for exceeding quotas and may be punished for falling behind. As a result, there is a tendency to exploit workers or to skimp on quality in order to obtain the quantity demanded. An exception to this rule is the production of military and scientific goods. Usually the best workers, engineers, and managers are assigned to this field. Results have been correspondingly good.

The Soviet worker has only limited freedom. For a long time, it was virtually impossible for him to quit a job without permission from the party. Even though this rule has been relaxed, housing difficulties tend to keep him in one place. Poor as his accommodations may be, he at least is certain of them so long as he remains with his current job. Wages vary according to the type of work and individual accomplishment. But even the better paid manual workers in the Soviet Union have the lowest living standards in all Europe. Because of this most wives also work. Yet the possession of money does not automatically insure food and clothing. Often stores are out of supplies. Long queues are the rule rather than the exception for many purchases. Nor can workers appeal to unions for redress of grievances, since their unions are party-controlled and aim to spur production rather than help their members. Strikes are virtually unheard of in the Soviet Union, although they have occurred in some of the satellite states.

Farm policies have been subject to some experimentation since Stalin's death, but the basic pattern has not changed. New state farms were opened in hitherto untilled areas of Siberia, with mixed success. In older farming areas, the collective farm is still the mainstay for food production. However, current plans point in the direction of more and more state farms, with the peasant deprived of what few possessions he had under the collective farm.

The economic results of these policies have been uneven. The Soviet Union has been able to achieve excellent results in high-priority areas, such as military production. Production for civilian use has been inadequate in quantity and poor in quality. Nikita Khrushchev did promise to equal or excel capitalist living standards as a result of socialist planning. It is unlikely that his successors will do better in this area, without a massive diversion of economic effort from the military field to the civilian economy. There are no immediate indications that such a shift is being planned.

In the internal political sphere, conditions have bettered considerably since the days of Stalin, but it is premature to say that a basic and permanent improvement has set in. Under Khrushchev limited political and ideological disagreement were possible, without drastic punishment for the dissenters. Political opponents of the Premier were dismissed from their posts and some were exiled to distant stations, but they were not imprisoned or executed. Criticism of policy by the intellectuals, particularly the poets, was tolerated at times. Suppression, when tried, was largely limited to denial of publishing rights. Yet there is no assurance that more lenient policies may not be revised under later rulers.

Relaxations from the iron rule of Stalin have not given Soviet citizens any appreciable advance toward democratic rights. There is practically no real freedom of speech or assembly. The state has a monopoly of press, radio, and education. Propaganda and indoctrination are still normal features of Soviet life. Persecution of religion in the U.S.S.R. is not so blatant as before, but the state-controlled Church exists only on sufferance. Other religious groups barely survive. The Catholic Church has been bitterly persecuted in the satellite nations, along with Lutherans and Jews.

The Soviet Union and World Communism. Prior to World War II, the Soviet Union endeavored to spread communism almost exclusively by subversion and propaganda. While it was often successful in gaining prestige and influence by such methods, it did not bring into being any permanent communist governments. The war changed the picture tremendously. Poland and the Baltic states were annexed by direct conquest. The Balkans were taken over by subversion backed by the forces of the

Red army. China, weakened by its long war with Japan and deprived of strong aid and guidance by the United States, could not resist the attacks of its communist armies. As a result of these events, the number of victims of communism increased to six times the prewar figure. One third of the human race, one billion persons, was in the shadow of the Red flag.

While the free world was slow in reacting to communist conquests, it finally developed a number of programs designed to prevent further aggression. A series of alliances in Europe, Asia, and the Near East made any new advance a direct challenge to the military might of the United States and its allies. Efforts by communist nations to win over the uncommitted peoples in countries formerly held as colonies were countered by diplomatic contacts, economic aid, and cultural and technical-assistance programs. When Communists in turn sought to use subversion, guerrilla warfare, and disguised intervention in Asia and Latin America, the United States developed counter measures. In spite of these reactions, Cuba was lost to communism, and Laos and South Vietnam were in serious jeopardy.

Paradoxically, while the communist threat continued to be a major factor in world politics, the communist world itself began to show serious signs of weakness and dissension. Food shortages forced both the Soviet Union and the People's Republic of China to purchase grain from capitalist nations. Indeed, a series of major economic and political blunders brought Communist China to the brink of collapse. Poland was plagued by unemployment. Czechoslovakia, formerly the economic showcase of the communist empire, became a drab shadow of its former self. Collectivized agriculture seemed to be a total failure, and industry in communist nations lagged far behind the growing economies of the Common Market and Japan.

To add to these internal difficulties, differences between the Chinese and Soviet communist parties broke into the open. The Chinese favored the orthodox Marxist-Leninist approach, with the emphasis upon revolutionary overthrow of capitalist nations. By contrast, the Russians advocated a more flexible approach, involving coexistence with capitalist peoples. While the Soviets did not back down from their goal of world communism, they were unwilling to risk nuclear war that might result from more aggressive tactics. They were content to use diplomacy, economic penetration, psychological warfare, subversion, and aid to guerrillas as means for extending their influence.

So severe was the split between the Soviet and the Chinese brands of communism that it divided communist parties throughout much of the world into warring factions. A minority of parties, mostly in Asia, took the Chinese side of the dispute. While the majority supported the Russian position, some remained neutral. In certain nations, such as India, there were both Chinese and Russian communist parties. To add to the distress of the communists, there was the danger that the party dispute might flow over into government policy of the two giant protagonists. The Soviet Union almost completely cut off its economic aid to its former ally. There were border incidents that could have escalated into armed conflict. It is not clear at this writing that the Soviet Union is prepared to honor its treaty obligations to defend the Chinese People's Republic, should it be drawn into clashes with United States armed forces.

Before the world was fully aware of the depth of the Sino-Soviet split, there were other signs of division in the communist orbit. The Italian Communist Party in particular advocated polycentrism, holding that fraternal communist parties should have considerable freedom to develop their own policies and programs, even though these may conflict with Soviet positions. They wished the Communist Party, U.S.S.R., to have a "primacy of honor, not of jurisdiction."

Finally, there were increasing signs of independence among nations that formerly were unquestioned satellites of the Soviet Union. Albania defiantly joined the Chinese side. Rumania asserted its economic independence and political neutrality. Hungary sought to re-establish its contacts with the free world, largely broken as a consequence of the brutal suppression of the 1956 uprising. Poland also showed some willingness to chart its own course of action, even though it sided with the Soviets in their clash with the Chinese.

Consequently, it is no exaggeration to say that the free world today is presented with a unique challenge and opportunity. The challenge is to react to these new developments in such a way as to bring about internal changes in the communist world in the direction of freedom and peace. As the Iron Curtain is being lifted more and more, there are opportunities for trade and cultural contacts which could lead to increasing dependence of some communist states on Western rather than Russian good will. These ties could lead to lasting changes within these communist nations, as well as to a better climate for world peace. Such an opportunity was apparently foreseen by Pope John XXIII, as will be noted later in this chapter.

Communism in the United States. The Communist Party, U.S.A., plays its appointed role in the international communist conspiracy. It is hardly expected to arrange for the revolutionary overthrow of the United States government. But it can help recruit espionage agents; endeavor to infiltrate government, labor, the entertainment and communication fields, and similar power centers; and devise methods for confusing and influencing American public opinion.

The current size of the communist party here is not accurately known, but the best estimates place its strength at about 7000 members. This is the lowest total in many years, although top membership never exceeded 100,000, even in the palmiest days. In addition to formal members, there are fellow travelers — persons who think and act like communists, but who are not actually subject to party discipline. Next there are the relatively large number of individuals who can often be duped by communist causes. Usually such persons are susceptible only in one or two areas, such as peace, labor policy, or racial issues. The number of fellow travelers and dupes cannot be estimated accurately. The director of the Federal Bureau of Investigation often states that there are ten fellow travelers for every party member. It is doubtful, however, that any constant ratio exists. Unfavorable events, such as the Korean War, the denunciation of Stalin, revelation of Soviet anti-Semitism, and the Hungarian revolt, tend to cut sharply the number of fellow travelers and dupes. The reverse is also true, as was noted during World War II, when Soviet popularity reached a peak in this country.

In assessing the internal threat of the Communist Party, U.S.A., three important points must be kept in mind: the problem of espionage; ties between the Communist Party here and world communism; and the ability of the Party to exploit serious national difficulties, such as unemployment and racial tensions.

Espionage by communist agents is a major business in the United States. While the most formidable operations are conducted by Soviet officials, we should not overlook the activities of nations allied to the Soviet Union. Diplomatic and consular aides accredited to the United States often direct such activities. Diplomats assigned to the United Nations have also been engaged in espionage. This is a serious problem, the more so since Americans tend to be an open people and talk freely about matters that might interest foreign agents.

Various devices are used to recruit agents from the ranks of American citizens at home or abroad. Sometimes the approach is relatively crude, involving bribery or blackmail. Persons with relatives in communist nations may occasionally be intimidated by threats that their loved ones will suffer if they do not co-operate, although the overwhelming majority are completely loyal to their adopted country. At other times misguided idealism may lead some persons to give information to communist powers. A scientist, for example, might feel that an American monopoly of certain weapons is a threat to world peace. Hence he gives classified information to Soviet agents. Most informants are not communists, although some notorious spies were members of the Communist Party here.

While the Communist Party, U.S.A., is not presently a major factor in espionage operations, it nevertheless fully supports Soviet policy when this conflicts with American positions. Accordingly, it must be considered as a fifth column in our midst. It is constantly seeking to subvert our national interests. As a result, the Federal Bureau of Investigation is compelled to spend a substantial amount of time and energy in monitoring communist activities here.

Moreover, there is always the chance that communists will successfully exploit our national difficulties, such as unemployment and racial tensions. There is strong evidence that communists were among the extremist groups that helped to incite racial rioting in American cities in 1964. However, most of these publicly identified as communists belonged to splinter parties allied with the Chinese position, rather than the Communist Party, U.S.A. Nevertheless, it is known that the Moscow-directed party has been using increased tensions to infiltrate civil-rights movements and to stir up agitation and strife.

These observations on communist activity here indicate that an attitude of vigilance and caution is warranted. At the same time, we should be strictly accurate in our assessment of the problem. Wild exaggerations and false denunciations only tend to divide the American people when unity is vitally needed in the struggle against world communism, either of the Moscow or the Peiping variety.

Groups which have been asserting that almost every top official in Washington — executive, legislative, and judicial — is under communist control are not only uttering arrant nonsense, they are subverting national unity far more successfully than any communists. One can disagree with economic policies involving greater centralization of power in Washington, without using the formula "liberalism equals socialism equals communism." Moreover, the fact that in the 1930's and 1940's many persons naïvely co-operated in communist-front activities does not mean that our churches and universities today are hotbeds of communism. We can question the judgment of persons who advocated certain policies without doubting their loyalty. Simple justice should make us realize that treason is among the most serious crimes a citizen can commit. To make such charges without compelling evidence is itself criminal.

It is a paradox that the communist party can have any status at all in the United States, considering the universal rejection of communism and fear of the Soviet Union among the American public. Communist achievements can be explained in two ways. First, there is the extraordinary talent of communists for propaganda and agitation. They have shown real genius in presenting issues cleverly and obtaining sympathizers who have no knowledge of the real source of these views. Second, communists have benefited from the habit of many Americans of going to extremes. Few among us seem to have the patience for calm and careful study of this problem. The result is that some opponents of communism make exaggerated and inaccurate statements. This creates sympathy in the general community and makes it susceptible to the civil-rights arguments raised by the communists. In the ensuing clash between the opposing camps, communists are often free to work with a minimum of hindrance.

The Free World Fights Communism. The impact of communism upon the world is so many-sided that no single method of countering it is likely to be successful. For example, it is relatively easy in the United States to answer Marxist theory. Our economic system is proof that a free, private economy can raise the living standards of workers. It can achieve sound democratic remedies for abuses. Such arguments are less effective in some parts of Europe, and in much of Asia, Africa, and Latin America. These areas see too much of the nineteenth-century brand of capitalism, with exploitation and sharp contrasts between the very poor and the enormously wealthy, to be impressed by arguments against the class struggle and the theory of surplus value. Vigorous social reform and real efforts to raise living standards are needed in these areas, if Marxism is to be countered.

Again, in the United States the argument that communism sacrifices essential spiritual values is fully appreciated. Even were the Soviet Union to exceed our own living standards, we would consider the cost too high, because freedom is more prized than luxury. But in nations in which the average man has few freedoms, except in theory, he may take a different

view of communist propaganda. Even proof that communism is materialistic and godless does not always have the impact it might have. Many
persons consider our own culture as sensual and materialistic. Hence they
feel that there is little difference between communist and free powers in
this regard. The free world needs more sensitive information services and
more extensive programs for educating foreign students and exchanging
visitors, if it is to win the war for the minds of uncommitted peoples.

But the struggle against communism is not merely a struggle against an
ideology. We must never forget the immense military, diplomatic, economic, and subversive resources of the Soviet Union and related communist nations. The military threat is obvious, and the free world has
reacted along two major lines. It has endeavored to keep equally strong or
stronger armed forces, with nuclear weapons and missiles to deliver them.
It has reinforced its defensive position by a world-wide series of alliances
and pacts. At the same time, it has remained willing to seek disarmament
and peaceful settlement of differences. Thus, the communist world is
confronted with the choice between massive retaliation against aggression
and the willingness of other nations to work out a durable and just peace.

The diplomatic, economic, and subversive offensive of communism is
more difficult to meet. Communists can be ruthless in exploiting complex
disputes, such as Arab-Israeli tensions or various colonial situations, whereas their opponents often find it difficult to unite on a policy regarding
such problems. Communists can use trade and aid as weapons, while the
West is often internally divided on economic measures. Moreover, Western measures of technical assistance to developing nations have been non-
political. By contrast, communists fully exploit any aid they give. The
noncommunist world does not have its agents and native parties in the
strategic areas which the communists are trying to win over. But the communists have highly organized and well-trained communist natives as their
allies in seeking to subvert newly developing nations. Great resourcefulness, intelligence, and flexibility are needed to counter this infiltration.
One promising method involves stepped-up programs of exchange of persons and student scholarships for Asia and Africa. The free world should
train future leaders in developing nations and give them a full understanding of the values of democracy and freedom.

In countering communism, we would make a mistake were we to ignore
the small but effective communist party in the United States. Loyalty and
security programs, exposure of communist tactics and propaganda, and
properly conducted congressional investigations still remain necessary.

There are too many evidences of past and even present communist successes for us to remain complacent. But we must approach this task with sanity and moderation. There seems to be little justification, for example, for efforts to dig up past communist connections of persons who presently have broken with the movement. Such tactics create strong resentments and may well explain why many persons are prejudiced against anticommunist programs. The test of any security program or investigation effort should be the present views of a person and the present security of the United States. Mistakes made in the past, particularly when the climate of opinion was vastly different, should not, without serious justification, be judged by present-day standards.

Likewise, it would be a mistake to ignore the possibilities for change within the communist empire. There are evidences of internal strains within the Soviet Union and its satellites. It is unlikely that any of these pressures will lead to successful revolt, unless the Soviet army were to rise up and take charge. But astute diplomacy, the wise use of exchange programs, and the acceptance of every opportunity to present the views of free nations to those within the communist world could do much to intensify pressures for greater freedom. If there is any chance that communism can be changed from within, the opportunity should be seized.

These prospects for change explain statements and policies of Pope John XXIII, often misunderstood in many parts of the world. *Pacem in Terris* was particularly subject to diverse interpretations. It is a profoundly antimarxist encyclical based on the spiritual and moral nature of man and society. Its ringing declarations in favor of the rights of the individual and freedom in society cannot be reconciled with any alleged weakening of the Church's position on communism.

But it is one thing to oppose communism as an ideology, and another to assume that every communist state, and its leaders, is totally and irrevocably dominated by this ideology. After all, Marx and Lenin taught communists how to seize power, but they offered little guidance for leaders confronted with the problem of running a complex economic system. When reality and ideology clash, we can at least hope that reality and truth will ultimately prevail. The very divergences that are appearing in the communist world show the validity of this analysis.

On this basis the Pope was willing to negotiate with communist powers in the effort to restore some freedom of worship in lands subject to cruel persecution. He also urged leaders of nations to negotiate for peace, and to seek bases for trust and understanding. Such conduct should be governed by prudence and, in the case of Catholic experts, by loyal submission to the authority of the Church.

Undoubtedly the approach of Pope John differed from that of his predecessors, Popes Pius XI and Pius XII. But he confronted different problems and changed world attitudes. The earlier pontiffs were compelled to warn a too trusting world against the deceptive and evil nature of communism. Pope Pius XI could thunder against communism in these words: "No one who would save Christian civilization may collaborate with it in any undertaking whatsoever" (A.C., No. 58). But a more enlightened world is not so likely to be deceived by communist wiles. It is better equipped to work for peace and for internal changes in communist nations.

So long as the only alternatives for the world are armed containment of communism and the prospect of a war of liberation that could escalate into a nuclear holocaust, there seems to be little hope for mankind. The former choice means an immense and continuing burden of armaments. The latter could involve the destruction of civilization. Given these choices, should one question the wisdom of the Pope in seeking a third way? History has repeatedly shown that reality and truth erode false ideologies, even when these are the bases of government. It is not enough merely to hope that such will be the case in communist countries, but nations should work prudently but actively to bring about these changes.

The real problem with communism today is, as Pope Paul VI noted, the almost insuperable obstacles which communist regimes place in the way of real dialogue. There is an absence of sufficient freedom of thought and action. Church leaders face the ever-present danger that discussions may be distorted into propaganda attacks against religion. Those who expect immediate and startling results from contacts and negotiations are bound to be disappointed. The fall of Khrushchev is an indication that the Soviet world has elements of the uncertain and the unpredictable. But for the sake of peace and religious freedom, responsible Church leaders are willing to engage in dialogue. When Vatican Council II faced the problem of atheism, the council fathers suggested that the ultimate answer is the witness of an integral Christian life. In the *Constitution on the Church in the Modern World* (No. 21), they state:

> The remedy which must be applied to atheism, however, is to be sought in a proper presentation of the Church's teaching as well as in the integral life of the Church and her members. For it is the function of the Church, led by

the Holy Spirit who renews and purifies her ceaselessly, to make God the Father and His Incarnate Son present and in a sense visible. This result is achieved chiefly by the witness of a living and mature faith, namely, one trained to see difficulties clearly and to master them. Very many martyrs have given luminous witness to this faith and continue to do so. This faith needs to prove its fruitfulness by penetrating the believer's entire life, including its worldly dimensions, and by activating him toward justice and love, especially regarding the needy. What does the most to reveal God's presence, however, is the brotherly charity of the faithful who are united in spirit as they work together for the faith of the gospel and who prove themselves a sign of unity.

No easy task confronts the world as it faces the problems inherent in world communist movements. This issue can be met only by strength, leadership, intelligence, and sacrifice. The Christian world must meet its greatest challenge. Courage and dedication alone will meet this challenge and save the world from apocalyptic ruin.

READINGS*

J. Y. Calvez and J. Perrin, *The Church and Social Justice*, Chaps. 16–17.
R. N. Carew Hunt, *The Theory and Practice of Communism.*
J. F. Cronin, "Communism: Threat to Freedom."
V. Ferkiss, *Communism Today: Belief and Practice*
J. E. Hoover, *A Study of Communism.*
F. J. Sheed, *Communism and Man.*

---

* For further readings, see List No. 5 in the Appendix.

Chapter VII

THE IDEAL SOCIAL ORDER

CO-OPERATION, NOT CONFLICT

Leo XIII, Rerum Novarum

28. It is a capital evil with respect to the question We are discussing to take for granted that the one class of society is of itself hostile to the other, as if nature had set rich and poor against each other to fight fiercely in implacable war. This is so abhorrent to reason and truth that the exact opposite is true; for just as in the human body the different members harmonize with one another, whence arises that disposition of parts and proportion in the human figure rightly called symmetry, so likewise nature has commanded in the case of the state that the two classes mentioned should agree harmoniously and should properly form equally balanced counterparts to each other. Each needs the other completely: neither capital can do without labor, nor labor without capital. Concord begets beauty and order in things. Conversely, from perpetual strife there must arise disorder accompanied by bestial cruelty. But for putting an end to conflict and for cutting away its very roots, there is wondrous and multiple power in Christian institutions.

33. But the Church, with Jesus Christ as her teacher and leader, seeks greater things than this; namely, by commanding something more perfect, she aims at joining the two social classes to each other in closest neighborliness and friendship.

Pius XII, Address to Catholic Employers, May 7, 1949

We have just made reference to the preoccupations of those who are engaged in industrial production. Mistaken and disastrous in its consequences is the prejudice, alas! too widely held, which sees in these problems an irreducible clash of rival interests. The opposition is only apparent. In the economic domain management and labor are linked in a community of action and interest. To disregard this mutual bond, to strive to break it, can only betray a pretension to blind and preposterous despotism. Employers and workers are not implacable adversaries. They are co-operators in a common task. They eat, so to speak, at the same table, seeing that they must live, in the last analysis, from the gross or net profits of the national economy. . . .

From this it follows that both parties are interested in seeing to it that the costs of national production are in proportion to its output. But since the interest is common, why should it not manifest itself in a common outward expression? Why should it not be allowable to assign to the workers a just share of responsibility in the establishment and development of the national economy?

John XXIII, To Christian Association of Industrialists and Managers, January 30, 1959

. . . Industrialists, managers, and workers are not, and must not be, irreconcilable competitors. They are co-workers in a common undertaking that demands first of all mutual understanding and a sincere effort to overcome the temptation on each one's part to seek his own profit to the detriment of the others sharing in the common effort. It is a question of justice and a question of the application of the Christian spirit.

ORGANIZED ECONOMIC LIFE

Pius XI, Quadragesimo Anno

81. First and foremost, the state and every good citizen ought to look to and strive toward this end: that the conflict between the hostile classes be abolished and harmonious co-operation of the Industries and Professions be encouraged and promoted.

82. The social policy of the state, therefore, must devote itself to the re-establishment of the Industries and Professions. In actual fact, human society now, for the reason that it is founded on classes with divergent aims and hence opposed to one another and therefore inclined to enmity and strife, continues to be in a violent condition and is unstable and uncertain.

83. But complete cure will not come until this opposition has been abolished and well-ordered members of the social body — Industries and Professions — are constituted in which men may have their place, not according to the position each has in the labor market but according to the respective social functions which each performs. For under nature's guidance it comes to pass that just as those who are joined together by nearness of habitation establish towns, so those who follow the same Industry or Profession — whether in the economic or other field — form guilds or associations, so that many are wont to consider these self-governing organizations, if not essential, at least natural to civil society.

84. Because order, as St. Thomas well explains, is unity arising from the harmonious arrangement of many objects, a true, genuine social order demands that the various members of a society be united together by some strong bond. This unifying force is present not only in the producing of goods or the rendering of services — in which the employers and employees of an identical Industry or Profession collaborate jointly — but also in that common good, to achieve which all Industries and Professions together ought, each to the best of its ability, to co-operate amicably. And this unity will be the stronger and more effective, the more faithfully individuals and the Industries and Professions themselves strive to do their work and excel in it.

85. It is easily deduced from what has been said that the interests common to the whole Industry or Profession should hold first place in these guilds. The most important among these interests is to promote the co-operation in the highest degree of each industry and profession for the sake of the common good of the country. Concerning matters, however, in which particular points, involving advantage or detriment to employers or workers, may require special

care and protection, the two parties, when these cases arise, can deliberate separately or as the situation requires reach a decision separately.

97. What We have taught about the reconstruction and perfection of social order can surely in nowise be brought to realization without reform of morality, the very record of history clearly shows. For there was a social order once which, although indeed not perfect or in all respects ideal, nevertheless, met in a certain measure the requirements of right reason, considering the conditions and needs of the time. If that order has long since perished, that surely did not happen because the order could not have accommodated itself to changed conditions and needs by development and by a certain expansion, but rather because men, hardened by too much love of self, refused to open the order to the increasing masses as they should have done, or because, deceived by allurements of a false freedom and other errors, they became impatient of every authority and sought to reject every form of control.

Pius XI, On Atheistic Communism

32. The means of saving the world of today from the lamentable ruin into which amoral liberalism has plunged us, are neither the class struggle nor terror, nor yet the autocratic abuse of state power, but rather the infusion of social justice and the sentiment of Christian love into the social-economic order. We have indicated how a sound prosperity is to be restored according to the true principles of a sane corporative system which respects the proper hierarchic structure of society; and how all the occupational groups should be focused into a harmonious unity inspired by the principle of the common good. And the genuine and chief function of public and civil authority consists precisely in the efficacious furthering of this harmony and co-ordination of all social forces.

54. If, therefore, We consider the whole structure of economic life, as We have already pointed out in Our Encyclical *Quadragesimo Anno*, the reign of mutual collaboration between justice and charity in social-economic relations can only be achieved by a body of professional and interprofessional organizations, built on solidly Christian foundations, working together to effect, under forms adapted to different places and circumstances, what has been called the Corporation.

Pius XII, To Italian Workers, March 11, 1945

As for "the democratization of economy," it is equally endangered by monopolies — that is, by the economic tyranny of an anonymous conglomeration of private capital — and by the preponderant power of organized masses, ready to use their power to the detriment of justice and the rights of others.

The time has come to repudiate empty phrases, and to attempt to organize the forces of the people on a new basis; to raise them above the distinction between employers and would-be workers, and to realize that higher unity which is a bond between all those who co-operate in production, formed by their solidarity in the duty of working together for the common good and filling together the needs of the community. If this solidarity is extended to all branches of production, if it becomes the foundation for a better economic system, it will lead the working classes to obtain honestly their share of responsibility in the direction of the national economy. Thus, thanks to such harmonious co-ordination and co-operation; thanks to this closer unity of labor with the other elements of economic life, the worker will receive, as a result of his activity, a secure remuneration, sufficient to meet his needs and those of his family, with spiritual satisfaction and a powerful incentive toward self-improvement.

Pius XII, Letter to Semaines Sociales, July 18, 1947

Over and above the distinction between employer and employee, which threatens more seriously every day to become a pitiless separation, there is human labor itself: the work to be done, the job to which every man contributes something vital and personal, with a view to supplying society with goods and services adequate to its needs. It lies in the very nature of labor, understood in this sense, to draw men together in a genuine and intimate union, and to restore form and structure to a society which has become shapeless and unstable. This in turn would infuse new life into the relations between society and the state.

John XXIII, Mater et Magistra

37. Pius XI saw the re-establishment of the economic world within the framework of the moral order and the subordination of individual and group interests to the interests of the common good as the principal remedies for these evils. This, he taught, necessitated an orderly reconstruction of society, with the establishment of economic and vocational bodies which would be autonomous and independent of the state. Public authority should resume its duty of promoting the common good of all. Finally, there should be co-operation on a world scale for the economic welfare of all nations.

38. Thus Pius XI's teaching in this encyclical can be summed up under two heads. First he taught what the supreme criterion in economic matters ought not to be. It must not be the special interests of individuals or groups, nor unregulated competition, economic despotism, national prestige or imperialism, nor any other aim of this sort.

39. On the contrary, all forms of economic enterprise must be governed by the principles of social justice and charity.

40. The second point which We consider basic in the encyclical is his teaching that man's aim must be to achieve in social justice a national and international juridical order, with its network of public and private institutions, in which all economic activity can be conducted not merely for private gain but also in the interests of the common good.

67. So long as social relationships do in fact adhere to these principles within the framework of the moral order, their extension does not necessarily mean that individual citizens will be gravely discriminated against or excessively burdened. On the contrary, we can hope that they will help him to develop and perfect his own personal talents, and lead to that organic reconstruction of society which Our Predecessor Pius XI advocated in his encyclical Quadragesimo Anno as the indispensable prerequisite for the fulfillment of the rights and obligations of social life.

American Hierarchy, Pastoral Letter, 1919

In his pronouncement on Labor [Rerum Novarum] Pope Leo XIII describes the advantages to be derived by both employer and employee from "associations and organizations which draw the two classes more closely together." Such associations are especially needed at the present time. While the labor union or trade union has been, and still is, necessary in the struggle of the workers for fair wages and fair conditions of employment, we have to recognize that its history, methods, and objects have made it essentially a militant organization. The time seems now to have arrived when it should be, not supplanted, but supplemented by associations or conferences, composed jointly of employers and employees, which will place emphasis upon the common interests rather than the divergent aims of the two parties, upon co-operation rather than conflict. Through such arrangements, all classes would be greatly benefited. The worker would participate in those matters of industrial management which directly concern him and about which he possesses helpful knowledge; he would acquire an increased sense of personal dignity and personal responsibility, take greater interest and pride in his work, and become more efficient and more contented. The employer would have the benefit of willing co-operation from, and harmonious relations with, his employees. The consumer, in common with employer and employee, would share in the advantages of larger and steadier production. In a word, industry would be carried on as a co-operative enterprise for the common good, and not as a contest between two parties for a restricted product.

A FLEXIBLE PROGRAM

Leo XIII, Rerum Novarum

76. Furthermore, if citizens have free right to associate, as in fact they do, they also must have the right freely to adopt the organization and the rules which they judge most appropriate to achieve their purpose. We do not feel that the precise character in all details, which the aforementioned direction and organization of associations ought to have, can be determined by fast and fixed rules, since this is a matter to be decided rather in the light of the temperament of each people, of experiment and practice, of the nature and character of the work, of the extent of trade and commerce, and of other circumstances of a material and temporal kind all of which must be carefully considered.

Pius XI, Quadragesimo Anno

86. The teaching of Leo XIII on the form of political government, namely, that men are free to choose whatever form they please, provided that proper regard is had for the requirements of justice and of the common good, is equally applicable in due proportion, it is hardly necessary to say, to the guilds of the various Industries and Professions.

87. Moreover, just as inhabitants of a town are wont to found associations with the widest diversity of purposes, which each is quite free to join or not, so those engaged in the same industry or profession will combine

with one another into associations equally free for purposes connected in some manner with the pursuit of the calling itself. Since these free associations are clearly and lucidly explained by Our Predecessor of illustrious memory, We consider it enough to emphasize this one point: People are quite free not only to found such associations which are a matter of private order and private right, but also in respect to them "freely to adopt the organization and the rules which they judge most appropriate to achieve their purpose."

The same freedom must be asserted for founding associations that go beyond the boundaries of individual callings. And may these free organizations now flourishing and rejoicing in their salutary fruits, set before themselves the task of preparing the way, in conformity with the mind of Christian social teaching, for those larger and more important guilds, Industries and Professions, which We mentioned before, and make every possible effort to bring them to realization.

Code of Social Principles

82. If authority is necessary in the profession to regulate the activity of its members, it is still more necessary that there be a supreme authority over all the professions, with power to regulate their mutual relations and to direct their activity towards the common good. The social order, therefore, requires interprofessional organization on regional, national, and even international lines.

83. Experience shows that vocational groups are exposed to a grave danger: induced by a certain group selfishness, they tend to forget and to neglect their chief duty, which is to work together as effectively as possible for the general welfare of the country. Hence a just relationship of dependence should be established and maintained between the state, guardian of this welfare, and the vocational groups. Vocational organization should relieve the state of many tasks which at present weigh heavily upon it, without, however, absorbing or weakening it, but rather perfecting and strengthening it.

84. Once the vocational bodies have been established, three tasks will remain to be accomplished: (i) To unite kindred associations into federations; (ii) To gather together the vocational groups and federations under one supreme vocational authority; (iii) To bestow on this supreme authority the powers required for its purpose and thus to reach the culminating point towards which the vocational organization tends and in which it ought to find its full realization.

85. Yet, in order to be effective, they will have to adapt themselves to national temperament, to traditions, to the particular needs of each country and, at their beginning, to what occupational elements already exist. In the same manner, within each vocational group, account must be taken of the particular needs of that occupation.

86. Vocational organization does not exclude the freedom of trade unions and employers' associations.

THE PRINCIPLE OF SUBSIDIARITY

Pius XI, Quadragesimo Anno

79. Just as it is gravely wrong to take from individuals what they can accomplish by their own initiative and industry and give it to the community, so also it is an injustice and at the same time a grave evil and disturbance of right order to assign to a greater and higher association what lesser and subordinate organizations can do. For every social activity ought of its very nature to furnish help to the members of the body social, and never destroy and absorb them.

80. The supreme authority of the state ought, therefore, to let subordinate groups handle matters and concerns of lesser importance, which would otherwise dissipate its efforts greatly. Thereby the state will more freely, powerfully, and effectively do all those things that belong to it alone because it alone can do them: directing, watching, urging, restraining, as occasion requires and necessity demands. Therefore, those in power should be sure that the more perfectly a graduated order is kept among the various associations, in observance of the principle of "subsidiary function," the stronger social authority and effectiveness will be and the happier and more prosperous the condition of the state.

THE social teaching of the Church is clear and definite in regard to the nature of man and society, the purpose of economic life, and the virtues which should govern man the producer. It rejects both individualism and statism as totally inadequate to organize economic life according to God's plan for mankind. Instead, Pope Pius XI outlines a completely different approach to economic society.

The papal plan, in essence, calls for an organization of economic life, and indeed all social life, in terms of the common interests and goals of all producers and families. Workers and employers in each industry and profession would band together to co-operate for their own mutual interests and for the common good of the country. When this is accomplished, the economic system would reach its maximum efficiency. Production of wealth would attain the highest levels possible in terms of available skills and resources.

This type of organization would incorporate into economic society the principles of sound social morality. It would be formed on the basis of co-operation, not conflict. It would aim at seeking the common good, not merely the selfish interests of individuals and classes. In effect, it would afford an institutional framework for policies based on the virtue of social justice.

Pope Pius XI considered this proposal the heart of his program for social reform. He proposed it first in 1931 and reiterated it strongly in 1937. His successor, Pope Pius XII, likewise referred repeatedly to this form of economic life as the only hope for a thorough renewal of industrial society. In spite of this repeated emphasis, there are considerable elements of obscurity about the precise import of the papal program. Numerous efforts have been made to interpret and apply the principles laid down in *Quadragesimo Anno*. Yet no clear and universally accepted explanation has been produced as a result of these studies. Perhaps some light can be obtained by a study of the background of the papal proposal.[1]

Background Considerations. It is clear from the papal documents involved that a number of factors prompted the analysis summarized above. Some of these considerations involve negative and destructive elements in existing economic life against which the Pope was reacting. Others concern both historical and theoretical reasons for the proposed organization of industrial society.

One negative element is the class struggle. All the modern popes have insisted upon the folly and destructiveness of the internecine war between capital and labor. It is obvious that management and workers must cooperate in the actual production of goods and services. No one questions the fact that the prosperity of any given company is greatly affected by the degree of harmony and understanding in the factory. Yet there is rarely any organized effort to intensify and extend this process. Generally what co-operation exists is the product of understandings reached at the collective-bargaining table. But these understandings come from groups organized for entirely different purposes. Labor unions and their management counterparts seek primarily to protect the rights and interests of their partisans, not necessarily the common good of the industrial community.

Another negative element is unregulated competition, to the extent that it obtains in a given nation. Competition is an important part of economic life. It stimulates incentive, weeds out the slovenly and inefficient, and tends to vitalize and energize the economy. But it can also atomize producers and prevent the formation of organizations dedicated to their common interests. Too often its rigors lead businessmen to the other extreme, to the formation of monopolies or the seeking of arrangements to

---

[1] The Pope's program is generally called by American Catholics the Industry Council Plan. Industry councils are the equivalent of the *ordines* and *collegia ordinum* of *Quadragesimo Anno*, translated in the text used here as "industries" and "professions." Other terms used are "occupational groups," "vocational groups," "modern guilds," and "corporative society."

stifle competition completely. The ideal social order would avoid these extremes. Businessmen would compete, but within a framework of organization that protects both their mutual interests and the common good. Some mutual interests, for example, would be research, advertising, standards of quality, and the social obligations of the industry.

Finally, among the negative elements, is the relation of the modern state to society. This has varied from the extremes of *laissez-faire* indifference to totalitarian statism. We have neither in the United States, but we do have some other evils mentioned by the popes. One is the burdening of the state with an infinity of duties that could be handled, within a properly organized social order, by organized economic groups. If these groups were truly seeking the common good, and had sufficient powers, they could take over many of the regulatory and social functions now delegated to government bodies. To cite one example from a thousand possible instances, the meat industry could be organized to set up and administer proper standards for grading and branding meats.

Among the more positive considerations mentioned in papal documents is the success of medieval economic society during its golden period. Before decay set in, it had achieved methods of regulating economic life in accord with the principles of morality. Pope Pius XI did not state that this social order was perfect or ideal, but it did meet "in a certain measure the requirements of right reason, considering the conditions and needs of the time." It failed, not because of inherent weaknesses, but because of selfishness and rebellion against authority.

Undoubtedly another factor inspiring the Pope was the writings of Heinrich Pesch, the originator of the system called solidarism. He and his disciples and fellow Jesuits, Oswald von Nell-Breuning and Gustav Gundlach, saw clearly the dangerous trends in modern economic society. They called for a new approach more in accord with the demands of human nature, with both production and the organization of economic society based on the true needs of man and the family. There is sufficient similarity between papal proposals and the writings of these scholars to warrant the use of these sources in interpreting *Quadragesimo Anno*.[2]

Some writers have asserted that the papal proposals were based on the corporate state of Mussolini. Actually, nothing could be farther from the truth. The purpose of the reform of social order is to lessen, not

---

[2] See O. von Nell-Breuning, S.J., *Reorganization of Social Economy* (Milwaukee: Bruce, 1936), and R. E. Mulcahy, S.J., *The Economics of Heinrich Pesch* (New York: Holt, 1952).

increase, state control of economic life. The corporate state features excessive controls. Corporative society would restore controls to properly organized economic groups.

We mention these background factors to give a definite idea of the evils in society that industry councils would cure, and also to indicate possible parallels that might help clarify the encyclical presentation. The Pope wishes to substitute order for disorder, harmony for the class struggle, and decentralized power in place of concentration of political or economic might. He desires social institutions that will of themselves facilitate the practice of justice. This is the basic distinction between social order and a society that lacks such order, even though individuals in the latter may endeavor to practice virtue in their economic relationships.

Elements of Social Order. Certain points seem clear in regard to the proposed industry councils. First, they comprise industries and professions. They should not be considered in terms of labor-management collaboration at the factory level. This collaboration, of course, is desirable but it is not the type of co-operation discussed here. What is envisioned is the organization of an entire industry or occupation, such as steel, automobile production, or farming. All the members of the occupation will be represented in the organization. Workers and employers, for example, will both be on the council in any given industry.

The type of organization should be determined by those concerned, "provided that proper regard is had for the requirements of justice and of the common good." Hence it would be quite improper for any commentator to draw up a detailed blueprint of economic society and present this as the papal program. At best, any blueprint would be the author's considered application of basic principles to the needs of a particular time and place. For example, there has been some controversy over the position of labor unions in respect to an industrial council. Would they furnish the representatives of labor, or would some other method of selection be used? Such questions cannot be answered in advance. Prudential judgment, considering "the requirements of justice and the common good" under the circumstances, should give the answer in each instance.

The Pope makes a distinction between industry councils and "free associations" which are a "matter of private order and private right." The implication is clear that industry councils would not be considered free associations (such as labor unions, trade associations, or research councils), but rather semipublic bodies. This means that every member of the industry or occupation would be expected to belong to the councils and would be bound by their regulations.

Here we introduce a concept somewhat strange to Americal legal customs. We do not have many groups that have such regulatory powers over their members. The closest parallels would be the medical and the bar associations. Private organizations, of course, can impose rules upon their members. But normally no one is compelled to join them or to retain membership. We would need drastic revisions of our antitrust laws to accept such concepts of regulatory powers.

Industry councils would not supplant free associations. Present organizations should prepare the way for a social order based on co-operation for the common good. But they would continue to remain in being in order to handle matters that are the special concerns of management or labor, in contrast to those which reflect the mutual interests and the common problems of the industry or occupation.

The purpose of industry councils is the co-operation of all involved individuals in seeking the welfare of each industry or occupation, and their working together for the common good of all. Presumably this calls for some type of higher co-ordinating council, although Pope Pius XI was not explicit in this regard. He simply spoke of "that common good, to achieve which all Industries and Professions together ought, each to the best of its ability, to co-operate amicably." He also mentioned "professional and interprofessional organizations." Here again it would seem inadvisable to draw up blueprints prematurely. Decisions can be made at the proper time in accord with the demands of the common good.

The Pope did not specify how the councils should function in seeking the welfare of their industries or occupations and the common good. Their task would be to infuse justice into economic life. The means used would be determined by their prudent judgment, motivated by Christian principles, in the light of the laws, customs, and economic realities of the time.

There was a tendency among some earlier commentators to envision the councils as a giant economic planning body, with controls over investment, prices, profit, markets, and wages. It is difficult to see how such a type of organization would actually promote the common good. It would increase centralization of power if the government had to make the final decisions, as it undoubtedly would. Furthermore, such a system would be rejected by most people as merely another brand of socialism.

Prices, profit, investment, and markets seem to belong in the area of management economic decisions that Pope Pius XII characterized as within the competence of the owners of property. Wages would be determined mutually, but by the free associations representing management and labor. Of course, all these decisions have social aspects and should be made in the light of the common good as well as individual interests. But their social aspects do not make them mutual concerns of labor and management, to be decided on the industry level by industry councils. Rather the parties directly concerned have the prime responsibility to decide, subject to considerations of the common good, directed first by their own consciences and ultimately, when necessary, by the state as the supreme custodian of the common good.

Nevertheless, there are many industry-wide economic problems that would seem to fall within the competence of industry councils. These would include studies and policies designed to increase productivity, standards of justice that aim to keep competition within proper bounds, regional economic problems, and national problems such as the quest for economic stability and orderly economic growth. When problems transcend the boundaries of an individual industry or occupation, there would seem to be a need for a higher level of industry councils and undoubtedly some degree of government participation.

The examples just given, of course, represent interpretation and application of the encyclical program. The popes deliberately couched their counsels in general terms, leaving the utmost latitude for individual economies to apply them according to their special needs and customs. The essential point in any effort at interpretation and application is a conscientious effort on the part of any commentator first to keep faithful to the spirit of the entire body of papal teaching, and then never to confuse doctrinal teaching of the Church with his own economic analysis. This latter point is especially important when debatable schools of economic thought are being followed. Economic debate, when it does not involve moral principles, should be labeled properly, and not blanketed into interpretations of Catholic social teaching.

It may be objected that the type of co-operation sought by the Pope is impractical, given man's selfishness. This objection was foreseen, as Pope Pius XI explicitly stated that the reconstruction and perfection of social order "can surely in nowise be brought to realization without reform of morality." But reform of morality does not mean the rooting out of selfishness and greed from the hearts of all men. It means that there should be enough men of good will seeking to bring about a right social order, and having the power to draw up binding rules and regulations that would implement the demands of justice and charity. As was noted earlier, sound laws, customs, and institutions can bring about a good society, even though evil men may be members of that society.

Pope John XXIII on Social Order. When *Mater et Magistra* appeared Catholic commentators were struck by the apparently minor position afforded to his predecessors' proposals for organized economic life. A thesis that was given major prominence in *Quadragesimo Anno* was summarized in four short paragraphs by Pope John. Only once again did he refer to the organic reconstruction of society, as advocated by Pope Pius XI. There is no explicit reference to this topic in *Pacem in Terris*, although there are occasional comments on the value of "intermediary bodies."

Why this seeming downplaying of a proposal that earlier popes considered almost essential for lasting social reform? Pope John never offered an explanation of this reversal of emphasis, but enough is known about his general approach to social problems to explain his actions in this instance.

Pope John preferred a practical and pastoral approach to social problems. He did not care much for abstractions and ideologies. Hence he was inclined to face the world as it is and then to offer concrete and workable suggestions for both short-range and long-range improvements. He was strongly convinced that any worthwhile social changes would be the result of evolutionary development, not revolutionary change. The blueprints of an ideal society may be attractive indeed, but they rarely are accepted without change by any going economy.

Catholic social thinkers were often bogged down in impractical analysis and fruitless disputes, as they tried to apply the industry-council plan to a world that lacked many of the fundamental prerequisites for such an approach. They failed to appreciate sufficiently the counsels of Pope Pius XI that each society should be free to adapt the basic principles he outlined in accord with its own traditions and genius.

To avoid perpetuating sterile disputes and unrealistic efforts at reform, Pope John used the ideas of his predecessors, but expressed them in different language. He stressed the value of the principle of subsidiarity. He cautioned the state against unwarranted interference with private initiative. Employers were strongly urged to give workers a greater say in the conduct of the enterprise where they worked. Representatives of workers should be on national and international boards whose decisions have vital impact on economic life. As the world becomes more socialized, man should be alert to control this process in accord with justice and equity.

All of these points have been urged by many commentators as essential steps toward an organic reconstruction of society. But Pope John used the language of modern economics and sociology in preference to the more philosophical approach of his predecessors. Thus we may conclude that, far from abandoning the social-order approach of *Quadragesimo Anno*, Pope John gave these ideals new life by expressing them in a practical and workable fashion.

Steps Toward Social Justice. Granted the soundness of encyclical principles on social order, the important question is how they are to be promoted in the United States. It would be a mistake, in the light of American temperament and general patterns of historical change, to try to draw up an elaborate, detailed pattern which would be labeled the Industry Council Plan. Social change normally is evolutionary, not revolutionary. It involves modification of existing institutions, not the establishment of entirely new patterns. Pope Pius XI spoke of "preparing the way" for these councils and making "every possible effort to bring them to realization." Education and experimentation will bring us closer to our goal.

One field of action that should be increasingly emphasized is that of labor-management co-operation. This has been the subject of much research in recent decades, but almost exclusively at the level of the single plant or company. Management has studied new psychological techniques. Efforts have been made to instill in the worker pride in his job and pride in his company. The worker is consulted. Proposed changes are explained to him and he is given the opportunity to state his views on the subject. This stress on teamwork exists in unionized and nonunion plants alike.

Co-operation on the industry level is less common. The United Mine Workers have co-operated with management in seeking to expand markets for coal. Several unions in the clothing field have done commendable work in helping promote the products of their industry. But generally organized labor is not so co-operative. The tradition of many unions has been to seek gains for their members and to leave to the employer the problem of absorbing these costs and selling his product. Yet, in fairness to organized labor, it must be noted that the employer often influences union attitudes in regard to co-operation. If he is aloof and unfriendly, the union will remain at a distance.

The element of divergence is even greater so far as national economic policies are concerned. Employers charge that unions often restrict production, force price increases as a result of excessive wage demands, and fail to realize the profit needs of an expanding economy. Unions in turn justify wage increases as necessary to offset inflation or to increase purchasing power. They claim that profits are excessive. They further assert that mass markets are needed to stimulate investment. The value of these arguments will be considered in later chapters. But the wide divergence of opinion is a challenge to both sides to seek competent and independent analysis of their claims.

So long as these fundamental cleavages exist, it is not likely that they will be solved by any council made up of the conflicting parties. Discussion, as such, can only clear up misunderstandings. It rarely can lead to the removal of basic conflicts of interest. If we were to organize a national economic council in the United States today, for example, one would hardly expect business, labor, and farm groups to agree completely upon what constitutes the economic common good of the nation. Government would have to make the final decisions, as it does today.

Realism compels us to face these difficulties. But they are not insurmountable. One method for seeking greater unity is to seize every possible opportunity to bring together conflicting groups to discuss matters upon which they do not diverge. These could include questions of public policy — local, state, national, and international. One good example is the problem of race relations and discrimination in employment. Membership in public-service organizations is another suitable meeting ground. Contacts made in "neutral" activities can bring about personal understandings, which often carry over to the fields where conflict prevails.

Another method is to promote public debate of issues. When members of interest groups are challenged by expert and impartial critics, they are less likely to rely upon weak arguments or unfounded opinions. They are not able to argue that their opponents are clouding issues in order to promote their own interests. In this regard, the radio and television industries can render a public service by airing the economic conflicts that divide our nation. Once public opinion is informed and aroused on any point, even the strongest pressure groups are likely to give way.

We should not overlook the value of labor-management co-operation on the factory or company level. If real understanding and trust are reached at these levels, they are bound to influence broader policies. The plant manager today may be the corporation president tomorrow. A local union leader may advance to a position of national influence. Assuming that the majority of such executives are men of good will, they are bound to re-examine basic clashes with those whom they have grown to admire and trust.

In addition to promoting labor-management co-operation on a broad front, it is desirable to restudy our pattern of social controls. The purpose of this would be to substitute, where possible, self-regulation in place of government regulation. The question might be raised, for example, whether or not our organized security exchanges could take over some of the functions of the Securities and Exchange Commission. It may be that the financial community has progressed sufficiently in thirty-two years to warrant such trust. Such transfers of power need not be total, at least in the beginning. Government regulatory commissions could remain as watchdogs over the performance of private groups, with power to intervene when serious abuses arose.

The important point is that we develop an awareness regarding centers of power. The more that control is removed from individuals and smaller groups, the more difficult it is for the average citizen to influence those who exercise power. We should be consciously striving to keep real life in local government, local unions, and local units of large corporations. This does not mean that we blindly oppose any activities of the federal government or national groups. Rather it means that we consistently use the principle of subsidiarity — keeping power decentralized so far as this is consistent with the common good.

One method of moving toward an ideal social order is to utilize every available opportunity to insist upon the importance of the common good. The principle that business and labor should serve the general welfare is widely accepted, so far as public statements go. It is rare today that any economic conflict is carried out merely as a power struggle. To an ever increasing degree, the belligerent parties try to win the support of public opinion. They argue that their claims are right and that their position would benefit the nation. This recognition of the power of an aroused citizenry can be a valuable asset in the fight for social justice.

Those who are seeking a better social order can deal with various economic groups and their programs in terms of the impact upon the entire economy. They can argue for policies that benefit the nation, not merely a particular group. This is an understandable and acceptable approach in terms of American psychology. It is much more likely to produce results, in contrast to efforts to introduce an industry-council plan in one step.

In brief, we can be constantly aware of the main objectives of a just social order, and the main obstacles to it. The objectives, as listed in papal writings, are organized effort to seek the common good, and co-operation as a pattern in economic life. The obstacles most often cited are the class struggle, unsocial forms of competition, and various evils connected with the relation of the state to economic society — excessive concentration of power, efforts of economic groups to control the state, and misuse of civil power with resulting prejudice to the common good.

Policies that promote the objectives sought, or remove obstacles to their attainment, should be the main concern of Catholic social action. This will be the Church's answer to the social problem outlined in Chapter I. Thus we seek a social order in accord with God's purpose for man and in line with the social virtues. We offer a means to remedy past abuses and an alternative to unacceptable social and political systems.

The detailed analysis of capital, labor, property, and the state, in the section to follow, gives the rights and duties connected with each of these great institutions. As each conforms more and more to the demands of social justice, it is better prepared to take its proper place in a well-organized social order. Detailed problems connected with each topic must be judged in the light of our transcendent goal — the complete reform of economic society. The vision and insight of Pope Pius XI have given us a pattern for justice integrated in our economy. As we are guided by this vision, our contribution to social policy will gain in wisdom and enduring value.

READINGS*

J. Y. Calvez and J. Perrin, *The Church and Social Justice*, Chap. 19.
B. W. Dempsey, *The Functional Economy*, Chaps. 14–17.
H. Johnston, *Business Ethics*, Chap. 9.
J. Messner, *Social Ethics* (rev. ed.), pp. 143–150, 209–217, 436–446, 754–760, 789–795, 885–947.
O. von Nell-Breuning, *Reorganization of Social Economy*, Chaps. 10–12.

---

* For further readings, consult List No. 3 in the Appendix.

Part II

SOCIAL PRINCIPLES AND MAJOR SOCIOECONOMIC INSTITUTIONS

Chapter VIII

RIGHTS AND DUTIES OF CAPITAL

THE RIGHT TO PROFITS

Pius XI, Quadragesimo Anno

53. And in the application of natural resources to human use the law of nature, or rather God's will promulgated by it, demands that right order be observed. This order consists in this: that each thing have its proper owner. Hence it follows that unless a man is expending labor on his own property, the labor of one person and the property of another must be associated, for neither can produce anything without the other. Leo XIII certainly had this in mind when he wrote: "Neither capital can do without labor, nor labor without capital." Wherefore it is wholly false to ascribe to property alone or to labor alone whatever has been obtained through the combined effort of both, and it is wholly unjust for either, denying the efficacy of the other, to arrogate to itself whatever has been produced.

54. Property, that is, "capital," has undoubtedly long been able to appropriate too much to itself. Whatever was produced, whatever returns accrued, capital claimed for itself, hardly leaving to the worker enough to restore and renew his strength. For the doctrine was preached that all accumulation of capital falls by an absolutely insuperable economic law to the rich, and that by the same law the workers are given over and bound to perpetual want, to the scantiest of livelihoods. It is true, indeed, that things have not always and everywhere corresponded with this sort of teaching of the so-called Manchesterian Liberals; yet it cannot be denied that economic-social institutions have moved steadily in that direction. That these false ideas, these erroneous suppositions, have been vigorously assailed, and not by those alone who through them were being deprived of their innate right to obtain better conditions, will surprise no one.

55. And therefore, to the harassed workers there have come "intellectuals," as they are called, setting up in opposition to a fictitious law the equally fictitious moral principle that all products and profits, save only enough to repair and renew capital, belong by very right to the workers.

57. Therefore, the riches that economic-social developments constantly increase ought to be so distributed among individual persons and classes that the common advantage of all, which Leo XIII had praised, will be safeguarded; in other words, that the common good of all society will be kept inviolate. By this law of social justice, one class is forbidden to exclude the other from sharing in the benefits. Hence the class of the wealthy violates this law no less, when, as if free from care on account

of its wealth, it thinks it the right order of things for it to get everything and the worker nothing, than does the nonowning working class when, angered deeply at outraged justice and too ready to assert wrongly the one right it is conscious of, it demands for itself everything as if produced by its own hands, and attacks and seeks to abolish, therefore, all property and returns or incomes, of whatever kind they are or whatever the function they perform in human society, that have not been obtained by labor, and for no other reason save that they are of such a nature.

58. To each, therefore, must be given his own share of goods, and the distribution of created goods, which, as every discerning person knows, is laboring today under the gravest evils due to the huge disparity between the few exceedingly rich and the unnumbered propertyless, must be effectively called back to and brought into conformity with the norms of the common good, that is, social justice.

136. Those who are engaged in producing goods, therefore, are not forbidden to increase their fortune in a just and lawful manner; for it is only fair that he who renders service to the community and makes it richer should also, through the increased wealth of the community, be made richer himself according to his position, provided that all these things be sought with due respect for the laws of God and without impairing the rights of others and that they be employed in accordance with faith and right reason.

Pius XII, To the Italian Federation of Commerce, February 17, 1956

Every exchange of products, in fact, quite apart from satisfying definite needs and desires, makes it possible to put new means into operation, arouses latent and sometimes unexpected energies, and stimulates the spirit of enterprise and invention. This instinct, which is innate in mankind, of creating, improving, and making progress explains commercial activities as much as and more than the mere desire for gain.

John XXIII, Mater et Magistra

81. These demands of the common good [good faith in productive competition, cooperation in economic affairs, aid to underdeveloped lands], both on a national and a world level, must also be borne in mind when assessing the rate of return due as compensation to the company's management, and as interest or dividends to investors.

DUTIES OF OWNERS

Leo XIII, Graves de Communi

15. Certainly, the path of popular improvement is better assured and more quickly traversed, the more we have the co-operation of the well-to-do, with their wide opportunities of effectual aid. We would have them reflect upon the fact that they are not free to choose whether they will take up the cause of the poor or not; it is a matter of simple duty. Men live in a civic society not only for their own good, but also for the good of all. Some are too poor to contribute their share to the common stock; those, therefore, who can should contribute more generously. The

extent of this obligation is in proportion to the amount of riches received. The larger it is, the stricter must be the account we shall have to render to God, who gave it to us. We learn the same lesson from the plague that spreads its calamity and unless a remedy be applied in time, will break out to the ruin and destruction of all classes. He who neglects to take up the cause of the poor acts without regard to his personal interest as well as that of his country.

Leo XIII, Rerum Novarum

31. The following duties, on the other hand, concern rich men and employers: workers are not to be treated as slaves; justice demands that the dignity of human personality be respected in them, ennobled as it has been through what we call the Christian character. If we hearken to natural reason and to Christian philosophy, gainful occupations are not a mark of shame to man, but rather of respect, as they provide him with an honorable means of supporting life. It is shameful and inhuman, however, to use men as things of gain and to put no more value on them than what they are worth in muscle and energy.

Pius XI, On Atheistic Communism

50. Therefore, We turn again in a special way to you, Christian employers and industrialists, whose problem is often so difficult for the reason that you are saddled with the heavy heritage of an unjust economic regime whose ruinous influence has been felt through many generations. We bid you be mindful of your responsibility. It is unfortunately true that the manner of action in certain Catholic circles has done much to shake the faith of the working classes in the religion of Jesus Christ. These groups have refused to understand that Christian charity demands the recognition of certain rights due to the workingman, which the Church has explicitly acknowledged. What is to be thought of the action of those Catholic employers who in one place succeeded in preventing the reading of Our Encyclical, Quadragesimo Anno, in their local churches? Or of those Catholic industrialists who even to this day have shown themselves hostile to a labor movement that We Ourselves recommended? Is it not deplorable that the right of private property defended by the Church should so often have been used as a weapon to defraud the workingman of his just salary and his social rights?

Pius XII, Christmas Message, 1952

This solidarity of men with each other demands, not only in the name of brotherly love, but even of mutual advantage, that everything possible be done to maintain and increase employment. Therefore, let those who are able to invest capital consider in the light of the common good — and with due regard to their economic condition, to risks involved and opportunity offered — whether they can reconcile with their conscience their neglect and failure to make investments because of unreasonable caution.

John XXIII, Mater et Magistra

75. We must notice in this connection the system of self-financing adopted in many countries by large, or comparatively large firms. Because these companies are financing replacement and plant expansion out of their own profits, they grow at a very rapid rate. In such cases We believe that the workers should be allocated shares in the firms for which they work, especially when they are paid no more than a minimum wage.

77. Experience suggests many ways in which the demands of justice can be satisfied. Not to mention other ways, it is especially desirable today that workers gradually come to share in the ownership of their company, by ways and in the manner that seem most suitable. For today, even more than in the time of Our Predecessor, "every effort must be made that at least in future a just share only of the fruits of production be permitted to accumulate in the hands of the wealthy, and that an ample sufficiency be supplied to the workers."

SHARING WITH WORKERS

Pius XI, Quadragesimo Anno

64. First of all, those who declare that a contract of hiring and being hired is unjust of its own nature, and hence a partnership contract must take its place, are certainly in error and gravely misrepresent Our Predecessor whose Encyclical not only accepts working for wages or salaries but deals at some length with its regulation in accordance with the rules of justice.

65. We consider it more advisable, however, in the present condition of human society that, so far as is possible, the work contract be somewhat modified by a partnership contract, as is already being done in various ways and with no small advantage to workers and owners. Workers and other employees thus become sharers in ownership or management or participate in some fashion in the profits received.

Pius XII, To Catholic Employers, May 7, 1949

The owner of the means of production, whoever he be — individual owner, workers' association, or corporation — must always — within the limits of public economic law — retain control of his economic decisions

Pius XII, To Catholic International Congresses for Social Study and Social Action, June 3, 1950

The wisdom of Our Predecessor Pius XI has made that quite clear in the Encyclical Quadragesimo Anno, where he denies, in consequence, that there is any need in the nature of things to pattern the wage-contract on the contract of partnership. That is not to disavow the usefulness of what has thus far been achieved in this direction, "in various ways, to the no small gain of both wage-earners and employers." But in the light of principles and facts the right of economic joint-management lies beyond the field of these possible achievements.

Pius XII, To Austrian Catholics, September 14, 1952

. . . the pontiffs of the social encyclicals, and also We Ourselves, have declined to deduce, directly or indirectly, from the labor contract the right of the employee to participate in the ownership of the operating capital, and its corollary, the right of the worker to participate in decisions concerning operations of the plant (Mitbestimmung). This had to be denied because behind this question there stands that greater problem — the right of the individual and of the family to own property, which stems immediately from the human person. It is a right of personal dignity; a right, to be sure, accompanied by social obligations; a right, however, not merely a social function.

John XXIII, Mater et Magistra

91. We, no less than Our predecessors, are convinced that employees are justified in wishing to participate in the activity of the industrial concern for which they work. It is not, of course, possible to lay down hard and fast rules regarding the manner of such participation, for this must depend upon prevailing conditions, which vary from firm to firm and are frequently subject to rapid and substantial alteration. But We have no doubt as to the need for giving workers an active part in the business of the company for which they work — be it a private or a public one. Every effort must be made to ensure that the enterprise is indeed a true human community, concerned about the needs, the activities, and the standing of each of its members.

92. This demands that the relations between management and employees reflect understanding, appreciation, and good will on both sides. It demands, too, that all parties cooperate actively and loyally in the common enterprise, not so much for what they can get out of it for themselves, but as discharging a duty and rendering a service to their fellow men.

All this implies that the workers have their say in, and make their own contribution to, the efficient running and development of the enterprise.

As Pius XII remarked, "the economic and social function which every man aspires to fulfill, demands that the carrying on of the activity of each one is not completely subjected to the others."

Obviously, any firm which is concerned for the human dignity of its workers must also maintain a necessary and efficient unity of direction. But it must not treat those employees who spend their days in service with the firm as though they were mere cogs in the machinery, denying them any opportunity of expressing their wishes or bringing their experience to bear on the work in hand, and keeping them entirely passive in regard to decisions that regulate their activity.

93. We would observe, finally, that the present demand for workers to have a greater say in the conduct of the firm accords not only with man's nature, but also with recent progress in the economic, social, and political spheres.

94. For although many unjust and inhuman economic and social imbalances still exist in our day, and there are still many errors affecting the activity, aims, structure, and operation of economies the world over, it is an undeniable fact that, thanks to the driving impulse of scientific and technical advance, productive systems are today rapidly becoming more mod-

ernized and efficient— more so than ever before. Hence a greater technical skill is required of the workers, and more exacting professional qualifications. This means that they must be given more assistance, and more free time in which to complete their vocational training as well as to carry out more fittingly their cultural, moral, and religious education.

95. As a further consequence, the modern youth is enabled to devote a longer time to his basic schooling in the arts and sciences.

96. All this serves to create an environment in which workers are encouraged to assume greater responsibility in their own sphere of employment. In politics, too, it is of no small consequence that citizens are becoming daily more aware of their responsibility for furthering the common good in all spheres of life.

IN THE first part of this work, our intellectual camera used a broad focus. The "social question" was presented in sweeping outlines. The right and the duty of the Church to pronounce upon moral aspects of social and economic problems were explained. In furthering this concept, two chapters were devoted to the pertinent moral principles and virtues. Next, general social systems were examined, including papal directives for a sound approach to social order.

In the present section, our focus is narrowed. Important social institutions, such as capital, labor, the family, property, and the state, are scrutinized in terms of the demands of justice and charity. In each case, the emphasis is upon major current problems and rights and duties pertinent to current situations. Of necessity, the treatment is selective rather than comprehensive. Stress is laid upon actual present-day issues, rather than historical or abstract considerations. Thus, for example, in dealing with capital and business management, the main rights emphasized are those connected with salaries and profits. The duties treated are those toward labor and the public. A similar selectivity is practiced in the other chapters of Part II. It was deemed more important to concentrate upon vital issues of the day than to force each treatment into a preconceived uniform pattern.

Capital was chosen as the first topic primarily because of the tremendous impact that physical capital — billions invested in factories and machines — has made upon our standard of living. The term itself, as used in the encyclicals, has many meanings. Sometimes it refers to the capitalist class, in the sense of promoters, managers, or owners of productive property. At other times it means physical capital, or capital goods. Here allusion is made to the machinery, buildings, and natural resources used as agents of production. Still again, it can mean invested funds and the "profits" secured from such investment. For the sake of clarity, it is best to consider separately these different contributions to the productive process and the returns each deserves.

We must decide not only what are the proper returns for capital, but also to whom they should be allocated and in what proportion. In making this decision, both commutative justice and social justice should be consulted. To the extent that what is clearly due in strict justice can be defined, we should do so. In addition we should try to determine what the common good demands of capital.

OUR PROFIT SYSTEM

Management and Promotion.   Since the questions of profits and interest are highly complex, it is easier to consider first the reward to the capitalist as promoter or manager of a firm. It is possible that the promoter may contribute nothing from his own funds to a given enterprise. Yet he may have vision, daring, or experience which insures great success with the use of borrowed or invested money. A person of this nature makes a definite contribution to economic life and is entitled in justice to a reward for this function. Organization, correct calculation of risks, and awareness of opportunities are real values and add to the wealth of the community. One could even say that the speculator, often despised as a parasite, is not necessarily nonproductive of economic value. Stock exchanges and commodity markets, when properly regulated, smooth out the functioning of the price system and actually lessen risk to producers. The actual return imputed to the efforts of promoters is difficult to assess accurately. In a free economic system, however, the law of supply and demand tends to bring about a rough approximation of what the business community attributes to these agents. If labor is able to demand a proper wage, money capital receives its fair share, and management is suitably rewarded, the surplus remaining in a competitive enterprise is usually credited to the promoter.

Management of an enterprise is likewise a distinct function, not necessarily connected with the initial promotion of a firm or the furnishing of funds for its needs of physical capital. This distinction is clearly seen in the corporation, where day-by-day direction of the company may be in the hands of a president who is not even a stockholder. Broad policies may be laid down by a board of directors, representative of the stockholders, but the actual running of the firm is left to skilled management.

In many of the largest corporations, management controls the appointment of directors through the use of the proxy machinery. In small companies, the owners are usually their own managers. In such cases, their salary for management is lumped in with other "profits," but in fact the directing of a firm is distinct from both its promotion and its ownership.

The contribution of management is best seen when a succession of managers run the same company. It frequently happens that a firm may approach bankruptcy under poor management and make large profits under a new president, with economic conditions, market for the product, and wages remaining the same. In other cases, several competitive firms may be equally close to raw materials and market, have the same power and transportation facilities, pay the same wage rate, and yet one company may be highly successful and others barely survive. Obviously, such results reflect different management policies.

In view of the economic contribution made by management, it follows that salaries based on this contribution are not necessarily unjust. Some moralists are appalled at the differential between wages paid to workers and the salaries and bonuses given to corporation executives. Yet published salaries, and actual income after taxes, are often quite different. Under present tax laws, it is quite difficult to get rich on salaries, no matter how high they may seem. If the net salary incomes of most top corporation executives were apportioned equally among their workers, it would be unusual were this to add as much as ten dollars a year to the wages of each worker.

When we apply the rules of strict justice to corporation salaries, we conclude that they are not of themselves unjust. Good executives can earn millions of dollars annually for many firms. When they are paid a small portion of what they contribute, certainly we cannot say that their income is excessive. From the viewpoint of social justice and the common good, we note that good management helps provide jobs, worthwhile products, and vital economic incentives. All these contributions lead to a healthy economy and national prosperity.

These comments, of course, are generalizations about American business. Undoubtedly there are exceptions to the rules just stated. Some executives may obtain their positions through favoritism and may be overpaid in terms of their contributions. There are those whose policies are antisocial. While they may add to the financial soundness of their firms, they do not enhance the common good of the nation.

Given this defense of executive salaries, it is nonetheless socially desirable to emphasize incentives other than economic. Many public servants perform duties fully as complex as those of corporation executives, but receive only a minor fraction of the latters' salaries. This shows that service to the community, a sense of creative achievement, and similar nonmonetary incentives can also be attractive. If such attitudes could be created, there would be less need for disproportionate salaries, which may give rise to social tensions.

Profits. The term "profits" has many meanings in current usage and in the papal encyclicals. Many persons, particularly small businessmen, use the term to denote the net annual return from a firm. They do not calculate separately their salaries for managing the company. Economists, on the other hand, do not consider return on capital as profits. To them profits constitute a residue after wages, salaries, and other expenses have been paid; depreciation allowed on investment; and payment made for money invested or borrowed.

In these pages, profits are used to denote a return on money invested in a firm. They exclude salaries paid or imputed for management and also interest paid on borrowed money. This usage is closest to that of the encyclicals and hence makes interpretation and comment on these documents more accurate. Particular emphasis is laid upon corporate profits, since these are often subjects of controversy.

The right to profits must be judged both in terms of commutative and of social justice. In strict justice, capital makes a contribution to economic life by furnishing a necessary factor of production. Machines and raw materials contribute to the productive process by enhancing and multiplying the effectiveness of human labor. Capital goods are purchased as a result of the savings of investors and lenders, who reserve a part of their current income, thus diverting some economic effort from the making of goods for consumption to the making of goods for production. This contribution is made in prospect of at least two types of rewards. At the minimum, the sum contributed should be returned. The corporation does this for lenders by setting aside reserves for the retirement of its bonds. For investors, it keeps their property in good repair and may make depreciation allowances to cover the cost of capital equipment.

The second return to lenders and investors is a charge for the use of their money. The moral justification of this charge is treated subsequently in connection with interest. Interest to bondholders is called such, whereas with stockholders it is a part of their dividends, together with a payment for the added risk they assume and, at times, a share of profits in the strict, scientific sense. Stockholders should receive more than the going rate of interest in view of two types of risk. They run the chance of nonpayment in poor years (corporations today tend to use depression reserves more to keep the firm alive than to pay out dividends) and they may lose their principal if business changes lead to bankruptcy of their company.

While strict justice looks upon profits in terms of payment for service rendered, social justice weighs them in the light of the common good. Here the overruling consideration is the health of the economy taken as a whole. We must balance two factors: the need for adequate profits as an incentive for the business community; and the danger that excess profits may lead to overexpansion of capacity in certain industries and consequent strains upon the economy. In general, we should encourage renovation of obsolete plants. There should be adequate funds for research, so that new processes and products may be found. We should seek to stimulate economic expansion and the creation of additional jobs. Yet, at the same time, there is need for channeling sufficient income to workers so that they may be able to consume the products of modernized and expanded industry. The achievement of such a balance must to some degree depend upon experimentation. A high degree of statesmanship on the part of both business and labor will be required to work out the most appropriate distribution in each case.

Is it possible to be more concrete than this, and to express in practical terms what is a fair and honest profit level? This is not an easy task, but the following considerations may be helpful.

In terms of strict justice, we feel that investors have a right to more than the going interest rate, when they invest in stocks rather than bonds. Stockholders assume a greater risk. Hence a dividend rate that is double the rate paid on corporate bonds in a given company seems reasonable. Such a return is generally adequate to attract funds that a firm may need for growth. Historically, the average rate of return for American corporations over the past forty years has ranged between seven and eight per cent of net worth. This appears to be fair.

Where risk is greater, as in the case of new and experimental industries, higher returns would be justified. The return to the stockholder may also be expected to vary from year to year, reflecting changes in corporation profits. Hence any calculation of a proper dividend rate must be based on an average of good and bad years.

To avoid any misunderstanding, we note that the only pertinent profit rate, in terms of justice, is based on money invested in the firm. Many companies also issue profit figures as percentages of return on sales. This is a valuable accounting device for internal cost control, but it has absolutely no relevance to fairness of profit. A supermarket may be getting a good return if it makes one per cent on sales, whereas a furniture store may need twenty per cent on sales to secure a fair return on its investment. The turnover in the supermarket is so great that a small unit profit leads to a good return on invested funds. By contrast, jewelers and furniture stores must have a large unit mark-up to compensate for slow turnover.

When we consider fair profits in terms of social justice, the best criterion is the health of the industry. If it is expanding and paying good wages, the presumption is that the profit rate is at least adequate. When an industry finds it difficult to finance necessary research, and when it is unable to replace an obsolescent plant, obviously it is in difficulty and is not obtaining needed profits. Finally, when companies consistently receive more income than is needed for good wages and efficient operation, and pay exceptionally high dividends year after year, there is evidence of a monopolistic situation and exploitation of the consumer.

To be concrete, heavily competitive operations, such as agriculture and the clothing industry, generally receive subnormal profits. Basic manufacturing firms, steel and automobiles for example, have had at least an adequate profit level over recent years. Companies that produce ethical drugs have been accused of fixing prices and profits at levels far higher than their high research costs would justify.

The Right to Interest. The question of interest formerly loomed large in moral treatises. Pure interest was forbidden by medieval theologians because money was considered a consumption good which was used up in the process of spending. It was analogous to food. When a housewife borrows ten pounds of sugar, she is expected to repay that amount and no more. The sugar, in contrast to land, animals, or other productive property, does not produce an income that can be considered a title justifying an extra charge.

Medieval writers allowed extrinsic claims, such as a loss incurred, a gain forgone, or a premium to cover risk, as justification for interest. But a charge for the use of money as such was considered exploitive. The Church ban on interest charges was gradually relaxed as the complex world of business provided more and more extrinsic titles for a return on money. The presumption now is that any lender either passes up a possible gain, or at least incurs the sacrifice of losing the liquidity of his funds. Moreover, the common good of the community is served by the availability of loan capital. Indeed, our modern economic system could not function without it.

It is more difficult to determine what is a just rate of interest. Basic loan rates today are determined by supply and demand factors. The amount of money available for loans depends partly upon savings decisions by income receivers and partly upon funds released by central-banking systems (e.g., the Federal Reserve System). The demand for money is influenced by business conditions and by consumer needs for financing.

Since the general bank rate is influenced by central-banking decisions, the presumption is that it is a just rate, determined by considerations of the common economic good. In the United States, the governing board of our central-banking system is appointed by the President with the consent of Congress. Hence it is an agency of the state, committed to seek the common good.

Higher rates based on greater risks or higher collection costs are also morally justified. Even the relatively high rates of finance companies (3 per cent a month, or 36 per cent a year) may not be excessive, since these firms have high investigation, bookkeeping, and collection costs. Injustice is more likely to occur in some installment-sale practices. First, the buyer is often deceived as to the real charges he is incurring. Second, many contracts are so framed as to keep a borrower in constant debt. Most larger stores and sales agencies avoid such practices, but they are common among firms that cater to poor credit risks or less educated buyers. Such firms lend freely at exorbitant rates and let the courts become their collection agencies. Even worse are the "loan sharks" who prey upon improvident borrowers. It is not uncommon for such persons to lend "until payday" (for example, lending five dollars and collecting six), thus getting 20 per cent interest for a loan of a few days. This, of course, makes an annual rate in excess of 1000 per cent.

Usurious exploitation, while cruel and unjust, is not a major economic problem. It can be remedied by better laws (such as the New York State law calling for full disclosure of installment charges), promotion of credit unions, and by adequate economic education in our schools. Even then there will always remain a residue of truly improvident persons who cannot manage money or who gamble or drink away their incomes. These persons need moral guidance and possibly psychiatric treatment.

Laws and social institutions rarely help such cases. But society should be concerned with those who, through unavoidable necessity or even ignorance, are victimized by exploitive moneylenders.

Self-Financing of Industry. The discussion of self-financing by Pope John XXIII (*M.M.*, Nos. 75, 77) raised a problem generally overlooked by moralists. Who has the moral claim to property acquired by retained earnings in excess of normal depreciation reserves? The Pope treats the issue in the context of firms which pay workers only a minimum wage and use the excess to finance expansion. But there are two other ways in which this process is carried out. In one case, stockholders are paid no dividends or a smaller than normal amount, with the proceeds used for investment. In the other, stockholders receive average returns so that the funds presumably come from excessive prices charged to consumers.

In the situation envisioned by the Pope, it is clear that the workers concerned have a claim to ownership of the new facilities. By accepting less than normal wages, they contributed the money used for growth. This was the situation in West Germany during the years 1949–1959, when workers deliberately refrained from seeking better wages in order to enable industry to rebuild after World War II. Obviously they, rather than the stockholders, have a right to ownership of property so financed.

By contrast, when stockholders receive little or no dividends from an expanding firm, they have a clear claim to the capital gains resulting from this policy. Many American corporations have grown in this fashion. Others, however, have paid good wages and dividends and financed development from excess earnings. In this case, the presumption is that they are charging consumers exorbitant prices. Here neither stockholders or workers have a moral claim to the wealth so acquired. Such a situation calls for some type of governmental action to remedy the injustice involved, either pressures to force prices down or taxes to return excess profits to public use.

DUTIES OF OWNERS AND MANAGERS OF CAPITAL
Duties Toward Labor

The basic social obligation of "capital," in relation to workers, is to respect their human dignity. From this fundamental outlook, many detailed duties may be deduced. Thus, the claim of workers for a fair wage springs from their human dignity. Their right to form unions may be derived from this source. These and other considerations will be treated more at length in the chapters immediately following.

One suggestion, given by Popes Pius XI and John XXIII, may be discussed at this point. The earlier pontiff urged as desirable the introduction of some element of partnership into the work contract. This could be done by the workers' sharing in profits, management, or ownership, or some combination of these three items. Pope John stressed participation in management through a process of consultation in matters connected with production. This not only harmonizes with the human dignity of the workers, but it also reflects the fact that modern methods call for higher skills, and hence a more intelligent contribution by the average employee. The general concept of sharing has been widely discussed in the United States and various devices have been used to bring about closer unity between labor and management. We shall note the main proposals and the reaction of American workers to these devices.

Profit-Sharing. Profit-sharing normally involves the dividing of a portion of net profits among the workers in accord with a previously developed formula. Thus, in a given company, some figure may be taken as the fair compensation of stockholders, after suitable reserves had been set aside for bad years. It may then be agreed that of the net profits remaining, 60 per cent (to use an arbitrary figure) may be divided among workers, with the remainder going to salaried employees, executives, and, possibly, stockholders. This would be in addition to a fair wage determined by normal collective bargaining. Such a procedure emphasizes the common interests of workers and employers, gives labor an incentive to cooperate with management, and tends to increase workers' loyalty to the company employing them.

Some firms frankly emphasize the incentive element in profit-sharing. After a basic wage is fixed, supplementary returns depend upon increased production at lower cost. In this way, output is increased and hence workers can be paid at a higher annual rate. The Lincoln Electric Company, in Cleveland, is a strong proponent of this method. On the other hand, the incentive method of profit-sharing often causes much suspicion and even hostility on the part of organized labor. Many workers fear that this is a device to speed up production by developing a pace of operations which cannot be sustained indefinitely. To them, it is reminiscent of piece-rate methods in which unit rates were cut after employees earned a good salary by increasing output. They argue that labor shares the losses during depression times by virtue of unemployment; hence its basic wage should be independent of the ups and downs of the business cycle.

Since these objections are rather widespread and since many profit-sharing plans have failed, it is clear that caution should be used in approaching the problem. As far as any conclusion may be reached from the many plans tried in the United States, it is this: profit-sharing is not normally a good initial means to establish employee good will toward the employer; but if understanding and co-operation have been built up by other means, then profit-sharing is a sound auxiliary device for strengthening bonds already established. Where mutual trust already exists, the sharing of profits is a legitimate incentive to higher productivity, stability in employment, and greater employee loyalty.

A sound profit-incentive plan is based on the theory that there are untapped reserves in the working force which can be utilized through co-operation. Workers often have suggestions for new methods of production, devices to increase quality and cut down waste, safety programs, and the lessening of absenteeism and labor turnover. It may even happen that they could work faster without undue fatigue if the proper stimulus were applied. But the evolving of such patterns of co-operation is a complex psychological problem which will never be met by an unaided profit-sharing plan. Profit-sharing can be successful only if previously complete trust in management's integrity and competence has been developed.

One of the most successful forms of profit-sharing is the so-called Scanlon plan. The heart of this plan is the attempt to make the entire plant work as a team in increasing efficiency and lowering costs. Group rather than individual incentive is the keystone. Management and its workers jointly set a productive norm. They work together in cutting costs. Their teams are constantly screening suggestions and seeking better methods of performance. Results of this method have been remarkable, provided that a pattern of trust and co-operation pre-existed its adoption.

Somewhat different is the approach pioneered by the Kaiser Steel Corporation. Here workers share in savings resulting from cost reductions regardless of company profit. Under this plan it would be possible for employees to receive a bonus even if the firm was losing money. All that is required is evidence that costs have gone down.

Sharing Management. While the idea of profit-sharing has met with indifference on the part of business and some hostility from labor, suggestions for sharing management usually provoke violent reactions from business and indifference from a large part of labor. Business is acutely sensitive to the "prerogatives of management." It insists that responsibility must be centralized, meaning that it should rest in the hands of owners or their representatives. On the other hand, many labor unions are not interested in sharing any of management's burdens. On some specific points, such as the rate of production, they may demand a voice in what was formerly considered the exclusive field of management, but there is little general interest in any broad participation. This is even more true, as a rule, of the average worker in a factory. He has a limited conception of the broad problems of management and even less interest in assuming a share of them. Thus, at first glance, it might appear that proposals for management-sharing are unrealistic; convincing perhaps to intellectuals, but unappealing to those directly concerned.

Yet, in another sense, sharing of management not only is sound, it is one of the most important developments in recent years. Most of the adverse reaction springs from one limited interpretation of the proposal. Thus, it has been presented as involving employee representation on a board of corporate directors with (presumably) minority status. Business balks at such a notion and labor is not very interested in it. On the other hand, thousands of businessmen are becoming deeply interested in the "human-relations" literature and experience of the past twenty-five years. Learned studies have been made and experiments attempted to prove that "teamwork, communication, and participation" are necessary for a smoothly functioning industrial unit. Educational programs have been developed to make workers feel an identity with company interests and a sense of common responsibility in meeting problems.

In the literature mentioned above, there is great emphasis upon treating a worker as an individual, with full recognition of his personal traits. When a worker is hired, his aptitudes and desires are ascertained and he is fitted to a suitable job. He is trained, not only for his special work, but also in the broad problems of his company. He is made to feel that the firm's problems are his own. Communication is a two-way process. His point of view is solicited; and ultimate decisions are explained to him, not merely handed down as peremptory orders. The ultimate aim is teamwork between workers on all levels and management. Such practices at the factory level are harmonized with the union contract, and with the workers' representatives as definite parts of the pattern of consultation and teamwork.

It is also noteworthy that there is much postwar discussion of management-sharing, on the part of European Catholic groups. Europeans frequently make the distinction, in discussing this problem, between social and economic questions, with the workers having a clear right to participate in the former area, but less right to enter into economic decisions. Under the heading of social questions would come various personnel matters and the problems of social welfare. These considerations are often included in collective bargaining and social legislation in the United States. Economic matters include prices, output, profits, investment, and similar management decisions. American labor has not gone deeply into this field, except to the extent implied by collective bargaining over wages and other costs.

The results of European experiments, particularly those in Germany since codetermination was introduced by law in 1951, are not impressive. At any rate, the historical and cultural patterns behind such moves are quite different from those prevailing in the United States. Our temperament inclines toward partnership situations built on mutual trust, not those imposed by law.

Sharing Ownership. Sharing of ownership usually involves employee stockholding in corporations. Plans of this nature were tried extensively during the 1920's to promote worker interest in a firm. But the stock-market crash of 1929 caused most of these plans to founder. Some companies today retain the practice, particularly in connection with pension or profit-sharing plans. Sears, Roebuck, & Company is an outstanding example.

Most firms, however, have been reluctant to inaugurate stock-ownership plans. Their executives feel that stock prices are too unstable and that workers might become disillusioned when the value of their shares dropped. Moreover, ownership of stock does not give any substantial degree of participation in the control of a modern corporation. Stockholders are too scattered, as a rule, to exercise any personal supervision over the companies in which they have invested. In addition, most American workers are concerned with tangible wage returns, rather than the prospect of dividends.

It would be a mistake so to emphasize means and devices that the ultimate end is overlooked or slighted. The sharing of profits, management, or ownership belong in the category of means toward the end of further emphasizing the human dignity of the worker. Moreover, the form they may take is in large part a matter of experience and prudential judgment. It would seem that the trend of American experience is in the direction of emphasizing worker participation in management at the level where it has concrete and daily impact on his life. If workers are day-by-day partners in the productive process, and their unions are included in the area of broad co-operation, participation, and consultation, then we shall have a greater degree of partnership than has ever previously existed in the American economy.

Duties Toward the Public

Management must seek the public good, as well as proper relationships with its workers. One aspect of this has already been mentioned, the element of fair prices and reasonable profits. It is a matter of simple justice to give the consumer value for his money. Monopoly or practices in restraint of trade are exploitive. The selling of inferior products or any element of substantial deception of the consumer is unjust.

Beyond this, one of the great needs in the business world is a genuine feeling for the public economic good. Business, like labor and farmers, often becomes a captive of class psychology. As a result, it tends to equate the common good with its own immediate interests. "What is good for business is good for the nation." This attitude, for example, makes some business spokesmen seek tax cuts at a time when national defense precludes such relief. It leads others to oppose removal of trade barriers and to denounce foreign economic aid as a waste of taxpayers' money. It often produces a captious and negative attitude toward government.

Any of these positions may be supported by arguments that appear sound. The holding of any of them is not necessarily a sign of anti-social tendencies. Here the real test is why they are held. Is the businessman reading only arguments that favor his preconceptions? Is he seeking reasons to bolster the short-term interests of his company, and neglecting the national welfare? It is not easy to give general answers to such questions, but there are reasons to believe that it is readily possible for a businessman to drift into a narrow and self-centered position.

In the first place, his own psychology poses problems. By the nature of his calling, he is a man of self-reliance and independence. He is used to giving orders and making firm decisions. He has successfully relied on personal energy and resourcefulness to see him through difficulties. As a result, he is often temperamentally unprepared for the tortuous ways of politics and diplomacy. He wants direct action in fields where it often cannot be had. Then he feels frustrated and hostile and vents his feelings in denunciations of Washington or the United Nations.

Again, many businessmen are so tied down with their own problems that they do not have the time for general reading. They get their information in capsule form from business letters and special sources, such as their trade associations or national business groups. Many of these sources, unfortunately, cater to views designed to please their clients. The result is a reinforcement of originally narrow opinions by the ability to quote "experts" and "authorities."

In this connection, it is a paradoxical fact that often big business, so frequently damned as antisocial, is more advanced than the small businessman. Managers of large corporations of necessity acquire a national and even international point of view. They consult with economists and professional analysts of public policy. They even have some independence in regard to their stockholders and can often take a larger and more long-range viewpoint than is likely with small businessmen. At the same time, their prestige with smaller businessmen is so great that, as our allies in presenting a social philosophy, they are powerful forces for good. Hence the use of publications such as the *Harvard Business Review* or *Fortune*, and of statements by organizations such as the Committee on Economic Development or the American Management Association, are more effective than quoting material compiled by a government or labor group. In citing business leaders, it is often more compelling to use a mild but progressive assertion by acknowledged leaders than a stronger position urged by some highly publicized businessman who lacks real influence in his own community. Thus, a quotation from the Chamber of Commerce of the United States, noting that central fiscal and monetary policies are important in preventing depressions, is more useful than a powerful plea for economic planning by some businessman who is considered a maverick by his colleagues.

While we find in many businessmen a tendency toward parochialism, it is only fair to note that they are not the only offenders. The pressure of modern life tends to make persons in many occupations narrow and overspecialized. Labor leaders can be as guilty or as unfortunate as business leaders in this regard. It is important, in terms of Catholic social action, to have some degree of understanding for these human limitations. We can more readily convince people toward whom we have sympathy.

A final problem, much discussed in recent years, involves the ethics of American businessmen. Some of our large corporations have been subjected to the embarrassing disclosures that their executives engaged in secret price-fixing deals with officials from competing firms. There were stories of commercial bribery, theft of business secrets, and even the furnishing of call girls to prospective purchasers. Expensive entertaining was charged as a routine business expense. If these failings were simply matters of personal guilt on the part of the culprits, one would dismiss the incidents as examples of human weakness. There is, however, a social factor involved as well. Many executives claimed that the pressures for achievement, at whatever cost, led them into unethical conduct. To the extent that this is true, the boards of directors and top officials of the corporations involved are at least guilty of neglect of duty.

Given the power and prestige of business in American life, we do not hesitate to urge this community to become increasingly sensitive to its moral standards. Corruption in such a vital area can seriously weaken the entire nation. We have no wish to single out business, as if it were the only profession in our nation afflicted with unworthy members or double standards. Rather our appeal is in terms of *noblesse oblige*. A city on a mountaintop cannot be hidden.

READINGS*

J. Y. Calvez, *Social Thought of John XXIII*, Chap. 3.
J. Y. Calvez and J. Perrin, *The Church and Social Justice*, Chap. 11.
B. W. Dempsey, *The Functional Economy*, Chaps. 18, 20–21.
H. Johnston, *Business Ethics*, Chaps. 8–9.
J. Messner, *Social Ethics* (rev. ed.), pp. 366–367, 716–719, 747–882 (especially 834–868).
O. von Nell-Breuning, *Reorganization of Social Economy*, Chap. 7.
J. A. Ryan, *Distributive Justice*.
———— *A Better Economic Order*, Chap. 7.

---

* For further readings, consult List No. 6 in the Appendix.

Chapter IX

CAPITAL-LABOR RELATIONSHIPS

THE DIGNITY OF LABOR

Leo XIII, Rerum Novarum

31. Workers are not to be treated as slaves; justice demands that the dignity of the human personality be respected in them, ennobled as it has been through what we call the Christian character. If we hearken to natural reason and to Christian philosophy, gainful occupations are not a mark of shame to man, but rather of respect, as they provide him with an honorable means of supporting life.

Pius XII, Christmas Broadcast, 1942

1850. He who would have the star of peace shine out and stand over society should give to work the place assigned to it by God in the beginning. As an indispensable means toward gaining over the world that mastery which God wishes for His glory, all work has an inherent dignity and at the same time a close association with the perfection of the person; this is the noble dignity and privilege of work which is not in any way cheapened by the fatigue and the burden, which have to be borne as the effect of original sin, in obedience and submission to the will of God.

Pius XII, Christmas Message, 1955

Man can consider his work as a true instrument of his sanctification because by working he makes perfect in himself the image of God, fulfills his duty and the right to gain for himself and his dependents the necessary sustenance, and makes himself a useful contributor to society. Bringing this order into existence will obtain for him security, and, at the same time the "peace on earth" proclaimed by the angels.

Pius XII, To Directors of Chemical Products Organizations, January 10, 1958

Respectful of persons and their inalienable rights, conscious of the profound solidarity that makes him one with the most humble of his fellows, the man with a heart — the Christian above all — does not allow the judgment of economic facts and social situations in the light of the determinism of blind laws or of an inexorable historical evolutionism. He suffers deeply to see the worker of our day too often a stranger to his work, chained to a task which chokes him in an iron collar instead of giving him the opportunity to develop, no matter how modest that opportunity may be.

Competent people realize that the worker, when faced with a job which distorts or degrades his personality to the vanishing point, slows down his productive effort and thus reduces considerably the advantages gained twenty-five years ago by mechanization.

Psychologists have tried to classify the numerous influences which determine the behavior of the worker at his task.

It seems that the most outstanding of these is an active interest in his task, which engages the attention of the man and gives him the feeling of putting his personal resources into his work and developing them.

The worker then feels that he is using not only his muscular power but also his very soul, and that his labor is recompensed, first of all, by pride in the work accomplished, which grows within him.

Instead of seeing in his work only a means for making a living, he finds in it a sense of life and the measure of his personal and social being.

If from the point of view of productivity alone this factor merits the serious attention of industrial chiefs, it is even more impressive when one considers it from the more lofty point of view of the human conscience and its absolute responsibilities.

These responsibilities were succinctly expressed by Christ when He as Supreme Judge declared that, all that is done for the least of His, is as though it were done for Him (cf. Matt. 25, 40).

John XXIII, Mater et Magistra

82. Justice is to be observed not only in the distribution of wealth, but also in regard to the conditions in which men are engaged in producing this wealth. Every man has, of his very nature, a need to express himself in his work and thereby to perfect his own being.

83. Consequently, if the whole structure and organization of an economic system is such as to compromise human dignity, to lessen a man's sense of responsibility or rob him of opportunity for exercising personal initiative, then such a system, We maintain, is altogether unjust — no matter how much wealth it produces, or how justly and equitably such wealth is distributed.

John XXIII, Pacem in Terris

18. In the economic sphere, it is evident that a man has the inherent right not only to be given the opportunity to work, but also to be allowed the exercise of personal initiative in the work he does.

19. The conditions in which a man works form a necessary corollary to these rights. They must not be such as to weaken his physical or moral fibre, or militate against the proper development of adolescents to manhood. Women must be accorded such conditions of work as are consistent with their needs and responsibilities as wives and mothers.

THE RIGHT TO ORGANIZE

Leo XIII, Rerum Novarum

72. [For man is permitted by a right of nature to form private societies;] the state, on the other hand, has been instituted to protect and not to destroy natural right, and if it should forbid its citizens to enter into associations, it would clearly do something contradictory to itself, because both the state itself and private associations are begotten of one and the same principle, namely, that [men are by nature inclined to associate.]

76. Furthermore, if citizens have free right to associate, as in fact they do, they also must have the right freely to adopt the organization and the rules which they judge most appropriate to achieve their purpose. We do not feel that the precise character in all details which the aforementioned direction and organization of associations ought to have can be determined by fast and fixed rules, since this is a matter to be decided rather in the light of the temperament of each people, of experiment and practice, of the nature and character of the work, of the extent of trade and commerce, and of other circumstances of a material and temporal kind, all of which must be carefully considered. In summary, [let this be laid down as a general and constant law: workers' associations ought to be so constituted and so governed as to furnish the most suitable and most fitting means to attain the object proposed, which consists in this, that the individual members of the association secure, so far as possible, an increase in the goods of body, of soul, and of property.]

Pius XI, Quadragesimo Anno

30. They were with criminal injustice denying the natural right to form associations to those who needed it most to defend themselves from ill-treatment at the hands of the powerful. There were even some Catholics who looked askance at the efforts of workers to form associations of this type as if they smacked of a socialistic or revolutionary spirit.

35. Under these conditions, Catholics seem almost forced to join secular unions. These unions, however, should always profess justice and equity and give Catholic members full freedom to care for their own conscience and obey the laws of the Church. It is clearly the office of bishops, when they know that these associations are on account of circumstances necessary and are not dangerous to religion, to approve of Catholic workers joining them, keeping before their eyes, however, the principles and precautions laid down by Our Predecessor, Pius X, of holy memory. Among these precautions the first and chief is this: side by side with these unions there should always be associations zealously engaged in imbuing and forming their members in the teaching of religion and morality, so that they in turn may be able to permeate the unions with that good spirit which should direct them in all their activity. As a result, the religious associations will bear good fruit even beyond the circle of their own membership.

Pius XII, Sertum Laetitiae, November 1, 1939

1468. Because social relations is one of man's natural requirements and since it is legitimate to promote by common effort decent livelihood, it is not possible without injustice to deny or to limit either to the producers or to the laboring and farming classes the free faculty of uniting in associations by means of which they may defend their proper rights and secure the betterment of the goods of soul and of body, as well as the honest comforts of life. But to unions of this kind, which in past centuries have procured immortal glory for Christianity and for the professions an untarnishable splendor, one cannot everywhere impose an identical discipline and structure which therefore can be varied to meet the different temperament of the people and the diverse circumstances of time.

Pius XII, To Railroad Workers of Rome, June 26, 1955

No true Christian can find fault if you unite in strong organizations to defend your rights — while remaining aware of your duties — and to arrive at an improvement in your conditions of life. On the contrary, precisely because the harmonious action of all groups in the state is a Christian duty, [no individual citizen ought to become a victim of the arbitrary act or tyranny of others.] You are therefore acting in full conformity with the Church's social teaching when, by all means morally permissible, you vindicate your just rights.

We said by all means morally permissible. It is unnecessary to remind you that acts of violence which damage the liberty and the goods of others are not even contemplated by true Christians. When, therefore, they use the power of their organizations to win recognition for their rights, it is essential that, in the first place, they use the means suitable for the negotiation of a peaceful settlement. Then, in particular, there must be taken into consideration whether the results being aimed at are in reasonable proportion to the damage which could result from force.

John XXIII, Mater et Magistra

100. It is Our prerogative to be a Father, and there is a special place in Our thoughts and in Our heart for those professional groups and Christian associations of workers which exist and operate in so many parts of the world. We know the nature and extent of the difficulties under which these dearest sons of Ours are laboring, as they strive continually and effectually to promote in their own countries and throughout the world the material and moral interests of the working people.

101. They are fully deserving of Our praise. The importance of their work must be gauged not merely by its immediate and obvious results, but also by its effect on the working world as a whole, where it helps to spread sound principles of action and the wholesome influence of the Christian religion.

102. We wish further to praise those dear sons of Ours who in a true Christian spirit collaborate with other pro-

fessional groups and workers' associations which respect the natural law and the freedom of conscience of their members.

Vatican Council II, The Church in the Modern World

68. Among the basic rights of the human person must be counted the right of freely founding labor unions. These unions should be truly able to represent the workers and to contribute to the proper arrangement of economic life. [Another such right is that of taking part freely in the activity of these unions without risk or reprisal.] Through this sort of orderly participation, joined with an ongoing formation in economic and social matters, all will grow day by day in the awareness of their own function and responsibility. Thus they will be brought to feel that according to their own proper capacities and aptitudes they are associates in the whole task of economic and social development and in the attainment of the universal common good.

Hierarchy of Quebec, Pastoral Letter, February, 1950

100. Present circumstances render more pressing and more imperious the *obligation* for workers . . . to exercise this right [to join unions].

101. Every man has an obligation to seek to protect the security of his professional [economic] interests. He has the duty to seek to obtain for himself and his family all that is necessary in order to live a truly human life and to safeguard them against future hazards.

RIGHT TO WORK AND UNION SECURITY

Pius XII, Christmas Message, 1952

. . . access to employment or places of labor is made to depend on registration in certain parties, or in organizations which deal with the distribution of employment. Such discrimination is indicative of an inexact concept of the proper function of labor unions and their proper purpose, which is the protection of the interests of the salaried worker within modern society, which is becoming more and more anonymous and collectivist.

In fact, is not the essential purpose of unions the practical affirmation that man is the subject, and not the object, of social relations? Is it not to protect the individual against collective irresponsibility of anonymous proprietors? Is it not to represent the person of the worker against those who are inclined to consider him merely a productive agent with a certain price value?

How, therefore, can it be considered normal that the protection of the personal rights of the worker be placed more and more in the hands of an anonymous group, working through the agency of immense organizations which are of their very nature monopolies? The worker, thus wronged in the exercise of his personal rights, will surely find especially painful the oppression of his liberty and of his conscience, caught as he is in the wheels of a gigantic social machine.

Cardinal Cicognani, Letter to Canadian Social Week, August 16, 1963

There are occasions when this right of association may become a real duty for individuals, if their participation is required for the good of all.

Statement of Ohio Bishops, March 20, 1958

Man has a right and duty to work for his livelihood. This right cannot be circumscribed to the extent that a man loses his liberty of choice of a vocation; nor to the extent that he is deprived of an opportunity to support himself and his family. It does not follow that a man has the unconditional right to work in any and every industry or business at will.

For reasons of social justice it may be desirable and often advantageous to the common good that man's right be restricted by certain specified conditions. One of these imposed conditions may require that he belong to a labor union or at least be obliged to join the union subsequently, so as to share responsibility with his fellow workmen in support of the union.

Just as a citizen of the United States is free to live in Ohio, Kentucky, or Pennsylvania, yet is obliged to observe the laws of the particular state as a condition of citizenship, so also in respect to his right to work; he is free to work in any industry of his choice, but only on condition that he abides by the rules adopted by that particular industry as a condition of employment.

In other words, the right to work is a general right and cannot be denied to men in the aggregate; but the right to work in a specific industrial plant or business can be subject to special conditions.

If state statutes were to make such a condition of union maintenance mandatory, we would oppose them as unwise, if not unjust. If state statutes however were to forbid the enforcement of such a condition, when mutually accepted by management and labor through collective bargaining, then we would be equally opposed.

We believe it is unwise to encourage state intervention in this matter, whether it be in favor of "right-to-work" laws or against them.

There are certain abuses which sometimes creep into the labor movement, but we are convinced that "right-to-work" laws are not the proper means to correct them. Corruption of certain labor leaders has been one of these current abuses. The denial of the democratic processes and the denial thereby of responsibility to the rank and file of union membership, whether in election to office or in the determination of union policy, are prolific causes of these abuses.

COLLECTIVE BARGAINING

Leo XIII, Rerum Novarum

56. Labor which is too long and too hard and the belief that pay is inadequate not infrequently give workers cause to strike and become voluntarily idle. This evil, which is frequent and serious, ought to be remedied by public authority, because such interruption of work inflicts damage not only upon employers and upon the workers themselves, but also injures trade and commerce and the general interests of the State; and, since it is usually not far removed from violence and rioting, it very frequently jeopardizes public peace. In this matter it is more effective and salutary that

the authority of the law anticipate and completely prevent the evil from which it would seem that conflict between employers and workers is bound to arise.

Pius XII, To Christian Associations of Italian Workers, June 7, 1957

. . . only one word of advice is possible for the organized parties to the labor contract: it is better to bargain than to fight one another. This is the only conclusion they can adopt before their own consciences and the people at large.

Australian Hierarchy, Peace in Industry

⌈Under modern conditions, the right to organize in trade unions and the right to strike, under certain defined conditions, are inseparable.⌉

It would be futile to urge the formation of trade unions if the Church did not realize that this involves recognition of the right to strike, as a last resort, and when other measures of achieving social justice have failed.

Four conditions of a just strike have been laid down commonly by theologians: (1) The cause of a threatened strike must itself be just and rightful. (2) There must be sufficient hope of success. It is morally wrong to plunge workers into a strike in which they have no hope of success and from which they will emerge in a worse condition than before. Nevertheless it does not always follow that because a strike is lost it is in vain. (3) The benefit to be gained must not be out of proportion to the harm inflicted. In the case of strikes which seriously affect the entire community, the onus thus placed on those who decide to strike is therefore very great. (4) Before a strike is declared, every effort must first be made to settle the dispute peacefully through conciliation, arbitration, and other more peaceful methods.

Hierarchy of Quebec, Pastoral Letter, February, 1950

179. There are certain categories of workers who would seriously imperil the common good, were they to strike. In this not too frequent situation, the law may suppress or suspend the right to strike, but not without at the same time giving such workers some compensating methods which are adequate to obtain justice. The law should, for example, provide for compulsory arbitration, adequately safeguarded in regard to impartiality, effectiveness, and promptness of decision.

WORKERS IN SOCIETY

Leo XIII, Rerum Novarum

30. Among these duties the following concern the poor and the workers: To perform entirely and conscientiously whatever work has been voluntarily and equitably agreed upon; not in any way to injure the property or to harm the person of employers; in protecting their own interests, to refrain from violence and never to engage in rioting; not to associate with vicious men who craftily hold out exaggerated hopes and make huge promises, a course usually ending in vain regrets and in the destruction of wealth.

Pius XII, To Christian Association of Italian Workers, June 29, 1948

But if you are not to grow faint along the road, if you are to keep alive the flame that burns in your hearts, if especially you are to win over the young to your cause, you must keep always before your eyes the noble objective toward which your movement is on the march. Your ultimate purpose is the formation of authentic Christian workingmen, equally distinguished for skill in the practice of their profession and for fidelity in the practice of their religion; men who are capable of reconciling harmoniously the stubborn defense of their economic interests with the strictest sense of justice, and with the sincere disposition to collaborate with the other classes of society toward Christian reconstruction in every walk of social life.

Do not let yourselves deviate from this goal, which is more important than any purely transitory form of union organization. The future of the unions themselves depends on the faithfulness with which you pursue this goal. In fact, if ever they should aim at exclusive domination in the state and society, if they should seek to exercise absolute power over the worker, if they should reject the strict sense of justice and sincere good will to collaborate with the other social classes, they would betray the expectations and the hopes which every honest and conscientious worker places in them. What must be thought when a worker is kept from his labor because he is not *persona grata* to the union, when workers are forced to abstain from labor for political purposes, when they are led astray down not a few other mistaken paths that lead very far away indeed from the true good and often invoked unity of the working class?

John XXIII, Mater et Magistra

97. In modern times we have seen an extensive increase in the number of workers' associations, and their general recognition in the juridical codes of single states and on the international level. Members are no longer recruited in order to agitate, but rather to co-operate, principally by the method of collective bargaining. But it is worthwhile stressing here how timely and imperative it is that workers be given the opportunity to exert their influence throughout the state, and not just within the limits of their own spheres of employment.

98. The reason for this is that the individual productive concerns, regardless of their size, efficiency, and importance in the state, form but a part — an integral part — of a nation's entire economic and social life, upon which their own prosperity must depend.

99. Hence it is not the decisions made within the individual productive units which have the greatest bearing on the economy, but those made by public authorities and by institutions which tackle the various economic problems on a national or international basis. It is therefore very appropriate, or even necessary, that these public authorities and institutions bring the workers into their discussions, and those who represent the rights, demands and aspirations of the workingmen; and not confine their deliberations to those who merely represent the interests of management.

THE discussion of management's duties toward labor, presented in the preceding chapter, was professedly limited in scope. It dealt primarily with the suggestion of Pope Pius XI that the wage contract be supplemented by some form of partnership. It is appropriate now to extend this treatment by considering broader aspects and moral implications of the contacts between workers and management. We do this in two stages, treating first the worker as an individual dealing with his employer and then discussing their collective relationships in union-management affairs.

THE WORKER AND HIS INDIVIDUAL RIGHTS

Much has been said in earlier pages of this book about the rights of man and the dignity of the individual. These points were treated positively and directly in Chapter III, and indirectly in connection with the virtues of justice and charity and in our rejection of individualism and statism. Natural law teaches that man enjoys certain inherent rights, regardless of differences in individual ability and achievement. Our immediate concern is how this truth is applied in work situations that affect nearly seventy million Americans.

Work: A Right and a Duty. First of all, we note that work is a duty and a right for mankind. It is a duty, since most persons can only thus procure their means of livelihood. Even those who may not have the economic need to work must find an equivalent form of activity, or otherwise face physical, mental, and spiritual decline. Idleness is harmful to human character, whereas the discipline of work can develop many virtues, such as fortitude, patience, and brotherly co-operation.

Work participates in the miracle of creation, since man thereby brings into being new forms and materials not found in nature. Hence there is no need for the worker to feel ashamed of his lot, no matter how humble it may seem. Some of the most difficult types of work are most necessary for the general welfare. Few persons may like such tasks as street cleaning or garbage removal, yet the community would suffer intensely if such tasks were neglected. Again, domestic and personal service is often in disrepute today. To the extent that such attitudes are the result of low wages and poor working conditions in the past, they are quite natural. But it would be wrong to feel that direct personal service is inherently undignified and unworthy. Some of the most respected professions, such as medicine and teaching, embody personal service. A mother's devotion to children is one of the highest forms of this work.

If man has the duty to work as a means of earning his livelihood, he must also have the right to secure work. The God-implanted instinct of self-preservation warrants reasonable access to the wealth of the earth. In most cases, the appropriate form of access is through the creation of new wealth by work. Therefore we can say that man's right and duty to live in effect mean a right to work. This right is directed toward the economic system and owners of property in general. It is not a right to any specific job, but merely a moral claim against economic society. Society meets this claim when it makes every effort so to organize its laws, customs, and institutions that a maximum degree of employment consistent with the common good be created. Its aim should be a job opportunity for every willing and qualified worker.

Although the right to work is not a claim to any specific job, the question arises as to the possibilities of a strict right — in commutative justice — to a definite job, rather than a broad claim in social justice to a fair opportunity to earn a livelihood. Such a strict right, either to obtain or retain a job, can arise from a contract. But most persons, not being motion-picture or baseball stars, do not have contractual rights to a job. Are there, then, any strict rights that may be asserted either in getting or keeping a specific job?

Job Discrimination.   In the matter of obtaining a job, the moral problem is that of the responsibility of an employer who practices discrimination against work applicants. No individual applicant has a right to a particular job, but this does not mean that an employer may arbitrarily hire whom he pleases. Obviously he may not, if his discrimination is based on an unworthy motive. Employers are not necessarily bound to hire the most qualified applicants — a certain exercise of whim or irrationality in choice need not be reprehensible. But serious moral fault can be present when the grounds of rejection are immoral.

When a qualified applicant is refused an available job merely because of race, religion, national origin, union affiliation, or similar reasons, the refusing employer can be guilty of grave sin. He is at least violating the virtue of charity. He can also be co-operating in a collective act of injustice. Such can be the case, for example, if all employers in a community refuse skilled work to a qualified Negro, thus forcing him to accept unskilled work at lower pay. If individual employers feel that they are hopelessly coerced by unjust community pressures, they are bound in social justice to try to correct the situation that caused such pressures.[1]

A special problem of some concern today involves the hiring of persons over forty years of age. It is becoming increasingly difficult for workers in this age group to find new jobs, should they lose their former positions. Employers' objections to hiring them stem from pension plans, fear of sickness and injuries, and preference for more energetic and younger workers. Yet older workers bring skill and experience that often more than compensate for any difficulties involved in hiring them. They are usually stable and reliable. It is hoped that field studies being made regarding this problem will convince employers that they are seriously mistaken in regard to the disabilities of older workers. Just as industry learned to appreciate the assets of the handicapped worker, so likewise it can understand the real merits of older applicants for jobs.

Once a worker is hired and performs satisfactorily, he does not, barring some contractual arrangement, acquire a right in strict justice to retain his job. An employer who replaces him with a favored nephew may be acting contrary to charity and equity, but he is not breaching a strict right. To preclude actions of this nature, unions generally and rightly insist, as part of their contracts, upon seniority features and provisions for impartial review of discharges. Some moralists, however, would not accept the analysis just given. They hold that implied in the contract of hiring is the assumption that a worker may retain his job, so long as conditions do not change and his work remains satisfactory. If this condition is really a part of the work contract in modern times, then arbitrary and unwarranted discharge would be a violation of strict justice.

It would be unfortunate if the somewhat negative features of this treatment of the right to a job were to leave an impression that this right is meaningless. Serious rights and duties can exist apart from the claims of commutative justice. The fact that most of the duties connected with employment involve social justice, equity, and charity does not make them less binding. It merely indicates that different means may be needed to enforce them. Social justice, for example, may call for group action rather than unilateral efforts to remedy a situation.

Human Relations. Nor does reserve about the right to retain a job mean that any worker may be mistreated with impunity in this work. On

---

[1] The problem of discrimination, and techniques to be used in fighting it, will be treated later in Chapter XV.

the contrary, the dignity of man demands that the worker be considered as a moral equal who happens to be in a subordinate position. There is nothing inherently wrong in the idea of one person's being in authority over another. On the contrary, authority and subordination are necessary for orderly society. Parents should be able to give commands to their children. Policemen must have the power to direct traffic and keep public peace. But authority rightly used respects the rights of the person in an inferior position. It is used for his welfare, either directly or through his participation in the common good. This principle should be used as a test of industrial relations.

Recognition of the dignity of the worker in industrial life calls for many complex adjustments. At the very beginning of the employee relationship, the element of respect should enter. When a worker is hired, he should be treated as an individual, not merely as another name on the payroll. This means an effort to secure the right person for a job, careful explanation of his duties, opportunity to discover and correct his mistakes, transfer possibilities when needed, and a consistent program aimed at making a worker feel that he is a welcome partner in production. In-service training and advancement programs also help worker morale and minister to his human dignity. Finally, more enlightened firms have methods for taking care of the maladjusted and personality problems, ranging from workers who are merely "difficult" or odd to full-fledged alcoholics or the chronically antisocial.

It is important in this connection to note attitudes rather than techniques. The essential point is consideration of the basic dignity of employees; the means used may vary from plant to plant and from industry to industry. A sensitive employer will try to root out any element of unfairness in hiring workers, autocracy in the issuance of orders, a pace of operations too rapid for older workers, or any policies that prove to be irritants in labor-management relations. An employer should be benevolent, without being paternalistic. While kindness is important, consistent justice and equity are essential. Workers prefer fairness and a predictable set of principles, even though this means strict treatment, to changeable outbursts of good will and generosity. Likewise, if a choice were necessary, most would take equitable rules, minus the latest psychological techniques, in preference to techniques not backed up by principle. Of course, no dichotomy need exist here; it is possible to have both good principles and good techniques.

Even when the employer is fair in treating his workers, considered as individuals, he has not exhausted the possibilities inherent in their relationships. Workers rarely react to their work situation in a purely individualistic fashion. As a rule they form various types of social groupings, formal or informal, ranging from labor organizations to bowling teams or credit unions. Often strong loyalties to the groups concerned are developed. These loyalties need not conflict with loyalty to the company, unless management itself insists upon opposing a particular grouping. In most cases, the problem area is that involving the labor union. Because of the special importance of union-management relationships, the remainder of this chapter will be devoted to the complex issues they engender.

THE WORKER AND HIS UNION

Why Workers Organize. [Workers organize into labor unions for one primary reason: to deal more effectively with their employer.] Even when the employer is fair in his personnel policies, his employees may still need a union to protect their interests. The sheer complexity of many modern plants often makes it impossible to have good labor relations without the aid of independent representatives of the workers. There are too many layers of authority between top management and the man at the machine, too many opportunities for misunderstanding or misinterpretation of instructions, and too many occasions for damaging rumors to arise. [For the employer's own protection, he often needs experienced union leaders to handle grievances and negotiations.]

The case for the union is even stronger when an employer is not prepared to give his workers equitable treatment. In such cases, he has an enormous advantage over his employees, if they come to him as individuals. The average worker lacks the ability, experience, and knowledge necessary to present his case to an employer. He cannot usually marshal economic statistics to buttress a wage plea or quote legal authorities to support his rights. Even were he to make a good case, he has no economic power to back up his argument against an unyielding management. He needs the job more than the job needs him. By contrast, a union can give such workers economic information and legal aid. It also enables them to mount against the employer the serious economic threat of a concerted work stoppage. Under such circumstances the job does need the workers. Most employers are quite reluctant to provoke strikes, especially if they are not sure of the justice of their own position.

The right of workers to organize into unions of their own choosing is widely accepted both as a legal and a moral principle. Legally the right of organization is protected in the United States by federal law and often by state law as well. Morally, a labor union enjoys the general protection given by man's natural right of association, and the specific sanction given to a means necessary to secure certain basic human rights. Today it is rare for any responsible person in the United States to attack labor's right to organize. Even the most determined foes of unions deny that they oppose unionism as such.

We come to a more controversial point when we examine the question of a duty to join a union. Such a duty could arise because a labor union is necessary to secure essential ends for the worker, his family, or economic society. For example, it might be that only a union could obtain wage rates adequate for the health and welfare of the worker and the needs of his family. Or it might be argued that good unions are a first step in the direction of organized social order, as treated in Chapter VII. To prove these points, and thereby establish a duty to join a union, it is necessary to show that the union is uniquely able to secure a necessary end. This is often difficult to do without arguments so complex and involved that an opponent is rarely convinced. For instance, if the worker is satisfied with wages and working conditions in a nonunion plant, is one compelled to argue that he should develop "divine discontent" and seek changes? It is also possible that a worker may be dissatisfied, but unconvinced that unions would be effective or that they would not bring as many disadvantages as advantages. Finally, the argument that all must join unions in order to bring about a just social order begs the question in regard to the position of unions in relation to industry councils.

A more fruitful approach is to stress instead the virtue of social justice and the obligations it imposes upon all members of economic society. Undoubtedly the common good, under some circumstances, may be achieved only by the existence of a union in a particular plant and by universal participation in such a union. Even when a worker may be personally unconcerned with the goals sought by his fellow workers in organizing a union, he may not thereby remain indifferent. For example, he as a single worker may be content with his wage. But he must share the concern of married workers who contend that it is inadequate for their needs. Such obligations, in social justice and charity, are clear and beyond debate. It is better to emphasize definite duties of this nature rather than to hazard the more difficult task of establishing a universal duty to join unions. The end result may be the same in most cases, but the task of persuasion and conviction may be easier if we try the less ambitious approach. In view of the widely publicized charges that both communism and corruption have infected segments of the American labor movement in the past twenty years, an unqualified assertion that every worker has a duty to join a union may be a source of scandal to many of the faithful.

Duty to Recognize Unions. ⌊If workers have the right to form unions, employers have correlative duties to recognize such unions and to deal with them in collective bargaining.⌉ Such obligations are usually part of federal and state laws protecting union organization. But the moral principle goes further than most laws. For example, government bodies and nonprofit organizations are sometimes exempt from laws protecting unions. But there is no reason why employees of the government or of religious or charitable organizations should be considered second-class citizens in regard to union organization. Even where the right to strike may be surrendered (as with hospitals), it does not follow that collective bargaining is useless.

In general, employers should accept unions chosen freely by their workers. They have a moral and legal right to counsel their workers on the choice of a union, but they may not coerce them or interfere with them. If the union chosen turns out to be corrupt or communist-dominated, employers may be morally justified in fighting it or refusing to recognize it. Corrupt or communist influences may so divert a union from its legitimate ends that it ceases, in fact, to be primarily a labor union. But employers must be sure of their facts in regard to charges of this nature. Too often allegations of radicalism or corruption are made without sufficient evidence. Even when employers have moral certainty in regard to charges made against a union, they are still bound by law to deal with such a union, provided that it has fulfilled all the conditions required for National Labor Relations Board protection.

When churchmen act as employers, they have the same obligations toward workers as have other employers. Indeed, in the light of papal teaching, their conduct should be exemplary in regard to union recognition and collective bargaining. They would be expected to negotiate freely and willingly, invoke conciliation where differences have not been resolved, and even use arbitration in matters where its value is generally recognized. At the same time, it must be remembered that the Church as an employer has the same moral rights as other employers. Its negotiators may argue inability to pay, the need for safeguarding a going business, the case for considering ability above seniority in regard to promotions, and similar pleas. These representatives may fight union claims, even to the point of provoking a strike, when they are considered unjust. It is legitimate to refuse recognition to a communist-dominated or racketeering union. Good example does not involve automatic concession of every union claim. It simply means that Church employers practice the principles of social justice with fidelity and generosity.

Right-to-Work Laws. A particularly difficult problem connected with union organization involves right-to-work laws. These are laws which outlaw compulsory unionism. The nineteen or more states having such laws acknowledge labor's right to organize, but they forbid the union shop or any other device which forces a worker either to join a union or to retain membership after he has joined. It is argued, in favor of such laws, that it is un-American to force workers into unions. Furthermore, it is alleged that compulsory union membership favors racketeers and communists in unions. Workers are unable to leave such unions and thereby deprive vicious leaders of their support.

The traditional argument in favor of the union shop is that workers who receive the benefits of union protection should also pay the costs incurred by the union. It is also asserted that a union shop is the only real guarantee of workers' rights to organize, when the employer is hostile and there is a considerable degree of labor turnover. Otherwise, a union must spend all its time and energy organizing, merely to replace workers who have left the plant or the union. Finally, proponents of the union shop maintain that it is a precondition for labor-management peace. This is true because a union that lacks security must be constantly fighting management to justify its existence. A secure union, on the other hand, is free to work in a friendly and unaggressive fashion with employers.

The ethical arguments against compulsory union membership are not conclusive. The right to work is not an unconditional or unqualified right. It is usually surrounded by many social obligations, ranging from security checks to medical examinations, or from compulsory pension plans to requirements that workers buy company products. Nor are these limitations necessarily wrong. The right to work, like many other rights, must be exercised in the context of the common good.

It is true that the union shop probably makes it easier for racketeers and communists to maintain their power in a union. This point should not be exaggerated, however, since corrupt and Red-led unions seem to do as well in right-to-work states as do their more reputable fellows. At any rate, it is better to seek more direct methods for curing abuses within the union movement, and not to forbid a practice which long has fulfilled a legitimate need in American labor-management relations.

An unusual argument against the union shop is one directed exclusively to Catholics. It holds that the popes favor Catholic unions and merely tolerate neutral unions, at the same time demanding proper safeguards for the faith of the workers. Hence it is difficult enough to justify the joining of secular unions by Catholics, and impossible, they say, to excuse devices that force the faithful into such unions.

Catholic unions were originally formed to counter the virulently Marxist and antireligious unions of certain European nations. As such, they performed a needed function both of preserving the faith of workers and of indicating the Church's interest in the working class. No such unions were formed in Ireland, since there was little if any Marxist tradition in the Irish labor movement. By contrast there are Catholic unions in Quebec, but it is possible that they may merge with the secular A.F.L.-C.I.O. There has been no movement in the Catholic hierarchy of the United States in favor of Catholic unions. In view of such wide diversity of action throughout the world, known to the Holy See and at least tolerated by it, it seems a bit farfetched to bring up this point in connection with the right-to-work controversy.

The arguments cited in favor of the union shop are not absolute. They are presented in connection with American conditions at a given time. As such, they may not be valid in a nation where employers generally accept unions without question. They may even cease to be valid here, were conditions to change drastically. The best that one can do, in matters such as these, is to exercise the most careful prudential judgment as to what the common good demands in the circumstances. Others, holding the same Catholic principles, may see the facts differently and thus come to different conclusions. Principles are based on faith and authority, as well as upon sound reason. As such, they do not change. Policy, to the contrary, being based upon prudential judgment in concrete matters, allows for diversity and even disagreement.[2]

There is no doubt but that the Holy See has been concerned with monopolistic tendencies in labor unions. The June, 1948, address *To the Italian Workers*, two addresses in September, 1949 (*To Belgian Workers* and *To the German Catholics*), and the Christmas, 1952, message clearly indicate these concerns. The Pope is most unhappy about conjoining

[2] In the United States, the overwhelming majority of bishops and Catholic social scientists who have stated public views on right-to-work laws opposed such enactments. Several priests, however, have been articulate in favor of these laws.

"access to employment" with abusive political or social demands by unions. Certainly those who defend the union shop as best suited for labor peace in the United States should be equally vocal, as were the Ohio bishops, in insisting that proper measures be taken to see that the unions they defend are indeed worthy of such help.

A possible way out of the impasse connected with the union shop is what may be termed a "service-charge" agreement. Under this clause, all workers in the collective-bargaining unit pay a service charge to the union that bargains for them and handles their grievances. Membership in the union, however, is optional. Those who pay the slightly higher charge for union membership have the right to vote for officers, to vote on strike calls, and to share strike benefits and other privileges dispensed by the union.

American law has consistently favored the principle that a chosen bargaining agent should have exclusive rights to bargain for all members of the unit. The alternative here would be chaos in industrial relations. Since a chosen union is committed by law to serve all workers, whether members or not, it is reasonable to ask all workers to pay a fair charge for these services. Workers who object to union membership may remain outside, without being called "free loaders." They should have legal protection against excessive charges, in addition to their existing right to request decertification of an unsatisfactory union. Such an arrangement should give adequate security to unions and yet avoid the odium of compulsory union membership.

COLLECTIVE BARGAINING

The most common purpose of union organization is collective bargaining over wages, hours, and working conditions. Unions represent their members in seeking agreement upon a contract which governs their employment. This fact implies many rights and duties both in regard to unions and employers.

Aims of Collective Bargaining. Union-management negotiations in collective bargaining should seek to give both workers and employers their rights and their equitable claims in matters of wages, hours, and working conditions. Workers have a right to a just wage and hours and working conditions consonant with their human dignity. The employer has a right to a fair profit and responsible performance of work by his employees. Moreover, the public has a right to expect conscientious dealings on both sides, so that unnecessary strikes or lockouts will not cause serious inconvenience or even hardship. In addition to rights there are equitable claims. The worker is seeking higher standards of living than the minimum of strict justice. The employer desires wholehearted co-operation from his workers. And the public wishes to share in the gains achieved through increased productivity.

The real problems in collective bargaining usually fall within the domain of claims for better conditions, rather than the area of rights. The demand for a living wage, for hours which do not endanger health or interfere with family life, and for working conditions consonant with human dignity is not likely to cause serious theoretical objections from the employer. At most he might object that he is unable to meet all the demands, but he is not likely to contest their justice. Thus, the right to grievance machinery, assuring the worker of a system of appeals against conditions which he finds oppressive, is a matter of justice. It is a recognition of human dignity. Social justice likewise favors provisions regulating job security. Protection against arbitrary discharge is equitable. More controversial are seniority provisions regulating layoffs and promotions. In view of the fact that older workers are generally family men, it is consonant with human dignity to afford them job protection. The employer is benefited through the retention of a stable and contented working force. Likewise, it is equitable to invoke seniority in promotion where abilities are equal. The principle of absolute seniority in promotion, disregarding ability, is less acceptable. It might be legitimate where the nature of work is such that skills do not vary appreciably. But it would not be suitable in regard to promotion to executive positions where abilities are usually the controlling factor.

Other items in union contracts, such as paid vacations and holidays, are more in the nature of claims than rights. They raise the worker's standard of living and may legitimately be sought when the condition of business permits. But an employer who might give two week's vacation with pay would be within his rights in turning down a request for a third. The same reasoning would apply to claims such as pensions, a guarantee of work or wages, and medical insurance. If the employer is not paying a living wage, the workers may in justice demand either a living wage or its equivalent through pensions and medical plans. But where these are claims above the minimum standard, it is equally legitimate for workers to ask them and for employers to deny them. These are problems of equity rather than justice.

The fact that demands in collective bargaining often go beyond the realm of rights into the more shadowy ground of claims and interests does much to explain the difficult problems connected with strikes or lockouts. If every work stoppage were based upon clear problems of justice, it would be relatively simple to judge who was right and to provide machinery for enforcing the rights involved. In fact, however, it is extraordinarily difficult to judge the merits of a strike or a lockout.

Justice in Strikes. Strikes are to collective bargaining what quarrels are to married life. They are temporary breakdowns of unity, leading to widely varying results. They can clear the air and bring a new and better understanding. Or they may create lasting bitterness, smoldering beneath a surface truce. Finally, they can cause a complete break in relationships between the affected parties. Furthermore, like quarrels between spouses, they are often the source of serious suffering to innocent third parties. Because of the problems occasioned by industrial disputes, sound social principles circumscribe the right to strike with many qualifications.

That workers in general have the right to strike is usually conceded. Some authors are so concerned with possible evils that they consider the strike a weapon of extreme desperation, to be used only when its necessity is clear and overwhelming. Others are not so rigorous in demanding justification for work stoppages. The American public justifies strikes on the grounds that workers cannot be compelled to remain at the job. Moralists are more likely to emphasize the justice of workers' claims as the excusing circumstance. They permit a strike for a just cause when other means of securing fair treatment fail. Many writers compare a strike to war and pose similar conditions for its justification. The strike must be (1) for a just cause; (2) necessary because other means have failed; (3) such that the gains sought will outweigh the evils occasioned, with a reasonable hope for success in the strike; and (4) carried on by lawful and morally sanctioned means. These conditions imply many complex decisions.

A just cause involves at least some claim which is fair and equitable. As noted before, we do not limit collective bargaining (and consequently strikes) to matters of strict justice. Otherwise, workers would have little chance to improve their conditions. Indeed, the economy itself might suffer, since the constant goad of worker demands forces employers to use more efficient methods and thus benefit the entire nation. Between demands that are beyond doubt matters of justice and exactions that are clearly unjust lies a no man's land of claims and interests. Such claims may be pressed even to the point of a strike, but the employer who rejects them and permits the strike is not of necessity acting unjustly.

For this reason, and others, the concrete determination of the justice or equity of a strike issue is not easy. The critic must understand the realities of industrial relations to be able to appraise correctly the issues involved. Thus, a strike for noneconomic reasons, such as for union recognition, may be vitally important for the workers. Only when the union is recognized may they be sure that their rights can be enforced. Again, workers may strike over an unjustified discharge of a fellow worker. Here they feel that precedent is essential, in that if the principle of unjustified discharge is allowed, no worker may be safe. On the other hand, there have been strikes motivated by considerations of union or civic politics. It is unjust for a union leader to provoke a strike merely for the sake of his own personal pique or ambition. Political strikes, especially general strikes, are usually wrong, since there are better alternative methods in a democracy for securing political ends. They may not always be wrong, since sometimes they are a dramatic form of the right of petition, calling public attention to the inadequacy or injustice of administrative decisions. As an illustration, it sometimes happens that a legal means exists for settling a dispute without recourse to a strike, but that the use of this means involves intolerable delays, often for years. Direct efforts to secure a settlement seem justified here.

Even more difficult are problems connected with secondary, sympathy, and jurisdictional disputes. In these cases, the employer is often an innocent victim caught in the crossfire between warring parties. There is little difficulty when the employer of primary and secondary strikers is the same person. Thus, if Corporation A had a strike in its New York plant called for a just cause, workers in its Detroit plant could strike to enforce the just claim of their fellow employees. Again, if one employer in an industry had a strike, and workers for other employers in the same industry had reason to feel that conditions obtained through the strike would become general, they might reasonably go out for their own protection. Otherwise, they would be victims of the divide-and-conquer strategy. Father Clune goes further and justifies, on the principle of indirect voluntary, a strike against the main supplier of a mill which is trying to break a just strike through the use of strikebreakers.[3] But he would not concede the justice

---

[3] Cf. G. Clune, *Christian Social Reorganization* (Dublin: Browne and Nolan, 1940), pp. 416–417. The moral principle of the indirect voluntary permits a person to perform an action which is in itself morally good or indifferent, but from which an evil result may follow. This is permitted provided that the agent acts from correct motives, that the good result does not follow as a result of the evil, and that the reason for acting is sufficiently serious to outweigh the unintended but foreseen evil. Thus, a woman might, to save her life, permit radium treatments for cancer of the cervix, even though this might result in sterility.

of a sympathy strike merely because what hurts labor in one place hurts all workers. In other words, where workers have a real and tangible, even though indirect and secondary, interest in a just strike, this may be an excusing reason for them to go on strike. But if the interest is remote and fanciful, they would not be justified in striking.

Jurisdictional disputes are strikes over the allocation of work. They may be sanctioned where the employer has clearly violated a contract or the unwritten customs of the trade. But where he is merely an innocent party, a victim to the conflict of claims between two unions, such a strike does not seem just. In such cases social justice would call for resort to other methods, such as an impartial board to arbitrate the claims. If the affected parties cannot agree to disinterested judgment, then the state has the right and duty to enforce such an agreement.

A common cause of jurisdictional disputes is the action of specialty employers, often employing only one craft, in spreading out to fields traditionally handled by other crafts. Contractors may be as often the cause as the victim of such disputes. The complexity of these issues shows the wisdom of the Taft-Hartley clause which encouraged union-management machinery to solve them. On the whole these committees have done a good job. They have proved the value of subsidiarity.

Likewise, there are industries and occupations where the public interest is so paramount that strikes may not be tolerated or, at best, permitted as a last resort. Here the clear demands of the common good transcend the interests of the parties. In such cases alternate methods for solving the dispute must be set up, even though they involve techniques (such as compulsory arbitration) that would otherwise be unacceptable. One might here distinguish between an absolute and a relative public interest. In the first case, even one day's strike would be intolerable. This would be true of police, the army, firemen, emergency nurses in a hospital, electric power workers (if no service at all were maintained), or a total paralysis of all means of public transportation on a broad scale. In the second case, grave public inconvenience would be caused, but no disaster provided the strike were not prolonged unduly. This would be true of telephones, a major form of transportation, garbage collection, atomic energy production in time of international tension, war strikes in major industries, coal mining, oil transportation or production, milk and food delivery, or a limited strike in electric power production.

In the first instance, strikes should be prohibited by law, with compulsory settlement of disputes. In the second category, strikes should be delayed by law, with public hearings and other pressures for an equitable settlement and an emergency power to stop the strike when disaster threatened. It does not follow from this that all strikes by public workers are unjustified. Many public servants are not performing emergency duties. Often a strike is the only means for publicizing the conditions of underpaid or mistreated government workers. Federal or state laws to prohibit such strikes by public workers are unjust if they do not provide effective alternative means for meeting rights and equitable claims.

To summarize, in normal disputes between employers and their workers, a just cause for a strike may be found either in a right which has been denied or an equitable claim which is being pressed. This principle may be applied with limitations to secondary and sympathy strikes where the workers are striving for valid claims which otherwise might be lost. Even greater limitations should be imposed on jurisdictional strikes since satisfactory alternate methods for handling such disputes can be set up. Finally, in industries or occupations vitally affecting the public interest, the public good demands other means than a strike for deciding the justice of the case.

Other Conditions for a Strike. A strike for a just cause is not legitimate if other means of settlement are not exhausted. The normal means of settlement are negotiation, conciliation, and arbitration. Thus, it is unjust to call a "quickie" strike to settle a dispute, if no efforts have been made to negotiate the point. Damage is thus caused to the employer and the public, without reasonable attempts to forestall this evil. There may be cases where solid grounds exist to believe that negotiations would be useless and that the employer would use the time to prepare strikebreaking methods. In such a situation, a sudden strike might be justified. Normally, however, both parties should attempt to bargain in good faith until it is clear that no settlement can be reached. Genuine collective bargaining involves efforts by both sides to present reasonable offers and to discuss the merits of the issues in question. A take-it-or-leave-it attitude is permissible only after a complete breakdown of fair discussions. A certain amount of "padding" of claims or the use of poker-playing methods is not unfair, since such tactics are usually expected and discounted in advance.

When negotiations break down, federal or state conciliation machinery is usually available. At times, private parties may serve as mediators. Here again both groups are bound in justice to use such services, unless there are solid reasons to believe that conciliation is invoked merely to waste time and weaken the economic power of one party. Since there are profound psychological elements involved in the negotiation of contracts, it is often helpful to gain the aid of friendly or disinterested third persons.

If conciliation fails, it is possible to submit the dispute to judicial arbitration. Many industries have permanent arbitrators who handle contract disputes as well as grievances. In other cases, ad hoc arbitration is invoked when a situation reaches an impasse. On the other hand, most industries and labor unions are violently opposed to arbitration of issues, claims, and even rights in the negotiation of contracts. Employers claim that this means the abdication of basic managerial rights to an outsider who rarely can be as familiar with the industry as the parties directly concerned. Unions likewise are reluctant to entrust their rights or even claims to a third party. If disputes were only over rights, there would be less difficulty. But interests and claims are not easily subject to judicial decision. Even where economic rights are involved, such as a fair wage, an employer may be understandably reluctant to entrust to another a decision which may mean the life or death of the company.

Compulsory arbitration, enforced by law, amounts to complete government control over industry and labor, since the economics of collective bargaining are far-reaching in their implications. Moreover, the existence of an outside court often tends to break down normal collective bargaining. One party or the other merely goes through the motions, hoping to gain more from the outside agency than it could get directly. All these results are seriously contrary to the common good and hence involve a violation of social justice. Compulsory arbitration might more easily be justified in the administration of a contract previously reached by collective bargaining. The contract settles clearly defined and limited rights and claims, so that its carrying out is a matter of justice. Actually, most modern agreements do have such an arbitration clause.

Compulsory arbitration, with all its limitations, is likewise acceptable for jurisdictional disputes and absolute public interest disputes. In these cases, the evils caused by a strike outweigh the disadvantages attendant upon compulsory settlement of claims. Decisions in jurisdictional disputes are more akin to the interpretation of contracts and customs than they are to the awarding of claims. There is usually a body of precedent or analogy to similar situations which permits equitable decisions in such matters. In regard to absolute public-interest disputes, these industries or occupations are usually under a fair degree of government control already. Thus, compulsory arbitration would not here be extending appreciably the area of state penetration into private life.

The third major condition, that a strike should promise more good than the evil it occasions and that it have some chance of success, likewise must be judged in the light of industrial realities. Often workers remain on strike for a single cent an hour more than has been offered by the employer. It may take them years to gain what they seem to have lost in wages. Yet, there are intangibles involved in such situations which preclude an oversimplified treatment. Unions may feel that concessions made one year would be a precedent for further pressures later. There may be a principle of discrimination involved, with one union getting less than another. This could lead to the playing off of one against the other until both were rendered impotent. Or the surface cause of a dispute may be but a last straw in a long history of irritations, just as quarrels between individuals may erupt violently for apparently slight reasons. Thus, it is almost impossible to generalize as to which causes of strikes outweigh the attendant evils. This has to be done in each individual case by persons experienced in the ways of industrial life.

Finally, the last condition of a just strike is that it should be waged by morally acceptable means. It is not legitimate to engage in sabotage or other destruction of the employer's property. Nor is violence permissible, save in self-defense against clearly threatened violence from groups supporting the employer. If the employer uses strikebreakers against a just strike, the strikers would be permitted to boycott and attempt to persuade others to boycott goods so produced. This is merely inducing people not to cooperate in an unjust action by buying products made under unethical conditions. Picketing is lawful for the same reasons. Of course, there are forms of mass picketing which are conducive to violence. But mass picketing is not in itself wrong, since it has a legitimate purpose which may be intended. It is a more effective manner of advertising the strike. Striker morale and solidarity are aided when strikers see their fellows on the picket line. Not all strike violence is induced by strikers. In the past, and in some industrially backward parts of the country today, it was a standard employer tactic to provoke violence so as to discredit strikers.

If all the four conditions laid down are fulfilled, a strike may be just. Of course, it is impossible to make any generalization as to run-of-the-mill American strikes and to say whether or not they have often been just. Two points do have validity: with some exceptions, union leaders do not sanction strikes without serious reason, since the risk they run is too great; second, many newspapers do not give fair reports of the strikers' case, either through bias or through the necessary brevity found in tabloids or provincial papers largely interested in local news. Hence it is necessary to find the facts before judging.

If a strike (or lockout) appears to be justified by the criteria just outlined, we should blame any inconvenience caused by the strike or lockout upon the party who is responsible in the dispute. This, of course, need not be the party who ordered the stoppage. Moreover, we should not co-operate with the party at fault by any activity on our part. This could mean refusing to cross picket lines or buy "hot goods." Such an obligation would be particularly strong for a person in a position of influence, since his actions may well determine the success or failure of the work stoppage.

In conclusion, it might be said that the prevalence and importance of strikes is frequently overstressed. Strikes are dramatic, whereas industrial peace seems prosaic. Lincoln Steffens observed that any newspaper can "break" a police chief simply by reporting and headlining routine crime news. Similarly, a bad public opinion can be created in regard to unions by overemphasis upon exceptional strikes, to the neglect of continuing examples of labor-management co-operation. The percentage of total working time lost by strikes during the period of dramatic headlines (1947–1949) was 0.46. By 1963, the average had dropped to 0.13 per cent. These figures are somewhat low, since they measure only direct stoppages, not indirect effects. Nor do they allow for the unusual impact of highly critical strikes. But they do serve as a useful antidote to exaggeration.

THE DUTIES OF LABOR

Labor has duties as well as rights. It must deal fairly with employers. Unions should be honestly and effectively run. And, in all cases, the rights of the public must be observed.

Duties Toward Employers. A worker is bound in justice to work diligently and fairly in return for a decent wage. "An honest day's work for an honest day's pay" is the old maxim. Conscientious work means more than avoidance of loafing. It also involves care of property, concern with the quality of work, and a proper interest in the welfare of the employer.

Difficult practical problems arise in regard to such practices as stretching out work, "feather-bedding," or "made-work." Usually these practices are motivated by the effort to preserve and extend employment in a declining industry. Unfortunately, this approach is self-defeating, since it increases costs and hence accentuates the fall-off in demand for products or services.

Labor must learn that production of wealth is the only basis for its income. Increases gained through abuse of a monopoly position, without any gain of productivity, are morally wrong and economically suicidal.

Organized labor should recognize the evils of restrictive practices, whatever their subjective justification. More than any other practice, they give unions a bad name in the public mind. The public expects fair value when it pays a worker. It is understandably resentful when necessities are high priced because of work limitation. This is particularly the case in times of full employment. Here soldiering and feather-bedding may well be contrary to strict justice. At any time, the unions concerned would be wise to prepare a constructive, long-range program for remedying the conditions which have occasioned these practices.

In this light a special duty of workers, in social justice, is their willingness to co-operate with management to secure more efficient production. Labor-management co-operation is one of the main techniques for raising living standards. Moreover, it is desirable for its own sake since class hostility is contrary to the nature of industrial life. As was observed before, the uniting force of production is as important as the divisive force of distribution. This duty of co-operation implies a corresponding willingness of employers to do their share in meeting the legitimate demands of labor. Workers must be assured that generous efforts on their part will not mean that they will work themselves out of their jobs. The resulting increase must be distributed fairly among the workers, as well as among stockholders and consumers.

With all the faults of some unions, employers must bear a large share of the blame for an aggressive situation. They often get the type of union that their own conduct calls for. When they are "hard boiled" and try to break the union, it will become a fighting organization. If they are coldly impersonal, the union normally takes a strictly business attitude. Here one has an armed peace rather than either co-operation or conflict. Occasionally one finds collusion rather than real co-operation, the difference being that both sides unite in policies contrary to the public interest. More frequently there is a situation which might be called accommodation, where common interests are recognized but only in a limited fashion. Conflict and hostility are avoided, but positive friendliness and complete mutuality are absent. The test of full co-operation is progression beyond normal collective bargaining to the level of joint efforts to increase productivity and to lower costs. It is this final stage which is the aim of Catholic social teaching.

Duties in Regard to Unions. Workers have many duties as union members. Among these one of the most important is that they make the effort to see that their union follows sound principles. This involves attendance at meetings, conscientious voting in union elections, and even running for union office. Where unions have gone bad, either through communism or racketeering, there is nearly always a history of poorly attended union meetings. Workers are often content to let small cliques or factions run their unions, provided they get results. At times, this produces an entrenched bureaucracy which consolidates its power either through a political machine or by changing the union constitution. In this light, the obligation to take interest in union matters might well be compared to one's civic obligations, the more so since unions today are quasi-public institutions. Union members should not emulate corporation stockholders in the doubtful practice of evading responsibility behind the anonymity of a large organization.

At the same time, workers should avoid the opposite extreme of undue pressure on union officers. Holding union office is a task beset with many trials and rewarded with ingratitude and abuse. It is almost a vocation rather than an attractive profession. While some union leaders may live well, a majority works long hours, particularly at night, under extreme tension. For one overpaid union racketeer, there are hundreds of underpaid and overworked servants of workers. So true is this that there exists at times a problem of social justice in relation to union employees. Unions, like church and similar groups, occasionally expect their workers to toil long hours at inadequate pay for the sake of the cause.

Union officers in turn have duties toward their members. They owe them faithful and honest service, representing them with integrity and courage. They should consider themselves as servants of the workers. Any trend in the direction of autocracy and dictatorship violates the human dignity of the members. This does not mean that some discipline and leadership are not useful in unions. On the contrary, they are essential if the union is to function smoothly. Since public interest demands that labor organizations act as responsible and trustworthy groups, their leaders must have some power to enforce continuity of policy. It would be intolerable if any agreement were subject to repudiation by a small but vocal minority of members.

Union officials should insist that orderly methods be followed in handling grievances, with no wildcat and unauthorized strikes. They should have the courage to stand for sound policy. When their experience tells them that membership wishes are unwise, they should use all their ability to persuade the members to follow a wiser course.

These same officials should serve the interest of their members in relation to the employer. While they should explore all forms of labor-management co-operation, such activities must be open and upright. Collusive, underhand dealing with employers to the detriment of the workers is thoroughly dishonest. A union official who accepts secret payments from company officials to "go light" in his demands upon them is like a grafting public official. He betrays trust and is guilty of dishonesty. If the betrayal is serious, one might say that he has no right in justice to the salary which he takes from the union. He is receiving it only through fraud and deception. Of course, there is no objection to personal friendliness between union officials and corporation executives. A private chat at the dinner table might solve problems in an hour which would take weeks in a grievance committee. The motivation behind such meetings should be the controlling factor in judging their propriety.

Finally, officers of unions should be honest in handling the funds of the membership. It is desirable to have preliminary financial reports of a local on a quarterly basis, at least, with an annual detailed audit of funds both of the local and of the parent union. Members likewise should have fair opportunity to vote for their leaders in an honest election. In view of past abuses, there is a case for government regulation of such matters, in the attempt to preserve genuine democracy in unions. Labor groups today are no longer private associations; they are quasi-public bodies and hence have public responsibility.

All these observations are particularly pertinent in connection with Senate hearings on labor corruption, held during the years 1956–1958. These led to the passage of the Labor-Management Reporting and Disclosure Act of 1959 (Landrum-Griffin Act). This Act guarantees certain basic rights to union members such as the right to democratic procedures in the conduct of the union, protection against unfair assessments or disciplinary actions, and safeguards for those who seek outside help when treated unfairly by union officials. It requires extensive reports from such officials and also from employers. Strict controls are imposed on the use of union funds. Communists may not hold union office for five years after termination of party membership. Likewise certain convicted criminals are barred for five years after conviction. It should be noted in this connection that several unions have voluntarily established public-review boards, staffed by impartial outside experts, to insure fair and democratic procedures within these unions.

Duties Toward the Public. One of the aspects of labor's duties toward the public was examined earlier, in connection with the morality of strikes. Strikes called for trivial or unworthy reasons cause hardships to employers and to the public, without any compensating justification. In addition, unions should carefully examine their position in regard to charges of wage inflation. This point will be treated in the following chapter.

The internal conduct of labor unions, also studied previously, is a matter of public interest today. But good conduct is not merely a matter of avoiding corruption or autocracy. It also involves positive acceptance of community responsibilities and a certain maturity commensurate with labor's power. Most labor leaders are eager to assume such duties. They take their part in community-chest programs, Red Cross drives, and public-school activities. But the labor movement could acquire more finesse in public relations. It could drop the class-hostility approach in its press and speeches, particularly in areas where employers are reasonable in dealing with unions. There is no reason why the labor press should often read like a page from a nineteenth-century socialist publication. Business as a whole has shown more awareness of the need for good public relations than has the labor movement. Fine words may not always be backed up by deeds in the business community. But labor too often has concealed fine deeds behind the smokescreen of careless public utterances.

Pope John XXIII has outlined one outstanding area of public service which he considers appropriate for union officials. He argued that workers should be given the opportunity to exert their influence on a scale much broader than labor-management relations. Since economic decisions made by national governments and by international bodies are often more important for the welfare of individual companies than any action they take themselves, workers should have the right to participate in such broad-range policies. Here workers and their representatives act as a matter of full right, since they are dealing with public affairs, and not the private economic decisions of individual firms.

In the United States, organized labor has long been interested in national and international problems that affect the economy. Union officials follow proposed legislation with great care and often testify on measures before Congress. They likewise have participated in such international bodies as the International Labor Organization. Nor has their concern been exclusively the interest of labor itself. Unions have often argued for the general interest of the community, thus seeking peace and prosperity for all peoples. It is unfortunate that the public is often unaware of these civic-minded activities and hence fails to give proper credit to the union officials involved.

If business and labor both can develop a sense of broader interests and responsibilities, we can move toward replacing group individualism with a genuine sense of concern for the common good. Thus we approach, step by step, that happy unity of society which can bring industrial peace and economic prosperity.

READINGS*

J. Y. Calvez and J. Perrin, *The Church and Social Justice*, Chaps, 10–13, 18.
J. F. Cronin, *Christianity and Social Progress*, Chaps. 8–9.
J. F. Cronin and H. W. Flannery, *The Church and the Workingman*, Chaps. 3–4.
B. W. Dempsey, *The Functional Economy*, Chap. 13.
H. Johnston, *Business Ethics*, Chaps. 9, 11.
B. L. Masse, *Justice for All*, Chaps. 7–8.
J. Messner, *Social Ethics* (rev. ed.), pp. 834–840.

* For further readings, consult List No. 7 in the Appendix.

Chapter X

THE LIVING WAGE AND FULL EMPLOYMENT

THE LIVING WAGE

Leo XIII, Rerum Novarum

51. Nay, in this respect, [their energy and effectiveness are so important that it is incontestable that the wealth of nations arises from no other source than from the labor of workers. Equity therefore commands that public authority show proper concern for the worker so that from what he contributes to the common good he may receive what will enable him, housed, clothed, and secure, to live his life without hardship.] Whence it follows that all those measures ought to be favored which seem in any way capable of benefiting the condition of workers. Such solicitude is so far from injuring anyone, that it is destined rather to benefit all, because it is of absolute interest to the state that those citizens should not be miserable in every respect from whom such necessary goods proceed.

61. We shall now touch upon a matter of very great importance, and one which must be correctly understood in order to avoid falling into error on one side or the other. We are told that free consent fixes the amount of a wage; that therefore the employer, after paying the wage agreed to, would seem to have discharged his obligation and not to owe anything more; that only then would injustice be done if either the employer should refuse to pay the whole amount of the wage, or the worker should refuse to perform all the work to which he had committed himself; and that in these cases, but in no others, is it proper for the public authority to intervene to safeguard the rights of each party.

62. An impartial judge would not assent readily or without reservation to this reasoning, because it is not complete in all respects; one factor to be considered, and one of the greatest importance, is missing. To work is to expend one's energy for the purpose of securing the things necessary for the various needs of life and especially for its preservation. "In the sweat of thy face shalt thou eat bread." Accordingly, in man labor has two marks, as it were, implanted by nature, so that it is truly personal, because work energy inheres in the person and belongs completely to him by whom it is expended and for whose use it is destined by nature; and, secondly, that it is necessary, because man has need of the fruit of his labors to preserve his life, and nature itself, which must be most strictly obeyed, commands him to preserve it. If labor should be considered only under the aspect that it is personal, there is no doubt that it would be entirely in the worker's power to set

the amount of the agreed wage at too low a figure. For inasmuch as he performs work by his own free will, he can also by his own free will be satisfied with either a paltry wage for his work or even with none at all. But this matter must be judged far differently, if with the factor of personality we combine the factor of necessity, from which indeed the former is separable in thought but not in reality. In fact, to preserve one's life is a duty common to all individuals, and to neglect this duty is a crime. Hence arises necessarily the right of securing things to sustain life, and only a wage earned by his labor gives a poor man the means to acquire these things.

63. Let it be granted then that workers and employers may enter freely into agreements and, in particular, concerning the amount of the wage; yet there is always underlying such agreements an element of natural justice, and one greater and more ancient than the free consent of contracting parties, namely, that the wage shall not be less than enough to support a worker who is thrifty and upright. If, compelled by necessity or moved by fear of a worse evil, a worker accepts a harder condition, which although against his will he must accept because the employer or contractor imposes it, he certainly submits to force, against which justice cries out in protest.

Pius XI, Quadragesimo Anno

69. It is obvious that, as in the case of ownership, so in the case of work, especially work hired out to others, there is a social aspect also to be considered in addition to the personal or individual aspect. For man's productive effort cannot yield its fruit unless a truly social and organic body exists, unless a social and juridical order watches over the exercise of work, unless the various occupations, being interdependent, co-operate with and mutually complete one another, and, what is still more important, unless mind, material things, and work combine and form as it were a single whole. Therefore, where the social and individual nature of work is neglected, it will be impossible to evaluate work justly and pay it according to justice.

71. . . . Every effort must therefore be made that fathers of families receive a wage large enough to meet ordinary family needs adequately. But if this cannot always be done under existing circumstances, social justice

demands that changes be introduced as soon as possible whereby such a wage will be assured to every adult workingman. It will not be out of place here to render merited praise to all who, with a wise and useful purpose, have tried and tested various ways of adjusting the pay for work to family burdens in such a way that, as these increase, the former may be raised and indeed, if the contingency arises, there may be enough to meet extraordinary needs.

72. In determining the amount of the wage, the condition of a business and of the one carrying it on must also be taken into account; for it would be unjust to demand excessive wages which a business cannot stand without its ruin and consequent calamity to the workers. If, however, a business makes too little money, because of lack of energy or lack of initiative or because of indifference to technical and economic progress, that must not be regarded a just reason for reducing the compensation of the workers. But if the business in ques-

tion is not making enough money to pay the workers an equitable wage because it is being crushed by unjust burdens or forced to sell its product at less than a just price, those who are thus the cause of the injury are guilty of grave wrong, for they deprive workers of their just wage and force them under the pinch of necessity to accept a wage less than fair.

73. Let, then, both workers and employers strive with united strength and counsel to overcome the difficulties and obstacles and let a wise provision on the part of public authority aid them in so salutary a work. If, however, matters come to an extreme crisis, it must be finally considered whether the business can continue or the workers are to be cared for in some other way. In such a situation, certainly most serious, a feeling of close relationship and a Christian concord of minds ought to prevail and function effectively among employers and workers.

74. Lastly, the amount of the pay must be adjusted to the public economic good. We have shown above how much it helps the common good for workers and other employees, by setting aside some part of their income which remains after necessary expenditures, to attain gradually to the possession of a moderate amount of wealth.

Pius XI, On Atheistic Communism

32. We explained clearly [in *Quadragesimo Anno*] the right and dignity of labor, the relations of mutual aid and collaboration which should exist between those who possess capital and those who work, the salary due in strict justice to the worker for himself and for his family.

49. The wage earner is not to receive as alms what is his due in justice. And let no one attempt with trifling charitable donations to exempt himself from the great duties imposed by justice.

52. But social justice cannot be said to have been satisfied as long as working men are denied a salary that will enable them to secure proper sustenance for themselves and for their families; as long as they are denied the opportunity of acquiring a modest fortune and forestalling the plague of universal pauperism; as long as they cannot make suitable provision through public or private insurance for old age, for periods of illness and unemployment.

53. It happens all too frequently, however, under the salary system, that individual employers are helpless to ensure justice unless, with a view to its practice, they organize institutions the object of which is to prevent competition incompatible with fair treatment for the workers. Where this is true, it is the duty of contractors and employers to support and promote such necessary organizations as normal instruments enabling them to fulfill their obligations of justice. But the laborers, too, must be mindful of their duty to love and deal fairly with their employers, and persuade themselves that there is no better means of safeguarding their own interests.

Pius XI, Casti Connubii

123. And so, in the first place, every effort should be made to bring about that which Our Predecessor Leo XIII, of happy memory, has already insisted upon, namely, that in the state such economic and social meth-

ods should be adopted as will enable every head of a family to earn as much as, according to his station in life, is necessary for himself, his wife, and for the rearing of his children, for "the laborer deserves his wages" (Luke x, 7). To deny this, or to make light of what is equitable, is a grave injustice and is placed among the greatest sins by Holy Writ (Deut. xxiv, 14, 15); nor is it lawful to fix such a scanty wage as will be insufficient for the upkeep of the family in the circumstances in which it is placed.

126. If, however, for this purpose, private resources do not suffice, it is the duty of the public authority to supply for the insufficient forces of individual effort, particularly in a matter which is of such importance to the commonweal, touching as it does the maintenance of the family and married people.

Pius XII, To International Union of Family Organizations, September 20, 1949

The popes, in their social messages, have strongly favored the family or social wage, which gives the family the power to rear children in proportion to their increasing number. . . . Naturally, it is fitting to note that more attention is needed for large families: reduction of taxes, [granting] subsidies [and] allowances, considered not as pure gifts, but as a modest grant for the most valuable service rendered by the family, and especially the large family.

John XXIII, Mater et Magistra

71. We therefore consider it Our duty to reaffirm that the remuneration of work is not something that can be left to the laws of the marketplace; nor should it be a decision left to the will of the more powerful. It must be determined in accordance with justice and equity; which means that workers must be paid a wage which allows them to live a truly human life and to fulfill their family obligations in a worthy manner. Other factors too enter into the assessment of a just wage: namely, the effective contribution which each individual makes to the economic effort, the financial state of the company for which he works, the requirements of the general good of the particular country — having regard especially to the repercussions on the overall employment of the working force in the country as a whole — and finally the requirements of the common good of the universal family of nations of every kind, both large and small.

72. The above principles are valid always and everywhere. So much is clear. But their degree of applicability to concrete cases cannot be determined without reference to the quantity and quality of available resources; and these can — and in fact do — vary from country to country, and even, from time to time, within the same country.

78. But a further point needs emphasizing: Any adjustment between wages and profits must take into account the demands of the common good of the particular country and of the whole human family.

79. What are these demands? On the national level they include: employment of the greatest possible number of workers; care lest privileged

classes arise, even among the workers; maintenance of equilibrium between wages and prices; the need to make goods and services accessible to the greatest number; elimination, or at least the restriction, of inequalities in the various branches of the economy — that is, between agriculture, industry, and services; creation of a proper balance between economic expansion and the development of social services, especially through the activity of public authorities; the best possible adjustment of the means of production to the progress of science and technology; seeing to it that the benefits which make possible a more human way of life will be available not merely to the present generation but to the coming generations as well.

Hierarchy of Quebec, Pastoral Letter, February, 1950

131. In the present state of labor relations, a collective bargaining agreement negotiated with a labor union may be considered as the normal means for determining a just wage. It ceases to be such a norm, however, if imposed by undue pressure from any source.

Australian Hierarchy, Standard of Living, September, 1954

In social justice, as distinct from strict justice, the state must come to the relief of the family man. Nor should it be urged that the state is asked to give a gratuitous subsidy to the family. For apart from the duty of Christian charity, the man who marries and rears a family renders an important and vital service to the stability, progress and defense of the state, and the state should willingly discharge its debt. Indeed, in Australia the state acknowledges this obligation when it provides child endowments and other social benefits.

The worker with a family responsibility, therefore, in addition to the wage which he, like the single man, is entitled to get from his employer, will receive from public funds a social benefit allowance for his wife and for each child dependent on him.

To apply these general principles in practice, we suggest the following arrangement:

1. There should be a Standard Wage, which would be that of a single man. This would cover his essential needs of food, clothing and shelter. It would provide a modest amount for recreation, and enable him to make partial provision for marriage. It would enable him to begin to make suitable provision, through public and private insurance, for old age, for periods of illness and unemployment. It would provide some opportunity whereby the prudent man, by the practice of thrift, could acquire a moderate amount of property for himself. The same amount would be fixed for either sex.

2. On his marriage, the worker would be entitled to an increase in income to provide now for his wife in addition to himself, and to provide also for savings in anticipation of the birth of a child. He would also be entitled to a bonus to enable him to purchase in part his house and furniture.

3. On the birth of each child, he would be entitled to an added weekly payment to cover the cost of his dependent children. Endowments for dependents should remain so long as dependency exists.

AUTOMATION

Pius XII, To Christian Union of Executives and Businessmen, March 7, 1957

It is also foreseen that the age of automation will constantly reassert the pre-eminence of intellectual values among the productive class: knowledge, ingenuity, organization, foresight.

There is no doubt that the period of transition may result in an increase of unemployment among older workers, who are less adapted to new training; but younger laborers as well are faced with the same danger whenever a nation is forced to hasten its steps toward automation because of competition with other countries.

This is why it is necessary to make suitable plans, starting now, so that the dynamism of technology may not result in a public calamity. In every case, producers must accept the principle that technology is at the service of the economy, and not vice versa.

Pius XII, To Christian Associations of Italian Workers, June 7, 1957

Automation involves, above all, the danger of confusing technical productivity with economic productivity.

. . . automation achieves a fantastic increase in . . . productive capacities. But will it, on the other hand, involve a true growth of productivity in the national economy? By this we mean a lasting and sure attainment of conditions which will make possible the material and human well-being of every member of the population, and in which all those who contribute immediately — with their labor, their property, their capital — to the national economy will receive a return corresponding to their investment. Further, such a state of economic production ought to be capable of giving an easy solution to social tensions.

*   *   *

Another important point regarding social life which must be carefully weighed is the technological unemployment which might well arise, according to circumstances, with the introduction of automation.

*   *   *

But even if these problems could be satisfactorily solved in the long run, the fact remains that increase in technological unemployment even for a brief period would represent in some countries a loss that could not be lightly incurred. In this area it is not at all legitimate to adopt the false principle which in the past impelled certain statesmen to sacrifice an entire generation in view of the great advantages that would accrue to succeeding ones.

*   *   *

New criteria, therefore, will have to be adopted to estimate the value of the paid worker, and new types of workers will have to be considered. These will present domestic problems for the labor unions and may even affect their present form, especially if it is borne in mind that, in certain sectors of the national economy, the working class will not in the future be notably affected by automation.

*   *   *

He will also be saved from the false notion that a man works in order to enjoy leisure. In reality, a man has leisure — apart from the natural and honorable rest from toil, which is needed to enable him to perfect his faculties and to fulfill better his religious, social, and domestic duties — in order to make him physically and mentally more competent in his work.

Touching this matter, an unconsidered use of automation might give rise to no slight dangers, both with regard to personal morality and to the sound structure of production and consumption in the national economy.

Pius XII, Aspects of Automation, October 23, 1957

Now, if it is true that in the early stages the machine often enslaved man, who was supposed to control it, today machine tools have been perfected to a point where one can hope that an ever-increasing number of workers will be freed who have until now been subjected to the performance of purely material and monotonous tasks.

Cardinal Cicognani, Letter to Canadian Social Week, October 16, 1961

It is, therefore, a requirement of social justice that such application [of automation] be made in such a way that the immediate negative results should not be borne exclusively by workers or by certain groups of workers. Rather such negative results should weigh equally, or even more heavily, upon the investors of capital and, when appropriate, even upon all members of the political community, since all in the final analysis benefit by such changes of automation. This can the more surely be obtained when the workers, through their unions and organizations, are present and have a voice in the implementation of the processes of automation.

FULL EMPLOYMENT

Pius XI, Quadragesimo Anno

74. But another point, scarcely less important, and especially vital in our times, must not be overlooked: namely, that the opportunity to work be provided for those who are able and willing to work. This opportunity depends largely on the wage and salary rate, which can help as long as it is kept within proper limits, but which on the other hand can be an obstacle if it exceeds these limits. For everyone knows that an excessive lowering of wages, or their increase beyond due measure, causes unemployment. This evil, indeed, especially as we see it prolonged and injuring so many during the years of Our Pontificate, has plunged workers into misery and temptations, ruined the prosperity of nations, and put in jeopardy the public order, peace, and tranquillity of the whole world. Hence it is contrary to social justice when, for the sake of personal gain and without regard for the common good, wages and salaries are excessively lowered or raised; and this same social justice demands that wages and salaries be so managed, through agreement of plans and wills, insofar as can be done, as to offer to the greatest possible number the opportunity of getting work and obtaining suitable means of livelihood.

75. A right proportion among wages and salaries also contributes directly

to the same result; and with this is closely connected a right proportion in the prices at which the goods are sold that are produced by the various occupations, such as agriculture, manufacturing, and others. If all these relations are properly maintained, the various occupations will combine and coalesce into, as it were, a single body and like members of the body mutually aid and complete one another. For then only will the social economy be rightly established and attain its purposes when all and each are supplied with all the goods that the wealth and resources of nature, technical achievement, and the social organization of economic life can furnish. And these goods ought indeed to be enough both to meet the demands of necessity and decent comfort and to advance people to that happier and fuller condition of life which, when it is wisely cared for, is not only no hindrance to virtue but helps it greatly.

Pius XII, Christmas Message, 1952

In fact, the intention of guaranteeing full employment with a constantly rising standard of living may well evoke the anxious query, to what degree expansion is possible without provoking a catastrophe and, above all, without bringing in its wake mass unemployment. It seems, therefore, that efforts must be made to attain the highest possible level of employment, but at the same time means must be sought to insure its stability.

*   *   *

. . . where private initiative is inactive or inadequate, the public authorities are obliged to provide employment, so far as possible, by undertaking works of general utility, and to facilitate by counselling and other means the finding of employment by those who seek it.

Pius XII, To the International Association of Economists, September 9, 1956

. . . it is dangerous, for example, to increase industrial production without assuring the sale of the goods produced, to modify the volume of monetary circulation without taking into account the corresponding volume of commercial transactions, or to seek for full employment while neglecting to prevent the risk of inflation.

John XXIII, Mater et Magistra

150. Among citizens of the same political community there is often a marked degree of economic and social inequality. The main reason for this is the fact that they are living and working in different areas, some of which are more economically developed than others.

Where this situation obtains, justice and equity demand that public authority try to eliminate or reduce such imbalances. It should ensure that the less developed areas receive such essential public services as their circumstances require, in order to bring the standard of living in these areas into line with the national average. Furthermore, a suitable economic and social policy must be devised which will take into account the supply of labor, the drift of population, wages, taxes, credit, and the investing of money, especially in expanding industries. In short, it should be a policy designed to promote useful employment, enterprising initiative, and the exploitation of local resources.

151. But the justification of all government action is the common good. Public authority, therefore, must bear in mind the interests of the state as a whole; which means that it must promote all three areas of production — agriculture, industry, and services — simultaneously and evenly. Everything must be done to ensure that citizens of the less developed areas are treated as responsible human beings, and are allowed to play the major role in achieving their own economic, social, and cultural advancement.

152. Private enterprise too must contribute to an economic and social balance in the different areas of the same political community. Indeed, in accordance with "the principle of subsidiary function," public authority must encourage and assist private enterprise, entrusting to it, wherever possible, the continuation of economic development.

John XXIII, Pacem in Terris

32. For example, it is useless to admit that a man has a right to the necessities of life, unless we also do all in our power to supply him with means sufficient for his livelihood.

HITHERTO we have discussed primarily the procedural aspects of labor-management relationships, although one major substantive matter — working conditions — was considered in some detail. The present chapter treats of two additional major substantive issues: wages and stability of employment. All these, of course, are closely connected with the concept of human dignity. Only if the rate of pay is adequate to support really human existence, and the stability of employment is such that man can have reasonable assurance about the future, can we say that a job meets the essential demands springing from a worker's rights. A living wage for the worker and a condition of full employment that bolsters job security are both needed if economic life is to meet human needs.

THE LIVING WAGE

Moral Concept of a Living Wage. The introduction of the concept of a living wage was a great moral achievement for the Church in the nineteenth century. Prior to that time, other and harsher doctrines were accepted both in theory and in practice. Both classical economic theory and the realities of the day left the wages of labor to the price-fixing mechanism of a free market. Labor was treated as a commodity, with its wage governed exclusively by conditions of supply and demand. Furthermore, it was widely held that the wage fund available for the payment of workers was a relatively stable amount, so that the pressure of increased population would only lead to misery and starvation. The Iron Law of Wages was a shackle binding labor to unending wretchedness.

At the time, some moralists justified this condition, at least in terms of the virtue of strict justice, in that the labor contract was freely entered upon. A worker agreed to accept a given rate of pay by the fact that he willingly accepted the job. Perhaps in charity, or even in distributive justice, there might be a claim for more. But contractual justice was satisfied when the wage agreed upon was paid. Moreover, the equality of justice was met when the worker received the market value of his services as determined by supply and demand. Hence the going rate for labor was considered the just rate.

Karl Marx and the socialists reacted strongly to this trend, swinging to the other extreme. They held that all value arose through labor, so that the worker was entitled to the full amount of the value of the product. Socialism denied to capital any right to a return from gains achieved through the labor of workers. The appropriation of such surplus value was considered theft.

Popes Leo XIII and Pius XI opposed both extreme views. While Pope Leo stated that through the labor of workers states grow rich, his successor clarified his thought by noting that labor's contribution is wonderfully enhanced by machinery and other physical capital. Both upheld the right of management and investors to their just share from the joint product. But, at the same time, they denied the theory that labor was a commodity whose value was to be determined exclusively by the market. In ringing words, Pope Leo stated that over and above the wage contract there is natural justice, the imperious demand that the wage be sufficient to support the worker who is thrifty and upright. Here again, his illustrious successor added clarity, by specifying that this wage be sufficient to support not only the worker, but his family as well.

The argument given to justify the claim in justice for a living wage derives basically from the dignity of man. In the labor market, a worker is selling more than an economic service. He is offering his work as the only normal means he has for human existence. The wage he receives affords him the wherewithal to live as befits a man. This means, not only food, clothing, and shelter for himself, but also the requirements for family living, since family life is normal for most men. He must receive enough to live in decency at any given time and to make provisions for sickness, old age, and like contingencies of existence.

Hence in human labor there is an intrinsic value, reflecting human dignity and needs, which is quite distinct from the market value determined by supply and demand schedules. The monetary expression of this intrinsic value is termed a living wage, a wage adequate for family needs paid to the head of a household. This sum should establish a minimum wage for persons who are the support of families. Above this minimum, there may be differentials based on skill, zeal, initiative, resourcefulness, and similar qualities. The evaluation of such additional contributions may be left to collective bargaining, the market for these added inputs, and other traditional methods for setting wages.

The standard of a decent living wage varies according to time and place. It is relevant to the resources and economic organization of a given country. Of course, there is an absolute basic minimum of food, clothing, and shelter necessary to sustain life itself. But the higher standard of decent comfort is relative to the economic conditions of a nation. An American housewife and her teen-age daughters would feel a sense of real deprivation today if they did not have nylon stockings. Such might not be the case with a Central European peasant woman. Hence, there is no absolute, world-wide living wage.

It may be objected that, in American social life, there is excessive emphasis upon conventional standards of living which are far more costly than such absolute needs as adequate food, clothing, housing, medical care, and education. Thus, it is held that as incomes rise needs also rise. What is a luxury today may be a conventional necessity tomorrow. We are like squirrels in a cage, very active but going nowhere. There is some merit in this objection, but it can be carried too far. In the United States today some families lack the minimum in the field of absolute needs. Here the productive ability and the earnings of the main wage earners must be enhanced so that they can provide adequate food, clothing, housing, and medical care for their dependents. The first need in social justice is a proper structure of economic society, so that all able and willing heads of households can earn a living wage for the care of their families. When such a stage is reached, we can then face the problem of conventional necessities, adjusting our standards to the productive capacities of our economy.

An Obligation in Justice. Papal statements on a living wage ended some controversies among theologians, but they also created new ones.

Older writers sometimes asserted that an employer was obliged in justice to pay the contractual wage, and in charity a living wage. Now it seems clear that the payment of a living wage is a matter of justice. But is it commutative justice, with the obligation of restitution and strict bilateral claims against employers, or is it social justice, involving personal and group accountability, but not the obligation of restitution?

Those who hold that the obligation is one of strict justice can cite several encyclical passages to bolster their position. Popes Leo XIII and John XXIII insisted that wages should not be determined merely by the law of supply and demand. Work is more than a commodity; it has an intrinsic value based on the dignity of the human person and the necessity of a living wage for a fitting mode of life. At one point Pope Pius XI referred to the "salary due in strict justice to the worker for himself and for his family" (A.C., No. 32).

On the other hand, Pope Pius XI on several occasions tied in the payment of a living wage with social reforms that come under the heading of social justice rather than commutative. "Where the social and individual nature of work is neglected, it will be impossible to evaluate work justly and pay it according to justice" (Q.A., No. 69). "It happens all too frequently, however, under the salary system, that individual employers are helpless to insure justice unless, with a view to its practice, they organize institutions the object of which is to prevent competition incompatible with fair treatment for the workers" (A.C., No. 53).

Pope John XXIII, while insisting on the moral claim for a living wage, lists many economic factors which should be considered in determining wages. Among these are the contribution by the worker to production, the financial state of the company for which he works, the quantity and quality of available resources, and the many demands of national and international common good. The demands of the common good, of course, involve social justice.

It seems more consonant with the total picture of papal writings on this subject to reach these conclusions: (1) The worker has a moral claim to a family living wage. (2) Employers generally cannot meet this obligation unless the economic system is so organized that a just wage is feasible. (3) Hence they are obliged to seek such economic and social reforms as are required to insure a just wage — this is an obligation in social justice. (4) In the interim, the "equality of justice" is met by payment of a wage equal to the value of the worker's contribution to the firm's output. And ⑤ society should supplement inadequate earn-ings while the economic system is being reorganized; it should also through such instruments as social security — including health benefits, old-age pensions, unemployment insurance, and family allowances — meet the unusual needs of individual families and of persons who because of handicaps cannot produce enough to warrant the receiving of a living wage.[1]

The conclusions reached above harmonize with the interpretation of *Quadragesimo Anno* by the learned German Jesuit, Father Oswald von Nell-Breuning, who was a close adviser of Pope Pius XI in preparing this encyclical:

> If, however, the economic structure is disturbed, or if it proves to be impossible to give labor its proper place in the system, then the value of work done will more or less fall short of family requirements. Then the employer cannot be required, either on the basis of commutative justice or for some other reason, to pay family wages. On the contrary, in this instance he is unable to pay them. The attempt to pay them in spite of it would merely result in further dislocation of the economic structure, and would endanger the employer himself.[2]

On this reasoning, the employer is bound in strict justice only to pay a going wage, but in social justice he must co-operate with other economic agents to make a living wage possible.

Problems of Implementation. Even in prosperous firms and indus-tries, there may be serious problems involved in paying every worker, regardless of present family obligations, a living wage. This means in practice that, in order to have a suitable wage for heads of families, other wage earners must receive a substantial sum in excess of their personal needs. The economic implications of this demand have caused many writers to ask what type of wage we should seek as a result of reforms brought about through the practice of social justice. Should this be some absolute figure, designed to meet the needs of an average family in each country? Or should it be a flexible amount, tailored to the family needs of each worker through a family-allowance system or some equivalent device?

The idea of an absolute figure, based on the so-called average family,

---

[1] See J. F. Cronin and H. W. Flannery, *Labor and the Church* (New York: Hawthorn, 1965), for further background material on papal teaching regarding the living wage. See also J. F. Cronin, *Christianity and Social Progress* (Baltimore: Helicon, 1965), for extended comments on *Mater et Magistra*.

[2] *Reorganization of Social Economy*, p. 177. In reference to handicapped workers, see St. Thomas Aquinas, *Summa Theologiae*, II, II, 77, 1.

leads to serious economic difficulties. A wage set at this level provides substantial bonuses for single workers, for husbands with working wives, and for husbands with childless families. These in turn enjoy luxurious standards of living, which become the goal of the wage-earner who is the sole support of his family. We thus set upon an upward spiral which even the most productive economic system finds a staggering burden.

Pope John XXIII takes a different approach to the problem of setting wages. The worker's salary should reflect the value of his services and the financial state of the company which employs him. It should be set with the view of employing the largest possible number of workers. There should be no privileged class of workers. Inflation should be shunned by maintaining an "equilibrium between wages and prices." Wage rates should be approximately equal in industry, agriculture, and the services. Goods and services should be made accessible to the greater number. Technical changes should be welcomed. Natural resources must be conserved. And there should be balance between economic expansion and social services — in other words, as the economy expands, social security and public services should likewise grow.

According to this view, the prime consideration is a sound, productive, and balanced economy. By using the best technical methods, output can be increased and prices held down. If this does not suffice to remove imbalances, the government may use taxation and social-security measures to bring about a greater measure of equality. A social-security system, in its broadest aspects, should protect individuals and families faced with events that may lead to destitution, such as unemployment, sickness, old age, and exceptional family burdens. In this way social progress will keep pace with economic growth.

In the United States we do not have either health insurance or family allowances as part of our social-security system, although over sixty nations in the world today offer these benefits to their citizens. Until our nation is prepared for these broader forms of social security, it is possible to achieve some of these advantages in an indirect fashion. Our tax system, for example, does offer exemptions for dependents, as well as limited deductions for medical expenses. Fringe benefits in industry, particularly medical care, can be expanded to cover the family as well as the individual worker. By methods such as these, we can progress toward adapting family income to needs, even though we lack the more direct social-security programs so common in most of the world.

In addition, we should do much more to inculcate in our younger people realistic attitudes toward spending, saving, and living standards. If unmarried younger workers spend all their income in "having a good time," two serious evils result. First, they have no savings to fall back upon when they are married. Second, they develop impossible cravings in terms of living standards. Many young couples think it quite normal to buy an automobile, a house, and furniture during the first two or three years of marriage. They plunge so deeply into debt that any unforeseen contingency, such as unemployment, sickness, or even pregnancy may push them into insolvency.

Problems connected with a living wage and the dignity of labor should be a special concern of priests and religious who are in the position of employers. In the past, our record in this regard has not always been good. Church institutions have at times been notorious both for low wages and arbitrary practices, such as the discharge of workers who have given most of their lives to an institution, only to be let out either because of old age or a change of administration. Cynics have remarked that some in our midst apply vows of poverty to workers, even though Canon Law makes no provision for vicarious acceptance of religious vows. Undoubtedly, such situations occur with the best of motives. Church institutions rarely have adequate funds, so that their administrators understandably try to economize in the attempt to have the most money for the primary purpose of the venture. This would be especially true for schools, institutions of charity, and even some parishes. Yet charity should not be served at the expense of justice. We should give good example in regard to the social teaching of the Church as well as in matters of piety.

Many bishops now require that wages and working conditions be considered in letting construction contracts. It would be most desirable that when bids are let, the award go, not to the lowest bidder absolutely, but to the lowest bid from a reputable firm which pays decent wages and treats its workers fairly. Likewise, the Church as employer cannot afford to lag behind in other phases of industrial relations, such as proper hours, working conditions, grievance machinery, seniority provisions, protection from arbitrary discharge, security for old age, and such normal features of reasonable employment. These are usually matters of justice, not works of supererogation. We should be more reluctant than lay employers to seek excuse from such obligations on the grounds that we cannot afford to meet them.

Economics of a Living Wage. Thus far we have discussed the ethical obligation in regard to a living wage and the method by which it should be paid. The conclusions reached were that the obligation was primarily in terms of social justice and that some form of family-allowance method was most likely to bring about the results sought.

Since the primary obligation is in the area of social justice, it logically follows that we should ask: What changes are necessary to make possible the payment of a living wage? Some might reply that the most important and immediate change would be a family-allowance system, so that distribution of current production would be directed in favor of families, rather than in favor of the unmarried and the childless married couples. This may be true, but it is rather unlikely that such a basic change will come about in the United States in the near future. We should seek special family help as a long-range project, and yet ask ourselves what can be done immediately to help workers who are paid under our present system of wage rates geared to the job rather than family status.

If we examine our economic system as a whole, we find it quite impressive in terms of resources, machinery, management and technical skills, and the quality and quantity of labor. For over twenty years, we have been able to divert an important share of our resources to nonproductive uses, such as the building of our military strength, and also give some of our wealth in foreign-aid programs, and yet maintain a high and ever increasing standard of living.

Moreover, developments in such areas as atomic energy, the discovery of new materials, and advances in electronics and automation all promise more rather than less wealth in the future. We seem on the verge of scientific breakthroughs that will put virtually unlimited energy resources at our disposal and will provide either natural or synthetic materials for nearly all our needs. In addition, the efficiency of labor, already multiplied many times by machines and managerial skills, will skyrocket as automation becomes more common. The electronic and chemical processes that make automation possible add a new dimension to the machine. In the past, machines made available immense and tireless sources of energy applied under the guidance of a skilled worker. But automation transfers to the machine a power of direction, correction, and even "judgment," that seems to duplicate human intelligence to a limited degree, but with a speed, accuracy, and tirelessness that man is not capable of achieving.

The ultimate implications of automation are difficult to assess. If these processes are extended widely throughout our economic life, undoubtedly we can have both substantially higher living standards and new vistas of leisure. Physical productive capacity alone will not solve our economic problems, as is evident from difficulties connected with farm surpluses. But unless we are able to produce, we cannot advance far even with the best distribution methods in the world. On this basis, the physical and technical capabilities of our economic system are most relevant to living standards and a living wage.

World economic problems would be very simple if every increase in productive capacity would automatically mean more wealth, higher wages, and increasing living standards. Unfortunately economics is not that simple. Goods have to be sold at a price that will meet the cost of a producer. Here we run into one of the paradoxes that constantly frustrate those who dream of a simple economy of abundance. This paradox is the fact that, economically speaking, scarcity also has value. A person who can control the supply of wanted goods and services often makes out better, in the short run, by producing less rather than more. A manufacturer with a monopoly, or a union with strict control of the supply of workers in a given craft, can often "charge what the traffic will bear." They are paid, not primarily because of what they produce, but because of the artificial scarcity they have created. Of course these advantages are strictly short-run and self-defeating, like standing to get a better view of a football game. No society gets rich by restricting production. But individuals have become wealthy this way.

Over a long range, living standards can rise only by one method — increased output per worker. By education, good management, or by automation, the worker can turn out more in a given time with an unchanged or lower expenditure of energy. Thus labor costs per unit of product or service decline. This increase in productivity can be passed on directly to the worker in the form of higher wages. Or it can go to consumers as lower prices, to stockholders as higher profits, or to any combination of these factors. Other consequences also follow. It may happen that increased efficiency will mean that fewer workers will be needed or that less efficient plants can be retired. Such dislocations can cause hardships, but their ultimate effect is to keep all producers at top peaks of efficiency.

Policy Problems. The preceding treatment of the basic economics of a living wage is a highly simplified prelude to some important policy discussions. Two problems, in particular, are deserving of serious consideration: how union wage rates affect the distribution of productivity gains; and what is to be done about industries or occupations that do not easily adapt themselves to new processes and hence do not have productivity gains.

When we discuss union wages achieved through collective bargaining, we refer to the total package, including fringe benefits. These latter have mounted to such a degree that they often comprise one fifth of the total wage. Indeed, fringe benefits are sometimes a form of socialized saving, making less necessary personal saving for old age, sickness, unemployment, vacations, and the like. Yet workers often forget that they are getting these benefits, since they rarely affect take-home pay and current spending power.

The format of payment is in itself unimportant, provided we do not lose sight of total costs. Thus, when the guaranteed annual wage was asked of the automotive industry in 1955, few questioned the principles involved. Workers and their families eat by the year, not by the hour. It is highly desirable to have wage guarantees so that workers can plan their economic futures, including such major expenditures as the buying of a house. The practical problem was how to offer such guarantees without bankrupting an industry. The idea of limited, regular contributions to a fund to supplement unemployment compensation solved this difficulty. A limited guaranteed annual wage became a reality.

Where real problems arise is in industries where a tradition has arisen of substantial periodic wage gains, apparently in excess of any productivity increases within the industry. The leaders in this process are certain large industrial unions, such as those in the automotive, steel, and coal-mining fields. Similar patterns are followed by teamsters and many building-trade unions. The result of their demands is usually a round of price increases, leading to long-term inflationary trends in the nation. To some degree such wage demands are self-defeating, since higher prices may cancel some of the gains. Often, however, these unions are protected by cost-of-living clauses, so that the burden of inflation must be borne elsewhere.

Wages and Inflation. There seems to be neither moral nor economic justification for wage increases that are essentially inflationary. Inflation is a highly disruptive force in the economy. Any action that provokes it normally is contrary to the common good. It will be argued, of course, that the "bloated profits" of the large corporations can absorb these wage increases without the necessity of price rises. But the burden of proof here rests upon the union, since the corporate-profit sector of our economy has declined, in comparison with wages, in recent years.

Indeed, it is questionable that organized labor should even seek to capture the entirety of productivity gains for its members. Quite apart from the moral claims of capital (if new machines explain the productivity rise), there is the problem of workers in industries or occupations that do not lend themselves readily to automation or other devices to increase productivity. Are they to remain stagnant economically, while other workers make more and more gains? The answer is that, when the gap gets too great, teachers, policemen, barbers, and the like will demand wage increases. Since higher costs in these areas cannot be absorbed, they must be passed on and hence inflation is given another push upward.

This type of inflation could be avoided if productivity gains in industry were shared partly by the workers involved (as higher wages) and partly by consumers (as lower prices). Lower prices give some benefits to workers on fixed incomes or those in industries not having productivity increases. Lower prices in technologically advanced sectors also make a constant price level more feasible, since they permit price increases elsewhere in the economy when such are needed to help less favored groups.

All workers should share equitably in the benefits brought about by automation and similar methods for increasing production. The process just described will help bring this about. Of course, some industries resist pressures toward greater efficiency. Productivity in the building trades, for example, is notoriously low. High hourly wages, often coupled with restrictive labor practices; hand-production methods; multiple handling charges for materials; and obsolete building codes all contribute to low productivity in this field. Such practices cannot be justified in terms of social justice. They may even pose problems of conscience in terms of simple honesty.

While wage increases should be framed in terms of productivity gains, either in the industry or in the economy as a whole, this does not mean that workers must withhold their demands until the accountants have calculated the last penny of increased efficiency. A certain consistent pressure for higher standards forces employers to develop more efficient methods and thus make such standards feasible. But this pressure must be within reasonable bounds. No one, for example, expects the economy to bound ahead with an annual efficiency gain of 10 per cent, or even half that amount. Union wage demands that do not consider these facts are at best unrealistic and possibly are highly damaging to the economy.

In this regard, we must carefully evaluate the slogan often used in wage demands: "Wage increases mean more purchasing power needed to stimulate consumer buying." Such statements can be pure nonsense. If an industry cannot absorb wage increases without passing them on in the form of higher prices, then purchasing power has not increased at all. Only when wage increases can be absorbed without raising prices is there any net gain in purchasing power. It would be much truer to say that higher efficiency, leading to either lower prices or higher wages or both, is the only real source of increased purchasing power. Anything else is illusory.

We may conclude that sound wage increases either reflect or provoke productivity gains. Workers in high-wage industries should not seek increases in excess of efficiency gains. Generally they should take less, so that lower prices can be had. Workers in low-wage occupations may seek higher wages, either through union demands or minimum-wage laws, even in excess of productivity gains. Thus they share efficiency increases of other segments of the economy. They also force their own industries or occupations to seek lower costs and better use of the factors of production.

FULL EMPLOYMENT

Even more critical than the question of a living wage is the problem of employment security. Most men, if compelled to make a choice, would prefer a secure job with lower pay to a well-paying job whose future is uncertain. This is especially true of those who suffered during the great depression of the 1930's. Many, although able and willing to work, lost their life savings, their homes, and their other property. Their families suffered from anxiety, malnutrition, and even despair. It was a bleak tragedy to millions and they are not anxious to repeat it.

Three factors must be considered in the modern world when facing problems of unemployment. These are automation, depressed areas, and measures to insure a stable, growing economy.

Automation. Automation is now generally recognized as a basic new development in economic life, comparable to atomic energy or the miracles in chemistry so far as impact is concerned. Many students consider it something qualitatively different from past technological advances, since it uses processes not too dissimilar to thinking and judgment. Earlier machines often surpassed manual workers in speed, energy, and accuracy. But the computer and the automated machine take over functions that are basically intellectual in nature. Their extraordinary rapidity of operation permits them to perform in minutes the tasks that would take skilled workers hours. Or they can do in an hour what an expert mathematician would require years to accomplish.

In the past, breakthroughs in technology usually led to far more jobs than were displaced by the new machines. Today, the machines are often doing the work of skilled, semiskilled, and unskilled workers, without creating any comparable number of new jobs. Even where work does become available, it is normally of a type that the displaced workers are unable to perform. Computers need highly trained engineers, mathematicians, programers, and the like. As a result, although our economy is growing, there is an absolute decline in the work force in agriculture, mining, and manufacturing. Nor are office workers or service employees secure. Automated bookkeeping, accounting, checkwriting, and copying — and even self-service elevators — take their toll of jobs.

Automation is making an increasing impact on the American economy at the very time that a substantially increased number of young workers are coming into the work force. High postwar birthrates will affect the job market in the years following 1965. Even though total employment has passed 72 million and is growing at the rate of a million jobs a year, we are not sure that graduates of our high schools will be able to find work in the years to come.

Some automated firms have safeguarded the jobs of those presently employed by retaining these workers indefinitely, relying upon normal attrition to lead to an ultimate reduction in the work force. Others offer retraining programs so that workers can find new positions in the same company. The federal government is also offering retraining for displaced workers. Unless, however, the economy can expand sufficiently to absorb those displaced by automation, there will be demands for more drastic measures. It would not be surprising to find more serious consideration of the shorter work week as a means of spreading jobs. This has been opposed in the past as a confession of economic weakness. It was argued that we should expand in order to produce more goods and services, not spread existing levels of production among more workers. However, unless such expansion does in fact take place, pressures for a shorter work week will mount.

Depressed Areas. Pope John XXIII noted the problem of regional imbalance as one of the serious evils of our day. In the United States today there is considerable discussion of this problem. We have depressed areas caused by the decline in coal mining and by soil conditions unsuitable for agriculture. The entire Appalachian region is considered a depressed area.

In some instances, it is possible to remedy the situation by bringing in new industries. Ireland and Puerto Rico are classic examples of entire nations that have prospered through this device. Many cities in the United States have recovered from the loss of major industries by attracting new firms. Whole states in the South have grown rapidly. Often tax concessions are used as a lure, along with an abundant supply of labor. Rural areas, unsuitable for agriculture, can be developed as tourist attractions. New and better roads can often make mountain and lake regions more accessible to vacationers. If none of these devices seems feasible, it is possible to train workers for new jobs and relocate them and their families. This assumes, however, that new jobs are available. We now face this problem.

Economic Growth and Stability. Even a country as prosperous as the United States needs economic growth, not merely to provide jobs, but also to meet unmet needs. Our slums and decaying cities are one area which offers a challenge for further growth and renewal. We are short of doctors, nurses, teachers, and social workers. There is a need for competent mechanics and repairmen. Engineers are in short supply. Our colleges cannot expand rapidly enough to meet the clamor for admission. Even consumer goods can be produced more abundantly, as many families find reasons to justify a second or third automobile or television set. With higher living standards, more and more families can afford a summer home at a beach or in the mountains. Finally, our obligations to developing nations in other parts of the world can absorb substantial portions of our national production.

These are some of the needs. The problem is how to meet them within the framework of our economic system. Certainly, for reasons explained earlier, we expect that the bulk of these needs will be met through the private sector of the economy. It should furnish most of the jobs and hence most of the income needed to purchase goods and services. One method for stimulating growth in private business is through reform of the tax structure. Measures taken in the 1960's to further expansion of plants and replacement of obsolescent machinery, along with tax reductions for both industry and individuals, led to one of the most sustained periods of growth and prosperity in American history.

Many social needs can be met by combined public-private action. In urban renewal programs, for example, government may meet most of the cost of buying and razing run-down buildings. Cleared land is then sold at an attractive price to private investors. Government subsidies to private medical schools and colleges can help meet our educational needs. To the extent that the economy grows and prospers, there are tax revenues available for needed public services. Better education leads to more skilled and productive workers.

In addition to growth, we need stability. So far as possible, we want no recurrence of the great depressions of the past, or even the smaller recessions of recent years. Business and labor can contribute to stability by avoiding policies that lead to inflation, speculative build-up of business inventories, and other excesses that trigger a boom-and-bust cycle. There should be healthy competition so as to prevent dangerous practices, such as price-fixing, on the part of business and labor. Greater accuracy in government and private statistical reporting can warn of difficulties in time to take corrective action.

But, as Pope John noted, governmental decisions and actions on a national and international level are often even more important than the private policies of individual firms. Such matters as balance of payments, internal credit policies set by the Federal Reserve System, and the impact of a federal budget surplus or deficit are powerful factors influencing the health of the economy. Great wisdom and skill are needed in the conduct of trade, monetary, and fiscal policies in order to promote stability and growth.

Fortunately, our economic knowledge and experience have grown to such an extent that it now seems possible to "manage" the economy as needed. Tax policies can stimulate growth. Money management can help avoid either an excess of credit (leading to inflation) or a shortage (causing deflation and unemployment). The relationship between the total federal cash outflow (as distinct from the smaller administrative budget normally cited in the press) and the total inflow from taxes and other revenue sources has a tremendous impact on the economy. A cash surplus has a braking effect and a deficit tends to stimulate the private sector.

It is certainly premature to say that we have all the answers to the problems of unemployment and economic instability. But we have enormously increased our knowledge in this area of economics and have developed many new tools to use. Moreover, there is a much greater consensus between business and labor, and between liberals and conservatives, about the use of these tools. Hopefully, man can become the master, not the slave, of our intricate economic system.

READINGS*

J. F. Cronin, *Christianity and Social Progress*, Chaps. 6–7, 16.
J. F. Cronin and H. W. Flannery, *The Church and the Workingman*, Chap. 2.
B. W. Dempsey, *The Functional Economy*, Chaps. 11–12, 22.
H. Johnston, *Business Ethics*, Chap. 10.
B. L. Masse, *Justice for All*, Chap. 4.
J. Messner, *Social Ethics* (rev. ed.), pp. 796–812, 834–840, 924–928.
O. von Nell-Breuning, *Reorganization of Social Economy*, Chap. 9.
J. A. Ryan, *A Living Wage.*
———— *Distributive Justice*, Section 4.

---

* For further readings, see List No. 7 in the Appendix.

Chapter XI

THE ECONOMIC PROBLEMS OF THE FAMILY

LIVING STANDARDS

Pius XI, Casti Connubii

126. If families, particularly those in which there are many children, have not suitable dwellings; if the husband cannot find employment and means of livelihood; if the necessities of life cannot be purchased except at exorbitant prices; if even the mother of the family, to the great harm of the home, is compelled to go forth and seek a living by her own labors; if she, too, in the ordinary or even extraordinary labors of childbirth, is deprived of proper food, medicine, and the assistance of a skilled physician, it is patent to all to what an extent married people may lose heart, and how home life and the observance of God's commands are rendered difficult for them. Indeed it is obvious how great a peril can arise to the public security and to the welfare and very life of civil society itself when such men are reduced to such a condition of desperation that, having nothing which they fear to lose, they are emboldened to hope for chance advantage from the upheaval of the state and of established order.

127. Wherefore, those who have the care of the state and of the public good cannot neglect the needs of married people and their families, without bringing great harm upon the state and on the common welfare. Hence, in making the laws and in disposing of public funds they must do their utmost to relieve the needs of the poor, considering such a task as one of the most important of their administrative duties.

Pius XII, To Italian Workers, June 13, 1943

Our Predecessors and We Ourselves have not lost any opportunity of making all men understand by Our repeated instructions your personal and family needs, proclaiming as fundamental prerequisites of social concord those claims which you have so much at heart: a salary which will cover the living expenses of a family and such as to make it possible for the parents to fulfill their natural duty to rear healthily nourished and clothed children; a dwelling worthy of human persons; the possibility of securing for children sufficient instruction and a becoming education, of foreseeing and forestalling times of stress, sickness, and old age.

Pius XII, Christmas Message, 1952

We are thinking of the consequences of poverty, still more of the consequences of utter destitution. For some families there is a dying daily, a dying hourly; a dying multiplied, especially for parents, by the number of dear ones they behold suffering and wasting away. Meanwhile, sickness becomes more serious, because it is not properly treated; it strikes little ones in particular, because preventive measures are lacking.

Then there is the weakening and consequent physical deterioration of whole generations. Whole masses of population are brought up as enemies of law and order, so many poor girls gone astray, pushed down into the bottom of the abyss, because they believed that that was the only way out of their shameful poverty. Moreover, not rare is the case where it is wretched misery that leads to crime. Those who in their works of charity visit our prisons affirm constantly that not a few men, fundamentally decent, have gone to prison because extreme poverty has led them to commit some unpremeditated act.

WOMEN WORKERS

Leo XIII, Rerum Novarum

60. Finally, it is not right to demand of a woman or a child what a strong adult man is capable of doing or would be willing to do. Nay, as regards children, special care ought to be taken that the factory does not get hold of them before age has sufficiently matured their physical, intellectual, and moral powers. For budding strength in childhood, like greening verdure in spring, is crushed by premature harsh treatment; and under such circumstances all education of the child must needs be foregone. Certain occupations likewise are less fitted for women, who are intended by nature for work of the home — work indeed which especially protects modesty in women and accords by nature with the education of children and the well-being of the family.

Pius XI, Quadragesimo Anno

71. In the first place, the worker must be paid a wage sufficient to support him and his family. That the rest of the family should also contribute to the common support, according to the capacity of each, is certainly right, as can be observed especially in the families of farmers, but also in the families of many craftsmen and small shopkeepers. But to abuse the years of childhood and the limited strength of women is grossly wrong. Mothers, concentrating on household duties, should work primarily in the home or in its immediate vicinity. It is an intolerable abuse, and to be abolished at all cost, for mothers on account of the father's low wage to be forced to engage in gainful occupations outside the home to the neglect of their proper cares and duties, especially the training of children.

Pius XII, On Women's Duties, October 21, 1945

Indeed, We have on a former occasion pointed out that for the same work output a woman is entitled to the same wages as a man.

We see a woman who, in order to augment her husband's earnings, betakes herself also to a factory, leaving her house abandoned during her absence. The house, untidy and small perhaps before, becomes even more miserable for lack of care. Members of the family work separately in four quarters of the city and with different working hours. Scarcely ever do they find themselves together for dinner or rest after work — still less for prayer in common. What is left of family life? And what attractions can it offer to children?

As to the working classes, forced to earn daily bread, a woman might, if she reflected, realize that not rarely the supplementary wage which she earns by working outside the house is easily swallowed up by other expenses or even by waste which is ruinous to the family budget. The daughter who also goes out to work in a factory or office, deafened by the excited restless world in which she lives, dazzled by the tinsel of specious luxury, developing a thirst for shallow pleasures that distract but do not give satiety or repose in those revues or dance halls which are sprouting up everywhere, often for party propaganda purposes, and which corrupt youth, becomes a fashionable lady, despises the old nineteenth-century ways of life.

Pius XII, To the Federation of Italian Women, October 14, 1956

Because of this temporal goal, there is no field of human activity which must remain closed to woman; her horizons reach out to the regions of politics, labor, the arts, sports; but always in subordination to the primary functions which have been fixed by nature itself.

John XXIII, Pacem in Terris

19. Women must be accorded such conditions of work as are consistent with their needs and responsibilities as wives and mothers.

HOURS OF WORK

Leo XIII, Rerum Novarum

59. Now as concerns the protection of corporeal and physical goods, the oppressed workers, above all, ought to be liberated from the savagery of greedy men, who inordinately use human beings as things for gain. Assuredly, neither justice nor humanity can countenance the exaction of so much work that the spirit is dulled from excessive toil and that along with it the body sinks crushed from exhaustion. The working energy of a man, like his entire nature, is circumscribed by definite limits beyond which it cannot go. It is developed indeed by exercise and use, but only on condition that a man cease from work at regular intervals and rest. With respect to daily work, therefore, care ought to be taken not to extend it beyond the hours that human strength warrants. The length

of rest intervals ought to be decided on the basis of the varying nature of the work, of the circumstances of time and place, and of the physical condition of the workers themselves. Since the labor of those who quarry stone from the earth, or who mine iron, copper, and other underground materials, is much more severe and harmful to health, the working periods of such men ought to be correspondingly shortened. The seasons of the year also must be taken into account; for often a given kind of work is easy to endure in one season but cannot be endured at all in another, or not without the greatest difficulty.

60. Let it be the rule everywhere that workers be given as much leisure as will compensate for the energy consumed by toil, for rest from work is necessary to restore strength consumed by use. In every obligation which is mutually contracted between employers and workers, this condition, either written or tacit, is always present, that both kinds of rest be provided for; nor would it be equitable to make an agreement otherwise, because no one has the right to demand of, or to make an agreement with, anyone to neglect those duties which bind a man to God or to himself.

HOUSING

Pius XII, To Women of Italian Catholic Action, July 24, 1949

First of all, We say that everything that can contribute to a sound social policy for the good of the family and Christian youth can always count on the efficacious support of the Church.

We repeat now to you what We said to the men of Catholic Action some two years ago. The Catholic Church strongly supports the requirements of social justice. These requirements include provision for the people of the necessary houses, and above all for those who desire to found a family or are already doing so. Can there be conceived a social need of greater urgency? How sad it is to see young people, at the age when nature is more inclined to marriage, forced to wait years and years, merely because of the lack of a place to live, and always with the danger that in this nerve-wracking waiting their morals may deteriorate. Encourage, then, as much as you can, with your propaganda and your labors, the provision of houses so that the dignity of marriage and the Christian education of children may not suffer from this need.

Pius XII, To Autonomous Institute for Popular Housing, November 21, 1953

Public authorities ought, in regard to housing, as in other matters, seek to favor, and in no case oppose, private enterprise. In the case of popular housing especially, they should favor the enterprise of co-operatives.

Pius XII, To "Stations de Plein Air" Movement, May 3, 1957

Is it necessary to bring up the sad example of the exploitation of slum areas? Dilapidated, ramshackle houses without the most necessary hygienic installations sometimes yield a sizeable income to their owners without costing them a penny. Inevitably, they neglect to make necessary repairs in them for years on end.

Enough can never be said about the harm that these dwellings do to the families condemned to live in them. Deprived of air and of light, living in filth and in unspeakable commingling, adults and, above all, children quickly become the prey of contagious diseases which find a favorable soil in their weakened bodies. But the moral injuries are still more serious: immorality, juvenile delinquency, the loss of the taste for living and for working, interior rebellion against a society that tolerates such abuses, ignores human beings, and allows them to stagnate in this way, transformed gradually into wrecks.

Society itself must bear the consequences of this lack of foresight. Because it did not wish to prevent the evil and to provide a remedy in time, it will spend enormous sums to keep up an appearance of curbing delinquency and to pay expenses for prolonged confinement in sanatoriums and clinics. How many millions authorized for the cure of evils that it would be easier and less expensive to prevent!

*   *   *

Persons of good faith who have only an inadequate knowledge of the matter readily believe that the majority of those who live in the slums or who must be satisfied with an income below the essential minimum are there through their own fault or negligence, and that welfare organizations are capable of helping anyone in need of it. The fact is, existing institutions which address themselves chiefly, as We have already said, to those who can help themselves, ought to be adapted and their activity extended to those who, for any reason whatsoever, are incapable of benefiting by measures already in force.

John XXIII, To Members of UN Housing Committee, November 14, 1958

Reflect then, on the basis of this premise, how the heart of every Christian should consider the duty it has to provide a house for him who has none as one of the bases of charity in general and of every complete apostolate.

SOCIAL SECURITY

Pius XII, Christmas Message, 1950

For this reason We have repeatedly and with ever greater insistence proclaimed the fight against unemployment and the striving after a sound social security as an indispensable condition if all members of a nation, both high and low, are to be united in a single corporate body.

Pius XII, To the Italian Federation of Commerce, February 17, 1956

Undoubtedly, nowadays more than in the past, there is a growing desire to assure to all classes of society guarantees that will preserve them from the mishaps and chances inherent in the fluctuations of the economy; guarantees that will protect employment and its rewards; guarantees that will provide for sickness and incapacitating accidents that may reduce a man to idleness and deprive him of the means of livelihood. This solicitude is quite justified; but in many cases the present system of social security has not yet succeeded in putting an end to difficult situations or in healing wounds that are always open.

It is important, however, that the anxious desire for security should not prevail over the businessman's readiness to risk his resources to such an extent as to dry up every creative impulse; nor impose on enterprise operating conditions that are too burdensome; nor discourage those who devote their time and energy to commercial transactions.

John XXIII, Mater et Magistra

136. Systems of social insurance and social security can make a most effective contribution to the overall distribution of national income in accordance with the principles of justice and equity. They can therefore be instrumental in reducing imbalances between the different classes of citizens.

IN THE preceding chapter, the moral claim for a living wage was urged. In addition, there was also the comment that a family-allowance system is a more practical means for implementing this ideal than the alternative of a fixed wage based upon the needs of the so-called average or normal family. Yet it is only the part of realism to note the difficulties facing the family-allowance system, so far as acceptance here is concerned. Because of this difficulty, the present chapter offers comments upon the economic problems confronting the family under existing social conditions.

Living Standards. In judging the welfare of the family, it is necessary to make clear the standards used. The pages to follow give some of the indications of poverty as well as the bases for commonly accepted standards of family living. There follows a discussion of housing and medical costs, since these are two of the more important components of the family budget. Then we face the methods used by many families to augment their incomes: additional work by the main wage earner, work by wives and mothers, and work by children. After these situations have been evaluated, a brief exposition of social-insurance and the family-allowance plan is offered.

While there may be some elements of the subjective in such terms as poverty, frugal comfort, and luxury, there are nonetheless sufficient objective standards to warrant some conclusions about proper standards of living. Thus propriety would call for a minimum of three bedrooms for most families with children, one each for parents, boys, and girls. We expect separate kitchen and bathroom facilities for each family. The cost of renting or buying such facilities can be priced in different cities. Likewise, we can make up and price a typical breadbasket for a family of various sizes. The same applies to clothing, medical care, transportation, and sundries. In this way a budget can be drawn up that estimates the monetary cost of a given level of living.

The best known and most widely used of such budgets is issued by the Bureau of Labor Statistics, U. S. Department of Labor. It is revised periodically to give up-to-date figures on typical living costs for a family of four persons, consisting of husband, wife, and two minor children. On the basis of 1964 studies, this family would need $6,000, or slightly less than $120 a week.

There is some debate as to the nature of the BLS budget, and particularly whether or not families need less than this amount must be classified as poor. Actually, it is extremely difficult to determine poverty in terms of any given level of income. If we take a level of $4,000 as the absolute minimum for a family, then two fifths of Americans can be considered poor. Should we decide that the lowest fifth among income receivers are to be classed as poor, then the income level — using 1960 census figures — drops to about $3,000 a year or less.

Among the lowest fifth of family income receivers, the largest easily identifiable group is the aged, with about 2.6 million obtaining less than $3,000 cash income in 1959. Farmers and mothers in broken homes each comprise about 1.6 million poor families. About one million of the poor families are nonwhite. Then there is a catchall group of 3 million families which includes the unemployed, the unemployable, unskilled workers, illiterates, alcoholics, chronic gamblers, and handicapped persons.

Two features of American poverty are particularly significant. The first is that many of the poor escape notice in our complex society. A series of books and articles appearing during the years 1963–1964 dramatized this situation. For the first time, millions of Americans realized that real destitution prevails extensively in this extremely wealthy nation. Certainly a situation that afflicts one third of our nation should not have remained unobserved. It is a shocking illustration of the depersonalized nature of modern society that such extensive evils were completely overlooked by the bulk of our citizens.

The second significant fact is that much of this poverty is self-perpetuating. Some cities report third generations of families on relief.

Nor is this surprising, since children reared in slum conditions rarely receive a good education. They become school dropouts and swell the ranks of unskilled workers — the most difficult group to employ in modern America. No matter how high national income may reach and whatever the general level of prosperity, there seems to be a fairly stable level of impoverished families and individuals. This is real destitution, not the mere statistical fact that there will always be the "poorest one fifth" in any study of income.

Alleviating Poverty. Poverty connotes the idea of doing without at least some things that are generally considered essential. In a poor family, to cite one example, housing conditions may involve overcrowding, to the detriment of health and morale. It may be difficult, if not impossible, for children to have quiet and privacy for study. Their sleeping quarters may be overcrowded. They may be forced to use the streets as playgrounds, endangering their lives and often impairing their moral standards.

A poor family may lack essential foods. It may be forced to skimp on fruits, milk, meat, and fresh vegetables. As a result, diet may not be adequate for health. Yet this family cannot afford private medical care and must depend upon free clinics. Thus, it may or may not get medicines and treatment it needs. Poverty may also be felt in other ways, such as the quality and even quantity of clothing. It often is a barrier to educational advancement.

Poverty is obviously a major challenge in a nation that prides itself on its wealth and high living standards. But there is no single, automatic approach to this problem. Obviously it would be most desirable to prevent destitution from occurring in our midst. Next we seek measures to remove the causes of already existing poverty. Finally, we wish to be sure that those who, for various reasons, will be unable to earn suitable incomes can still live in a manner befitting human beings.

Of the classes of poor listed earlier, two groups can readily be helped by methods already in operation. For example, we shall describe in Chapter XVI the work of the Rural Areas Development Administration in aiding poor farmers. A broad extension of this program could do much to eradicate rural poverty. The second group is the aged. Improvement in social-security coverage and benefits, plus a better system of industrial pensions, could keep most older citizens from want.

So far as nonwhites are concerned, we will note in Chapter XV the complex nature of discrimination, particularly against Negroes. The

Negro needs his civil rights, incentive for education and better school facilities, job opportunities, and decent housing. These problems, and their solutions, will be treated at length later.

Where broken homes exist, particularly when mothers are the sole support of young children, most communities have welfare provisions to assist the family. It is normally desirable that children live with their mother, rather than in foster homes or institutions. Hence it is better to give aid to such mothers, instead of compelling them to work while children are quite young.

One of the most critical problems, so far as poverty is concerned, is the quality and amount of education received by children from poor homes. Many slum schools are poor in quality, with disspirited teachers unable or unwilling to give students the extra care they need. Home conditions make study almost impossible. Parents often give these children no motivation to study or advance in school. Many just remain physically present until the law permits them to drop out. Obviously the products of such an "education" will remain poor.

Intensive care programs for such students, volunteer tutoring, keeping the schools open for study after class hours, and similar devices have worked wonders in many cities. There is need for a "domestic peace corps" whereby volunteers will work with our most demoralized citizens and give them new hope and opportunity. In some areas adults have been persuaded to attend literacy classes and thereby increase their earning ability.

Unemployed youth can be offered the opportunity to attend special work camps. There they can learn various skills and, above all, escape the deadening effect of idleness during these critical years. In other cases, work programs at home can be developed to give our unemployed youth a chance to earn, and also to learn the discipline of work.

Many of these objectives were sought in the Economic Opportunity Act of 1964. This act provides for a job corps for dropouts, affording them remedial education in camps and residential schools. There is also a work training program for teenagers living at home. They can earn money at community projects while continuing their studies. College students may also benefit by a work-study program. Communities may receive federal loans for antipoverty programs. Finally, there is a domestic peace corps, Volunteers in Service to America (Vista). These will work in areas of deep poverty and special need.

Families with low incomes can often stretch their earnings by means of shrewd management. Many times this involves a willingness, and ability, to trade time and effort for little savings that can mount up. For example, in the budgets cited, food costs are important. But an ingenious cook can prepare less expensive items and still have good meals. The economy-minded will bypass convenient but expensive mixes and prepared foods and use their own time instead to prepare cakes, vegetables, and soups. But here we must be realistic and note that the busy mother of several young children may not have much energy for time-consuming, albeit economical, preparation of food. Nor may she be able to shop around for the best bargains.

Family needs emphasize the desirability of lower food costs, since they are so important in family budgets. Yet we must frankly admit that current trends are in the other direction. Every effort is being made, and rightly so, to increase farm income. Processing costs increase as consumers buy more and more of frozen and precooked foods. It is not easy to see where important savings can be made in this area, although isolated cases of excessive middleman charges may be turned up.

Whether or not a low-income family may better its lot by more shrewd spending, it at least should have the opportunity to try. Consumer education as part of high school social-science study, sewing lessons in adult-education courses, and similar aids may give families the option of using their time in the effort to secure savings in the purchase of food and clothing.

One point often overlooked in any consideration of poverty is the fact that many merchants cruelly exploit the poor. They sell them inferior goods at inflated prices and exorbitant credit charges. Parish credit unions and adult consumer-education courses could save millions for those who can least afford the losses they incur.

Housing Costs.   One of the most critical factors in family living costs is the high price of housing. No other area of our economy has suffered so much from inflated costs. It is estimated that a typical house that cost $8,000 in 1941 sold for $22,000 in 1964. Rental housing has likewise increased in cost. The result is that many families are paying heavy charges for housing, to the detriment of other demands upon the family salary. Others are forced to live in housing below the standards they can reasonably expect. Still others are crowded into slums where an entire family may have but one room.

There are many reasons for this debacle, but the most important stem from a combination of inefficiency and greed. The construction industry has often resisted change in regard to materials, working practices, and methods of production. Land costs are often high, and likewise money costs. City building codes may force obsolete and antiquated methods of production. Prefabrication is the exception and individual building the rule, at least for single dwellings. Hourly wages for labor are among the highest in the land, and productivity is often quite low, hampered by feather-bedding practices and work-stretching traditions. The result is that housing often has priced itself out of the market.

An important reversal of this trend was promised in 1958, when the building-trade unions and the construction industry announced long-range plans to use more efficient production methods. While the initial announcement concerned only heavy construction, it is expected that the policy will gradually be carried over into residential housing. It certainly is an unwelcome paradox that, in the richest and most progressive industrial nation of the world, antiquated methods should be used for the provision of one of the major necessities for family life.

Even if the cost of construction is cut drastically, it does not follow that the cost of housing will always be within the reach of the family purse. This is particularly the case when urban rental housing is involved, especially in areas of high land costs. In many cases it is impossible for private builders to construct rental housing at prices suitable even for "middle-income" tenants, to say nothing of rehousing slum occupants. When land is extremely high-priced, the only alternative to costly rents is a high density of occupancy — the very slum conditions that most cities seek to eliminate. For this reason, it is generally necessary that the federal or local governments assume part of the costs, thereby making low-rent facilities available. It is customary, in the case of low-income families, for local authorities (with federal help) to build public housing. This, in effect, is subsidized housing, since the rents charged do not pay the costs of land, construction, and operation. Where middle-income families are involved, some cities or states offer special tax arrangements for limited-dividend housing projects. For instance, they may be taxed at a rate based upon previous unimproved use, instead of the current value of the project.

Where downtown city areas are involved, it is important that new housing fit in with an adequate pattern of planning and urban renewal. Otherwise, the core areas of large cities tend to decline when population migrates to the suburbs. Huge investments in stores, churches, schools, and like properties become impaired in value or even worthless, as population shifts leave them stranded. Obviously it is sound economy to utilize valuable central-city properties instead of building duplicates in the suburbs, unless population growth (rather than movement) makes these necessary.

In discussing housing problems, and related subjects of urban renewal and rehabilitation, much of the treatment has been in the abstract, with no reference to concrete governmental programs for lending money to home buyers (FHA, VA), purchasing bank mortgage loans (FNMA), slum clearance, urban renewal, and public housing. These programs are extremely important for any understanding of current government aids to the housing market. Yet since they are subject to frequent changes in detail and emphasis, it was considered more desirable in these pages to deal with the principles concerned and to leave the details for study in available reference manuals.

Medical Care. The problem of medical care is currently surrounded by considerable controversy, much of it unnecessary in that it involves avoidable misunderstandings. In this discussion, three points will be treated: the physical availability of medical care, the costs of medical care, and general health insurance.

In the United States, at this writing, there are important shortages of medical facilities, particularly for rural regions and low-income states. In these cases, there are not enough doctors, nurses, clinics, technicians, and hospitals. It is unlikely that these needs can be met by private initiative, particularly in the low-income states. An argument can be made for federal subsidy both for the construction and equipping of buildings and for the training of necessary personnel. A further problem exists in cities where adequate facilities and trained personnel are available, but where their cost is excessive for low- and middle-income families. The most successful method for meeting this problem is the formation of clinics, whereby a number of specialists work in the same building under some type of common direction. This avoids unnecessary duplication of expensive equipment and makes thorough medical care available at the same price as is currently paid for less adequate treatment. At the same time, it does not lower doctors' incomes or interfere with their full freedom of practice. The promotion of such clinics would be a form of social justice especially suitable for Catholic doctors.

A valuable technique for handling medical costs for some moderate-income families is the institution of industrial or union group health plans. Since it has been estimated that the cost of sickness, in terms of lost industrial production, is about eight billion dollars a year, or a productivity decline of 5 to 7 per cent, management often calculates that such assistance saves money in the long run. Some firms feel that a direct money profit is made by such programs, while others consider the gain indirect, through better morale and industrial relations. One careful study made by the Industrial Hygiene Foundation showed that a chemical industry spent $21,335 in medical care and estimated its return at $87,032, or $4.08 for each dollar spent. There was less sickness, fewer accidents, and lower insurance costs. Labor turnover also declined. In addition to industry, some labor unions have secured medical care for their members. Thus, the Union Health Center of the International Ladies' Garment Workers Union occupies seven floors of a New York skyscraper. It has a staff of 143 doctors (11 of whom are full time), 40 nurses, 5 registered pharmacists, 4 junior pharmacists, and 30 technicians. This center served 42,352 persons in 1957 and 757,015 visits were made by these patients. No charge is made to Union members, and family dependents pay $1.25 a visit. Employer contributions pay most of the costs of the Union Health Center. The United Mine Workers Union also has elaborate health facilities, including a number of hospitals. Other unions use community services, such as Blue Cross or Blue Shield.

In regard to the costs of medical care, a distinction must be made between ordinary medical care and extraordinary problems. The cost of ordinary medical care is not unreasonable. The total amount spent for medical care in the United States is low, when compared with national expenditure for luxuries. Moreover, the rapid growth of prepayment plans indicates that the economic problems connected with certain types of illness are being met. Nevertheless, there is room for further improvement along these lines. Present-day coverage is more adequate for hospital care than for payment of doctors' bills and the cost of expensive medicines. Hence there is need both for extension of coverage in regard to existing plans and for rapid growth of plans which deal with fees and high-cost medicines. But sound social policy would dictate progress along lines which have proved their worth rather than radical experimentation with new devices.

Extraordinary medical care includes chronic illnesses, such as arthritis and certain forms of heart disease; crippling sickness, like poliomyelitis or mental illness; operations which are unusually costly; and disease which requires the constant use of high-cost drugs. Sickness of this type usually wrecks the finances of a family. If it strikes the main wage earner, income is cut off at the same time that needs are greatest. Moreover, such illness is not ordinarily met by present-day prepayment plans. Indeed, the prepayment method is not intrinsically suitable for these cases, since their incidence is scattered and unpredictable. The insurance method is the only logical device for such a situation, just as it is the only sound way for meeting the costs incidental to a fire. There are now available private insurance plans analogous to automobile collision insurance. An insurance company fixes a total annual amount to be paid by the patient, either directly or through prepayment plans, and covers all costs above this amount. Plans of this type deserve every encouragement.

There is one possible hazard to the prepayment and insurance systems that poses a moral question. At times patients demand unneeded care, even hospitalization, merely because they are covered. Again, certain doctors increase their fees when they know that a patient has medical coverage. The practice of causing unwarranted and unnecessary increases in the costs of medical plans threatens to endanger the stability of the entire program. Both patients and doctors alike are woefully shortsighted when they indulge in such improper activities.

The analysis just given does much to answer the question as to the advisability of national health insurance. If the approach advocated here is sound, there is no need for a detailed study of the arguments for or against such a plan. Clearly it is contrary to the principle of subsidiarity for the government to intervene in matters already being handled by private initiative. Even granting the present inadequacy of private approaches through prepayment plans and similar devices, it is better to aid methods which are basically sound rather than to replace them with a new and cumbersome approach. At the same time, the medical profession would be doing itself a great disservice were it to remain contented with a merely negative approach to the problem of the economics of medical care. It is not enough to fight proposals which it fears might lead to socialized medicine. The real problems which occasioned these proposals must be met adequately and within reasonable time. The state does have the moral right and duty to intervene in matters concerning the common good, when individual initiative fails to meet serious needs. It is primarily the duty of the medical profession to see that sound organization and adequate private payment plans answer the needs of the American public, so that in the future extensive government intervention will not even be seriously considered.

Related to the problem of health insurance is the controversy over medical care for the aged. Older persons, as a group, have higher than average medical expenses and lower than average incomes. Hence they face a serious problem of medical indigence. This is met, in many states, by a combined federal-state program of aid, based on proven need. But many persons rebel against a "means test" and forcing the aged to seek medical care as a dole. Consequently, there is strong agitation for a system of prepaid medical insurance for older persons. It is urged that this insurance be tied in with the social-security system, so that wage-earners may provide during their working years for the unusual costs of illness that beset many in their declining years. Although many doctors have opposed this proposal, it does seem more consonant with human dignity to have some type of prepaid medical insurance — private, governmental, or mixed — to meet the hazards frequently associated with old age.

The economic problems of medicine afford an excellent opportunity for social action by thousands of Catholic doctors. They are well aware of our teaching in regard to family life and also know the medical costs of bringing children into this world and rearing them to maturity. Such doctors are within their rights in opposing programs for medical care which they consider unsound and dangerous. But they should at the same time be in the forefront in proposing practical plans for making medical care available, through prepayment, to all families and individuals. They, better than laymen, can suggest methods for lowering the costs of such care without decreasing quality or denying to doctors their proper incomes. Finally, they can endorse the insurance method, whether private or public, for the field where it is really needed, namely, for extraordinary and almost catastrophic expenses from chronic or crippling illness. Such a positive approach would meet the needs of our time, without risking the real values of private initiative and local autonomy.

Making Ends Meet. A worker may confront the problem of high living costs in two ways. First, he might try, individually or through social action, to cut costs in key areas. This approach has been discussed in the pages immediately preceding. Second, he or his family, or both, may try to earn additional income. This may involve seeking added sources of income in return for additional work by the main bread-winner, who usually is the father of the family. Or it may involve work by married women whose husbands also work. Finally, it can raise the problem of child labor. By 1964, over half of American families had more than one pay check.

During World War II, the Korean War, and some phases of the post-Korean boom, it was possible for workers to earn considerable sums in the form of overtime pay. Most industrial workers are covered by the Fair Labor Standards Act (Wage and Hour Act) and thus usually receive time and one half for all time worked in excess of forty hours a week. If such overtime pay is available over a sustained period, many workers can accumulate substantial additional income. This permits such expenditures as down payments on a home, the purchase of a car, or payment for furniture. Moreover, as automation progresses in American industry, there will be increasing demands for a shorter work week without any pay decrease. This presents serious difficulties, but it is not economically impossible, provided that productivity per worker has risen enough to absorb the increased costs involved. If changes of this nature are made, it is likely that overtime pay will increase in importance as a source of additional family income.

In this regard, attention should be paid to the increasing practice of holding a second, part-time job. In factory argot, this is called "moonlighting." It is estimated that four million workers today do additional work for a few hours at night, or on Saturdays and Sundays, in order to supplement family income.

Besides work done for pay, we should consider as income any productive work done at home. The do-it-yourself technique is often a real source of savings, as amateurs do painting, papering, plastering, tile-laying, and related activities that formerly were confined to skilled workers. A home owner who knows how to use the "cold-tube" method safely in repairing a malfunctioning television set can often effect really substantial economies. Just as with the housewife's shopping and cooking, time and effort used in making repairs and improvements can mean money saved.

From a social viewpoint, such extra income-producing activities are not to be condemned, provided they are important for the family and do not lead to impairment of health or neglect of parental duties. If a worker is able during his years of greatest energy to pay for a house and accumulate furniture and like possessions, he is less likely to be under severe economic pressure as he advances in age and suffers a decline in energy and health.

The same principle applies to the problem of women workers, to be treated presently. It is good, rather than bad, when young, unmarried women work. Even if they expect to make marriage their career, it is good for them to learn the discipline of work. They can also save money for their marriage. Older unmarried women and widows may need to work in order to earn their living. Married women who are not mothers may work outside the home, provided they are willing and prepared to accept their normal responsibility of motherhood. In addition, they should be sure that these extra duties do not impose a strain upon their marriage. It is always wise, when possible, to consider any such income as a supplement, not to be included in deciding family living levels. Thus, this income could be used to pay for a home, furniture, or other capital expenses in contrast to day-by-day living costs.

Women Workers. The position of women in industry has varied considerably during modern times. With the advent of the industrial revolution, women were employed in factories and mines. Gradually, their place in the factory was yielded to men, except that in both world wars the trend was reversed. In 1964, there were over 24 million women in the labor force in the United States, or more than one third of the women over fourteen years of age. Among the occupations heavily staffed by women are: secretarial, sales, teaching, clerical work, work in restaurants, nursing, and various kinds of personal service. A sizable group of women (over 4,000,000) work in manufacturing, such as textiles and clothing, paper and printing, shoe manufacturing, glassmaking, electrical manufacturing, and metal, rubber, and chemical industries. Women do light assembly-line work. In some industries, such as tobacco manufacturing or women's clothing, women comprise about 70 per cent of the working force. A high percentage also obtains in knit goods, woolen and worsted goods, radio manufacturing, gas and electric fixtures, boots and shoes, and men's clothing. But even in the masculine stronghold of heavy industry, about 12 per cent of the workers are women. Half the women in the labor force are thirty-eight years old or older. A majority of working women are married and about 40 per cent of these have children under eighteen.

The position of women in the business world has many social implications. These include the question of proper wages and working conditions, the effect on the home, and the impact on the economy in general.

Women are frequently paid lower wages than men, even for the same occupations. Thus, women schoolteachers often receive lower salaries than men doing the same task. The argument used is that men are more efficient, that they need the higher wages to support families, and that women do not remain in an industry or occupation long enough to be considered other than learners or apprentices. On the other hand, there is no question but that women are used to supplant male workers and thus depress the wage rate. Women often accept lower wages because they enter the working force either under some pressure or with the idea that the job is temporary. Married women workers frequently seek only a supplementary income, while single girls, often living at home, will accept lower wages since their expenses are lower. When these groups take jobs which are competitive with those of men, undoubtedly they depress standards. Moreover, the elements of pressure or temporary employment make them less amenable to unionization or other steps to raise wages. The net result is competitive lowering of living standards.

Some protection against wage discrimination is given in the Federal Equal Pay Act of 1963, which is an amendment to the Fair Labor Standards Act. This means that women in occupations affecting interstate commerce must receive equal pay for the same type of work as that performed by men. In addition, 24 states have equal-pay laws for private employment and 16 have equal-pay programs for schoolteachers.

Women need special consideration in the matter of working conditions. They need periodic rest intervals, a more liberal sickleave policy, and also maternity leaves. As a rule, nightwork is considered unsuitable for women. They are less able than men to work long hours. Because of this, most states have laws regulating the employment of women. These laws may specify the maximum number of hours per day and week, rest periods, and similar considerations. Over half the states also have minimum-wage laws for women. Standards for minimum wages usually assume a self-supporting single woman, thus taking a middle ground between the single woman living at home and the married woman supporting a family. Most laws are flexible, considering both the cost of living and the economic status of an industry.

Those whose duty it is to advise young girls and married women in the matter of employment might well ponder the address on Women's Duties given by Pope Pius XII on October 21, 1945. With moving eloquence and insight, the Holy Father noted that a woman cannot be happy in a social order which does violence to her nature. Her whole being tends toward motherhood and family life. Even when by vocation, either freely chosen or in submission to Divine Providence, she may never have a family of her own, she can still choose a form of spiritual motherhood in her choice of occupation. Through such professions as teaching, nursing, or social work, she can dedicate her life to the care of others. If she is forced, on the contrary, to do work more suitable for the masculine temperament, she does violence to her nature and becomes frustrated and unhappy.

Child Labor. Another possible source of supplementary family income is work by children of the family. Until recent years, most of the emphasis in regard to child labor concerned its abuses and consequent undesirability. With the serious problems of juvenile delinquency that have beset the United States in the 1960's, it is likely that there will be more stress upon the formative effects of hard work as a source of discipline and character building. It is still useful to note abuses that may exist in regard to immature workers. But we note these evils only to seek sound forms of work, not to discourage any constructive activity by the young or to promote the purposeless forms of idleness that often lead to delinquency. When discussing dangers in child labor, we observe physical, moral, and cultural problems that may arise as a result of wrong types of work for youth.

Work by children is physically dangerous when it taxes their strength and exposes them to sickness or, at least, to a stunting of their normal development. Such is the case with work too difficult for their years, risky in terms of possible accidents or in unsuitable surroundings in the matter of either place or time. Factory work is generally unhealthy for boys under eighteen. Labor in the fields in itself is better, but often the long hours and exhausting tasks are too much for the growing boy. Even light work which carries on into the night can mean loss of sleep and hence be debilitating. Moreover, if a child works so incessantly in his free time that he has no time for recreation, he will suffer physically. Hence, it is wrong to expect full-time hard work from children still in early adolescence. Part-time work likewise should be such as not to impose too great a strain at a time when energy reserves may be low.

Child labor is morally dangerous when performed in surroundings which present unusual temptations to crime or vice. From the moral viewpoint, indiscriminate mingling of young boys with older workers in factories would be generally unwise. The tone of conversation in the average factory is hardly that of a Holy Name meeting. While adults with decent standards develop a certain protective indifference to such language, the situation is otherwise with young boys, even in this sophisticated age. A similar problem obtains with street trades, such as those of newsboys and bootblacks, especially when boys work until late in the night to catch the after-theater crowd. Night surroundings in large cities can often be corrupting.

Another drawback to certain forms of child labor is the neglect of education which they involve. This ranges from outright withdrawal from school to carelessness in regard to studies. It is generally felt in the United States that a high school education or its equivalent should be available to all children. While there may be some who lack the minimum talent or interest necessary for such training, it is still desirable that they secure a better preparation for life, perhaps in a trade school. Certainly it is unjust when a student who is willing and able to receive a standard of education considered normal in this country is deprived of this opportunity because of family poverty.

There are two moral aspects to child labor. The first is that no child should be permitted to work under conditions which are detrimental to his health, morals, or basic education. Such work injures him and hence is contrary to his human dignity. Second, it is unjust when economic conditions force a child to work because total family income is insufficient to maintain decent standards. The father of a family should normally receive wages sufficient to support his family in frugal comfort. This does not mean that children should be forbidden work suitable to their age and strength. The discipline of moderate work is good training for children. They may learn habits of industry and responsibility. The income received may permit the family or the children small luxuries otherwise unobtainable. In some circumstances, it may be possible for a boy, through afterschool and summer work, to save enough to go to college. Again, in the absence of a family-allowance system, older children in large families may work to supplement a wage adequate for an average family but unsuitable in their case. Even in this situation, the family-allowance method might be better in principle.

Child labor in the United States is regulated by the Fair Labor Standards Act, which forbids the employment of minors under the age of sixteen in mining and manufacturing or at any work during school hours. Minors between the ages sixteen and eighteen may not be employed in hazardous occupations. Employment certificates may be secured by children between fourteen and sixteen, when the work will not interfere with their education or physical development. This law, however, applies only to occupations involved in interstate commerce. Children employed by their parents in occupations other than manufacturing and mining are exempt from the act. In 1965, 3.8 million young persons in the 14–17 year age bracket were in the work force. About half this group was either working full time or seeking such employment.

Even more meaningful than the figures quoted is the fact that both federal and state governments do not have adequate appropriations to enforce the laws upon the statute books. As a result, many abuses flourish even when regulatory laws have been passed to prevent them. In addition, many laws have loopholes to favor certain groups, such as farmers, so that coverage is often incomplete.

Social Insurance.   Not all income supplements create social problems. This is particularly the case with the so-called "fringe benefits" attached to the pay check, and also to social security and related programs. Fringe benefits, such as pensions, health plans, and paid vacations, constitute a real income gain to the worker, even though he may not always realize this fact. In effect, these benefits, plus social security, remove to a considerable degree the necessity for saving for sickness, old age, and unemployment. Hence a worker can devote a larger percentage of his pay to current needs.

In theory, it can be argued that workers should be paid enough that they can save for their own health and retirement needs. Actually, the whole trend of modern life is in the other direction. High-pressure advertising induces the worker to spend what he has and often to mortgage his future by installment purchases. We could not easily reverse this trend. In some cases, it may not even be desirable to try. For instance, we can probably have better medical care through industrial health plans or through group insurance than any worker could secure with the same funds spent piecemeal.

Likewise, it can be argued that the insurance principle is sound when dealing with the problem of unemployment. When a hazard is unpredictable in precise incidence as regards the individual, although predictable for a group, it is much easier to provide for this hazard through insurance rather than by individual saving. Workers are morally justified in seeking a level of unemployment benefits that permits a family to maintain its basic living standards. The reason that this is sought today through collective bargaining rather than through increases in state legislative benefits is partly economic and partly political. Economically some industries are in a good position to give supplementary unemployment benefits. From the viewpoint of politics, it is often easier to get gains through collective bargaining than to seek similar benefits through legislation. State legislators often view unemployment compensation with a jaundiced eye, as if it were a premium paid for idleness. Employers, on the other hand, are often more realistic in understanding that joblessness is unavoidable. Moreover, they are usually anxious to keep their work force intact when forced to lay off workers temporarily. Hence many of them, at least, are quite willing that their workers receive good benefits while unavoidably idle.

The Federal Advisory Council on Employment Security recommended at the close of 1958 that major changes be made in our unemployment compensation system. They favored a flat 30-week period of benefits, with benefits to average either half the worker's wage or two-thirds of the state's average weekly wage, whichever is lower. This would necessitate a major increase in practically every state in the Union. In addition, there was a call for simplifying and standardizing eligibility requirements. These proposals recognized the real importance of unemployment compensation to our economic system. It is more than a humanitarian measure; it is also a factor of stability in business fluctuations.

Finally, the combination of the industrial pension and federal old-age-and-survivors' benefits can often make the difference between destitution and security in old age. What was considered fantastic when proposed as the Townsend Plan some decades ago is almost a reality today — the availability of really suitable pensions for older persons without any means test or similar limitation. The time may come when the complex payment systems of today, both federal and private, will be replaced by pooled contributions based on the simple idea that the working force should take care of retired workers at any given time. We could thus avoid the tremendous bookkeeping problems, posed by present methods, as well as the economic implications of investing tens of billions for funded pension systems. Individuals and their employers could pay into this system according to their incomes. Payments to retired persons would be in terms of average previous income, regardless of how it was earned or for whom the pensioner worked. In this way there would be no need for huge investments and no problem of a pension tying a worker to a particular company for a lifetime.

In the meantime, certain adjustments are needed in the existing system of Old Age and Survivors' Insurance. For example the menace of inflation should be faced by some form of escalator clause tied to benefits. The extent of coverage should be still further broadened to include all persons in federal employment and the small groups of employed and self-employed still excluded from benefits. Finally, the age at which widows may receive payments should be further reduced. It is unrealistic, in most instances, to expect a widow to be self-supporting to the age of sixty-two.

Family Allowances.   In connection with the economic problems posed by a living wage, it was noted that there are strong arguments for a system of family allowances. Thus the wage received (including allowances) would be geared to family needs. We would not then burden our economic system with the heavy, if not impossible, task of paying all workers a wage that will enable family heads among them to support their children. In order to understand how such a system might help with family economic problems, it is useful to note here a few facts about different systems and to consider the controversies over the best method for instituting such allowances.

Practically every industrial nation in the world has some form of aid for families. Over sixty, including our neighbor, Canada, have direct allowances for children. Others have tax benefits, medical assistance, and other grants designed to help parents meet their burdens. These methods of help are based on several well-known facts. First, there is the fact that in our modern urban civilization children are an economic liability, not an asset. In earlier times, when farm and small-town life was predominant, large families were less of a burden, because children could work at home or near the home. Now it is often difficult for children to find suitable work, especially if they are young.

Second, total incomes for families with a large number of children tend to be low. One reason for this is that such families often have only one breadwinner, since the mother cannot be employed outside the home. Another factor is that the father is often relatively young and has not reached the peak of his earning capacity. Hence we find that families with the greatest needs are often low down on the family-income scale.

Apart from the element of need, some countries justify family help on the grounds that an expanding population is a national asset. Often it is a military necessity. It may be an economic advantage. Given the fact that so many families are childless, it is usually necessary to have a sizable number of large families (over four children) in order to maintain even a constant population level. On this ground, it can be argued that large families contribute to the general welfare and should in turn be rewarded for their contribution. Even totalitarian nations, such as the Soviet Union, have family allowances. Since it is notorious that such nations have little concern for human life or misery, one assumes that they support families as a source of national strength.

The form of allowance varies from country to country. Some give aid for all children, others for the third and following children, and so forth. Some systems decrease benefits per child as family size increases, others do not. Canada completely ignores the element of need, aiding even the children of the wealthy. The cost of aid may be met by general taxes or by special levies upon payrolls.

The types of argument used in the preceding chapter would favor an aid program closely tied up with the employer-employee relationship. Two reasons favor this, as contrasted with a state program based largely upon general taxation. One reason for payroll financing is the moral obligation of a living wage. This obligation is tied up with a work situation, not with the civic status of the worker. Hence employers, and workers also, should contribute to a fund designed to equalize family burdens. A second argument for the payroll-financed type of allowance plan is that it fits in more with the principle of subsidiarity. A state program would be another step in the direction of the welfare state. But here we must face up to the difficulty posed by low-wage industries. Obviously, an employer-financed plan would need supplementing from some general fund, if such industries were to pay an adequate wage to married workers with families.[1]

If a family-allowance system were to be inaugurated in the United States, there are good grounds for starting any system of payment with the third child. So much of our economic thinking has been in terms of the two-child family as normal, as indicated in the budgets analyzed earlier, that we can take for granted that most wages are supposed to meet this type of family obligation. A system of this nature would be less costly and less revolutionary in terms of established customs. Hence it would have a far better chance of being adopted than the theoretically better system of assistance for all family needs.

When the cost of family allowances is being considered, it is well to remember that contributions to the family may permit of savings in community social-service programs. Many existing welfare and relief programs could be curtailed if not abolished. In addition, there would be an enormous gain in terms of morale, as families got these services as

---

[1] For a temperate and factual analysis of the family-allowance program, see James C. Vadakin, *Family Allowances* (Miami, Fla.: University of Miami, 1959).

matters of right, not because of their indigence. It may well be that, strictly on the basis of cost, aid to families may turn out to be a long-run saving to the community.

READINGS*

A. H. Clemens, *Marriage and the Family*, Chap. 17.
J. F. Cronin and H. W. Flannery, *The Church and the Workingman*, Chaps. 5–6.
B. L. Masse, *Justice for All*, Chap. 5.
J. Messner, *Social Ethics* (rev. ed.), pp. 397–427.
C. S. Mihanovich and others, *Marriage and the Family*, Chap. 5.

* For further readings, see List No. 8 in the Appendix.

Chapter XII

PROPERTY

PROPERTY IN MODERN LIFE

John XXIII, Mater et Magistra

43. Concerning the use of material goods, Our Predecessor declared that the right of every man to use these for his own sustenance is prior to every other economic right, even that of private property. The right to the private possession of material goods is admittedly a natural one; nevertheless, in the objective order established by God, the right to property cannot stand in the way of the axiomatic principle that "the goods which were created by God for all men should flow to all alike, according to the principles of justice and charity."

104. It is well known that in recent years in the larger industrial concerns a distinction has been growing between the ownership of productive goods and the responsibility of company managers. This has created considerable problems for public authorities, whose duty it is to see that the aims pursued by the leaders of the principal organizations — especially those which have an important part to play in the national economy — do not conflict in any way with the interests of the common good. Experience shows that these problems arise whether the capital which makes possible these vast undertakings belongs to private citizens or to public corporations.

105. It is also true that more and more people today, through belonging to insurance groups and systems of social security, find that they can face the future with confidence — the sort of confidence which formerly resulted from their possession of a certain amount of property.

106. And another thing happening today is that people are aiming at proficiency in their trade or profession rather than the acquisition of private property. They think more highly of an income which derives from work and the rights consequent upon work, than of an income which derives from capital and the rights of capital.

107. And this as it should be. Work, which is the immediate expression of a human personality, must always be rated higher than the possession of external goods which of their very nature are merely instrumental. This view of work is certainly an indication of an advance that has been made in our civilization.

Confirmation of the right of ownership

108. What, then, of that social and economic principle so vigorously asserted and defended by Our predecessors: man's natural right to own

private property, including productive goods? Is this no longer operative today, or has it lost some of its validity in view of the economic conditions We have described above? This is the doubt that has arisen in many minds.

109. There is no reason for such a doubt to persist. The right of private ownership of goods, including productive goods, has permanent validity. It is part of the natural order, which teaches that the individual is prior to society and that society must be ordered to the good of the individual.

Moreover, it would be quite useless to insist on free and personal initiative in the economic field, while at the same time withdrawing man's right to dispose freely of the means indispensable to the achievement of such initiative.

Further, history and experience testify that in those political regimes which do not recognize the rights of private ownership of goods, productive included, the exercise of freedom in almost every other direction is suppressed or stifled. This suggests, surely, that the exercise of freedom finds its guarantee and incentive in the right of ownership.

110. This explains why social and political movements for the harmonizing of justice and freedom in society, some would maintain. It is inherent though until recently opposed to the private ownership of productive goods, are today reconsidering their position in the light of a clearer understanding of social history, and are in fact now declaring themselves in favor of this right.

Always vast field for personal charity

120. In recent years the state and other agencies of public law have extended, and are continuing to extend, the sphere of their activity and initiative. But this does not mean that the doctrine of the social function of private ownership is out of date, as in the very right of private ownership.

Then, too, a further consideration arises. Tragic situations and urgent problems of an intimate and personal nature are continually arising which the state with all its machinery is unable to remedy or assist. There will always remain, therefore, a vast field for the exercise of human sympathy and the Christian charity of individuals. We would observe, finally, that the efforts of individuals or of groups of private citizens, are definitely more effective in promoting spiritual values than is the activity of public authority.

Vatican Council II, The Church in the Modern World

71. Private ownership or some other kind of dominion over material goods provides everyone with a wholly necessary area of independence, and should be regarded as an extension of human freedom. Finally, since it adds incentives for carrying on one's function and duty, it constitutes a kind of prerequisite for civil liberties.

PROPERTY RIGHTS: SOCIAL AND INDIVIDUAL

Pius XI, Quadragesimo Anno

45. First, then, let it be considered as certain and established that neither Leo nor those theologians who have taught under the guidance and authority of the Church have ever denied or questioned the twofold

character of ownership, usually called individual and social according as it regards either separate persons or the common good. For they have always unanimously maintained that nature, rather the Creator Himself, has given man the right of private ownership, not only that individuals may be able to provide for themselves and their families, but also that the goods which the Creator destined for the entire family of mankind may through this institution truly serve this purpose. All this can be achieved in nowise except through the maintenance of a certain and definite order.

46. Accordingly, twin rocks of shipwreck must be carefully avoided. For, as one is wrecked upon, or comes close to, what is known as "individualism" by denying or minimizing the social and public character of the right of property, so by rejecting or minimizing the private and individual character of this same right, one inevitably runs into "collectivism" or at least closely approaches its tenets.

49. It follows from what We have termed the individual and at the same time social character of ownership, that men must consider in this matter not only their own advantage but also the common good. To define these duties in detail when necessity requires and the natural law has not done so, is the function of those in charge of the state. Therefore, public authority, under the guiding light always of the natural and divine law, can determine more accurately upon consideration of the true requirements of the common good, what is permitted and what is not permitted to owners in the use of their property. Moreover, Leo XIII wisely taught "that God has left the limits of private possessions to be fixed by the industry of men and institutions of peoples."

TAXATION

Leo XIII, Rerum Novarum

67. But these advantages can be attained only if private wealth is not drained away by crushing taxes of every kind. For since the right of possessing goods privately has been conferred not by man's law, but by nature, public authority cannot abolish it, but can only control its exercise and bring it into conformity with the common weal. Public authority, therefore, would act unjustly and inhumanly, if in the name of taxes it should appropriate from the property of private individuals more than is equitable.

Pius XI, On Atheistic Communism

75. The state must take every measure necessary to supply employment particularly for the heads of families and for the young. To achieve this end demanded by the pressing needs of the common welfare, the wealthy classes must be induced to assume those burdens without which human society cannot be saved nor they themselves remain secure. However, measures taken by the state with this end in view ought to be of such a nature that they will really affect those who possess more than their share of capital resources, and who continue to accumulate them to the grievous detriment of others.

Pius XII, To International Association for Financial and Fiscal Law, October 2, 1956

There can be no doubt concerning the duty of each citizen to bear a part of the public expense. It is the obligation of the state, however — insofar as it is charged with protecting and promoting the common good of citizens — to assess upon its citizens only necessary levies which are, furthermore, proportionate to their means. Taxation can never become, then, a convenient way for public authority to make up a deficit brought on by an improvident administration, or a means of favoring one industry or branch of business at the expense of another of equal utility. The state must forbid itself any waste of public funds; it must forestall abuse and injustice on the part of its employees, as well as evasion by those who are legitimately taxed.

Modern states tend today to multiply their interventions and to make themselves answerable for an increasing number of services; they exercise a tighter control over the economy; they intervene to a greater extent in the social protection of many classes of workers. Thus their need for money mounts in proportion to the degree to which they enlarge their administrations. Excessively heavy impositions often oppress private initiative, check the development of industry and commerce, and work to the detriment of good will.

*   *   *

May taxes continue to be adjusted, with increasingly sensitive and adequate criteria, to the true capabilities of the individual. Taxation will no longer, then, be regarded as a constantly excessive and more or less arbitrary burden. It will come to represent — in a state better organized and equipped for achieving the harmonious performance of society's various activities — a humble, perhaps, and very material, but nonetheless indispensable, aspect of civic unity and individual support of the common welfare.

John XXIII, Mater et Magistra

132. In a system of taxation based on justice and equity it is fundamental that the burdens be proportioned to the capacity of the people contributing.

DUTIES OF PROPERTY OWNERS

Leo XIII, Rerum Novarum

36. To own goods privately, as We saw above, is a right natural to man, and to exercise this right, especially in life in society, is not only lawful, but clearly necessary. "It is lawful for man to own his own things. It is even necessary for human life." But if the question be asked: How ought man use his possessions, the Church replies without hesitation: "As to this point, man ought not regard external goods as his own, but as common so that, in fact, a person should readily share them when he sees others in need. Wherefore the Apostle says: 'Charge the rich of this world . . . to give readily, to share with others'" (Summa, II, II, 66, 2). No one, certainly, is obliged to assist others out of what is required for his own neces-

sary use or for that of his family, or even to give to others what he himself needs to maintain his station in life becomingly and decently: "No one is obliged to live unbecomingly." But when the demands of necessity and propriety have been sufficiently met, it is a duty to give to the poor out of that which remains. "Give that which remains as alms." These are duties not of justice, except in cases of extreme need, but of Christian charity, which obviously cannot be enforced by legal action. But the laws and judgments of men yield precedence to the law and judgment of Christ the Lord, who in many ways urges the practice of almsgiving: "It is more blessed to give than to receive," and who will judge a kindness done or denied to the poor as done or denied to Himself. "As long as you did it for one of these, the least of My brethren, you did it for Me." The substance of all this is the following: whoever has received from the bounty of God a greater share of goods, whether corporal and external, or of the soul, has received them for this purpose, namely, that he employ them for his own perfection and, likewise, as a servant of Divine Providence, for the benefit of others.

Pius XI, Quadragesimo Anno

47. In order to place definite limits on the controversies that have arisen over ownership and its inherent duties there must be first laid down as a foundation a principle established by Leo XIII: the right of property is distinct from its use. That justice called commutative commands sacred respect for the division of possessions and forbids invasion of others' rights through the exceeding of the limits of one's own property; but the duty of owners to use their property only in a right way does not come under this type of justice, but under other virtues, obligations of which "cannot be enforced by legal action." Therefore, they are in error who assert that ownership and its right use are limited by the same boundaries; and it is much farther still from the truth to hold that a right to property is destroyed or lost by reason of abuse or nonuse.

48. Those, therefore, are doing a work that is truly salutary and worthy of all praise who, while preserving harmony among themselves and the integrity of the traditional teaching of the Church, seek to define the inner nature of these duties and their limits whereby either the right of property itself or its use, that is, the exercise of ownership, is circumscribed by the necessities of social living. On the other hand, those who seek to restrict the individual character of ownership to such a degree that in fact they destroy it are mistaken and in error.

50. Furthermore, a person's superfluous income, that is, income which he does not need to sustain life fittingly and with dignity, is not left wholly to his own free determination. Rather the Sacred Scriptures and the Fathers of the Church constantly declare in the most explicit language that the rich are bound by a very grave precept to practice almsgiving, beneficence, and munificence.

51. Expending larger incomes so that opportunity for gainful work may be abundant, provided, however, that this work is applied to producing really useful goods, ought to be considered, as We deduce from the principles of the Angelic Doctor, an outstanding exemplification of the virtue of munificence and one particularly suited to the needs of the times.

A JUST DISTRIBUTION OF PROPERTY

Leo XIII, Rerum Novarum

65. We have seen, in fact, that the whole question under consideration cannot be settled effectually unless it is assumed and established as a principle, that the right of private property must be regarded as sacred.

Wherefore, the law ought to favor this right and, so far as it can, see that the largest possible number among the masses of the population prefer to own property.

Pius XI, Quadragesimo Anno

57. Therefore, the riches that the economic-social developments constantly increase ought to be so distributed among individual persons and classes that the common advantage of all, which Leo XIII had praised, will be safeguarded; in other words, that the common good of all society will be kept inviolate.

58. To each, therefore, must be given his own share of goods, and the distribution of goods which, as every discerning person knows, is laboring today under the gravest evils due to the huge disparity between the few exceedingly rich and the unnumbered propertyless, must be effectively called back to and brought into conformity with the norms of the common good, that is, social justice.

60. The immense multitude of the nonowning workers on the one hand, and the enormous riches of certain very wealthy men on the other, establish an unanswerable argument that the riches which are so abundantly produced in our age of "industrialism," as it is called, are not rightly

distributed and equitably made available to the various classes of people.

61. Therefore, with all our strength and effort we must strive that at least in the future the abundant fruits of production will accrue equitably to those who are rich and will be distributed in ample sufficiency among the workers . . . that they may increase their property by thrift, that they may bear, by wise management of this increase in property, the burdens of family life with greater ease and security, and that, emerging from that insecure lot in life in whose uncertainties nonowning workers are cast, they may be able not only to endure the vicissitudes of earthly existence, but also have assurance that when their lives are ended they will provide in some measure for those they leave after them.

63. . . . It will be impossible to put these principles into practice unless the nonowning workers through industry and thrift advance to the state of possessing some little property.

Pius XI, On Atheistic Communism

50. Is it not deplorable that the right of private property defended by the Church should so often have

been used as a weapon to defraud the workingman of his just salary and his social rights?

Pius XII, Christmas Broadcast, 1942

1840. The dignity of the human person, then, requires normally, as a natural foundation of life, the right to the use of the goods of the earth. To this right corresponds the fundamental obligation to grant private ownership of property, if possible, to all. Positive legislation regulating private ownership may change and more or less restrict its use. But if legislation is to play its part in the pacification of the community, it must prevent the worker, who is or will be a father of a family, from being condemned to an economic dependence and slavery which is irreconcilable with his rights as a person.

Pius XII, Radio Address, September 1, 1944

But the Church aims rather at securing that the institution of private property be such as it should be according to the designs of God's wisdom and the dispositions of nature: an element of social order, a necessary presupposition to human initiative, an incentive to work to the advantage of life's purpose here and hereafter, and hence of the liberty and the dignity of man, created in the likeness of God, who, from the beginning, assigned him for his benefit domination over material things.

The social and economic policy of the future, the controlling power of the state, of local bodies, of professional institutions cannot permanently secure their end, which is the genuine productivity of social life and the normal returns on national economy, except by respecting and safeguarding the vital function of private property in its personal and social values.

*   *   *

For the same purpose small and medium holdings in agriculture, in the arts and trades, in commerce and industry should be guaranteed and promoted; co-operative unions should ensure for them the advantages of big business; where big business even today shows itself more productive, there should be given the possibility of tempering the labor contract with a contract of co-ownership.

Pius XII, To Spanish Employers and Workers, March 11, 1951

The Church defends the right of private property, a right she considers fundamentally inalienable. But she insists also on the need for a more just distribution of property and deplores the unnatural social situation in which an enormous mass of impoverished people live beside a small group of very rich and privileged. There always will be economic inequalities. But all those who in any way are able to influence the progress of society must aim to obtain a situation which permits people who do the best they can not only to live, but to save. There are many factors which must contribute to a greater diffusion of property. But the principal one always will be a just salary. You know very well, beloved children, that a just salary and a better distribution of natural wealth constitute two of the most impelling demands in the social program of the Church.

John XXIII, Mater et Magistra

115. Now, if ever, is the time to insist on a more widespread distribution of property, in view of the rapid economic development of an increasing number of states. It will not be difficult for the body politic, by the adoption of various techniques of proved efficiency, to pursue an economic and social policy which facilitates the widest possible distribution of private property in terms of durable consumer goods, houses, land, tools and equipment (in the case of craftsmen and owners of family farms), and shares in medium and large business concerns. This policy is in fact being pursued with considerable success by several of the socially and economically advanced nations.

Australian Hierarchy, Socialization, 1948

In the economic sphere, it is therefore a most important task of government to encourage that type of economic organization in which the family and the home may prosper. The normal economic order — that order which is best adapted to the real needs of mankind — is one in which the majority of men are working proprietors; that is to say, where they earn a living for themselves and their families by working their own property, whether that property is a farm, a shop, a workshop, or a factory. This is the best economic order precisely because the institution of the family is strongest where this system prevails. This type of economic order may be adapted to enterprises which require more capital than one family can contribute. Where the amount of capital actually needed for the conduct of the business is greater than one man can supply, the necessary capital is best made up in the form of a partnership in which each of the partners has an effective share of control.

THE RIGHT TO PRIVATE PROPERTY

PROPERTY is of necessity one of the foundations of economic life. Its accumulation makes men of wealth. Its widespread distribution normally brings about a stable society. Men risk their lives to acquire or to conserve it, while others, fearing the passion for wealth, take solemn vows relinquishing the right of ownership. To many, it is a bastion of security and a guarantee of freedom. It is no wonder, then, that the concept of property rights normally determines the entirety of a social philosophy. The rights of man and of the state are so closely correlated with those of property that often the one can be deduced from the other.

Disputes over the rights of property were among the major factors occasioning the social encyclicals. The socialists reacted to the abuse of property by calling for state ownership of all productive wealth. Proudhon said: "Property is theft." To which Bishop von Ketteler replied: "The notorious dictum, 'property is theft,' is something more than a mere lie; besides a great lie, it contains a terrible truth. Scorn and derision will not dispose of it. . . . As deep calleth unto deep, so one sin against nature calls forth another. Out of the distorted right of ownership, the false doctrine of communism was begotten."[1] Then came *Rerum Novarum*, which vindicated the right of property against socialism, but also denounced abuses by property owners. Even within the Church, controversy continued, with some holding that the right of property was contingent upon its proper use. But, when *Quadragesimo Anno* was issued, it clearly upheld the right of property, defined its individual and social character, noted the powers of the state in regard to it, and even more strongly denounced abuses connected with it. Finally, the repeated discourses and encyclicals of Pope Pius XII stressed both the need for more equitable distribution of property and the ideal that most men become owners of property.

The Right to Ownership. The classical treatment of property is found in the *Summa Theologiae* of St. Thomas Aquinas. The arguments of St. Thomas for private property have lost none of their luster through the centuries. His position may be quoted in full:

> Two things are competent to man in respect to exterior things. One is the power to procure and dispense them, and in this regard it is lawful for man to possess property. Moreover, this is necessary for human life for three reasons. First, because every man is more careful to procure what is for himself alone than that which is common to many or to all; since each one would shirk the labor and leave to another that which concerns the community, as happens when there are a great number of servants. Secondly, because human affairs are conducted in a more orderly fashion if each man is charged with taking care of some particular thing himself, whereas there would be confusion if everyone had to look after any one thing indeterminately. Thirdly, because a more peaceful state is ensured to man if each is contented with his own. Hence it is to be observed that quarrels arise more frequently where there is no division of things possessed.
>
> The second thing that is competent to man with regard to external things is their use. In this respect man ought to possess external things, not as his own, but as common, so that, to wit, he is ready to communicate them to others in their need.[2]

These arguments are based on such enduring qualities of human nature that they possess the virtue of timelessness.

---

[1] Sermon on "The Christian Idea of the Rights of Property," cited in J. J. Laux, *Ketteler's Social Reform* (Philadelphia: Dolphin Press, 1912), pp. 38–39.

[2] *Summa*, II, II, 66, 2; cf. W. J. McDonald, *The Social Value of Property According to St. Thomas Aquinas* (Washington: Catholic University, 1939), and Suarez, *De Legibus*, II, 17–19.

The first argument is that private property fosters initiative, whereas common ownership leads to slovenly neglect. This element of human interest in one's own is so obvious that proof is unnecessary. Even children tend to treasure their own toys. A businessman will slave to make his firm a success, whereas the hired manager (unless a personal incentive is present) tends to be careless and timeserving. In colleges and like communities, common property is often neglected. The community car often lacks gas, gets infrequent oil changes, and receives much more abuse than usually happens when an auto is privately owned. People generally take care of their own lawns and yet are careless in littering public parks. Government-owned business is often unimaginative and routine, whereas private business tends to be enterprising and resourceful. There are exceptions to these statements, but usually only where some equivalent motive substitutes for pride of ownership. A manager may be ambitious for success, feeling that his record will bring promotion. He may fear the penalties of failure. The instinct of self-seeking is deep. It may be modified by Christian altruism, but only in a few persons is altruism so dominant that they take care of common goods as if they were their own. So long as human nature remains in this pattern, and fallen nature is prone to evil, private ownership will be more successful than common possessions.

Second, private ownership leads to an orderly handling of human affairs. The distinction of ownership leads to a division of duties. The man who owns a farm will cultivate it. The proprietor of a store will order goods and sell them. If ownership were indeterminate, men would follow their impulses and instincts in a most haphazard fashion. In pleasant weather, there would be an inordinate number taking care of the fishing needs of the community. If snow blocked the streets, most men would prefer to meet their indoor duties, rather than clear off the snow. The alternative to this chaos would be central organization of life by the state. But if all economic power were centered in the state, freedom would be lost. In the absence of universal altruism, the normal method of getting men to work is the use of fear and compulsion. Experiences in the Soviet Union bear this out. The communists first tried the ideal of "from each according to his ability, to each according to his needs." But the system soon degenerated into a cruel incentive system for labor, with a reign of absolute terror superimposed.

Finally, private possessions tend to promote a peaceful society. If goods were held in common, there would be frequent quarrels over the most desirable things. Farmers would fight to cultivate the best land. Workers would want the most pleasant jobs. Each would seek a share of distribution more favorable to himself. The result would be mob rule, with the strongest or the most cunning holding the best positions. Even in religious communities, under a vow of poverty and practicing the virtue of charity, there are strains and tensions because of common possessions. With only one morning newspaper in the common room, some may be unhappy because a colleague persists in reading every word. Not all will agree on the programs to be seen on the community television. These sacrifices are endured and sublimated through religious ideals, but they would be occasions of quarrels outside the monastery walls. Hence, common ownership does not readily accord with fallen nature, except in cases where people voluntarily embrace a life involving the counsels of perfection.

The Thomistic arguments for private property are based upon an analysis of certain enduring traits of human nature. They should be supplemented, however, by the pronouncements of the "social popes," especially those which emphasize property as necessary both for the freedom of the individual and the stability of the family. Pope Pius XII particularly noted that property widely distributed affords an economic basis for political and other freedoms. Pope Leo XIII stressed the value of property ownership as an economic foundation for family stability.

If the right of property is upheld, then it follows logically that the property owner must receive the normal return from his possessions. Where these possessions consist of capital goods, this return is called profit. Money, considered as the equivalent of capital, is productive of interest. Both these types of return were treated in Chapter VIII. There remains one further method of realizing upon property, namely, rent.

Rent is a return based on the value of land, whether this value derives from fertility of soil or location of property. In strict economic usage, rent applies only to land, not to buildings that rest on the land or even to improvements, such as irrigation, that enhance its usefulness. By contrast, in the ordinary "rent" that an apartment dweller pays, an economist finds not only a charge for land, but also interest on capital investment, payment for the costs of management, and normal maintenance and depreciation charges.

Some persons have questioned the moral right of landowners to collect rent. These objectors argue that the special worth that constitutes a basis for rent (as defined above) depends upon natural fertility and artificial location values and not upon any contribution by the owner. Accordingly, he has no moral right to appropriate what is a result of divine bounty or of the enterprise of others. Fertility is a God-given attribute of soil, and location is dependent upon community developments.

Two answers can be offered to the attacks upon economic rent. First, any validity in the arguments cited applies only to the original occupant of the land who held it until it acquired substantial value. Any subsequent purchaser presumably has paid the full value of the land and hence is entitled to a return on his investment. Second, if the so-called unearned increment were to be taxed away or otherwise denied owners, all land would lose its value to an owner. This would have the practical effect of denying private property in land. Such a drastic limitation of property rights can hardly be reconciled with the powerful natural-law arguments in favor of private ownership. It is better to permit unearned gains to property owners, if the alternative is the limitation of the institution of private property in such a drastic manner.

Pope John XXIII faced more sophisticated arguments against the traditional view of private property. Many scholars held that the separation of ownership and control in large corporations, the desire of many persons to seek security through pensions and social insurance instead of property, and the fact that work skills are the greatest source of independence for many workers — all these lessen the validity of traditional arguments for property. The Pope insists, however, that there still remain pressing reasons to consider private property a bulwark of individual freedom. While some classical arguments in its favor may not be quite so convincing today, nevertheless society needs private property as basic support for both political and economic freedom.

Individual and Social Aspects of Property. St. Thomas stated that while ownership may be private, use should be common, so that an owner is ready to communicate his goods to others in their need. Pope Pius XI made this point more exact by distinguishing between the individual and the social aspects of property. While individual ownership is a right, social obligations also attach to property. These social duties may be evident from the nature of the common good or they may be specified by positive law, whether divine or human. The state normally determines, in the absence of natural or divine law, what should be the duties of owners. Thus, it directs property into its proper place in the universal pattern of the common good. In so acting, government should be careful not to destroy the right of ownership in the guise of regulation or taxation.

That property has a social aspect is evident from even casual consideration. When a man buys an automobile, he acquires a personal possession. It is his to use or to leave idle, to sell or to give. But the ownership and use of a car also involves clear social responsibilities. The owner, in most states, must register his title and acquire license tags. Before he is allowed to drive, he normally must have a permit and this usually involves an examination on his ability to drive and his knowledge of traffic laws. In using the car, he is bound by traffic regulations. He must drive on the right side of the street, at proper speed, and observe signal lights and signs. His brakes and headlights must be in order. In some states, he must secure periodic inspections of the car. All these requirements exist because the common good demands such regulation of private property in automobiles. If people drive haphazardly, lives are endangered and traffic is hopelessly entangled. Social obligations here are clear and binding.

As a general rule, it might be stated that the social aspect of property increases insofar as it affects persons other than its owners. Things which are close to the individual and do not normally affect others do not have important social connotations. Ordinarily such items as personal clothing, furniture in the home, or a tractor on the farm have little social import. But improper clothing offends public decency. A television set in the home should not blare loudly at night. If a tractor is driven on the public highways, its driver must observe traffic rules.

There are types of property which necessarily involve social obligations. Thus, a large factory may employ thousands of workers. It can be a major influence in the community. Its products may be used throughout the nation or even the world. Even if this factory were owned by a single individual, he could not be blind to the many duties implied by the type of ownership he enjoys. This is all the more true where a corporation owns such property, since corporation law gives shareholders the rights of ownership, but exempts them from many of its duties. Stockholders are not legally liable for the debts of the company (except that its property, their equity, may be sold to pay debts) nor are they legally responsible for the actions of their officers. Indeed, courts have upheld boards of directors that refused information requested by stockholders, when the divulging of such information would be contrary to the company's interests. Thus, we have in the large corporation ownership shorn of much of the right of control. The "property" of the stockholder is more a contingent claim upon profits than a title of effective ownership.

Two conclusions follow from this situation. First, the personal responsibility of the stockholder in regard to the large corporation is generally minimal. If he lacks power to control decisions, he can hardly be blamed for such decisions. The most that moralists could realistically expect in such situations is that, when a corporation is acting unjustly, good men do not profit from such injustice by buying or retaining stock in such a company. Second, there are special grounds for government action to specify and enforce social obligations, when property ownership and responsibility are divorced. Here more than ever the social aspects of property must be considered.

Regulation must not be carried to such an extreme that it degenerates into collectivism. This would be a denial of the individual aspect of property rights, a threat to human liberty, and hence a false interpretation of the common good. The community exists to serve its members, not to dominate over them or absorb them. But restraint does not mean a passive, laissez-faire attitude by the state, since this would be an abdication to individualism and a denial of the common good. A careful balance between the extremes of individualism and collectivism must be kept at all times. Naturally the emphasis on state intervention will vary according to circumstances of time and place. A small, self-sufficient country with a good balance between agriculture and industry needs less public stress on social duties than does a larger nation with difficult social problems. Again, the impact of social obligations is usually greater in times of war or emergency than in periods of peace and normal times. In a period of war, both the social aspect of property and the right of the state to direct its use for the common good are intensified.

We should not emphasize the function of the state in specifying the social aspects of property to the neglect of obligations springing from natural and divine law. Certain natural rights which are possessed by individuals involve limitations on the use of property. Even in the absence of law, an owner is obligated to consider these social implications of property use. Thus, labor's right to organize and to seek a living wage is bound to affect the employer's use of his productive property. A farmer who cultivates his land in such a way as to cause erosion on other farms is acting unsocially. A mining firm that endangers lives or property by its methods of extraction is doing wrong. Owners likewise have a duty to avoid unnecessary work on Sunday, so that their employees can attend divine worship. While the state may enforce such obligations in view of the common good, they also oblige individual consciences under social justice and other virtues, even in the absence of public law.

Taxation. Papal treatment of taxation is not extensive. Pope Leo XIII warns against confiscatory taxes which destroy property rights in the guise of collecting public funds. Pope Pius XI notes that this warning does not preclude progressive taxation, bearing heavily on the wealthy. Sharing the common burdens in accord with ability to pay, far from destroying property, safeguards it against the possibility of violent revolution. Pope Pius XII emphasizes the need for preserving economic incentive and directing taxes in terms of an efficient economic organization that provides the material basis for cultural and spiritual values. Finally, Pope John XXIII stressed the fact that social progress must keep pace with economic progress. Taxation and social security programs can aid in securing this balance.

The complexity of modern life and the heavy cost of war and preparation against war necessarily involve a high cost of government. Thus, in the United States today about 30 per cent of the national income goes for taxation and in other countries the amount is even higher. Most of these costs are necessary, although savings would be possible through greater efficiency in some phases of government. Accordingly, a high level of taxation seems inevitable. The only method of relieving the relative burden would be a continuing increase in the general national income. A 100-billion-dollar federal budget would be less troublesome if the national income were seven hundred billion instead of five hundred.

It happens that taxation is in turn one of the important determinants of the level of national income. If taxes were so directed as to absorb practically all the savings of the community, there would be no investment and no economic expansion. The economy would be stagnant and unemployment would rise, since industry could not provide for a growing working population. Hence two factors must be balanced in working out a just system of taxation. The tests of equality of sacrifice and payment according to ability would dictate progressive income taxes, which naturally bear most heavily upon the wealthier classes. Yet the need for retaining the profit incentive and of stimulating investment is also vital, if the economic system is to expand and provide more jobs. Hence taxation should not preclude all saving in the group which is prone to invest, nor should it make investment impossible by so taxing gains that the risk becomes prohibitive.

Practically all taxes have social aspects. Thus, sales taxes bear most heavily on low-income groups and so discourage consumption and bring about lower living standards. Taxes on a commodity or service tend to lessen the use of the goods or services. Sometimes this restriction may be deliberate, as with liquor or tobacco. At other times, imposts of this kind may have been enacted for emergency reasons (as with wartime "luxury taxes") and retained merely because of revenue needs. The entire pattern of an industry can be changed by taxation. When some states adopted chain-store taxes which rose progressively with the number of stores owned by a single firm, they practically broke up chain ownership. The relative positions of butter and oleomargarine are largely determined by tax laws. Tariffs and export taxes have great economic effects. Unfortunately, it often happens that such laws are enacted without full consideration of their effect upon the common good.

Since taxation is of far-reaching importance, the United States should re-examine its entire fiscal policy. Even if there were not known abuses, the sheer size of federal, state, and local budgets would make this imperative. Methods which worked well when government costs were less than 10 per cent of national income might not be feasible today. We rightly had a Hoover Commission to study the most efficient way of reorganizing the federal government. An equally distinguished and representative group could well consider our entire fiscal program. Present taxes discourage equity financing and small business, channel economic expansion into the form of enlarging existing corporations, reward debt financing in preference to the more socially desirable equity financing, and place heavy burdens on industries which already find survival difficult. The tremendous impact of government cash collections on the ups and downs of business has received inadequate study. Under any system, the burden of present-day government is bound to be great. But wise tax laws can so distribute and regulate this burden that business incentive will be retained and unnecessary shocks avoided.

Another moral aspect of taxation concerns the duty in conscience of the individual taxpayer in regard to tax laws. Should he consider such laws as being merely "penal," not binding in conscience, but subjecting him to the hazard of prosecution if he is caught evading taxes? Or should he consider taxes in general as moral obligations?

Theologians differ in answering the questions just raised. It would not be feasible here to go into all the complex arguments used on both sides. But it may be useful to comment upon a psychological attitude that runs through many of the discussions. Those who hold that tax laws do not bind in conscience often reflect the views of older theologians who faced a different political situation from that of the modern world. In older times taxes might rightly have been considered as impositions of a sovereign often used to finance his luxuries, wars of conquest, and so forth. In modern democratic societies, taxes should be more nearly tied to the needs of the common good and hence involve the virtue of social justice. If the citizen feels that his contributions are being misused, he can use political means for correcting the abuses. Accordingly, it follows that social (contributive) justice demands that citizens pay taxes as a matter of conscience. The contrary view, practiced in many countries, leads to many injustices and unfair distribution of tax burdens. A democratic political society can hardly thrive if large groups of citizens fail to contribute to the needs of a nation.

Duties of Owners. In addition to the general responsibility for using property in accord with the common good, owners have certain specific obligations in respect to their wealth. Pope Pius XI notes that the wealthy are bound to use their superfluous income in the practice of almsgiving, beneficence, and munificence. His language in this passage is strong: *gravissimo teneantur divites praecepto.* The Latin terms *praeceptum* and *grave* are both normally used only for the most serious obligations, although the Latin superlative is sometimes weaker than the positive. Thus, all moralists use the phrase *praeceptum sub gravi* as connoting a duty obliging under pain of mortal sin. This obligation is not in justice but under other virtues, such as charity.

Superfluous income has been defined as the excess over an amount needed to live becomingly in accord with one's state in life. At the same time, moralists have not refined this definition by precise rules as to what is "becoming" in various states. Nor have they clarified the moral conditions involved in advancing to a state of great wealth. In this somewhat inadequately explored field, certain conclusions might be offered. A man with ability and enterprise might, through the use of morally acceptable means, advance to a state of wealth. As he progresses, it would be legitimate to reinvest his savings in the business so as to promote its expansion, at the same time meeting the normal demands of charity appropriate to his income level.

His personal motivation should not be evil. Thus, he should avoid disordered pride, ambition, or avarice. He might be inspired by satisfaction in achievement, desire to help his family, and interest in the community. The building of an enterprise which produces useful goods or services and furnishes needed employment is morally sound. If this process brings great wealth, the owner might then live in accord with healthy community standards for persons in his position. While lavish display, motivated by pride or vanity, would be wrong, yet such luxuries as a large house, servants, two cars, and a winter trip to a warm climate would not necessarily be inappropriate. He might give his children the best of education and protect his family by large insurance policies.

At all times, however, such a wealthy man should be concerned over the needs of charity in his community and nation. Superfluous wealth, above the customary needs of his station, should be considered as money held in trust, to be used in accord with the virtues of almsgiving, beneficence, and munificence. Two of these virtues were treated earlier in Chapter IV. Beneficence implies the Christian virtue of charity, giving help not merely because it is a duty, but rather in terms of love of neighbor. St. Thomas and the popes insist that the helping of the needy out of one's superfluous income is a strict obligation, which could oblige under pain of mortal sin if the need were great and the wealthy man the only source of relief. But it is much more desirable to have a spirit of generous giving, springing from a compassionate heart. This is the true Christian ideal.

A WIDER DIFFUSION OF OWNERSHIP

The Ideal of Distributed Ownership. While the popes have defended the institution of private property, they have not supported past and present practices of distribution of both income and wealth. Each of the four great social popes has solemnly pronounced the need for a better diffusion of ownership. Pope Leo XIII made the advantages of actual ownership the major arguments for private property. Pope Pius XI reiterated the need for more equitable distribution of wealth and income and attacked existing abuses in this regard. It remained for Pope Pius XII to carry this argument further and to apply it to small business and other forms of distributed productive property. He likewise attacked directly the concentration of economic life into giant cities and huge industrial enterprises. Pope John XXIII was quite specific in calling for better distribution of durable consumer goods and craftsmen's tools.

The central argument for property diffusion is freedom. Long ago, St. Thomas Aquinas noted that the difference between freedom and slavery lies in property ownership. He said that the despot rules over slaves, who cannot resist his rule, since they own nothing. But government over free men is different, since, "although they are subjected to the rule of their president, nevertheless they have something of thir own, whereby they are able to resist the power of the ruler."[3] When the state owns all productive wealth, as under communism, the subject is of necessity a slave. Likewise, when the most important kind of wealth in a community is owned by a few, the many suffer a real limitation of their freedom. Thus, in the United States, to apply the words of *Quadragesimo Anno*, immense power and despotic economic domination have been concentrated in the hands of a few, and these few are not the owners, but the managers of invested wealth.

There have been adequate studies to prove that less than a thousand large corporations own most of the corporate business wealth in the United States. Their strategic control of vital raw materials and essential industries gives them great power over the hundreds of thousands of smaller corporations and the millions of unincorporated businesses and farms. Moreover, such firms have showed great ability to maintain profits during recession periods. Hence they survive, while smaller companies may go bankrupt. While ownership of corporations is technically vested in the hands of their stockholders (about ten million), actual control in large firms rests with self-perpetuating boards of directors, powerful minority stockholders, large investment banking houses, and giant insurance companies. By way of reaction, there have arisen giant labor unions, farmers organizations, and government regulatory agencies. Thus, the individual is lost sight of in battles between mammoths.

A very real problem in regard to concentration of property and economic power stems from the enormous resources of pension funds. Already private retirement funds account for over 47 billion dollars in investments, and the total figure is growing at an amazing pace. Since a substantial portion of these funds is invested in common stocks, the relatively few banks and insurance companies that control these investments may soon control the bulk of productive property in the United States. When our private pension funds reach the 100-billion-dollar level, a goal which many think they will attain by 1975, we may have a degree of concentration of economic power that would make the older trusts and combines seem puny by comparison. Paradoxically, this concentration largely resulted from union-sponsored efforts to give the worker additional security in his old age. The worker has his security, but the price he has paid for these gains could be high. Not only has the process led to enormous centralization of funds, but it has also made the worker highly dependent upon both the company and the union for the collection of his benefits. He

---

[3] *Summa*, I, 81, 3, ad 2.

is no longer free to quit the job or defy the union, unless he wishes to jeopardize the equity he has built up in retirement funds.

There is no intention in the analysis just concluded to leave the impression that scheming financial interests are trying to reduce America to slavery. On the contrary, each step in this drama is compatible with a benign interpretation. The efficiency of large-scale business is often enough to explain its predominance in industry. The fact that stock ownership is widely scattered is the basis for concentration of control in the hands of corporate insiders or holders of large blocks of stock. And the desire to have the best investment advice possible underlies the funneling of billions of pension funds into a small number of New York banks. Nevertheless, whatever may be the motives, the basic fact is that enormous concentrations of power characterize our present economic system.

The fact that the great abuses of the 1920's are now past does not alter the fundamental situation. Business has a far greater sense of public responsibility. Government regulation has been salutary and effective. Labor and the farmers have made great gains. Even the small businessman has been able to hold his own in many fields. But we must consider how many workers are employed by large corporations where of necessity it is difficult to treat them as individuals. Many executives, drawing large salaries, are essentially employees of great chains or sprawling industries. Even the top management of billion-dollar corporations may be subject to the control of absentee financial ownership, more interested in assured profits than in the welfare of its workers or even executives. We cannot honestly say that these men have lost their freedom, but it has been minimized to an unhealthy degree.

Moreover giantism has aggravated concentration into large cities, in which the obstacles to a normal family life are greater. It is difficult for many to own or rent homes suitable for several growing children, where they would have wholesome opportunities for play and association with other children. On the farms, there are the migrants and the sharecroppers who often live in poverty with little hope of owning the land they till. All this is not to deny the real advantages of mechanization and mass production. But we have grown far beyond the optimum size needed for economic efficiency and have ended up with unsocial power concentrations. More recently, both economic reasons and the fear of atomic war have prompted some decentralization and diffusion of industry. But a complex and far-reaching problem remains.

Distribution of Wealth and Income in America. It is difficult to obtain figures on the actual distribution of wealth in the United States. It is even more of a problem to interpret facts and to put them in proper perspective. Available information indicates some trends toward greater economic concentration, especially in cases where corporate mergers are involved. The Department of Justice may act to prevent a merger, or to dissolve merged companies, if this action is necessary to prevent restraint of trade. However, there is a considerable difference between concentration that brings legal inference of monopoly and a trend that diminishes small holdings of property, even though it may be legal under the Clayton Act, as amended in 1950 to restrict mergers in restraint of trade.

Special attention should be paid to the impact of tax laws upon business concentration. Tax policies may stimulate mergers for many reasons. One is the possibility that profits can be "plowed back" into the firm and later realized as capital gains (at lower rates) rather than as income, when a firm is merged with another. Even the existence of losses may make a firm attractive to a prospective buyer, who can use such deficits to offset earnings of more prosperous companies in the merger. Something is fundamentally wrong when our tax policies so control business that normal considerations of profit or loss become secondary in weighing the usefulness of a firm.

In judging trends toward concentration of ownership in productive property, we must at all times keep a proper perspective. It would be a mistake to be so obsessed by the real or imagined efficiency of big business that we failed to see the social values of small firms and distributed ownership. We can concede the real merits of big business and yet also realize the value of smaller firms. Likewise, we should not always feel that smaller companies need special assistance lest they collapse. There is a considerable degree of vitality in this sector of our economy. It is troubled with high mortality rates, yet we should distinguish between normal business failures and a long-term trend away from small enterprise. We may have the former without being plagued with the latter.

The time is ripe for a careful and objective reconsideration of the structure of our economy. We must evaluate the factors that have produced bigness and economic concentration. Then we must decide whether or not we wish to pay this price for the economic gains of large enterprise.

When we come to the question of income distribution, however, an entirely different picture presents itself. Here there are definite indications of a trend toward equalization. This started as a result of tax laws that make it extremely difficult to retain income, once a fairly modest level is reached. Nevertheless, this trend toward greater equality of incomes is offset by continuing incidence of poverty, as was noted in the previous chapter. Since future pressures will be in the direction of lower rather than higher tax rates, the drive for equality will be judged more by the effectiveness of the war on poverty than by any further equalizing tax measures.

In the effort to give an accurate picture, two different types of income statistics are presented in the tables below. Table 1, National Income by Distributive Shares, shows the relative returns to various classes in selected postwar years. Figures are given in billions of dollars, with percentages of total income given at the right of each figure. In this way, gains or losses of the different groups can be noted.

Table 1

NATIONAL INCOME BY DISTRIBUTIVE SHARES

	1953		1957		1963	
	Billions of dollars	Per cent of total	Billions of dollars	Per cent of total	Billions of dollars	Per cent of total
Total national income	302.1	100.0	358.2	100.0	478.5	100.0
Compensation of employees	208.1	68.8	254.4	71.0	340.3	71.1
Business and professional	25.9	8.6	28.7	8.0	37.6	7.9
Farm	13.3	4.4	12.1	3.4	13.0	2.7
Rental income of persons	10.2	3.4	10.4	2.9	12.3	2.6
Corporate profits before taxes; adjusted for inventory gains or losses	36.0	11.9	39.7	11.1	50.8	10.6
Net interest	8.7	2.9	12.8	3.6	24.4	5.1

Another useful study is the material presented in Table 2, showing the upward shift in family incomes during the thirteen years, 1950–1962. Allowing both for increase in prices and increase in the number of families, there is nonetheless a gain of 20 per cent in average real income and a notable shift of families into higher income brackets. Income, as used in this table, is total income before taxes, including imputed income and income in kind. Families include unattached individuals maintaining a separate household.

Table 2

CHANGES IN FAMILY INCOME: 1950–1962

	Per cent of families in each income bracket		Per cent of total income received	
	1950	1962	1950	1962
Under $2,000	23.2	12.0	6.1	1.8
$2,000– 3,999	34.2	18.3	23.1	7.7
$4,000– 5,999	24.0	20.4	26.3	14.1
$6,000– 7,499	7.9	14.1	11.8	13.0
$7,500– 9,999	5.6	15.7	10.8	18.6
$10,000–14,999	3.1	12.3	8.4	20.2
$15,000 and over	2.0	7.2	13.5	24.6

Of the two subjects studied in this section, the matter of wealth distribution is currently more important than that of income distribution. Concentration of control over vital productive wealth means enormous centralization of power and diminution of effective freedom. By contrast, the degree of income concentration under present tax laws is not clearly excessive. Social problems derived from low incomes exist, but the remedy is not generally redistribution of the present income total. As noted in Chapter X, higher incomes ultimately come from increased production, achieved through better economic organization, higher investment levels, and labor-management co-operation. Accordingly, emphasis in the section to follow will be on better distribution of productive wealth, not income.

Remedies for Concentration of Productive Wealth. A glance through the quotations from the writings and addresses of Pope Pius XII indicates the preoccupation of this great Pontiff with the problem of diffusion of ownership. Indeed, this emphasis on widespread ownership of productive wealth is the great social contribution made by Pope Pius XII. Facing this problem in terms of American conditions, a social scientist usually comes up with two broad lines of solution. The first consists of preventing further concentration and of endeavoring to break up existing giants. The second is the more positive and constructive approach of trying to foster small business and individual ownership, without necessarily attacking present-day giants. Both techniques have their merits and difficulties. Indeed, this is a difficult social problem.

In some fields, bigness is essential. Until recent technological developments made small firms possible, steel was basically a large industry. The capital investment and equipment needed was such that only large corporations could enter the field. Mass production of automobiles is likewise, by its very nature, a large industry. But even in the mass-production fields, there is often greater centralization than is required by the economics of the situation. The technical nature of production usually involves an optimum size. When a firm expands beyond that size, it is merely duplicating efficient producing units. Often the same output can be produced by a number of smaller firms at optimum size. This is the evil of the merger movement, which absorbs such efficient companies. But they may have no choice, currently, since they are presented with attractive offers of purchase on the one hand and the threat of destructive and unfair competition on the other. Vigorous enforcement of antitrust and antimerger acts can help to slow down or possibly even reverse movements toward unsocial concentration.

Careful study should be made of the trend toward concentration made possible by the accumulation of pension funds. There have been no charges that banks or insurance companies abuse the powers that their position of trusteeship confers. Nevertheless a potential for abuse remains present. One possible remedy, to be considered when conditions make it necessary, would be the neutralizing of the voting power conferred by pension funds invested in common stocks. Trustees would be compelled by law to secure a court order to permit such voting, when they must take action in order to safeguard their investments.

On the more positive plane of aiding small business, government purchasing policies can be effective. In some fields, government is one of the greatest buyers in the country. A broad policy of favoring small business can be laid down to all departments, with a certain area of discretion permitted on bids. Thus, instead of rigidly adhering to the policy of awarding contracts to the lowest bidder, it may be possible to purchase supplies by prorating orders among the lowest third of the bidders, with a certain priority to small industries and suppliers. Long-range military programs can fit into this pattern, the more so since modern warfare makes dispersal advisable. Moreover, government research and advisory services for business can give special emphasis to the needs of small business, since such firms do not often have the funds for research.

Much more needs to be done to enable small firms to obtain initial financing, especially through the sale of stock. It is difficult for such firms to find investors. Often the cost of floating securities is prohibitive when small amounts (less than $100,000) are involved (nearly 30 per cent, as compared with a general average of 10 per cent). Investors understandably gravitate toward offerings by established companies. Two devices may be used to make funds more available for small business. One is tax exemption (from surtax but not regular rates) for investors who gain income by investing in such small firms. The other is the encouragement of development corporations founded to lend risk capital to promising ventures, meanwhile exercising supervision over the fledgling companies. Once such development corporations showed evidence of stability and good management, they might be considered suitable investments for pension funds, thus promoting distribution rather than concentration of wealth.

Two promising steps were taken in 1958 to aid small business. One involved tax concessions. Now money invested in "small business stock" is placed in a special category. If the investment goes sour, the loss may be used to offset ordinary income up to $25,000 ($50,000 on a joint return). Small corporations may elect to be taxed like partnerships. Heirs can spread estate taxes over ten years. The second step is the setting up of development banks, such as the corporations urged above. These banks will specialize in risk capital for small business. The banks will have some government financial aid, but will be privately controlled. Initial response to these ventures indicates that, at last, really substantial help for small business will become available. Thus we can continue and even expand the gratifying growth of small business which, in spite of obstacles, increased by one-third since 1941.

Regardless of the techniques adopted, it is essential that we always keep in mind the values produced by widespread ownership of productive property. Ownership leads to economic independence, and this in turn is an important foundation of political democracy. The modern world has suffered too much already from the erosion of freedoms. For the sake of human dignity and the rights that all hold sacred, it is urgent that we do all within our power to protect and enhance the liberty we cherish.

READINGS*

J. Y. Calvez, *Social Thought of John XXIII*, Chap. 2.
J. Y. Calvez and J. Perrin, *The Church and Social Justice*, Chap. 9.
J. F. Cronin, *Christianity and Social Progress*, Chaps. 10–11.
B. W. Dempsey, *The Functional Economy*, Chaps. 9–10.
H. Johnston, *Business Ethics*, Chap. 3.
B. L. Masse, *Justice for All*, Chap. 3.
J. Messner, *Social Ethics* (rev. ed.), pp. 679–692, 821–834, 849–868.
O. von Nell-Breuning, *Reorganization of Social Economy*, Chap. 6.
J. A. Ryan, *Distributive Justice*, Chaps. 1–8, 20–21.

---

* For further readings, consult List No. 9 in the Appendix.

Chapter XIII

THE STATE IN ECONOMIC LIFE

PUBLIC AUTHORITY

Vatican Council II, The Church in the Modern World

74. It is therefore obvious that the political community and public authority are based on human nature and hence belong to an order of things divinely foreordained. At the same time the choice of government and the method of selecting leaders is left to the free will of citizens.

Leo XIII, Immortale Dei

2. Man's natural instinct moves him to live in civil society. Isolated, he cannot provide himself with the necessary requirements of life, nor procure the means of developing his mental and moral faculties. It is, therefore, divinely ordained that he should lead his life — be it domestic, social, or civil — in contact with his fellow men, where alone his several wants can be adequately supplied. But no society can remain united without someone in command, directing all to strive earnestly for the common good. Hence, every civilized community must have a ruling authority, and this authority, no less than society itself, has its source in nature, and consequently has God for its author. It follows, then, that all public power must proceed from God: for God alone is the true and supreme Lord of the world.

*   *   *

Furthermore, the civil power must not be subservient to the advantage of any one individual, or of some few persons, inasmuch as it was established for the common good of all.

Leo XIII, Rerum Novarum*

48. Therefore, those governing the state ought primarily to devote themselves to the service of individual groups and of the whole commonwealth, and through the entire scheme of laws and institutions to cause both public and individual well-being to develop spontaneously out of the very structure and administration of the state. For this is the duty of wise

* See also quotations on subsidiarity, Chapter VII.

statesmanship and the essential office of those in charge of the state. Now, states are made prosperous especially by wholesome morality, properly ordered family life, protection of religion and justice, moderate imposition and equitable distribution of public burdens, progressive development of industry and trade, thriving agriculture, and by all other things of this nature, which the more actively they are promoted, the better and happier the life of the citizens is destined to be. Therefore, by virtue of these things, it is within the competence of the rulers of the state that, as they benefit other groups, they also improve in particular the condition of the workers. Furthermore, they do this with full right and without laying themselves open to any charge of unwarranted interference. For the state is bound by the very law of its office to serve the common interest. And the richer the benefits which come from this general providence on the part of the state, the less necessary it will be to experiment with other measures for the well-being of workers.

52. Nevertheless, those who govern must see to it that they protect the community and its constituent parts: the community, because nature has entrusted its safeguarding to the sovereign power in the state to such an extent that the protection of the public welfare is not only the supreme law, but is the entire cause and reason for sovereignty; and the constituent parts, because philosophy and Christian faith agree that the administration of the state has from nature as its purpose, not the benefit of those to whom it has been entrusted, but the benefit of those who have been entrusted to it. If, therefore, any injury has been done to or threatens either the common good or the interests of individual groups, which injury cannot in any other way be repaired or prevented, it is necessary for public authority to intervene.

75. Let the state protect these lawfully associated bodies of citizens; let it not, however, interfere with their private concerns and order of life; for vital activity is set in motion by an inner principle, and it is very easily destroyed, as We know, by intrusion from without.

Pius XI, Quadragesimo Anno

78. When we speak of the reform of institutions, the state comes chiefly to mind, not as if universal well-being were to be expected from its activity, but because things have come to such a pass through the evil of what we have termed "individualism," that, following upon the overthrow and near extinction of that rich social life which was once highly developed through associations of various kinds, there remain virtually only individuals and the state. This is to the great harm of the state itself; for, with a structure of social governance lost, and with the taking over of all the burdens which the wrecked associations once bore, the state has been overwhelmed and crushed by almost infinite tasks and duties.

110. The public institutions themselves, of peoples, moreover, ought to make all human society conform to the needs of the common good, that is, to the norm of social justice. If this is done, that most important division of social life, namely, economic activity, cannot fail likewise to return to right and sound order.

Pius XI, On Atheistic Communism

30. Man cannot be exempted from his divinely imposed obligations toward civil society, and the representatives of authority have the right to coerce him when he refuses without reason to do his duty. Society, on the other hand, cannot defraud man of his God-granted rights. . . . Nor can society systematically void these rights by making their use impossible.

32. The genuine and chief function of public and civil authority consists precisely in the efficacious furthering of this harmony and co-ordination of all social forces.

33. Both man and civil society derive their origin from the Creator, who has mutually ordained them one to the other. Hence neither can be exempted from their correlative obligations, nor deny or diminish each other's rights. The Creator Himself has regulated this mutual relationship in its fundamental lines. . . .

75. It must likewise be the special care of the state to create those material conditions of life without which an orderly society cannot exist.

76. The state itself, mindful of its responsibility before God and society, should be a model of prudence and sobriety in the administration of the commonwealth. Today more than ever the acute world crisis demands that those who dispose of immense funds, built upon the sweat and toil of millions, keep constantly and singly in mind the common good. State functionaries and all employees are obliged in conscience to perform their duties faithfully and unselfishly, imitating the brilliant example of distinguished men of the past and of our own day, who with unremitting labor sacrificed their all for the good of their country.

Pius XII, Christmas Message, 1944

If then, we consider the extent and nature of the sacrifices demanded of all the citizens, especially in our day when the activity of the state is so vast and decisive, the democratic form of government appears to many as a postulate of nature imposed by reason itself.*

Pius XII, To the Holy Roman Rota, October 2, 1945

Equally unsatisfactory . . . is that conception of civil power which may be termed "authoritarian," for this shuts out citizens from any effective share or influence in the formation of the social will. Consequently it splits the nation into two categories, that of the rulers and that of the ruled, whose relations to each other are reduced to those of a purely mechanical kind, governed by force, or else based on purely biological foundations.

Letter of Papal Secretariat of State to French Social Week, July, 1963

Thanks to an authentic democracy, concord is achieved between the two complementary movements of personalization and socialism. Each man participates, that is, takes his responsible part, in the elaboration of a common destiny which governs in part the fulfillment of his personal destiny.

* See also Pius XII, *Summi Pontificatus*, Nos. 1420, 1429, quoted in Chapter V.

Thus understood, democracy can be recognized in every government that is not totalitarian. It includes a balance, which admits of variations, between the national representation and the initiative of those who govern; it calls for some freely-constituted, intermediary bodies, recognized and protected by law, normally consulted on matters within their competence; it calls for a loyally-informed electoral body, qualified to judge the policy of those to whom it gives its mandate, and to judge the programs of its candidates; it calls for rights and duties clearly defined and whose exercise is effectively protected; it calls for judges whose independence is sufficiently guaranteed to allow them to discharge their duties impartially, in the light and under the responsibility of their conscience; it calls, finally, for basic laws, respected by all, which insure the continuity of the national life.

John XXIII, Pacem in Terris

37. Now the order which prevails in human society is wholly incorporeal in nature. Its foundation is truth, and it must be brought into effect by justice. It needs to be animated and perfected by men's love for one another, and, while preserving freedom intact, it must make for an equilibrium in society which is increasingly more human in character.

60. It is generally accepted today that the common good is best safeguarded when personal rights and duties are guaranteed. The chief concern of civil authorities must therefore be to ensure that these rights are recognized, respected, co-ordinated, defended and promoted, and that each individual is enabled to perform his duties more easily. For "to safeguard the inviolable rights of the human person, and to facilitate the performance of his duties, is the principal duty of every public authority."

61. Thus any government which refused to recognize human rights or acted in violation of them, would not only fail in its duty; its decrees would be wholly lacking in binding force.

67. For the rest, it is not possible to give a general ruling on the most suitable form of government, or the ways in which civil authorities can most effectively fulfill their legislative, administrative, and judicial functions.

68. In determining what form a particular government shall take, and the way in which it shall function, a major consideration will be the prevailing circumstances and the condition of the people; and these are things which vary in different places and at different times.

We think, however, that it is in keeping with human nature for the State to be given a form which embodies a threefold division of public office properly corresponding to the three main functions of public authority. In such a State a precise legal framework is provided, not only for the official functions of government, but also for the mutual relations between citizens and public officials. This will obviously afford a sure protection to citizens, both in the safeguarding of their rights and in the fulfillment of their duties.

69. If, however, this juridical and political structure is to realize its potential benefits, it is absolutely essential that public officials do their utmost to solve the problems that arise; and they must do so by using policies and techniques which it is within their competence to implement, and which suit the actual condition of the State. It is also essential that, despite

constantly changing conditions, legislators never disregard the moral law or constitutional provision, nor act at variance with the exigencies of the common good. And as justice must be the guiding principle in the administration of the State, and executives must thoroughly understand the law and carefully weigh all attendant circumstances, so too in the courts: justice must be administered impartially, and judges must be wholly incorrupt and uninfluenced by the solicitations of interested parties. The good order of society also requires that individuals and subsidiary groups within the State be effectively protected by law in the affirmation of their rights and the performance of their duties, both in their relations with each other and with government officials.

75. There is every indication at the present time that these aims and ideals are giving rise to various demands concerning the juridical organization of States. The first is this: that a clear and precisely worded charter of fundamental human rights be formulated and incorporated into the State's general constitutions.

76. Secondly, each State must have a public constitution, couched in juridical terms, laying down clear rules relating to the designation of public officials, their reciprocal relations, spheres of competence and prescribed methods of operation.

77. The final demand is that relations between citizens and public authorities be described in terms of rights and duties. It must be clearly laid down that the principal function of public authorities is to recognize, respect, co-ordinate, safeguard and promote citizens' rights and duties.

PROBLEMS OF THE MODERN STATE — DUTIES OF CITIZENS

Vatican Council II, The Church in the Modern World

75. It is in full accord with human nature that juridical-political structures should, with ever better success and without any discrimination, afford all their citizens the chance to participate freely and actively in establishing the constitutional bases of a political community, governing the state, determining the scope and purpose of various institutions, and choosing leaders. Hence let all citizens be mindful of their simultaneous right and duty to vote freely in the interest of advancing the common good. The Church regards as worthy of praise and consideration the work of those who, as a service to others, dedicate themselves to the welfare of the state and undertake the burdens of this task.

*   *   *

Let all Christians appreciate their special and personal vocation in the political community. This vocation requires that they give conspicuous example of devotion to the sense of duty and of service to the advancement of the common good. Thus they can also show in practice how authority is to be harmonized with freedom, personal initiative with consideration for the bonds uniting whole social body, and necessary unity with beneficial diversity.

Christians should recognize that various legitimate though conflicting views can be held concerning the regulation of temporal affairs. They should respect their fellow citizens when they promote such views honorably even by group action. Political parties should foster whatever they judge necessary for the common good. But they should never prefer their own advantage over this same common good.

Civic and political education is today supremely necessary for the people, especially young people. Such education should be painstakingly provided, so that all citizens can make their contribution to the political community. Let those who are suited for it, or can become so, prepare themselves for the difficult but most honorable art of politics.

Let them work to exercise this art without thought of personal convenience and without benefit of bribery. Prudently and honorably let them fight against injustice and oppression, the arbitrary rule of one man or one party, and lack of tolerance. Let them devote themselves to the welfare of all sincerely and fairly, indeed with charity and political courage.

John XXIII, To Italian Catholic Jurists, December 11, 1958

. . . since the center of gravity of a democracy normally constituted resides in this popular representation, from which the currents radiate out into every field of public life — for good as well as for evil — the question of the moral nobility, practical competence, of intellectual capacity of deputies of parliament, is for every people in a democratic rule a question of life or death, of prosperity or decadence, of improvement or perpetual misery.

John XXIII, Pacem in Terris

26. Finally, man's personal dignity involves his right to take an active part in public life, and to make his own contribution to the common welfare of his fellow citizens. As Pope Pius XII said, "man as such, far from being an object or, as it were, an inert element in society, is rather its subject, its basis and its purpose; and so must he be esteemed."

27. As a human person he is entitled to the legal protection of his rights, and such protection must be effective, unbiased, and strictly just. To quote again Pope Pius XII: "In consequence of that juridical order willed by God, man has his own inalienable right to juridical security. To him is assigned a certain, well-defined sphere of law, immune from arbitrary attack."

73. A natural consequence of men's dignity is unquestionably their right to take an active part in government, though their degree of participation will necessarily depend on the stage of development reached by the political community of which they are members.

74. For the rest, this right to take part in government opens out to men a new and extensive field of opportunity for service. A situation is created in which civic authorities can, from the greater frequency of their contacts and discussions with the citizens, gain a clearer idea of what policies are in fact effectual for the common good; and in a system which allows for a regular succession of public officials, the authority of these officials, far from growing old and feeble, takes on a new vitality in keeping with the progressive development of human society.

146. Here once more We exhort Our sons to take an active part in public life, and to work together for the benefit of the whole human race, as well as for their own political com-

munities. It is vitally necessary for them to endeavor, in the light of Christian faith and with love as their guide, to ensure that every institution, whether economic, social, cultural or political, be such as not to obstruct but rather to facilitate man's self-betterment, both in the natural and in the supernatural order.

PUBLIC OWNERSHIP — SOCIAL LEGISLATION

Vatican Council II, The Church in the Modern World

71. The right of private control, however, is not opposed to the right inherent in various forms of public ownership. Still, goods can be transferred to the public domain only by the competent authority, according to the demands and within the limits of the common good, and with fair compensation. It is a further right of public authority to guard against any misuse of private property which injures the common good.

Pius XI, Quadragesimo Anno

114. For certain kinds of property, it is rightly contended, ought to be reserved to the state, since they carry with them a dominating power so great that they cannot without danger to the general welfare be entrusted to private individuals.

115. Such just demands and desires have nothing in them now which is inconsistent with Christian truth, and much less are they special to socialism. Those who work solely toward such ends have, therefore, no reason to become Socialists.

Pius XII, To Catholic Employers, May 7, 1949

Meanwhile feverish attempts are under way to work out other juridical types of organization for the social economy, and at the moment preference favors state enterprise and the nationalization of industry. There can be no question that the Church also admits — within certain just limits — state ownership and management, judging that "certain forms of property may legitimately be reserved to the public authority: those which represent a dominating power so great that it cannot without danger to the general welfare be entrusted to private individuals" (Quadragesimo Anno). But to make of this state enterprise the normal rule for public economic organization would mean reversing the order of things. Actually it is the mission of public law to serve private rights, not to absorb them. The economy is not of its nature — not more, for that matter, than any other human activity — a state institution. It is, on the contrary, the living product of the free initiative of individuals and of their freely established associations.

Leo XIII, Rerum Novarum

53. . . . the law ought not undertake more, nor should it go farther, than the remedy of evils or the removal of danger requires.

54. Rights indeed, by whomsoever possessed, must be religiously protected; and public authority, in warding off injuries and punishing wrongs,

ought to see to it that individuals may have and hold what belongs to them. In protecting the rights of private individuals, however, special consideration must be given to the weak and the poor. For the nation, as it were, of the rich, is guarded by its own defenses and is in less need of governmental protection, whereas the suffering multitude, without the means to protect itself, relies especially on the protection of the state. Wherefore, since wage workers are numbered among the great mass of the needy, the state must include them under its special care and foresight.

Pius XI, Quadragesimo Anno

28. A new branch of law, wholly unknown to the earlier time, has arisen from the continuous and unwearied labor to protect vigorously the sacred rights of the workers that flow from their dignity as men and as Christians. These laws undertake the protection of life, health, strength, family, homes, workshops, wages, and labor hazards, in fine, everything which pertains to the condition of wage workers, with special concern for women and children. Even though these laws do not conform exactly everywhere and in all respects to Leo's recommendations, still it is undeniable that much in them savors of the Encyclical, *On the Condition of Workers*, to which great credit must be given for whatever improvement has been achieved in the workers' conditions.

Pius XII, Address to the Society for the Construction of Waterworks, April 13, 1956

. . . the Church . . . opposes, on the basis of moral principles, everyone who would attribute to the state excessive control over the economic life of its citizens.

Where this interference is not restrained, there can be no adequate solution of the social question. Where this interference is extended to "total planning," certain aims are realized, but only at the cost of inestimable losses brought about by an insane and destructive urge. The just liberties of the individual are destroyed. The serenity of labor is disturbed. The sacred character of the family is violated. The love of country is corrupted. The precious patrimony of religion is obliterated.

Vatican Council II, The Church in the Modern World

75. Because of the increased complexity of modern circumstances, government is more often required to intervene in social and economic affairs, by way of bringing about conditions more likely to help citizens and groups freely attain to complete human fulfillment with greater effect. The proper relationship between socialization on the one hand and personal independence and development on the other can be variously interpreted according to the locales in question and the degree of progress achieved by a given people.

When the exercise of rights is temporarily curtailed on the behalf of the common good, it should be restored as quickly as possible after the emergency passes. In any case it harms humanity when government takes on

totalitarian or dictatorial forms injurious to the rights of persons or social groups.

John XXIII, Mater et Magistra

20. As for the state, its whole raison d'être is the realization of the common good in the temporal order. It cannot, therefore, hold aloof from economic matters. On the contrary, it must do all in its power to promote the production of a sufficient supply of material goods, "the use of which is necessary for the practice of virtue." It has also the duty to protect the rights of all its people, and particularly of its weaker members, the workers, women and children. It can never be right for the state to shirk its obligation of working actively for the betterment of the condition of the workingman.

21. It is furthermore the duty of the state to ensure that terms of employment are regulated in accordance with justice and equity, and to safeguard the human dignity of workers by making sure that they are not required to work in an environment which may prove harmful to their material and spiritual interests.

54. The present advance in scientific knowledge and productive technology clearly puts it within the power of the public authority to a much greater degree than ever before to reduce imbalances which may exist between different branches of the economy or between different regions within the same country or even between the different peoples of the world. It also puts into the hands of public authority a greater means for limiting fluctuations in the econ-

omy and for providing effective measures to prevent the recurrence of mass unemployment. Hence the insistent demands on those in authority — since they are responsible for the common good — to increase the degree and scope of their activities in the economic sphere, and to devise ways and means and set the necessary machinery in motion for the attainment of this end.

55. But however extensive and far-reaching the influence of the state on the economy may be, it must never be exerted to the extent of depriving the individual citizen of his freedom of action. It must rather augment his freedom while effectively guaranteeing the protection of his essential personal rights. Among these is a man's right and duty to be primarily responsible for his own upkeep and that of his family. Hence every economic system must permit and facilitate the free development of productive activity.

56. Moreover, as history itself testifies with ever increasing clarity, there can be no such thing as a well-ordered and prosperous society unless individual citizens and the state co-operate in the economy. Both sides must work together in harmony, and their respective efforts must be proportioned to the needs of the common good in the prevailing circumstances and conditions of human life.*

John XXIII, Pacem in Terris

63. In addition, heads of States must make a positive contribution to the creation of an over-all climate in

which the individual can both safeguard his own rights and fulfill his duties, and can do so readily. For if

* See also excerpts cited in Chapter V, under "Capitalism."

there is one thing we have learned in the school of experience, it is surely this: that in the modern world especially, political, economic and cultural inequities among citizens become more widespread when public authorities fail to take appropriate action in these spheres. And the consequence is that human rights and duties are thus rendered totally ineffective.

64. The public administration must therefore give considerable care and thought to the question of social as well as economic progress, and to the development of essential services in keeping with the expansion of the productive system. Such services include road-building, transportation, communications, drinking-water, housing, medical care, ample facilities for the practice of religion, and aids to recreation. The government must also see to the provision of insurance facilities, to obviate any likelihood of a citizen's being unable to maintain a decent standard of living in the event of some misfortune, or greatly increased family responsibilities.

The government is also required to show no less energy and efficiency in the matter of providing opportunities for suitable employment, graded to the capacity of the workers. It must make sure that working men are paid a just and equitable wage, and are allowed a sense of responsibility in the industrial concerns for which they work. It must facilitate the formation of intermediate groups, so that the social life of the people may become more fruitful and less constrained. And finally, it must ensure that everyone has the means and opportunity of sharing as far as possible in cultural benefits.

THE function of the state in economic life has been the subject of frequent allusions throughout the course of this book. From the beginning, man's social nature has been stressed, with political action noted as one of the major manifestations of social life. The virtues of social and distributive justice involve the state. Again, the unsound philosophies of economic life, condemned earlier, showed their major symptoms in their attitudes toward the state. By contrast, the Catholic ideal of economic life assigned an important though limited function to civil authority. Moreover, when the concrete problems of capital, labor, and property were treated, questions of public policy and social legislation arose frequently. Accordingly, it is quite appropriate at this point to offer an explicit and orderly treatment of civil power, especially with reference to economic affairs.

Civil Authority. The Church has steadily affirmed the divine origin and the pre-eminent authority, in its sphere, of the civil state. This must seem remarkable to those not familiar with Catholic dogma, since it would appear that throughout history the Church has been more often in conflict than in alliance with various governments. From the persecutions of early Rome, through the uneasy struggles of the Middle Ages and the sharp conflicts with nascent nationalism at the time of the Protestant Revolt, to the decisive opposition to modern statism, the Church, one, holy, catholic, and apostolic, has found occasion to fulminate against civil powers. Yet it has stood equally firm against those who would deny or unduly limit the authority of civil rulers. Anarchism and nihilism were rejected by Pope Pius IX in the same syllabus that condemned communism. The social contract of Rousseau, and the doctrine that the ultimate and only source of civil power is the people, have been rejected with the same firmness as that displayed toward the nazi and communist teaching that the state is absolute in its powers, with the individual merely a creature of the state.

Man is by nature both a social and a political animal. And, since God made human nature, it can be stated that societies deeply rooted in that nature, such as the family and the state, have their origin in God. Even external religious ceremonies have stressed the sacred character of public power. The ancient kings of Israel were anointed by the high priest, a custom which still prevails with modifications in many Christian states. Our liturgy carries prayers for kings, emperors, and rulers. They are permitted within the sanctuary at solemn services and accorded special honors. True, some may understandably find it difficult to discern the aura of sacredness about civil power in a day when political machines choose rulers, when graft and corruption are not uncommon, and when many laws are passed for private advantage rather than the common good and hence may not be just laws. But the Church, in defending civil power, has not thereby sanctioned the personal character of rulers. Moreover, in a democracy there is little excuse for a purely negative attitude toward government. If it is not good, it is within our power and among our duties to make it good. At any rate, the presumption is always in favor of government and law, with the burden of proof on him who decides to disregard authority.

As noted earlier, the doctrine of the divine origin of civil authority does not preclude the democratic selection of rulers. Indeed, the great Christian writers, Aquinas, Suarez, and Bellarmine, have stressed the importance of the consent of the governed in making laws and choosing rulers. The widespread American impression that the Middle Ages were times of autocracy does not allow for the immense power of customary law, based on the will of the people, in that period.

The notion of the divine origin of civil power flatly contradicts the theory of the "social contract," popularized by Rousseau and widely held today. The modern world swings between two extremes: statism, which makes society a law unto itself, independent of divine law and political control by its citizens; and political individualism, which considers society as the temporary depository of powers surrendered for a time by the citizens. One extreme exaggerates civil power; the other so minimizes it as to lead to the danger of anarchy. The middle position upholds the authority of government, at the same time maintaining the right of citizens to choose their rulers and to instruct them in their policies. Whatever the form of government, it must rule justly, for the common good, and in conformity with natural law and divine positive law.

While Catholics abhor statism and American Catholics are strongly prodemocratic, we are not always so careful to avoid political individualism. Too often we share the common attitude that government is something apart from us which imposes unwelcome restrictions which we evade when we can. We stress the corruption and inefficiency of government, as if we were not responsible for the condition of democratic government. Many times our moral theology texts teach a casuistry in regard to law, taxes, and the social obligations of citizens which is ill-suited for modern times. Possibly such casuistry was applicable in other circumstances to nondemocratic governments, where evasion and passive resistance were often the citizen's only recourse against state tyranny. But in modern times, where the citizen has the right to participate in lawmaking and where social obligations are so diverse and vital, casuistry and negativism are out of place. Likewise, where citizens can pick their rulers, it is unseemly to be carping against political corruption and inefficiency. We have a duty to do something about it, and not merely to withdraw by way of purely negative criticism.

Finally, we should note that the concept of society is broader than that of the state. National society includes the organized people of a region, with their government, their families, and their various social groups in diverse spheres of life. In this society, civil government is supreme in its sphere. Its main function is to promote the common good in the material and cultural orders. While it is supreme, it is not to be all-absorbing. It must foster and stimulate lesser social groups, not swallow them up. It may govern and direct their activities in the light of the general welfare, but control should not be usurpation. Its august authority in matters within its competence does not give it the power to invade fields reserved to lesser or equal social groups. There are sacred individual rights which the state must respect. It must be even more reserved in dealing with the family. In purely religious matters, the Church is an independent society not subject to civil control.

Dictatorship, Democracy, and Nationalism. References to government thus far have been in terms of function rather than form. A ruler is to govern justly under law. This applies alike to presidents and prime ministers, to kings and emperors, to dictators and commissars. Traditionally the Church has not concerned itself with the type of rule, provided it was indeed a rule of justice and law. Even in the case of totalitarian governments, the objections raised have been on the basis of the denial of fundamental rights of the individual, the family, and the Church, rather than in terms of voting rights or political forms.

The historical and philosophical reasons for this attitude are not difficult to understand. It is a simple matter of history that mankind often has been ruled by tribal chiefs, kings, emperors, or dictators. As we glance over the entirety of man's span upon earth, there seems to be little doubt that the democratic pattern, as we know it today, has been the exception rather than the rule. This is certainly the case, if we place emphasis upon the free choice of rulers as a prime element of democracy. Even if we consider consent to law as more basic in the democratic process, it is still doubtful that the bulk of mankind has often been in a position to control its political destiny.

Unquestionably, deficiencies in education, communications, and economic development may explain many of the limitations that encompassed political life in earlier centuries. Generally speaking, a certain degree of education is needed for intelligent participation in the choosing and guidance of rulers. Those who cannot read and write may find themselves unable to know what issues are at stake and what the views of candidates are on major matters. Even with the help of radio and television — aids not available everywhere even today — there is no substitute for the ability to read and understand arguments, since the influence of the spoken word is fleeting. Printing itself is a relatively modern invention. Moreover, even when problems of education and communication are solved, there remains the need for an economic basis for political freedom. If the great majority of people are completely dependent upon a very few for their livelihood, it is not likely that this majority will enjoy a high degree of liberty. He who furnishes the wherewithal to eat is likely to determine the political destiny of a people.

These points are stressed, not to play down the value of democracy, but rather to indicate some of its necessary prerequisites. Democracy is to political life what maturity is to the lives of individuals. There is nothing reprehensible in parental guidance of children. On the contrary, parents would be derelict if they did not furnish such guidance. Nonetheless, an individual may rightly rejoice when he has reached a stage of maturity and can enjoy independence and freedom from parental control. Likewise, it is understandable that at certain times and places, men were unable to rule themselves. But it is desirable that they should be prepared for this broader freedom, so that they may have in political affairs the maturity and fullness of decision that they as adults enjoy in their personal affairs.

Two types of government, in particular, come to mind in connection with the observations just made. One is political dictatorship as noted in Chapter V. There was some hesitation on the part of the Church in condemning outright such dictatorships, mainly because of the wide variety of backgrounds involved and certain questions about the earlier effectiveness of the democratic process in such nations. Whatever may have been the initial justifications for a dictatorship, little excuse can be found for its indefinite prolongation in a culturally advanced nation. If such a state were truly seeking the common good of its citizens, it would strive to prepare them so that they would be ready to assume the maturity of full political responsibility.

The second type of government of special interest is the nation newly emerged or seeking to emerge from colonial control. Throughout the extensive areas often characterized as "underdeveloped," there is today "a revolution of rising expectations." Even where such peoples often lack the literacy, communication facilities, and economic independence that form such useful foundations for political democracy, they are nonetheless determined to break with the patterns of the past and to share in the bounty that the Creator intended for all mankind. Caught in the rising tide of nationalism, they demand both political independence from colonial powers and also their rightful place in the world of commerce and industry. There is no point at this late stage in emphasizing for them the need to prepare for both political democracy and economic growth. These nations are not inclined to move slowly. They are seeking quick action and workable short cuts. If the democratic world does not offer effective aid to such peoples, they know that they can turn to communist nations that are eager to help. The precise form of aid needed will be discussed later, in connection with international economic life. Our immediate concern is to note that these nations demand material achievement, and they will choose the political forms that seem most likely to promote such achievement.

In both these situations, free men have an important stake in promoting and safeguarding democracy. Whatever may have been the justifications for other forms of government in earlier times, there is one primary reason why democracy is virtually essential today. This reason is that, under a democracy, mistakes in government can be corrected. By contrast, the techniques of dictatorship have been so refined today that it is most difficult to overthrow a tyrant. In older times, the armed citizen was the equal of a soldier. Today an army under dictatorial control can crush a citizen uprising. The shortcomings in communications of earlier years were not unmixed evils. While they may have made it more difficult for men to unite for political action, they also prevented the monopoly of information such as that held by the modern totalitarian state. Once a dictator gains control over radio, television, the press, and the schools, it is difficult to get the truth that alone can make men free. The power of the modern state is too pervasive for anything but a democracy.

Dangers to Democracy. Even the most casual observation should suffice to make clear the fact that free men may not rest content with the externals of the democratic process. Freedom can be lost in fact even when men are still permitted to vote and go through the motions of choosing their rulers. Three evils in particular should be considered particularly dangerous. These are apathy, self-seeking, and impatience with the rule of law.

Apathy is the failure to participate actively and appropriately in the democratic process. It is contrary to the demand of social justice that all citizens join in seeking the common good of the community. It is essentially a process of dodging responsibility by unwillingness to assume one's civic obligations. The duty of a citizen is not primarily one of voting for top officials at general elections. While a general election is a dramatic stage of the process of choosing rulers, it is often a relatively minor part of the political process. Far more important in the long run are the early electoral stages at which candidates for office are considered and nominated. At these stages the many possibilities are narrowed down to one candidate per party for each office. The building up of a candidate within a political party is the really critical stage of democracy. Equally important is the effort to communicate with an elected official so as to influence his decisions along lines considered sound and equitable. Only by such a continuous process of influencing political decision can democracy be fully effective.

When a citizen endeavors to influence the conduct of government, his actions should be motivated by desire for the general welfare, not by concern with his own selfish interests. The desire for privilege and the setting up of dual standards in regard to law are among the more corrosive forces that democracy must face. When respected citizens use their contacts to "fix" traffic tickets or to obtain special services from government, it is difficult to convince others that law is the embodiment of even-handed justice. This is especially the case when, as sometimes happens, crime may be involved. When a person of standing is exonerated in a drunken-driving homicide case, whereas some poor person spends years in jail for a relatively small theft, respect for law and government is the ultimate victim.

Equally dangerous is impatience with law and the tedious processes often needed to secure justice. Undoubtedly it can be argued that we in America go too far in erecting legal protections for accused persons. Justice is not served when the guilty evade punishment as a result of minor technicalities. But, when we condemn possible abuse of due process, we must always be prepared to defend the rule of law as the ultimate test of democracy and liberty. In recent years the communist problem has posed a serious temptation to seek short cuts that may in the long run lessen our liberties. One danger, for example, is the use of congressional committees for functions of questionable legality. One might question the legislative purpose, for example, of a congressional inquiry that had the effect of uncovering communists in a local school system. Since Congress has no control over local education, how does it have the right to inquire about communist affiliations of teachers in such schools? Emotionally we sympathize with any steps that lead to investigation, exposure, and "neutralization" of such communists. But is this a function of a committee of our *national* legislature?

A somewhat related problem concerns the use of our Bill of Rights, and specifically the Fifth Amendment, by persons connected with communist causes. Much nonsense has been written on both sides of this issue. Some would leave the impression that "invocation of the Fifth" is a minor matter, comparable to brushing of one's teeth. This school of thought apparently would permit no inferences whatever from the use of the amendment. At the other extreme are those who consider "taking the Fifth" as the equivalent to a plea of guilty to the most atrocious crimes that may have been raised at a hearing.

Two simple points of law should clear up some of the worst misunderstandings about the Fifth Amendment. First, it may legally be used only when a witness fears that testimony may incriminate him in a subsequent action. It may not be used to protect friends or to cover up any shameful behavior that is not legally incriminating to the person testifying. Hence the use of this amendment automatically indicates the existence of incriminating evidence. On the other hand, the fear of incriminating evidence is not the same as the admission of a crime. Incriminating evidence simply is evidence that could be used to convict a person of a crime. But such a person may be innocent! To cite an example, a husband may have had a particularly violent quarrel with his wife. In anger he leaves home and wanders the streets aimlessly. He returns home and finds his wife dead from a bullet wound, apparently a suicide. The police view it otherwise, and he is charged with murder. In these circumstances, any admission of the quarrel would be incriminating, even though actually no crime was committed by the accused.

A second point of law is that a witness is considered to have waived his immunity if he freely gives testimony on any essential aspect of the subject under investigation. Thus, a witness might not be permitted to deny espionage activity and later "take the Fifth" in regard to membership in the communist party. He must use the amendment in all matters related to communism if he uses it at all. If membership in the communist party could be incriminating in his case, his lawyer might also advise him to use the amendment in regard to questions about espionage, sabotage, or treason, even though testimony about these matters would not be directly incriminating. Hence it does not follow that there is incriminating evidence, even as defined above, in regard to each question where the defendant uses the Fifth Amendment.

If it is true that "eternal vigilance is the price of freedom," then all free men must be prepared at all times to work at home to retain our liberties, just as they willingly fight abroad when a foreign enemy threatens these freedoms. Sensitive concern for all the processes of democracy is of the utmost importance. The surest and safest way to prove devotion to the ideals of our nation is seek justice for all and privilege for none. It is for this reason that many persons who have no sympathy for communism nevertheless fight for the civil rights of communists. Once freedom is threatened in any sector, we surrender hard-won rights.

Government in Economic Life. When *Rerum Novarum* was written, the philosophy of individualism and *laissez faire* was still strong in the world. It was only natural that in this document Pope Leo XIII should stress the duty of government to intervene in the interests of the common good. The Pope insisted upon the power and obligation of the state to protect poor and defenseless workers. This teaching was reiterated in *Quadragesimo Anno*, with words of praise for the social legislation enacted in the intervening years, some of it inspired by Leonine doctrine. In the meantime, however, the ugly specter of statism had appeared, so that Pope Pius XI considered it opportune to give more detailed treatment to the economic function of government. Further clarification in important matters has been added by Pope Pius XII.

The power of the state to intervene in economic life springs directly from its supreme concern over the common good and is controlled and regulated by that principle. This authority might be considered under both negative and positive aspects. Negatively, the state has the right and duty to intervene when any situation threatens the common good. Among the illustrations given in *Rerum Novarum* are the limitations of the hours of work, protection of working women and children, safeguarding the health of workers when it is threatened by bad working conditions, and the prevention of disorders due to strikes. In *Casti Connubii*, Pope Pius XI mentions problems connected with family life, such as housing, medical care, adequate food, and decent wages. Pope Pius XII, in his 1945 address to Italian workers, gives social insurance as an illustration of proper state action. In all these cases, "the law ought not to undertake more, nor should it go farther, than the remedy of evils or the removal of danger requires" (*R.N.*, No. 53).

The controlling principle is the common good, or the welfare of society as a whole and of its constituent parts as members of the social group. When the rights of any group are threatened or the human dignity of persons violated, the state should intervene. In the light of history, it was only natural that the emphasis should have been on protecting the rights of workers. They were the victims of abuses in the economic society which developed after the industrial revolution. Now that labor has acquired considerable power, however, it in turn may need regulation. The state may be required to protect small or large business. In principle, apart from the wisdom of its provisions or the timeliness of its enactment, the Taft-Hartley Act is as justifiable as the Social Security Act or the Employment Act of 1946.

In acting to prevent abuses the state should follow the principles of subsidiarity and minimum intervention. It is not the function of government to procure all good or prevent all evil, but only to deal with matters affecting the general welfare. Hence, a higher authority should not step in where a lesser group is able and willing to meet the needs of the moment. The federal government should not act where the states are doing an efficient job in handling a given situation. Nor should it impose a pattern upon private activities such as labor-management relations, when collective bargaining or like private arrangements are securing results consonant with the common good. Furthermore, when intervention is necessary, it should be at the minimum level required by conditions. An abuse which could be remedied by public control measures would not justify nationalization of an industry. The misuse of a power would not normally justify its abolition, unless this was the only possible method of preventing serious harm.

Changing conditions affect the scope of state authority. In times of peace and stable prosperity, government has less occasion to exercise its power than it would in a period of war or a major depression. The concept of reserve and emergency powers, so deeply imbedded in our laws, is basically sound. But government intervention is not a normal or desirable condition. One might go further and assert that many of the negative state functions should be considered in the light of lesser evils. It would be more desirable that various social groups, under the supreme coordinating power of the state, would themselves establish conditions which make remedial legislation unnecessary. This is the positive function of public authority.

As noted in Chapter VII, the primary and positive duty of government is to promote an organic social order which by its nature tends to procure the public economic good. The modern state is the victim of centuries of individualism. Society has been atomized into thousands of conflicting groups, each seeking its own interest, with few concerned with the general welfare. As a result, the state has been forced to step into countless situations and remedy conditions which were hurting society. This burdening of modern government has injured the state itself, through loading it down with innumerable tasks, and has hindered it from exercising its primary mission of aiding lesser groups to govern themselves. Furthermore, it has contributed to the giantism of modern life, which is endangering the freedom of individuals. The fact that such actions have been necessary in the circumstances does not make them more desirable in the light of Christian ideals. Until organic reform is achieved, we may legitimately continue to promote suitable social legislation, but our first emphasis should be upon a fundamental change in our social structure in favor of smaller, self-governing societies.

Church teaching is not blindly opposed to all nationalization of property. When private ownership would be contrary to the public interest, the state must protect the common good by nationalizing (with compensation) the property in question. An obvious example is the central bank of a nation, controlling as it does the money supply of the economy. Likewise, the state may, under certain circumstances, supply protection or services which private industry fails to provide. If such actions bring the label of the "welfare state," they are nonetheless within the legitimate demands of the common good. Where the real danger arises is when state actions of this nature are considered as desirable in themselves, rather than as reluctant alternatives accepted because the private sector of the economy was unable or unwilling to do its duty.

Pope John XXIII on the Nature and Functions of Government. The approach of Pope John to the problems of government was more concrete and pastoral than those of his predecessors. Consequently, there was a certain shift in emphasis in regard to both democracy and the welfare function of the state. While repeating the balanced arguments of the earlier encyclicals and noting their warnings, yet he seemed more inclined to take chances with democracy and social reform than to caution against excesses in these areas. In particular, *Pacem in Terris* should finally lay to rest the controversies and ambiguities stemming from papal reaction to the new democracies in the confused circumstances of the nineteenth century. It is true that Pope Pius XII eulogized the democratic form of government in his Christmas message of 1944. But Pope John's encyclical on peace is specific, precise, and unreserved in its acceptance of the modern democracy.

Necessarily the encyclical states that one cannot determine once and for all the most suitable form of government. Traditionally the Church has remained neutral in regard to various types of political organization, asking only that rulers act justly and according to law. But the present encyclical clearly implies that democracy is the best form of government.

It "is in keeping with the innate demands of human nature" that there should be a threefold division of powers: legislative, executive, and judicial. The state should have a charter or constitution that spells out the human rights of the citizens and specifies the precise powers and duties of the different branches of government. Authority should be exercised according to law and with full respect for the rights and duties of citizens. Ministers of government should hold office only for a limited time.

Although the Church has recognized the legitimacy of various forms of government, it is proper to note that participation in public affairs is a right that stems from the dignity of the human person. Indeed, it is not merely a right, it is also a duty. It is true that the extent of participation will depend upon the level of development of a country. Yet those who exercise absolute rule over citizens, whether as king, dictator, or aristocrat, should prepare their subjects to participate in political life so that eventually they may rule themselves.

Both social encyclicals of Pope John spell out the rights and duties of the state in regard to economic life. The earlier encyclical gives an excellent summary of previous papal teachings in this area. It then notes two specific functions which are of the highest importance today. These are reducing imbalances among various regions and sectors of the economy, and the smoothing of the business cycle together with the prevention of mass unemployment. Public authority is better able today, because of advances in economic knowledge and gains in technical achievement, to secure these results. Consequently, the duty of government to promote the common good calls for effective action in these spheres. But this authority should not be exercised in an autocratic way. The state should protect the personal rights of citizens. Both the citizen and the state should co-operate and work in harmony, in a manner indicated by the present needs of the common good.

Pacem in Terris puts particular stress on the duty of government to reduce inequalities in regard to economic, political, and cultural affairs. Social progress should be given equal priority with economic progress. Essential public services should be available to all citizens. Government should see that the people have adequate social insurance, not only to cover misfortunes, but also to aid when family responsibilities are increased. Suitable employment and just wages should be available to all. However, it does not necessarily follow that each of these advantages should be directly provided by the state. When the state fosters the development of intermediate groups, these "will make social life richer and more effective."

It would not be accurate to call these directives a plea for the welfare state. Nothing is stated here that was not advocated in principle in the social encyclicals of recent popes. Where Pope John is different is largely in the specific nature of his examples. These illustrations embody many features that some conservatives characterize as part of the welfare state. But the precise genius of Pope John is his encouragement of citizens to preserve traditional values of initiative and independence, while recognizing that the complexity of modern society involves necessarily a greater degree of social control than was required in the nineteenth century. He does not fight developments, he only asks that they be kept in proper balance.

Whether or not this is a "shift to the left" is largely a matter of semantics. Pope John emphasizes individual initiative and the principle of subsidiarity, but he does this in the context of the modern world. He accepts the complexity of modern society, and the consequent increase of influences and controls affecting the individual, as an accomplished fact. But he does not hold that these trends, of necessity, must compromise basic freedoms or prevent adequate decentralization of power.

READINGS*

J. Y. Calvez, *Social Thought of Pope John XXIII*, Chap. 4.
J. Y. Calvez and J. Perrin, *The Church and Social Justice*, Chap. 15.
J. F. Cronin and H. W. Flannery, *The Church and the Workingman*, Chap. 6.
H. Johnston, *Business Ethics*, Chap. 12.
J. G. Kerwin, *Politics, Government, and the Catholic.*
——— *Catholic Viewpoint on Church and State.*
B. L. Masse, *Justice for All*, Chap. 6.
J. Messner, *Social Ethics* (rev. ed.), pp. 147–314, 474–744, 936–947, 948–980.
P. Riga, *Peace on Earth*, Part II.
H. R. Rommen, *The State in Catholic Thought.*

---

* For further readings, consult List No. 10 in the Appendix.

Part III

SOCIAL PRINCIPLES AND SELECTED SOCIAL AND POLITICAL PROBLEMS

Chapter XIV

INTERNATIONAL POLITICAL AND ECONOMIC LIFE

INTERDEPENDENCE OF NATIONS

Pius XI, Ubi Arcano Dei

20. For the love of country and of race, though a spur to many deeds of virtue and of heroism when guided by Christianity, may become also the seed of widespread injustice and iniquity when it transgresses the bounds of right and justice, developing into a spirit of excessive nationalism. They who fall into this error surely forget that all peoples, as members of the universal Christian family, are linked together by the common ties of brotherhood; that other nations also have a right to live and seek prosperity. . . .

Pius XII, Summi Pontificatus, October 20, 1939

1429. A disposition, in fact, of the divinely sanctioned natural order divides the human race into social groups, nations or states, which are mutually independent in organization and in the direction of their internal life. But for all that, the human race is bound together by reciprocal ties, moral and juridical, into a great commonwealth directed to the good of all nations and ruled by special laws which protect its unity and promote its prosperity. Now no one can fail to see how the claim to absolute autonomy for the state stands in open opposition to this natural law that is inherent in man — nay, denies it utterly — and, therefore, leaves the stability of international relations at the mercy of the will of rulers, while it destroys the possibility of true union and fruitful collaboration directed to the general good.

Pius XII, Nell' Alba, Christmas, 1941

1758. First: within the limits of a new order founded on moral principles there is no room for violation of the freedom, integrity, and security of other states, no matter what may be their territorial extension or their capacity for defense. If it is inevitable that the powerful states should, by reason of their greater potentialities and their power, play leading roles in the formation of economic groups, comprising not only themselves but smaller and weaker states as well, it is nevertheless indispensable that in the

293

interests of the common good they, and all others, respect the rights of those smaller states to political freedom, to economic development, and to the adequate protection, in the case of conflicts between nations, of that neutrality which is theirs according to the natural as well as international law. In this way, and in this way only, shall they be able to obtain a fitting share of the common good and assure the material and spiritual welfare of the peoples concerned.

Pius XII, To Italian Catholic Jurists, December 8, 1953

In this community of nations, then, every state becomes a part of the system of international law, and hence of natural law, which is both foundation and crown of the whole. Thus the individual nation no longer is — nor in fact was it ever — "sovereign," in the sense of being entirely without restrictions. "Sovereignty" in the true sense means self-rule and exclusive competence concerning what has to be done and how it is to be done in regard to the affairs of a definite territory, always within the framework of international law, without however becoming dependent on the juridical system of any other state. Every state is immediately subject to international law. States which would lack this fullness of power, or whose independence of the power of any other state would not be guaranteed by international law, would not be sovereign. But no state could complain about a limitation of its sovereignty if it were denied the power of acting arbitrarily and without regard for other states. Sovereignty is not a divinization of the state, or omnipotence of the state in the Hegelian sense, or after the manner of absolute juridical positivism.

John XXIII, Mater et Magistra

200. The progress of science and technology in every aspect of life has led, particularly today, to increased relationships between nations, and made the nations more and more dependent on one another.

201. As a rule no single commonwealth has sufficient resources at its command to solve the more important scientific, technical, economic, social, political, and cultural problems which confront it at the present time. These problems are necessarily the concern of a whole group of nations, and possibly of the whole world.

202. Individual political commu-nities may indeed enjoy a high degree of culture and civilization. They may have a large and industrious population, an advanced economic structure, great natural resources and extensive territories. Yet, even so, in isolation from the rest of the world they are quite incapable of finding an adequate solution to their major problems. The nations, therefore, must work with each other for their mutual development and perfection. They can help themselves only in so far as they succeed in helping one another. That is why international understanding and co-operation are so necessary.

John XXIII, Pacem in Terris

88. So, too, on the international level: some nations may have attained to a superior degree of scientific, cultural and economic development. But that does not entitle them to exert unjust political domination over other

nations. It means that they have to make a greater contribution to the common cause of social progress.

91. Relations between states must furthermore be regulated by justice. This necessitates both the recognition of their mutual rights, and, at the same time, the fulfilment of their respective duties.

92. States have the right to existence, to self-development, and to the means necessary to achieve this. They have the right to play the leading part in the process of their own development, and the right to their good name and due honors. Consequently, states are likewise in duty bound to safeguard all such rights effectively, and to avoid any action that could violate them. And just as individual men may not pursue their own private interests in a way that is unfair and detrimental to others, so too it would be criminal in a state to aim at improving itself by the use of methods which involve other nations in injury and unjust oppression.

98. Since relationships between states must be regulated in accordance with the principles of truth and justice, states must further these relationships by taking positive steps to pool their material and spiritual resources. In many cases this can be achieved by all kinds of mutual collaboration; and this is already happening in our own day in the economic, social, political, educational, health and athletic spheres — and with beneficial results. We must bear in mind that of its very nature civil authority exists, not to confine men within the frontiers of their own nations, but primarily to protect the common good of the state, which certainly cannot be divorced from the common good of the entire human family.

99. Thus, in pursuing their own interests, civil societies, far from causing injury to others, must join plans and forces whenever the efforts of particular states cannot achieve the desired goal. But in doing so great care must be taken. What is beneficial to some states may prove detrimental rather than advantageous to others.

118. In their deliberations together, let men of outstanding wisdom and influence give serious thought to the problem of achieving a more human adjustment of relations between states throughout the world. It must be an adjustment that is based on mutual trust, sincerity in negotiation, and the faithful fulfilment of obligations assumed. Every aspect of the problem must be examined, so that eventually there may emerge some point of agreement from which to initiate treaties which are sincere, lasting, and beneficial in their effects.

130. Recent progress in science and technology has had a profound influence on man's way of life. This progress is a spur to men all over the world to extend their collaboration and association with one another in these days when material resources, travel from one country to another, and technical information have so vastly increased. This has led to a phenomenal growth in relationships between individuals, families and intermediate associations belonging to the various nations, and between the public authorities of the various political communities. There is also a growing economic interdependence between states. National economies are gradually becoming so interdependent that a kind of world economy is being born from the simultaneous integration of the economies of individual states. And finally, each country's social progress, order, security and peace are necessarily linked with the social progress, order, security and peace of every other country.

131. From this it is clear that no state can fittingly pursue its own interests in isolation from the rest, nor, under such circumstances, can it develop itself as it should. The prosperity and progress of any state is in part consequence, and in part cause, of the prosperity and progress of all other states.

A universal public authority

137. Today the universal common good presents us with problems which are world-wide in their dimensions; problems, therefore, which cannot be solved except by a public authority with power, organization and means co-extensive with these problems, and with a world-wide sphere of activity. Consequently the moral order itself demands the establishment of some such general form of public authority.

138. But this general authority equipped with world-wide power and adequate means for achieving the universal common good cannot be imposed by force. It must be set up with the consent of all nations. If its work is to be effective, it must operate with fairness, absolute impartiality, and with dedication to the common good of all peoples. The forcible imposition by the more powerful nations of a universal authority of this kind would inevitably arouse fears of its being used as an instrument to serve the interests of the few or to take the side of a single nation, and thus the influence and effectiveness of its activity would be undermined. For even though nations may differ widely in material progress and military strength, they are very sensitive as regards their juridical equality and the excellence of their own way of life. They are right, therefore, in their reluctance to submit to an authority imposed by force, established without their co-operation, or not accepted of their own accord.

The universal common good and personal rights

139. The common good of individual states is something that cannot be determined without reference to the human person, and the same is true of the common good of all states taken together. Hence the public authority of the world community must likewise have as its special aim the recognition, respect, safeguarding and promotion of the rights of the human person. This can be done by direct action, if need be, or by the creation throughout the world of the sort of conditions in which rulers of individual states can more easily carry out their specific functions.

140. The same principle of subsidiarity which governs the relations between public authorities and individuals, families and intermediate societies in a single state, must also apply to the relations between the public authority of the world community and the public authorities of each political community. The special function of this universal authority must be to evaluate and find a solution to economic, social, political and cultural problems which affect the universal common good. These are problems which, because of their extreme gravity, vastness and urgency, must be considered too difficult for the rulers of individual states to solve with any degree of success.

141. But it is no part of the duty of universal authority to limit the sphere of action of the public authority of individual states, or to arrogate any of their functions to itself. On the contrary, its essential purpose is to create world conditions in which the public authorities of each nation, its citizens and intermediate groups, can carry out their tasks, fulfil their duties and claim their rights with greater security.

Paul VI, Address to Secretary General Thant, of the United Nations, July 11, 1963

Mr. Secretary General of the United Nations, the Holy See . . . holds a very high conception of that international organization. It considers it to be the fruit of a civilization to which the Catholic religion, with its driving center the Holy See, gave the vital principles.

It considers it an instrument of brotherhood between nations, which the Holy See has always desired and promoted, and hence a brotherhood intended to favor progress and peace among men. It considers the United Nations as the steadily developing and improving form of the balanced and unified life of all humanity in its historical and earthly order.

The universality proper to the Catholic Church, with its pulsing heart here in Rome, seems in a way to be reflected from the spiritual sphere into the temporal sphere of the United Nations. The ideologies of those who belong to the United Nations are certainly multiple and diverse, and the Catholic Church regards them with due attention. But the convergence of so many peoples, so many races, so many states in a single organization, intended to avert the evils of war and to favor the good things of peace, is a fact which the Holy See considers as corresponding to its concept of humanity, and included within the area of its spiritual mission to the world.

POPULATION PROBLEMS

John XXIII, Mater et Magistra

185. How can economic development and the supply of food keep pace with the continual rise in population? This is a question which constantly obtrudes itself today — a world problem, as well as one for the poverty-stricken nations.

186. As a world problem, the case is put thus: According to sufficiently reliable statistics the next few decades will see a very great increase in human population, whereas economic development will proceed at a slower rate. Hence, we are told, if nothing is done to check this rise in population, the world will be faced in the not too distant future with an increasing shortage in the necessities of life.

187. As it affects the less developed countries, the problem is stated thus: The resources of modern hygiene and medicine will very shortly bring about a notable decrease in the mortality rate, especially among infants, while the birth rate — which in such countries is usually high — will tend to remain more or less constant, at least for a considerable period. The excess of births over deaths will therefore show a steep rise, whereas there will be no corresponding incease in the productive efficiency of the economy. Accordingly, the standard of living in these poorer countries cannot possibly improve. It must surely worsen, even to the point of extreme hardship. Hence there are those who hold the opinion that, in order to prevent a serious crisis from developing, the conception and birth of children should be secretly avoided, or in any event, curbed in some way.

188. Truth to tell, we do not seem to be faced with any immediate or imminent world problem arising from

the disproportion between the increase of population and the supply of food. Arguments to this effect are based on such unreliable and controversial data that they can only be of very uncertain validity.

189. Besides, the resources which God in His goodness and wisdom has implanted in Nature are well-nigh inexhaustible, and He has at the same time given man the intelligence to discover ways and means of exploiting these resources for his own advantage and his own livelihood. Hence, the real solution of the problem is not to be found in expedients which offend against the divinely established moral order and which attack human life at its very source, but in a renewed scientific and technical effort on man's part to deepen and extend his dominion over Nature. The progress of science and technology that has already been achieved opens up almost limitless horizons in this field.

190. As for the problems which face the poorer nations in various parts of the world, We realize, of course, that these are very real. They are caused, more often than not, by a deficient economic and social organization, which does not offer living conditions proportionate to the increase in population. They are caused, also, by the lack of effective solidarity among such peoples.

191. But granting this, We must nevertheless state most emphatically that no statement of the problem and no solution to it is acceptable which does violence to man's essential dignity; those who propose such solutions base them on an utterly materialistic conception of man himself and his life.

Only possible solution

192. The only possible solution to this question is one which envisages the social and economic progress both of individuals and of the whole of human society, and which respects and promotes true human values. First consideration must obviously be given to those values which concern man's dignity generally, and the immense worth of each individual human life. Attention must then be turned to the need for worldwide co-operation among men, with a view to a fruitful and well-regulated interchange of useful knowledge, capital, and manpower.

199. A provident God grants sufficient means to the human race to find a dignified solution to the problems attendant upon the transmission of human life. But these problems can become difficult of solution, or even insoluble, if man, led astray in mind and perverted in will, turns to such means as are opposed to right reason, and seeks ends that are contrary to his social nature and the intentions of Providence.

INTERNATIONAL ECONOMIC PROBLEMS

Pius XI, Quadragesimo Anno

89. Furthermore, since the various nations largely depend on one another in economic matters and need one another's help, they should strive with a united purpose and effort to promote by wisely conceived pacts and institutions a prosperous and happy international co-operation in economic life.

Pius XI, On Atheistic Communism

76. In international trade relations let all means be sedulously employed for the removal of those artificial barriers to economic life which are the effects of distrust and hatred. All must remember that the peoples of the earth form but one family in God.

John XXIII, Mater et Magistra

80. The demands of the common good on the international level include: the avoidance of all forms of unfair competition between the economies of different countries; the fostering of mutual collaboration and good will; and effective co-operation in the development of economically less advanced communities.

153. It is not out of place to remark here on a problem which exists in quite a number of countries, namely, a gross disproportion between land and population. In some countries arable land abounds, but there is a scarcity of population; whereas in other countries the position is reversed: the population is large, arable land scarce.

154. Again, some countries use primitive methods of agriculture, with the result that, for all their abundance of natural resources, they are not able to produce enough food to feed their population; whereas other countries, using modern methods of agriculture, produce a surplus of food which has an adverse effect on the economy.

155. It is therefore obvious that the solidarity of the human race and Christian brotherhood demand the elimination as far as possible of these discrepancies. With this object in view, people all over the world must co-operate actively with one another in all sorts of ways, so as to facilitate the movement of goods, capital, and men from one country to another. We shall have more to say on this point later on.

156. Here We would like to express Our sincere appreciation of the work which the F.A.O. has undertaken to establish effective collaboration among nations, to promote the modernization of agriculture especially in less developed countries, and to alleviate the suffering of hunger-stricken peoples.

Obligation of the wealthy nations

157. Probably the most difficult problem today concerns the relationship between political communities that are economically advanced and those in the process of development. Whereas the standard of living is high in the former, the latter are subject to extreme poverty. The solidarity which binds all men together as members of a common family makes it impossible for wealthy nations to look with indifference upon the hunger, misery and poverty of other nations whose citizens are unable to enjoy even elementary human rights. The nations of the world are becoming more and more dependent on one another and it will not be possible to preserve a lasting peace so long as glaring economic and social imbalances persist.

158. Mindful of Our position as the father of all peoples, We feel constrained to repeat here what We said on another occasion: "We are all equally responsible for the undernourished peoples. [Hence], it is necessary to educate one's conscience to the sense of responsibility which weighs upon each and every one, especially upon those who are more blessed with this world's goods."

160. It is therefore a great source of joy to Us to see those nations which enjoy a high degree of economic wealth helping the nations not so well provided, so that they may more effectively raise their standard of living.

161. Justice and humanity demand that those countries which produce consumer goods, especially farm products, in excess of their own needs should come to the assistance of those other countries where large sections of the population are suffering from want and hunger. It is nothing less than an outrage to justice and humanity to destroy or to squander goods that other people need for their very lives.

162. We are, of course, well aware that overproduction, especially in agriculture, can cause economic harm to a certain section of the population. But it does not follow that one is thereby exonerated from extending emergency aid to those who need it. On the contrary, everything must be done to minimize the ill effects of overproduction, and to spread the burden equitably over the entire population.

Scientific, technical, and financial co-operation

163. Of itself, however, emergency aid will not go far in relieving want and famine when these are caused — as they so often are — by the primitive state of a nation's economy. The only permanent remedy for this is to make use of every possible means of providing these citizens with the scientific, technical, and professional training they need, and to put at their disposal the necessary capital for speeding up their economic development with the help of modern methods.

164. We are aware how deeply the public conscience has been affected in recent years by the urgent need of supporting the economic development and social progress of those countries which are still struggling against poverty and economic disabilities.

165. International and regional organizations, national and private societies, all are working toward this goal, increasing day by day the measure of their own technical co-operation in all productive spheres. By their combined efforts thousands of young people are being given facilities for attending the universities of the more advanced countries, and acquiring an up-to-date scientific, technical, and professional training. World banking institutes, individual states and private persons are helping to furnish the capital for an ever richer network of economic enterprises in the less wealthy countries. It is a magnificent work that they are doing, and We are most happy to take this occasion of giving it the praise that it deserves. It is a work, however, which needs to be increased, and We hope that the years ahead will see the wealthier nations making even greater efforts for the scientific, technical, and economic advancement of those political communities whose development is still only in its initial stages.

166. We consider it Our duty to give further advice on this matter.

Learning from other nations

167. In the first place, those nations which are still only at the beginning of their journey along the road to economic development would do well to consider carefully the experiences of the wealthier nations which have traversed this road before them.

168. Increase in production and productive efficiency is, of course, sound policy, and indeed a vital necessity. However, it is no less necessary — and justice itself demands — that the riches produced be distributed

fairly among all members of the political community. This means that everything must be done to ensure that social progress keeps pace with economic progress. Again, every sector of the economy — agriculture, industry and the services — must progress evenly and simultaneously.

169. The developing nations, obviously, have certain unmistakable characteristics of their own, resulting from the nature of the particular region and the natural dispositions of their citizens, with their time-honored traditions and customs.

170. In helping these nations, therefore, the more advanced communities must recognize and respect this individuality. They must beware of making the assistance they give an excuse for forcing these people into their own national mold.

Offering disinterested aid

171. There is also a further temptation which the economically developed nations must resist: that of giving technical and financial aid with a view to gaining control over the political situation in the poorer countries, and furthering their own plans for world domination.

172. Let us be quite clear on this point. A nation that acted from these motives would in fact be introducing a new form of colonialism — cleverly disguised, no doubt, but actually reflecting that older, outdated type from which many nations have recently emerged. Such action would, moreover, have a harmful impact on international relations, and constitute a menace to world peace.

173. Necessity, therefore, and justice demand that all such technical and financial aid be given without thought of domination, but rather for the purpose of helping the less developed nations to achieve their own economic and social growth.

174. If this can be achieved, then a precious contribution will have been made to the formation of a world community, in which each individual nation, conscious of its rights and duties, can work on terms of equality with the rest for the attainment of universal prosperity.

John XXIII, Pacem in Terris

102. We advocate . . . the policy of bringing the work to the workers, wherever possible, rather than bringing workers to the scene of the work. In this way many people will be afforded an opportunity of increasing their resources without being exposed to the painful necessity of uprooting themselves from their own homes, settling in a strange environment, and forming new social contacts.

CONSIDERATION of the major institutions of socioeconomic life does not exhaust the obligations imposed by justice and charity in the modern world. Problems connected with international political and economic life, the racial crisis of our times, and issues revolving around rural life are all vitally important. Likewise it is essential to discuss the application of social principles to social action, in the context of Catholic life in the United States.

All these subjects are urgent. Nor are they as unconnected as they may appear at first glance. While racial and rural problems are treated in the domestic context, they have vital international implications. Finally, it is logical to raise as a concluding question: What are we as Catholics to do about the problems discussed throughout the book? This question is answered in terms of principles and general forms of social action, rather than in detail, since movements and organizations tend both to differ from place to place and also to change with the passage of time.

As Catholics, we should have no doubts about our concern with international problems. The very term "catholic" means universal and the interest of the Church knows no boundaries of nation or race. In recent years, however, the problems of world peace and world economic development have intensified this concern, as is evident from the quotations taken from the encyclicals of Pope John XXIII. Social justice is a world-wide problem.

A World Society.   One of the most difficult concepts for many persons to grasp is that of a world society and the consequent demand for a juridical order to deal with the various relationships among nations. One reason for this difficulty is the failure to note the distinction between society and state, as noted in Chapter XIII. We can recognize the existence of a world society and still admit the obstacles that surround any attempt to secure a world government to supplement the sovereign nations of today. A world society is a fact; one-world government is but a dream at this time.

The world is truly a community, in the first place, because of the unity of mankind under the fatherhood of God. We are all brothers, one to another. Over and above differences in race, culture, and national origin is the common humanity of all men. This unity is far more evident today because progress in communications has broken down the barriers of distance that once made isolation possible. Moreover, there are common problems to challenge every nation of the world. Among these, the most urgent are those connected with world peace and prosperity.

World peace is more critically needed than ever before in the history of the world, since war has become unbelievably cruel and devastating. With hydrogen weapons likely to be delivered by intercontinental missiles, any war could cause the death of tens of millions and the destruction of entire nations. Indeed, a prolonged and all-out nuclear attack might so poison the atmosphere with radioactive dust that the survival of the entire human race could be threatened. Certainly dangers of this magnitude emphasize the unqualified necessity for peaceful solutions of disputes among nations.

Economic problems of the world are almost as acute as its political problems. In Chapter XIII, a reference was made to the "revolution of rising expectations." On the one hand, millions whose lands have known centuries of poverty have suddenly awakened to the possibilities of economic progress. They desire not only the necessities of life, but some of the comforts and even luxuries that others enjoy. Concurrent with this rise in expectations there has been a population explosion of considerable magnitude. This has largely been the result of dramatic increases of life expectancy caused by new developments in medicine. Hence in many areas, economic gains have been canceled out by the sharp pressure of population upon resources.

To meet these problems, we must apply upon an international scale many of the principles of justice and charity that we have studied in relation to national economies. First we note that, since mankind forms a world society, we must expect relationships within that society to conform to the moral law. Justice, in its many forms, and charity should be the basis of a juridical order that governs the conduct of nations in world affairs. The alternatives that confront us are clear: we have a choice between order and law, on the one hand, and force on the other.

If the relations among the peoples of the world are to be settled by law rather than force, we must expect that no nation will claim a sovereignty so absolute that it considers all its decisions as beyond review or question. Just as the basic freedom of individuals is not lost when they submit to the rule of law within a nation, so the sovereignty of nations is not compromised by the establishment of some lawful means for handling international problems. Experience of mankind has shown that these problems usually fall into either of two categories: matters of interest and matters of right. Where claims and interests are involved, the normal procedures for settlements of difficulties or disputes involve the use of negotiation and conciliation. Since these are not matters of right, we do not use arbitration or courts of law. But when matters of strict right do arise, there should be a court for the determination of such rights.

At the present moment, the world does have machinery, however imperfect, to meet the needs outlined above. The United Nations, with its General Assembly and its Security Council, and the various international groups either subsidiary to it or at least in relationship to it, do make an attempt to handle problems in a peaceful fashion. Political disputes and those dealing with claims and interests are usually referred to the General Assembly and the Security Council. Legal problems are handled by the International Court of Justice.

Some persons have been highly critical of the work of the United Nations because it has not been able to solve such difficult problems as East-West disputes or Arab-Israeli tensions. It is not logical, however, to abandon world efforts to promote peace just because they have failed to solve these extraordinarily complex challenges that have confronted the UN. We do not give up marriage counseling efforts just because some attempts fail and the parties end up in divorce courts. The United Nations did not create East-West tensions, nor would the dissolution of the UN contribute to their solution.

Many readers of *Pacem in Terris* were confused over the call for a universal public authority (Nos. 137–141). What is the relationship of this to the United Nations? A careful reading of the encyclical gives an answer to this question. The Pope first expresses the ideal of a supranational authority that could meet worldwide problems. He notes how this should be constituted and gives the rules that should govern its operation in relation to its sovereign state members. Immediately following this discussion, the Encyclical considers the United Nations and its problems. Concluding that treatment is a plea that the UN develop in structure and operation so that it can properly face its tasks (No. 145). It would seem clear from this that the Pope hopes that the UN will ultimately grow into a true world government of the type he described earlier.

Nevertheless, realism compels us to confess that we are just beginning to erect the framework of a juridical order to govern international affairs. Power relationships rather than justice too often dictate settlements of disputes. On the more hopeful side, we are slowly building a corps of international civil servants and a body of legal precedents, that can be considered as the beginnings of the rule of justice in world relationships.

International Economic Problems. A wide variety of economic problems confront the world today. Among the more important are population and migration problems, productivity and economic growth in "developing" nations, financial and technical assistance to such nations, and the promotion of international trade. To help in meeting these needs there exist such an enormous number of agencies and programs that it would take almost an entire book to describe them adequately. In the international sphere we have, in addition to the Economic and Social

Council of the United Nations, various related groups such as the International Labor Organization, the Food and Agriculture Organization, and the World Health Organization. UNESCO and the International Refugee Organization also have their economic aspects. Then there are regional groupings, such as the European Iron and Coal Organization, Euratom, and the European Economic Community (European Common Market). Even individual nations have their programs. Thus, the United States has its own technical assistance and foreign-aid activities.

Since the number of organizations and programs is so great, it is better in this limited space to deal only in terms of the problems involved and the principles invoked for their solution. There will be no attempt to pinpoint the precise contribution of any given nation or international organization.

To mention first one of the most difficult of all problems, there is the question of the explosive pressure of population upon resources. Such a pressure exists here and now because world health measures have lowered the death rate far more rapidly than economic measures have increased the production of food and fibers. This problem is most acute in Asia. It can be met by any of a combination of four measures: (1) bringing food and fibers to the people from surpluses elsewhere; (2) moving people to idle land areas so they can cultivate their own food; (3) increasing productivity of these peoples in their present home areas; and (4) using morally acceptable measures to adjust the birth rate so that population growth will remain within limits set by resources.

Meeting the Population Problem. Bringing of food and fibers from nations with surplus stocks to peoples in need is not always easy. Even if the exporting nation were willing to give its products, there would still be obstacles of transportation and processing. Sometimes the surplus material is not acceptable because of local customs. It may be difficult, for example, to get some Asian peoples to use wheat instead of rice. Southern Europeans may not like potatoes. Since milk and egg products must be shipped in dried form, they too may not be acceptable. Thus, we may continue to be faced with a paradox of surplus foods in Canada and the United States, while people elsewhere may be in desperate need. Certainly we should be ready to contribute from our abundance, but we must also realize that such contributions may not solve the long-range problems of poverty in some parts of the world.

Emigration poses serious political problems when it involves huge numbers of potential migrants. When surplus population is calculated in tens or hundreds of millions, as may well be the case with India and China, emigration is hardly a feasible solution. It would call for the availability of enormous tracts of fertile but unused land, a fantastically involved shipping operation, willingness on the part of host nations to receive millions completely alien in language and customs, and the availability of funds to finance the operation. This type of solution is understandable when relatively small numbers are concerned, such as the surplus population from Italy or the refugees from Iron Curtain countries. But it is hardly a solution for Asian population pressures.

Another solution that seems very simple at first glance may involve its own share of problems. Reference is made to the suggestion that we step up productivity in the nations now troubled by population pressures upon food resources. This is being done, to some degree, by programs of technical assistance. Often, however, the obstacle to increased production is not so much technical as economic. Land may be owned by a wealthy few who may not be willing to have it cultivated or who may not wish to change social and economic conditions of tenants. Usurious rates for loans may pose effective obstacles to the purchase of land or even of simple tools needed for more efficient production. Hence political and social changes of a type that cannot be imposed by international bodies may often be prerequisites for important gains in economic life in many parts of the world.

The practical difficulties that other proposed solutions involve explain why many population experts favor measures to control the birth rate, so that children will not be brought into the world only to face misery and starvation. When propositions of this sort are advocated, the instinct among many Catholics is to oppose them, since there is every likelihood that they will be conjoined with proposals for the use of contraceptive means for family limitation. Yet we must distinguish between the principle of family limitation or population control and the means used to achieve these ends. The principle that economic, social, or eugenic indications might counsel family planning or population control is not contrary to Catholic teaching. On the contrary, it has been explicitly accepted by Pope Pius XII. It is nothing more than using reason to control instinct in a very important phase of life. Only the use of wrong methods, such as contraception, is per se forbidden in this area. Nevertheless, the difficulties surrounding the use of morally acceptable methods of family planning, under our present state of scientific knowledge, will lead many population experts to favor contraception as the only acceptable means to be used. This in turn forces Catholics into what many outsiders consider a purely negative position, opposing the "only feasible" means of population control, and not offering any acceptable alternative.

In view of the dogmatically necessary stand on contraception and the difficulties this raises, Catholics should redouble their efforts to remove obstacles to other methods for meeting this problem. In particular, continuing interest in bringing surplus products to needy peoples, support for technical-assistance programs, and efforts to secure land reform can all help in raising the economic level of peasants now confronted with the grim threat of undernourishment or even starvation.

In this connection, the highest tribute should be paid to two Catholic organizations in the United States, the Catholic Association for International Peace and the National Catholic Rural Life Conference. Both groups have been indefatigable, not only in educating their members and the general public, but also in keeping in close touch with government agencies interested in problems of developing nations. Special attention should be drawn to the 1951 International Catholic Congress on Problems of Rural Life, sponsored by the NCRLC. Its findings are available in an outstanding document, "Christianity and the Land." Also notable were the First Latin American Catholic Congress on Rural Life Problems, in 1953, and the Caribbean Area Catholic Congress on Rural Life Problems, in 1955. "Conclusions" from these conferences were also published by the NCRLC. Nor should we overlook the splendid work of the American Catholic missionary societies, The Papal Volunteers for Latin America (PAVLA), and the Mission Secretariat of the Society for the Propagation of the Faith. All these groups are interested in every phase of economic development: migration, technical assistance, health, and education, in addition to strictly rural problems.

Economic Development. Population presents only one of the many social and economic problems of "developing" nations. A score or more of nations, newly released from the bonds of colonialism, now desire economic development as well as political independence. They wish their equitable share in the riches that modern technology can produce. The achievement of this goal calls for a variety of steps, depending in part on the history and resources of a nation. In general, however, such peoples want native manufacturing to supplement agricultural production or extractive industries. They prefer not to depend upon one commodity, no matter how much it is in demand. They have seen the fate of nations that depended upon such commodities as natural rubber, tin, copper, and coffee. Because of the uncertainties of such markets, these new nations wish a more varied output and some approach to self-sufficiency.

The achievement of these goals is to a considerable degree dependent upon both the natural and human resources of a country. In general, a nation needs to have or secure adequate transportation facilities, power resources, some industrial raw materials, and natives trained in technology, engineering, and business management. These in turn pose problems of financing and training. If the first need is for public facilities, such as ports, roads, schools, and medical clinics, then outside funds are not normally available on a business basis. Long-term loans can often be secured, however, on a combined economic and political foundation. Thus the Soviet Union or the United States may offer such loans primarily to secure or keep the political allegiance of a nation. In such cases, interest rates may be artificially low and repayment may be accepted in commodities produced by the borrowing nation, even though the lender may not readily find an outlet for the items it receives in payment. Of course, it would be desirable to keep Cold War politics out of the picture and to make such loans available merely as a human duty of the "have" nations toward the "have-nots." Such altruism is not the controlling factor at the present moment.[1]

Likewise, the availability of technical training, especially in the form of scholarships for technicians, engineers, and business students, is also bound up with the world political situation. In many areas, the critical problem is to determine who teaches the chemists, engineers, and scientists of tomorrow. Training at home in the form of technical assistance is to some degree divorced from world tensions. Important programs of technical assistance are being carried out under the supervision of United Nations bodies, such as the Food and Agriculture Organization or the International Labor Organization. At the same time, the United States and the Soviet Union have their own programs, somewhat more oriented to the contest for the allegiance of mankind.

When a nation wishes to develop manufacturing and extractive industries, it may face a choice between domestic and foreign sources for funds and guidance. If the decision is to have locally controlled development, there may be a further choice between private industry and nationalized industry. The argument for domestic financing of industry is that it

---

[1] See M. F. Millikan and W. W. Rostow, A Proposal: Key to an Effective Foreign Policy (New York: Harper, 1957). A more conservative view is given by P. T. Bauer, Economic Analysis and Policy in Underdeveloped Countries (Durham, N. C.: University of North Carolina Press, 1957).

precludes the economic imperialism that characterized industrial developments of colonial times. In addition, there may be pressure for nationalization of basic industries in the interests of centralized economic planning and short cuts toward economic growth. Those who favor outside capital argue that industry is no longer shortsighted, as it was in the nineteenth century, and that outside firms will bring "know-how" as well as money. Proponents of this latter view tend also to favor the Western World in the Cold War. Those who reject foreign firms, or even local private business, are more likely to be "neutralist" with procommunist leanings.

It would be a mistake to look at these problems from oversimplified and doctrinaire points of view. On the one hand, the need is great. Half of humanity receives less than 10 per cent of the world income. Less than one third has enough food for minimum caloric needs. Life expectancy in the less developed regions is less than half that of industrial Europe and North America. Yet, on the other hand, a poorly planned program often does more harm than good. Forced industrialization, rapid changes in age-old habits, imposition of foreign standards rather than development of native wants, all these create dislocations rather than cure evils. The best forms of growth accelerate and intensify sound native patterns, at the same time providing adequate opportunity for readjustment when innovations are truly necessary.

Whatever decisions are made, they are likely to determine the course of history for the next century in great areas of the world. For this reason, self-interest reinforces the demand of Christian principles that we seek to help these developing nations. It is not merely a matter of keeping them from the clutches of communism. Even if this were not a threat, we would have legitimate grounds for concern over the type of government and economy that would control the lives of hundreds of millions in Asia and Africa. At the least, we would want forms that were compatible with democracy in the political sphere and socially oriented free enterprise in the economic sphere.

Above all, we should approach these problems in the spirit of Pope John XXIII. He emphasized strongly the moral aspects of aid to developing nations. While praising existing programs in this area, he called for renewed and expanded efforts. Yet he cautioned that such assistance should not degenerate, as a result of Cold War politics, into a new form of imperialism. Nor should giving nations seek to impose their cultural patterns upon recipients of aid.

International Trade. Thus far, our emphasis has been primarily upon the economic problems of developing nations. We should not overlook, however, the trade needs of countries that have already reached a degree of economic maturity. Trade among nations is normal. Varieties of climate, resources, aptitudes, and skills make some exchange among different peoples essential. Even great and richly endowed nations and empires have not achieved economic self-sufficiency. From the broader viewpoint of the common good of peoples, there is a still stronger case for reasonable freedom of trade relations. Some nations lack resources, so that their only hope for a decent standard of living is the exchange of products made with their labor for the goods of more fortunate peoples. Richer nations have an obligation in charity and social justice to consider the needs of poorer countries. In this way, the great riches of the world will accrue fairly to all.

From an ethical viewpoint, it is necessary to adopt a middle ground between extreme nationalism and excessive internationalism. The love of one's country is normal and laudable. But this should not be carried to the point where it becomes a worship of the nation, to the derogation of the rights and claims of other sovereign peoples. At the other extreme, those who deride national independence as outmoded are unrealistic. Culture, tradition, race, customs, and language often form a strong bond uniting people into a single nation. It would be expecting the unusual from human nature to think that these bonds can be ignored.

In the nineteenth century many economists argued strongly for unlimited free trade. But the automatic mechanism of the market often created serious internal problems in various nations. Any international crisis or upset in foreign-exchange markets could lead to domestic depression or inflation. Consequently many nations reacted in the direction of economic nationalism. Trade was often bogged down in a welter of quotas, blocked currency, bilateral negotiations, barter agreements, and similar efforts to build one nation's economy at the expense of others. This in turn caused economic tension and increased the danger of war. Fortunately the various steps toward increased international trade, to be described shortly, reversed this trend and led to co-operative efforts to promote sounder trade relationships.

Principles for World Trade. Sound international economic relations must respect two major principles: first, it must be acknowledged that each nation has a right to internal security and stability; and, second, each nation must be ready to co-operate with others for the common good of all. The first principle rejects nineteenth-century automatism, while the second is contrary to twentieth-century autarky. If these principles are applied to economic life, a sound program can be developed.

National security demands that international trade, although necessary, should take a subsidiary position. Insofar as this is possible, the internal economy of a nation should not be subject to the vagaries of world trade. Certainly, the domestic monetary and price systems should be immunized from serious shocks resulting from short-range and random fluctuations in foreign exchange or trade. In principle, the present arrangements under the International Monetary Fund are sound. They provide for reasonable controls over currency fluctuations, instead of a purely automatic system.

It is also legitimate to seek some measure of protection for domestic industries through tariffs and quotas. But these must not be abused to the extent of stifling all trade. If nations wish to sell abroad, they must also buy. It is economic folly to be pushing sales in other nations and yet erecting barriers so that they will be unable to sell to us so as to pay for what they bought. Protection of domestic industry should be reasonable. It should conserve heavy capital investment and safeguard against unfair foreign competition. But it should not foster domestic monopoly or penalize the consumers of a nation in the interests of a favored few producers.

As a general rule, when a domestic industry is efficient and capable of meeting most national needs, it should receive protection. When it is small and inefficient, it is unwise to try to remove competition and thus subsidize high-cost production. Should this latter course be necessary for military reasons, in the light of national security, it is better to subsidize the domestic industry directly instead of making all consumers pay more because of tariffs.

An important step toward freedom of trade was taken in 1958 when six nations of Western Europe signed a pact for the ultimate abolition of custom barriers and any other economic obstacles within their boundaries. Under this agreement, after a period of ten years goods and workers alike can move freely with no concern over national barriers. The purpose of this program is to secure for Europe a market of sufficient size to warrant the economies of mass production. In addition, it will tend to force industries to modernize, since they will no longer be cushioned against the effects of competition.

Another move in the direction of normal free trade is the projected International Trade Organization, sponsored by the United Nations and submitted to the member nations in 1948. The I.T.O. would have five main objectives: (1) maintaining full employment and economic growth within each member nation; (2) encouraging economic development and reconstruction throughout the world; (3) modification of trade barriers and commercial restrictions; (4) prevention of restrictive business practices; and (5) the control of intergovernment commodity agreements through mutual understandings, consultation, and co-operation. These principles can be accepted as sound and in harmony with the ideals of international common good. Such an organization, together with the International Monetary Fund and the International Bank for Reconstruction and Development, would promote the welfare of peoples and lay an economic foundation for world peace.

Whether we like it or not, the world today is on the threshhold of major changes. Patterns that were accepted without question a few decades back are now rejected with contempt. People do not ask whether the road ahead will be easy or difficult. They have simply decided to move ahead, without calculation of price. From one end of the world to another, mankind seems to have discovered or rediscovered human dignity and the rights that accrue to all men. The challenge to us who enjoy the long tradition of Christian thought, and in addition the privileges of a democratic way of life, is to give of our treasure and experience alike to those who need and seek guidance. If we do this, mankind can look forward to a golden era of peace and prosperity. Should we fail, we and our children may pay a bitter price in a world torn by dissension and possibly gripped by the awful tyranny of communism.

READINGS*

J. Y. Calvez, *Social Thought of John XXIII*, Chap. 6.
J. Y. Calvez and J. Perrin, *The Church and Social Justice*, Chap. 14.
J. F. Cronin, *Christianity and Social Progress*, Chaps. 17–23.
H. W. Flannery, *Patterns for Peace*.
B. L. Masse, *Justice for All*, Chap. 10.
J. Messner, *Social Ethics* (rev. ed.), pp. 693–744, 948–980.
P. Riga, *Peace on Earth*, Parts III–IV.

---

* For further readings, consult List No. 11 in the Appendix.

Chapter XV

RACIAL DISCRIMINATION AND RACIAL JUSTICE

Vatican Council II, The Church in the Modern World

29. True, all men are not alike from the point of view of varying physical power and the diversity of intellectual and moral resources. Nevertheless, with respect to the fundamental rights of the person, every type of discrimination, whether social or cultural, whether based on sex, race, color, social condition, language or religion, is to be overcome and eradicated as contrary to God's intent.

Pius XII, Mystici Corporis, June 29, 1943

73. How can we claim to love the divine Redeemer, if we hate those whom He has redeemed with His precious blood, so that He might make them members of His Mystical Body? For that reason the beloved disciple warns us: "If any man say: I love God, and hateth his brother, he is a liar. For he that loveth not his brother whom he seeth, how can he love God whom he seeth not? And this commandment we have from God, that he who loveth God love also his brother." Rather one should say that the more we become "members one of another," "mutually one for another," the closer we shall be united with God, with Christ; as on the other hand the more ardent the love that binds us to God and our divine Head, the closer we shall be united to each other in the bonds of charity.

Pius XII, To Negro Publishers, May 27, 1946

In this you have the key to the solution of the problem that vexes you. All men are brothered in Jesus Christ; for He, though God, became also man, became a member of the human family, a brother of all.

This fact, the expression of infinite, universal love, is the true bond of fraternal charity which should unite men and nations. May it be welded ever more firmly through the efforts of all men of good will.

With this prayer in our heart and with deep, fatherly affection we invoke on you, on all who are dear to you, and on all who labor with you in charity to further the cause of interracial justice, the blessing of Almighty God.

Pius XII, To Delegates of Italian Catholic Action, July 16, 1952

Catholics likewise are educated from childhood to consider all men of whatever area, nation or color as creatures and images of God, redeemed by Christ and called to an eternal destiny, to pray for and to love them.

Pius XII, To Delegates of Apostolate of the Sea, September 7, 1956

God did not create a human family made up of segregated, dissociated, mutually independent members. No; He would have them all united by the bond of total love of Him and consequent self-dedication to assisting each other to maintain that bond intact. How better could you show your love for your neighbor than by striving to procure for him what is his greatest boon, love of His Lord and Creator.

Pius XII, To Hematological Congress, September 5, 1958

It is only too well known, alas, to what excesses pride of race and racial hate can lead. The Church has always been energetically opposed to attempts of genocide or practices arising from what is called the "color bar."

John XXIII, Pacem in Terris

44. Today, on the contrary, the conviction is widespread that all men are equal in natural dignity; and so, on the doctrinal and theoretical level, at least, no form of approval is being given to racial discrimination. All this is of supreme significance for the formation of a human society animated by the principles We have mentioned above, for man's awareness of his rights must inevitably lead him to the recognition of his duties. The possession of rights involves the duty of implementing those rights, for they are the expression of a man's personal dignity. And the possession of rights also involves their recognition and respect by other people.*

48. . . . all men are equal in natural dignity . . .

86. The first point to be settled is that mutual ties between states must be governed by truth. Truth calls for the elimination of every trace of racial discrimination, and the consequent recognition of the inviolable principle that all states are by nature equal in dignity.

100. Furthermore, the universal common good requires the encouragement in all nations of every kind of reciprocation between citizens and their intermediate societies. There are many parts of the world where we find groupings of people of more or less different ethnic origin. Nothing must be allowed to prevent reciprocal relations between them. Indeed such a prohibition would flout the very spirit of an age which has done so much to nullify the distances separating peoples. Nor must one overlook the fact that whatever their ethnic background, men possess, besides the special characteristics which distinguish them from other men, other very important elements in common

---

* Many commentators have caused confusion by treating the phrase "on the doctrinal and theoretical level, at least" as the expression of Pope John's thinking. The context makes clear that the Pope here is expressing the trends in modern states, not giving his own views. Only in the second part of the paragraph, dealing with the sacredness of rights, does the Pope give his own teaching.

with the rest of mankind. And these can form the basis of their progressive development and self-realization, especially in regard to spiritual values.

They have, therefore, the right and duty to carry on their lives with others in society.

Paul VI, Address to President Kennedy, July 2, 1963

We are ever mindful in Our prayers of the efforts to insure to all your citizens the equal benefits of citizenship, which have as their foundations the equality of all men because of their dignity as persons and children of God.

Vatican Council II, Message to Humanity, October 20, 1962

We proclaim that all men are brothers, irrespective of the race or nation to which they belong.

Vatican Council II, Constitution on the Church

32. In Christ and in the Church, therefore, there is no inequality on the basis of race or country, social status or sex, because "there is neither Jew nor Greek; there is neither male nor female. For you are all 'one' in Christ Jesus" (Gal 3, 28 Gk; cf. Col 3, 11).

Vatican Council II, On Non-Christian Religions

5. We cannot truly call on God, the Father of all, if we refuse to treat in a brotherly way any man, created as he is in the image of God. Man's relation to God the Father and his relation to men his brothers are so linked together that Scripture says: "He who does not love does not know God" (1 John 4, 8).

No foundation therefore remains for any theory or practice that leads to discrimination between man and man or people and people, so far as their human dignity and the rights flowing from it are concerned.

The Church reproves, as foreign to the mind of Christ, any discrimination against men or harassment of them because of their race, color, condition of life, or religion.

American Hierarchy, Discrimination and the Christian Conscience, November, 1958

* * *

Our nation now stands divided by the problem of compulsory segregation of the races and the opposing demand for racial justice. No region of our land is immune from strife and division resulting from this problem. In one area, the key issue may concern the schools. In another it may be conflicts over housing. Job discrimination may be the focal point in still other sectors. But all these issues have one main point in common. They reflect the determination of our Negro people, and we hope the overwhelming majority of our white citizens, to see that our colored citizens obtain their full rights as given to them by God, the Creator of all, and guaranteed by the democratic traditions of our nation.

* * *

The heart of the race question is moral and religious. It concerns the rights of man and our attitude toward our fellow man. If our attitude is governed by the great Christian law of love of neighbor and respect for his rights, then we can work out harmoniously the techniques for making legal, educational, economic, and social adjustments. But if our hearts are poisoned by hatred, or even by indifference toward the welfare and rights of our fellow men, then our nation faces a grave internal crisis.

*   *   *

Our Christian faith is of its nature universal. It knows not the distinctions of race, color, or nationhood. The missionaries of the Church have spread throughout the world, visiting with equal impartiality nations such as China and India, whose ancient cultures antedate the coming of the Savior, and the primitive tribes of the Americas. The love of Christ, and the love of the Christian, knows no bounds.

*   *   *

Even those who do not accept our Christian tradition should at least acknowledge that God has implanted in the souls of all men some knowledge of the natural moral law and a respect for its teachings. Reason alone taught philosophers through the ages respect for the sacred dignity of each human being and the fundamental rights of man. Every man has an equal right to life, to justice before the law, to marry and rear a family under human conditions, and to an equitable opportunity to use the goods of this earth for his needs and those of his family.

From these solemn truths, there follow certain conclusions vital for a proper approach to the problems that trouble us today. First, we must repeat the principle — embodied in our Declaration of Independence — that all men are equal in the sight of God. By equal we mean that they are created by God and redeemed by His Divine Son, that they are bound by His Law, and that God desires them as His friends in the eternity of Heaven. This fact confers upon all men human dignity and human rights.

Men are unequal in talent and achievement. They differ in culture and personal characteristics. Some are saintly, some seem to be evil, most are men of good will, though beset with human frailty. On the basis of personal differences we may distinguish among our fellow men, remembering always the admonition: "Let him who is without sin . . . cast the first stone . . . " (Jn. 8, 7). But discrimination based on the accidental fact of race or color, and as such injurious to human rights regardless of personal qualities or achievements, cannot be reconciled with the truth that God has created all men with equal rights and equal dignity.

Secondly, we are bound to love our fellow man. The Christian love we bespeak is not a matter of emotional likes or dislikes. It is a firm purpose to do good to all men, to the extent that ability and opportunity permit.

Among all races and national groups, class distinctions are inevitably made on the basis of like-mindedness or a community of interests. Such distinctions are normal and constitute a universal social phenomenon. They are accidental, however, and are subject to change as conditions change. It is unreasonable and injurious to the rights of others that a factor such as race, by and of itself, should be made a cause of discrimination and a basis for unequal treatment in our mutual relations.

The question then arises: Can enforced segregation be reconciled with the Christian view of our fellow man? In our judgment it cannot, and this for two fundamental reasons.

1) Legal segregation, or any form

of compulsory segregation, in itself and by its very nature imposes a stigma of inferiority upon the segregated people. Even if the now obsolete Court doctrine of "separate but equal" had been carried out to the fullest extent, so that all public and semipublic facilities were in fact equal, there is nonetheless the judgment that an entire race, by the sole fact of race and regardless of individual qualities, is not fit to associate on equal terms with members of another race. We cannot reconcile such a judgment with the Christian view of man's nature and rights.

* * *

2) It is a matter of historical fact that segregation in our country has led to oppressive conditions and the denial of basic human rights for the Negro. This is evident in the fundamental fields of education, job opportunity, and housing. Flowing from these areas of neglect and discrimination are problems of health and the sordid train of evils so often associated with the consequent slum conditions.

* * *

One of the tragedies of racial oppression is that the evils we have cited are being used as excuses to continue the very conditions that so strongly fostered such evils. Today we are told that Negroes, Indians, and also some Spanish-speaking Americans differ too much in culture and achievements to be assimilated into our schools, factories, and neighborhoods. Some decades back the same charge was made against the immigrant, Irish, Jewish, Italian, Polish, Hungarian, German, Russian. In both instances differences were used by some as a basis for discrimination and even for bigoted ill-treatment. The immigrant, fortunately, has achieved his rightful status in the American community. Economic opportunity was wide open and educational equality was not denied to him.

Negro citizens seek these same opportunities. They wish an education that does not carry with it any stigma of inferiority. They wish economic advancement based on merit and skill. They wish their civil rights as American citizens. They wish acceptance based upon proved ability and achievement. No one who truly loves God's children will deny them this opportunity.

To work for this principle amid passions and misunderstandings will not be easy. It will take courage. But quiet and persevering courage has always been the mark of a true follower of Christ.

We urge that concrete plans in this field be based on prudence. Prudence may be called a virtue that inclines us to view problems in their proper perspective. It aids us to use the proper means to secure our aim.

The problems we inherit today are rooted in decades, even centuries, of custom and cultural patterns. Changes in deep-rooted attitudes are not made overnight. When we are confronted with complex and far-reaching evils, it is not a sign of weakness or timidity to distinguish among remedies and reforms. Some changes are more necessary that others. Some are relatively easy to achieve. Others seem impossible at this time. What may succeed in one area may fail in another.

It is a sign of wisdom, rather than weakness, to study carefully the problems we face, to prepare for advances, and to bypass the non-essential if it interferes with essential progress. We may well deplore a gradualism that is merely a cloak for inaction. But we equally deplore rash impetuosity that would sacrifice the achievements of decades in ill-timed and ill-considered ventures. In concrete matters we distinguish between prudence and inaction by asking the question: Are we sincerely and earnestly acting to solve these problems? We distinguish between prudence and rashness by seeking the prayerful and considered judgment of experienced counselors who have achieved success in meeting similar problems.

For this reason we hope and earnestly pray that responsible and sober-minded Americans of all religious faiths, in all areas of our land, will seize the mantle of leadership from the agitator and the racist. It is vital that we act now and act decisively. All must act quietly, courageously, and prayerfully before it is too late.

For the welfare of our nation we call upon all to root out from their hearts bitterness and hatred. The tasks we face are indeed difficult. But hearts inspired by Christian love will surmount these difficulties.

Clearly, then, these problems are vital and urgent. May God give this nation the grace to meet the challenge it faces. For the sake of generations of future Americans, and indeed of all humanity, we cannot fail.

American Hierarchy, on Racial Harmony, August, 1963

We know that public authority is obliged to help correct the evils of unjust discrimination practiced against any group or class. We also recognize that every minority group in America seeking its lawful rights has the obligation of respecting the lawful rights of others.

*   *   *

These truths being understood no Catholic with a good Christian conscience can fail to recognize the rights of all citizens to vote. Moreover, we must provide for all, equal opportunity for employment, full participation in our public and private educational facilities, proper housing, and adequate welfare assistance when needed.

*   *   *

It is clear that the racial question confronts the conscience of every man, no matter what his degree of direct or indirect involvement. Indeed, the conscience of the nation is on trial. The most crucial test of love of God is love of neighbor.

*   *   *

We can show our Christian charity by a quiet and courageous determination to make the quest for racial harmony a matter of personal involvement. We must go beyond slogans and generalizations about color, and realize that all of us are human beings, men, women, and children, all sharing the same human nature and dignity, with the same desires, hopes, and feelings. We should try to know and understand one another.

To do this we must meet and talk openly and sincerely and calmly about our mutual problems and concerns. There are many ways in which such meetings can come about peacefully and naturally and fruitfully. For example those in the same type of work can readily discuss the problems caused by racial barriers. Physicians of one race can talk with those of another. So can businessmen, teachers, lawyers, secretaries, farmers, clerks, and other workers. Parish and diocesan societies, political gatherings, and civic and neighborhood associations can be common meeting grounds.

Our important task is to break down the barriers that have caused such grievous misunderstandings in the past. When barriers have existed for many decades, deep misunderstandings have all too often arisen. These should be faced, not in a spirit of debate, but with a desire to open doors of understanding.

It is only by open and free exchange of ideas that we can understand the rights and obligations that prevail on both sides. Such knowledge is the prelude to action that will remove the artificial barriers of race. We must act to remove obstacles that impede the rights and opportunities of our Negro brethren. We should do our part to see that voting, jobs, housing, education and public facilities are freely available to every American.

We can do this in our own area of work, in our neighborhood, in our community. We may act through various lay organizations of the church, as well as with civic groups of every type. In many parts of the nation there are interracial committees representing the major religious faiths as well as the important aspects of civic life. We bless and endorse such efforts to secure interracial harmony and to implement it in every day affairs.

But civic action will be more fruitful, and its results more lasting, if all our citizens openly and explicitly proclaim the religious basis of racial justice and love. Accordingly we repeat simply: Love one another, for this is the law of God. Revere in every man his human dignity, for this is a gift of God.

United, as men and women of every faith and race, we can heal the ancient wounds of division. Thus our nation will reflect its true greatness, a greatness founded on the moral principle that all men are free and equal under God.

RACIAL tensions constituted the nation's primary domestic problem in the mid-1960's. They were more serious than unemployment and poverty, even though there was close correlation between these issues. Although they first erupted as civil-rights struggles in the South, they soon moved to the North in the form of open rioting in several cities. The South practiced segregation and in some areas denied to the Negro his voting rights. In the North there was *de facto* segregation in housing and consequently in some schools. But the really corrosive problem there was unemployment, slum living, and embittered hopelessness.

Exploded Myths. Disquieting as were these eruptions, they did clear the air so far as the civil-rights issue was concerned. They exploded many myths widely accepted throughout our nation. And they served to uncover hidden areas of prejudice, while at the same time they inspired many groups hitherto passive at top levels to act strongly and decisively for the rights of man. Northerners who complacently condemned the South for segregation were often exposed as bigots when they shamefully mistreated Negro families that moved into their neighborhood. Yet, on the plus side, churches and synagogues became active on all levels in seeking full equality both of rights and opportunities for oppressed minority groups.

Another lost myth is the view that the Negro has been content with his lot and that outside agitators alone are responsible for the headlines of recent years. Perhaps the best answer to that illusion is to cite the large migration of Negroes from the South. We may also note the case of the 1957 bus boycott in Montgomery, Alabama. There an entire Negro community, at considerable cost both in terms of money and hardship, boycotted a segregated bus system until finally Negroes were able to secure fair treatment. This action, and dozens like it, show the true temper of the American Negro. Given even the semblance of leadership and opportunity, Negroes will fight for equality and justice. What was mistaken for docility and acquiescence was simply the prudent restraint that captive and conquered peoples show until the time is ripe for liberation. The communists were surprised when the workers of East Berlin, of Poland, and of Hungary revolted. They too were supposed to have been resigned to their lot.

A final myth that is a casualty of racial tensions is the thought that these problems can be easily solved by a few laws or committees. It is now abundantly clear that racial feelings in the Southern United States are deep and pervasive. They are too rooted in history to be removed overnight. Likewise, the Northern cities that permit a ghetto pattern of Negro housing segregation are building problems far more serious than many seem to realize. This is especially true where there is large-scale migration from Southern farms to Northern cities. This involves serious cultural adjustments, and potential clashes, quite independently of any specific racial elements. Assimilation is always difficult when large groups and sharp differences in education, cultural background, and work habits are involved.

What we face in the United States now is a many-sided problem. The forward movement of the Negro people is irreversible. Even under the best of circumstances, it would be a difficult path. As it is, a century or more of inferior education, housing, job opportunities, and social status have left their marks in terms of cultural differences. In the South, these factors will be emphasized by those who favor the *status* quo. In the North, they may provoke disillusionment on the part of the naïve who feel that the problems of a New York, a Detroit, or a Chicago can be met by methods adapted to simpler problems of a few decades back, when the Negro minority was a relatively small group that assimilated with no difficulty. In this connection, we must also note that these cities have troubles with many low-income white migrants from the South.

Now that the picture is presented in clearer focus, it is possible to examine the principles and problems involved. This in turn will permit a realistic program for seeking racial justice. Once such a program is formulated, our Christian conscience can seek its full implementation.

Racial Justice. In one sense, there should be no special principles to apply to racial matters. It should be self-evident that all men are equal in the sight of Almighty God. There is one Father of all mankind, and under Him we are brothers, one to another. Christ died to redeem all men. We are all called to be members of His Mystical Body. To a true Christian, anything that would deny or even qualify the unity of the human race is utterly inadmissible.

What the believer holds as a tenet flowing from his Christian faith, the anthropologist affirms as a scientific fact. Generally accepted tests for intelligence and learning ability indicate that there are no basic differences along racial lines. To be blunt, Negroes are quite as intelligent, basically, as whites. "Proofs" to the contrary, based on problems arising when schools are integrated or when a rural Negro is suddenly introduced into an urban, industrial community, are simply failures to distinguish between inherent abilities and acquired cultural patterns.

It is obvious that a person, no matter what his color, who is illiterate and who has the slow reactions of the untutored is going to appear to some disadvantage when compared with an educated, sophisticated urban type. Likewise, when a whole people has been submerged and given a second-class status, they are not likely to come up with all the virtues (such as they were) of the Court of Versailles, simply because the Supreme Court has stricken down certain legal barriers to equality. These limitations are cultural traits that can be changed in time. They are not fundamental disabilities.

Too often we tend to judge differences in the context of a particular problem, and forget that equal or greater differences exist elsewhere. Thus, with the focus upon the racial problem in the United States, presumably we are sensitive to any facts indicating cultural differences between Negro and white. But it would be most helpful, and illuminating, were we to carry the study further and note differences within nations that do not have the Negro as a substantial minority. The traveler in Ireland will note sharp contrasts when he moves from Dublin, to Cork, to Galway. The tourist in Germany may not find too much in common, in terms of certain cultural patterns, among the inhabitants of Berlin, Cologne, and Munich. The "typical" Italian is quite different, oftentimes, depending upon his native city, whether it be Milan, Rome, or Naples. Those who like or dislike Chinese cooking should realize that most of the time they are served Cantonese foods, and that these are quite different from the cooking of the Shanghai or Peiping regions.

It is not necessarily wrong to distinguish among persons on the basis of such individual qualities. An excellent card player, for example, is not being unjust or unkind when he seeks partners of equal ability. Indeed, he might be less than kind were he not to discriminate. But if he were to pass up an excellent Negro partner in favor of an indifferent white player, then it is likely that he is rejecting the Negro because of color only. Such a decision certainly is contrary to the Christian concept of his relations with his fellow man. At the least, it is a violation of the law of charity. It can well, under certain circumstances, be a violation of justice.

Today, in the United States, segregation is discrimination and hence unjust. Many persons object to a flat statement of this nature, implying that it in effect reflects moral relativism. They argue that "separate but equal" was both law and custom for many decades, accepted in practice by Church and state alike. It is amazing, they assert, that suddenly what was common practice in a great part of the nation should become a sin. How could the Catholic churches, for example, enforce segregated seating but a few decades back and now declare that this same practice is contrary to God's will?

The objection thus raised is more plausible than solid. It has always been a sin to mistreat, degrade, and abuse one's fellow man. When a man is denied vital opportunities and basic rights because of the accident of color, an injustice is done to that man. However, it is not always clear that a given pattern of action is contrary to justice and charity. This is the more true when available alternatives might lead to much worse violation of essential rights. When the American Negro was freed from slavery, he was ill prepared to exercise the rights that suddenly were accorded to him. He was, through no fault of his own, the symbol of a bitter defeat accorded the Southern states in the War Between the States. It is arguable, at least, that under such conditions a segregated pattern of life was a lesser evil. He was protected from a pattern of bitter strife such as we see today, at a time when he was much less prepared to fight for his rights. Actually, however, many "Jim Crow" laws are relatively recent and were resisted by the more educated white citizens. Discrimination is strongest in the "poor-white" groups.

Regardless of these arguments, today the evidence is clear that segregation is the greater, not the lesser, evil. It leads to inferior education, housing, job opportunities, and medical care. Indirectly, at least, it is responsible for much ignorance, crime, and vice, since people who live under degrading conditions are likely to be affected by their surroundings. Every argument that is used against integration, based on cultural clashes between colored and white, is actually an indictment of the segregation that produced such patterns. Separate but equal facilities are in fact a myth; if they are separate, they are almost inevitably unequal. For this reason, we now say that it would be wrong to tolerate any longer a pattern that has proved to be harmful.

It is not moral relativism to change judgments as experience makes clear that certain assumptions are no longer valid. For example, both St. Thomas Aquinas and Suarez listed slavery among the basic human institutions. Indeed, the practice was considered a comparative act of mercy, in contrast to the alternative sometimes practiced of slaying prisoners of war. Today it is doubtful that even the strongest defenders of segregation would come out in favor of slavery. What they fail to realize, however, is that the moral conscience of mankind has now come to realize that segregation is also an evil practice, little better than slavery.

Implications of Justice. When we assert that the Negro must be accorded the same human rights as are recognized in others, we must accept certain practical implications, such as the seven points which follow:

1. He has full and unqualified rights to any facilities furnished from public tax money, including access to all schools and libraries. These must be available on the same reasonable conditions afforded to others, on a nonsegregated basis.

2. He must be accorded full civil rights, with specific emphasis upon the right to vote and to participate in juries. He must also have the right to assemble peaceably and to petition for his rights by all lawful means, including peaceful demonstrations.

3. Public policy should protect his right to secure a job on a nondiscriminatory basis, with full opportunity to join a union, advance in the job, receive necessary in-service training, and even reach supervisory and executive levels, if qualified. A contrary public policy would be adverse to the common good and hence unjust.

4. Public policy should protect his right to nondiscriminatory access to housing, either on a rental or purchase basis. This applies to private as well as public housing.

5. The doctrine of equality implies nondiscriminatory access to any

other facility available to the general white public on the basis of willingness to pay the costs involved. Examples would be department stores, restaurants, motion picture houses, and hotels.

6. No minority group has the right to complain if selective admission is practiced according to reasonable rules which are impartially administered to everyone. A school, for example, might limit admissions to pupils resident in the school district. Unless there were injustice in drawing up the district lines, pupils might not reasonably complain of such a limitation. Here we differ from those groups who have argued that de facto school segregation in the North leads to discriminatory education. There is justice in their complaint, but the evil can be remedied by improving the quality of schooling in slum areas, rather than by transporting children in large numbers across the lines of school districts.

7. No minority or other group has the right to complain when strictly private and primarily social groups restrict membership or invitations to congenial persons. This applies to private homes, clubs, and private societies. It does not apply to labor unions. In all likelihood, it should not apply to school fraternities or sororities, since these are — like labor unions — not entirely private groups today.

Most of these rights were in fact given federal protection by the Civil Rights Act of 1964. Housing was not covered in the Act, but executive orders have forbidden discrimination in public housing and in federally financed private housing.

The connection between the statements made above and the principle of racial equality may not always be self-evident. For this reason, it is helpful to examine each of the major areas involved, to see how discrimination and injustice have been practiced, and what must be done to remedy them.

Schooling and Civil Rights. It should be self-evident that tax-supported facilities and civil rights should be available to all citizens without discrimination. Unfortunately, this has not always been the case. Public facilities have often been segregated. And basic civil rights, especially the rights to vote, to serve on juries, and to receive equal justice before the law, have been shamefully disregarded.

In practice, segregated facilities often meant that Negroes received inferior quality of treatment. Generally, their schools were poorer, their teachers less prepared, and their libraries inadequate. In Washington, D. C., for example, it was found upon integration that the average Negro student at a given grade level was, in effect, two to three grades behind white students at the same level. Surprisingly, segregationists used this fact to prove that integration does not work. It should be patent that it is rather an argument that separate is in fact unequal. This is true even, as occasionally happens, when the Negro is actually given better facilities from a physical standpoint than are accorded to white students in the area. Beautiful surroundings cannot erase the stigma of inferiority.

Inferior education is the first step in perpetuating a practice of discrimination. Obviously if the Negro is not so well educated as the white, he is handicapped in seeking suitable jobs and other opportunities to advance. His cultural inferiority, a product of inferior schooling, is then used to justify further discrimination and thus a continuation of the vicious circle. Undoubtedly this was the reason that impelled the Supreme Court in 1954 to rule that segregated schooling violated the Fourteenth Amendment.

While there were certain arguments for tolerating segregation in education, few persons of any prominence have tried publicly to justify denial of Negro rights in the matter of voting, jury service, and the receipt of a fair trial. Arguments of this nature would be such an obvious contravention of the Bill of Rights that even the most prejudiced could hardly be expected to uphold them publicly. In practice, however, conditions have been quite contrary to the standards set by our Constitution. Negroes have been widely disfranchised in many Southern states, sometimes by arbitrary application of literacy and competence tests, often by sheer economic pressure against Negroes who registered and voted. In addition, there is frequently a double standard of law for crimes committed by Negroes and by whites. Lynching has ceased to be a problem, but white judges and juries are far more lenient, as a rule, with "their own" than with colored defendants. Unfortunately, the Negro criminal is often regarded as lacking in basic human qualities and rights.

It need hardly be noted that the Fifteenth Amendment and our basic concept of democracy are completely incompatible with the conditions just described. Moreover, as a practical matter, it may be most difficult for the Negro to secure his rights in other areas, if he does not have an effective right to vote. Southern states that have substantial Negro registration and voting usually prove to be the states that are most attentive to other civil rights of the Negro. In the long run, the right to vote will be critical in determining whether or not the Negro will secure all his rights and opportunities.

Job Discrimination. No less important is the right of the colored worker to get a suitable job. Education will benefit him little, for example, if he is relegated to the most menial and poorest-paying jobs. He may be a skilled mechanic, but can only find work as a porter or unskilled manual laborer. Obviously under such conditions he cannot earn the income that will make possible good housing, medical care, and educational opportunities for his children. He will be condemned to poverty, no matter what his abilities and training.

Clearly such a situation is contrary to public policy, even when private employers are involved. It is a generally accepted principle of law that private actions that are contrary to the public interest may be enjoined by statute. For example, a contract entered into by a minor may not be enforceable, since the government wishes to protect the young against any abuse of their tender years. A gambling debt generally is no basis for a court action, since the state does not wish to encourage gambling. Traffic fines are not deductible expenses in operating a car, even though the car is used exclusively for business. On a similar basis, the government has a right, and often a duty, to see that private employment practices do not perpetuate racial discrimination.

Full job rights mean the opportunity to prepare for a job, including a chance to get the training needed; equal access to job openings on a non-discriminatory basis; right to join a union, when this is helpful, unqualified freedom to apply for on-job training; and unrestricted opportunities for advancement. More simply, ability should be recognized, regardless of race.

A sizable number of states and cities now have antidiscrimination laws. Most of them are based on the principle that education and persuasion should be used at first, with penal provisions available in case of persistent and flagrant noncompliance. As a result of the wise use of these laws, barriers of discrimination have been more and more breached and the areas of job opportunity have been extended.

Of equal value is the practice of using the enormous buying power of the federal government as a weapon against discrimination. The President's Committee on Equal Employment Opportunity, for example, holds hearings and endeavors to persuade employers holding government contracts to give out all jobs, and job opportunities, without any element of partiality or unfairness. This Committee can be of particular value in areas, such as the South, where it is most unlikely that local legislation will be available to enjoin job discrimination.

Sometimes it is objected that the legal approach to job discrimination is a mistake, since one cannot eradicate prejudice by law. It is true, of course, that laws cannot control anyone's feelings, but they can make quite a difference when actions are involved. Laws cannot make a communist feel more loyal to the United States than he does to the U.S.S.R. They cannot compel a thief to respect in his mind the rights of property owners. They have no power to force the lustful man to control his thoughts. But in each of these cases, they can and should enjoin actions that are contrary to the common good. So it is with racial prejudice. Laws cannot control how people feel. That is a matter for education and religious training. But laws should keep these feelings from overflowing into practices that do harm to millions of Americans.

What the law commands should be reinforced by the demands of a Christian conscience.

On the level of principle, it would seem that job discrimination for racial and religious reasons is clearly against the virtue of charity and very probably against justice. That any group of citizens should be relegated to an inferior position because of color or cultural background is obviously contrary to the Christian principle of brotherhood. More than this, widespread denial of job opportunity is definitely unjust. Men have in justice a right to a job consonant with their ability and human dignity. If a skilled Negro mechanic is forced to work as a common laborer, he is being denied his rights. Likewise, if he is paid less for the same kind of work performed by equally trained whites in his locality, he is being defrauded. It is difficult to see how such discrimination does not involve justice.

The question as to which type of justice is involved is more obscure. Earlier it was stated that a worker does not normally have a claim in strict justice to be hired for any particular job. His right to a job obtains in regard to the economic system as a whole rather than any given employer. If such is the case, then an employer does not sin against strict justice in denying a job to a properly qualified worker because of race, religion, or national origin. But social justice requires that all concerned work as circumstances permit to change the institutions which bring about the evil of discrimination. Social justice applies here, in that rights are being denied under circumstances definitely contrary to the common good. When a group is being deprived of basic rights, the common good demands that steps be taken to remedy the evil. The appropriate steps are matters of technique and prudential judgment. Such steps would include education and fair-employment practice legislation. At the same time, we should not overlook the serious personal obligation of employers and workers, at least in charity, to avoid discrimination in employment patterns. Personal example, as well as education and legislation to change faulty institutions, can be a means of achieving social justice in this field.

Housing for Minorities. Many Negroes, and to some degree other groups such as the Spanish-speaking or Asians, find that even a good job may not give them and their families adequate opportunities. This is particularly the case when they are denied access to good housing. Here is where the North is often more gravely at fault than is the South. In New York and Chicago, for example, Negroes have found extreme difficulties in getting private rental housing, except in certain ghetto areas. The result is that families that can afford good housing are often forced to live in hovels and slums. In these areas, families often pay higher rents for a few broken-down rooms than a white family would pay for a comfortable apartment.

The evils of discrimination in housing are many. In the first place, this is an important factor in creating or preserving slum conditions in many cities. This practice makes it extraordinarily difficult for a talented Negro family to advance culturally and socially. Incentive is killed, so that only the strongest-willed persist in the upward path. Others fall back into a "what's the use" attitude, and accordingly try to get the most enjoyment out of the present, since it is hopeless to plan for the future. The Negro family that dares to move to white neighborhoods is often snubbed, if not actually mobbed. This leaves lifelong scars. Although "restricted covenants" are no longer enforceable at law, many ways are still found to enforce segregation in housing.

Two arguments are sometimes used to condone or even support present practices. One is the argument that people have a right to choose their neighbors. The other is the allegation that racial groups moving into an area depress property values.

As a matter of general principle, there may be nothing wrong with the argument that people should have the right to choose their neighbors. What is wrong in this context is that the basis of choice be color alone, without any regard to personal qualities or abilities. It is incongruous, for example, when a university trained Chinese couple, who have thousands of years of culture as their national inheritance, is refused housing in an area where any white persons, no matter how low their cultural backgrounds, can automatically qualify. If people want to form communities composed exclusively of couples addicted to square dancing, or of families of atomic physicists, or of devotees of "Charlie Brown," these may be acceptable, if somewhat bizarre, reasons for picking one's neighbors. But race is not acceptable, either on a basis of moral principle or of public policy.

Likewise, families have a right to protect the value of their property, even to the point of trying to avoid having "undesirable" neighbors. Again, the problem remains of what in fact should be considered undesirable. If what is feared is overcrowding and similar slum conditions, proper zoning laws can handle the problem. Zoning can also handle any danger that sharp cultural changes will be imposed upon a neighborhood. This is true because, as a rule, economic and cultural levels are related. If the economic pattern of a neighborhood is maintained — for example, no boardinghouses, no apartments, and so forth — it is quite likely that its cultural level will not be changed, regardless of the race of the groups entering that neighborhood.

Neighborhoods deteriorate because of inadequate zoning protection, plus panic selling by former owners. The pattern is rather simple. The first house for Negroes is bought, almost regardless of price. Then white owners panic and try to sell their houses immediately. Obviously their bargaining power is almost nil, so they get little for their houses (hence the charge that Negroes cause value to decline). Then the real-estate groups sell the houses at huge profits to Negro tenants. Often the prices they charge are so exorbitant that overcrowding is forced, and slum conditions ensue. All this seems to prove that Negro in-migration deteriorates a neighborhood. Yet, if nobody panicked in the first place, none of these events would have occurred. Any Negro in-migration would be confined to those whose economic and cultural backgrounds would make them quite acceptable, save to the prejudiced, in their new neighborhood.

Housing problems can be handled in either of two ways. The first and better method is one of voluntary adjustment to neighborhoods that are mixed racially. This can be done, with proper preparation. As noted before, proper zoning standards can help. But the really important point is that people in the neighborhood agree that they will accept racially mixed housing, and that they will continue the same neighborhood patterns as before, with their new neighbors accepted as full equals. This may be an ambitious program, but it is not impossible. It has proved a success where it has been tried.

The other alternative is the use of law to make housing sale and rental a matter of public policy, just as jobs are today in some jurisdictions. New

York City was the pioneer in regulatory legislation, but its pattern will undoubtedly be adopted elsewhere. In New York, it is no longer legal to discriminate on the basis of race even in private rental housing. Because of this, it is possible for well-paid Negroes and Puerto Ricans to break from the ghettos that formerly confined them. They not only have the physical comforts of better housing, but they also have the psychic satisfaction of being freed from the confines of racially segregated living.

Public Facilities. When the Civil Rights Act of 1964 was under consideration, one of the main objections to its provisions for equal access to public facilities was the argument that property rights were being destroyed by insistence upon equal access. These claims show a basic misunderstanding of both law and of moral principles. The English common law, which is the basis of our legal system, held that innkeepers and similar purveyors to the public must serve all orderly persons without discrimination. When property is made available for public use at a fee, it ceases to be completely private.

Morally, as we noted in Chapter XII, property must be considered under both individual and social aspects. To the extent that the use of property affects the rights of others, the owner's rights are limited to some degree. Racial discrimination involves the denial of a fundamental right to equality. Segregation in public facilities inflicts on the Negro not only the insult of exclusion, but serious hardships as well. Negro travelers have often been unsure where they could obtain food, lodging, and gasoline.

We note in this connection that the civil-rights demonstrations of the mid 1960's tended to blur the fine distinctions regarding essential and peripheral rights. There were kneel-ins in churches, wade-ins in beaches, and insistence upon the use of public recreational areas, even when other facilities were open to Negroes. The mentality of the demonstrators was simple: if segregation is wrong, then it must disappear from every area of life.

Social Equality. Surprisingly, the one area in which integration may not legally be enforced is the area which most segregationists use as an argument for their practices. They argue that integration, once commenced, will lead to a complete fusion of the races. Yet it is not true that "once you break down the barriers, there is no telling where they will stop." The barriers of overt discrimination have long since disappeared for Irish, Italians, and Poles, for example, but very few of them belong to the Union Club or appear in social registers or blue books. There are certain clubs to which no amount of money would be sufficient to buy admission. Birds of a feather can always find effective ways to flock together, without the intrusion of other varieties.

There is even less weight to the argument that equal access to public facilities will lead to mixed marriages and dilution of "racial purity." Racial purity is being diluted with sufficient regularity as it is, without benefit of clergy. The fact that the father is nearly always white may have Mendelian significance, but to the average observer the offspring appear the same. But all this is incidental; the main point is that in our culture marriages are arranged almost exclusively by the potential bride and groom. The man proposes, the woman consents, and the wedding date is fixed. If the parties are of sufficient age to give presumptively valid consent, neither the law nor the general public should generally have any further interest in the matter. The Supreme Court is not in a position to force interracial marriages — only the consenting parties make a marriage. On the other hand, the law should not interpose barriers to marriage because of color.

If there is no legal interest in social equality (except for borderline cases, such as resort hotels, that may be considered public facilities), the question may arise as to the moral implication of discrimination in social matters. This question is difficult to answer categorically, since much depends upon motive and circumstances. There is nothing wrong per se in seeking congenial company for social relationships. One person may prefer a quiet club, another wants a young and gay set. There are Beethoven clubs, Mozart clubs, and French clubs. Some persons gather to improve the breed of horses. Others, like the mythical Ferdinand, would rather be alone to enjoy the beauty of the flowers.

In a world that is not doing too well in keeping existing moral obligations, there is little point in trying to find new ones for people to evade. Since there are no grounds to claim any *right* to the social companionship of another, the most we can demand is that we try not to be unkind or offensive if we choose one companion, or group of companions, in preference to another. We would act from wrong motives if we rejected the social companionship of a person, otherwise quite acceptable, purely on the basis of color. But the motivation (other than fear of flouting public opinion) that prompts such a decision undoubtedly leads to dozens of other wrong decisions in vital areas where clear rights are involved.

The place to attack evils of this sort is where they are clear and unmistakable, not in borderline situations. Otherwise we would be fighting the wrong war in the wrong place at the wrong time.

Racial Tensions. In view of the fact that the present chapter has advocated strong steps toward racial equality, some thought should be given to the racial tensions this would provoke. This problem is not readily solved by leaning from the ivory tower and proclaiming: "Let justice be done, though the heavens fall." Such an approach can be very comforting to righteous folk who already have adequate bomb shelters, but consideration must be given to the less fortunate persons on the firing line. Unquestionably, in applying the principles given here, we must give proper thought to the ensuing community reactions. It is not merely a matter of what is to be done, but also how it is to be done most effectively. Prudence is also among the cardinal virtues.

The fact that correction of an evil will provoke unrest and possible violence is not necessarily a reason for inaction. At times we are impelled to tolerate one evil, lest by seeking to correct it, far greater evils be unleashed. But there are other times when we must fight the fight for justice, regardless of consequences. When *Catholic Social Action* was written 17 years ago, it was possible to counsel "a moderate and gradual approach," noting that "moderation is not inertia or passivity," and yet say: "only in rare and exceptional cases is it permissible to acquiesce in a major evil on the ground that action against it may bring even greater evils."[1] The world has changed enormously in the intervening decade. The Cold War is as cold as chilly levels of Sputnik-filled outer space, and racial discrimination is a weapon in this war. The Supreme Court has put the prestige of the Constitution itself in the battle against discrimination. When the stakes are this high, we cannot listen to the counsels of the timorous. On the threefold grounds of moral right, the world struggle against communism, and internal respect for law within our borders, the only answer today is "God wills it," as the crusade against prejudice and discrimination marches on.

Racial tension is a fact, but it is not a one-sided fact. For every advocate of the *status quo* who is unhappy over possible change, there are as many if not more persons who hold that race relations must be patterned upon justice. If there is a clash between these points of view, it is more likely that those who are thoroughly convinced of the justice of their cause will win out.

---

[1] *Op. cit.,* p. 171.

Reform Procedures. Racial reform today involves action on many fronts. While certain general principles may be urged, it is also true that programs must at times be tailored to the needs of individual communities. It is obvious from what has already been said that the approach in the South must be different from that in the North. In general it is sound policy to study the most successful programs in our part of the country. We can learn from the experience of others the approaches, techniques, and methods that are most likely to work. Often we can learn from others' failures to avoid repeating the same mistakes.

Priority might well be given to steps toward job equality, especially when this can be secured through the medium of government contracts. A sizable number of national corporations have established branch plants in Southern states in recent years. This not only increases the demand for labor, but it often places hiring control in the hands of officials who have no particular prejudices against the colored. Judicious pressures by federal agencies upon such firms can mean an important economic breakthrough for the Southern Negro. This in turn may lessen some of the housing problems in the North, since massive migrations of unskilled workers are bound to cause difficulties, independently of any racial aspects of the problem.

It is most important that consistent pressures be set up in the area of civil rights, and especially voter registration. If the Negro vote becomes important politically in many areas, there is every likelihood that different attitudes will prevail in regard to schooling, justice before the courts, and equal use of public facilities.

Schooling is a problem both in the South and in the North. The South faces the need for removing the last segments of segregation. In the North, there is the problem of poor facilities and demoralized teachers in our slum schools. It has been shown that intensive care, after-school facilities for study, and volunteer tutoring can do much to improve the educational level of deprived students. Full use of the Economic Opportunity Act of 1964 can help either to prevent school dropouts or to persuade dropouts to return for further schooling.

In some cities the problem of slums is extremely urgent. There is need for slum clearance, public housing, and the breaking of barriers on the part of real-estate agents and lenders that prevent Negroes from securing good housing in suburban areas.

For slum dwellers, there is often the need for job opportunity as well as equality. Absence of prejudice in hiring means little to those who have few skills to offer a prospective employer. Many employers are willing to offer on-the-job training for suitable applicants. While we do not endorse the use of quotas in minority employment, yet the absence of Negroes in certain firms or in certain jobs does warrant some inquiry as to the reasons for this situation.

Religion and Race. One of the most encouraging developments in race relations during the 1960's was the tremendously stepped-up activities of religious bodies in the area of racial justice. A highly successful National Conference on Religion and Race, held in 1963, was the beginning of a closely co-ordinated interreligious effort to secure rights for Negroes. Interreligious, interracial groups were formed in scores of cities and sometimes on a regional or state level. The major religious bodies worked strongly and in harmony to secure the passage of the Civil Rights Act of 1964. They are continuing this joint action in such areas as housing, employment, and education. Likewise, they are co-operating with the Community Relations Service, established under the Civil Rights Act to mediate disputes involving race.

The significant aspect of these new developments is the fact that race-relations programs now involve the power structures of churches and synagogues. The National Council of Churches, the United Church of Christ, the Presbyterian Church, and the Episcopal Church expanded their staffs and poured millions of dollars into race relations. Jewish groups fought discrimination throughout the land. In the Catholic community, scores of cardinals, archbishops, and bishops issued pastoral letters and accepted positions on interreligious, interracial committees. Race relations is no longer considered a fringe activity for a few dedicated specialists.

A number of important activities can be carried out by religious groups, either acting alone or jointly with civic human-relations bodies. One project of considerable promise is the interracial home visitation program, carried out by parishes, schools, clubs, and the like. It has been shown that one of the main bases of prejudice is ignorance and misunderstanding. When the races meet in a meaningful fashion, many false preconceptions are removed. This often eases the path to more substantive programs, such as housing integration or job opportunity.

Religious groups can use their tremendous economic power to persuade contractors and suppliers to practice employment justice. It can be made a matter of church and synagogue policy to inquire into hiring and promotion practices and to reward those firms that have sound and constructive programs. Another possibility is that religious bodies with large investment programs can be active stockholders and urge the companies whose securities they hold to adopt fair employment practices.

In the area of housing, religious bodies can hold meetings to explain why proper housing integration is not only morally right, but also not harmful to property values. Pledges can be solicited to indicate that well behaved neighbors of all races will be welcomed. Steps can be taken to persuade real estate agents and lenders to facilitate good housing for Negroes. There is even a proposal for "tithing for fair housing," asking investors to set aside ten per cent of their funds for use in sound, integrated housing projects.

The National Council of Churches sponsored a project for helping Negroes in Mississippi to register and vote. Teams of volunteers were sent to this state to assist Negroes to acquire the knowledge necessary to pass the registration test. In addition, many religious leaders took part in civil-rights demonstrations, showing their solidarity with their Negro brethren. In the Negro community, churchmen took positions of leadership in developing programs of nonviolent demonstrations and resistance.

Two cautions may be noted in connection with interreligious, interracial action. It is essential that we work *with* the Negro community, and not merely *for* its interests. Patronizing is not only offensive, but it can lead to misdirected effort. Often the white religious community does not even know who are the real leaders of the Negro community. If there is any doubt, it is usually wise to consult the National Association for the Advancement of Colored People or the National Urban League.

In interreligious action, it is also essential to discover the top leadership in other religious bodies. Many mistakes have been made when it was assumed that certain prominent individuals were leaders of a religious group, when in fact the real leadership was elsewhere. In case of doubt, it is wise to consult the National Council of Churches or the Synagogue Council of America. When carrying out programs, one should not burden the leadership with innumerable problems of detail. For example, it is good to have a local bishop on the organizing committee and the top policy committee of an interreligious group. But an executive committee should be formed to handle detailed, day-by-day activities, thus sparing the time and the prestige of top leadership.

The problems of our day, critical as they are, can also be considered as opportunities. They are opportunities for the American people to purge from the national conscience the sin of oppression. They are opportunities for the moral and religious leaders of our nation to give a type of leadership that will truly reflect their deep conviction of the equality of all men under God. If our nation fails this test, the foes of democracy throughout the world can say that we preach freedom and practice discrimination. If our religious leaders fail to lead in this crisis, they too will be charged as failing to practice what they preach, of being selective in condemning evil and promoting good, and of seeking the easy way out and not the stern path of the Cross. No greater peacetime challenge has ever confronted the United States. Our stature in history may well be judged by our manner of meeting it.

READINGS*

D. M. Cantwell, The Challenge of Interracial Justice.
E. F. Frazier, The Negro in the United States.
J. LaFarge, The Catholic Viewpoint on Race Relations.
J. T. Leonard, Theology and Race Relations.
G. Myrdal, An American Dilemma.
R. Senser, Primer on Interracial Justice.

* For further readings, consult List No. 12 in the Appendix.

Chapter XVI

CATHOLIC RURAL PHILOSOPHY

CURRENT RURAL PROBLEMS

John XXII, Mater et Magistra

123. First, with regard to agriculture, it would not appear that the rural population as a whole is decreasing, but it is an undeniable fact that many people are moving away from their farms into more thickly populated areas as well as into the cities themselves. When we realize that this movement of population is going on in nearly every part of the world, often on a large scale, we begin to appreciate the complexity of the human problems involved and their difficulty of solution.

124. We know that as an economy develops, the number of people engaged in agriculture decreases, while the percentage employed in industry and the various services rises. Nevertheless, We believe that very often this movement of population from farming to industry has other causes besides those dependent upon economic expansion. Among these there is the desire to escape from confining surroundings which offer little prospect of a more comfortable way of life. There is the lure of novelty and adventure which has taken such a hold on the present generation, the attractive prospect of easy money, of greater freedom and the enjoyment of all the amenities of town and city life. But a contributory cause of this movement away from the country is

doubtless the fact that farming has become a depressed occupation. It is inadequate both in productive efficiency and in the standard of living it provides.

125. Nearly every country, therefore, is faced with this fundamental problem: What can be done to reduce the disproportion in productive efficiency between agriculture on the one hand, and industry and services on the other; and to ensure that agricultural living standards approximate as closely as possible those enjoyed by city dwellers who draw their resources either from industry or from the services in which they are engaged? What can be done to persuade agricultural workers that, far from being inferior to other people, they have every opportunity of developing their personality through their work, and can look forward to the future with confidence?

126. It seems to Us opportune to indicate certain directives that can contribute to a solution of this problem: directives which We believe have value whatever may be the historical environment in which one acts — on condition, obviously, that they be applied in the manner and to the degree allowed, suggested, or even demanded by the circumstances.

SOME REMEDIES

John XXIII, Mater et Magistra

127. In the first place, considerable thought must be given, especially by public authorities, to the suitable development of essential facilities in country areas — such as roads, transportation, means of communication, drinking water, housing, health services, elementary, technical, and professional education, religious and recreational facilities, and the supply of modern installations and furnishings for the farm residence. Such services as these are necessary nowadays if a becoming standard of living is to be maintained. In those country areas where they are lacking, economic and social progress is either prevented or greatly impeded, with the result that nothing can be done to retard the drift of population away from the land, and it even becomes difficult to make a good appraisal of the numbers involved.

128. If a country is to develop economically, it must do so gradually, maintaining an even balance between all sectors of the economy. Agriculture, therefore, must be allowed to make use of the same reforms in the method and type of production and in the conduct of the business side of the venture as are permitted or required in the economic system as a whole. All such reforms should correspond as nearly as possible with those introduced in industry and the various services.

129. In this way, agriculture will absorb a larger amount of industrial goods and require a better system of services. But at the same time it will provide both industry and the services and the country as a whole with the type of products which, in quantity and quality, best meet the needs of the consumer and contribute to the stability of the purchasing power of money — a major consideration in the orderly development of the entire economic system.

130. One advantage which would result from the adoption of this plan would be that it would be easier to keep track of the movement of the working force set free by the progressive modernization of agriculture. Facilities could then be provided for the training of such people for their new kind of work, and they would not be left without economic aid and the mental and spiritual assistance they need to ensure their proper integration in their new social milieu.

The need for a suitable economic policy

131. In addition, a sound agricultural program is needed if public authority is to maintain an evenly balanced progress in the various branches of the economy. This must take into account tax policies, credit, social insurance, prices, the fostering of ancillary industries, and the adjustment of the structure of farming as a business enterprise.

132. In a system of taxation based on justice and equity it is fundamental that the burdens be proportioned to the capacity of the people contributing.

133. But the common good also requires that public authorities, in assessing the amount of tax payable, take cognizance of the peculiar difficulties of farmers. They have to wait longer than most people for their returns, and these are exposed to

greater hazards. Consequently, farmers find greater difficulty in obtaining the capital necessary to increase returns.

134. For this reason, too, investors are more inclined to put their money in industry rather than agriculture. Farmers are unable to pay high rates of interest. Indeed, they cannot as a rule make the trading profit necessary to furnish capital for the conduct and development of their own business. It is therefore necessary, for reasons of the common good, for public authorities to evolve a special credit policy and to form credit banks which will guarantee such capital to farmers at a moderate rate of interest.

Social insurance and social security

135. In agriculture the existence of two forms of insurance may be necessary: one concerned with agricultural produce, the other with the farm workers and their families. We realize that agricultural workers earn less per capita than workers in industry and the services, but that is no reason why it should be considered socially just and equitable to set up systems of social insurance in which the allowances granted to farm workers and their families are substantially lower than those payable to other classes of workers. Insurance programs that are established for the general public should not differ markedly whatever be the economic sector in which the individuals work or the source of their income.

136. Systems of social insurance and social security can make a most effective contribution to the overall distribution of national income in accordance with the principles of justice and equity. They can therefore be instrumental in reducing imbalances between the different classes of citizens.

Price protection

137. Given the special nature of agricultural produce, modern economists must devise a suitable means of price protection. Ideally, such price protection should be enforced by the interested parties themselves, though supervision by the public authority cannot be altogether dispensed with.

138. On this subject it must not be forgotten that the price of agricultural produce represents chiefly the reward of the farmer's labor rather than a return on invested capital.

139. Hence, in *Quadragesimo Anno* Pope Pius XI rightly observed that "a proper proportion between different wages is also a matter of importance." He continued: "And intimately connected with this is a proper proportion between the prices charged for the products of the various economic groups, agricultural, industrial, and so forth."

140. While it is true that farm produce is mainly intended for the satisfaction of man's primary needs, and the price should therefore be within the means of all consumers, this cannot be used as an argument for keeping a section of the population — farm workers — in a permanent state of economic and social inferiority, depriving them of the wherewithal for a decent standard of living. This would be diametrically opposed to the common good.

141. Moreover, the time has come to promote in agricultural regions the establishment of those industries and services which are concerned with the preservation, processing, and transportation of farm products. Enterprises relating to other sectors of the economy might also be established there. In this case the rural population would have another means of income at their disposal, a means which they could exploit in the social milieu to which they are accustomed.

FAMILY FARMS

John XXIII, Mater et Magistra

142. It is not possible to determine a *priori* what the structure of farm life should be, since rural conditions vary so much from place to place and from country to country throughout the world. But if we hold to a human and Christian concept of man and the family, we are bound to consider as an ideal that form of enterprise which is modelled on the basis of a community of persons working together for the advancement of their mutual interests in accordance with the principles of justice and Christian teaching. We are bound above all to consider as an ideal the kind of farm which is owned and managed by the family. Every effort must be made in the prevailing circumstances to give effective encouragement to farming enterprises of this nature.

143. But if the family farm is not to go bankrupt it must make enough money to keep the family in reasonable comfort. To ensure this, farmers must be given up-to-date instruction on the latest methods of cultivation, and the assistance of experts must be put at their disposal. They should also form a flourishing system of co-operative undertakings, and organize themselves professionally to take an effective part in public life, both on the administrative and the political level.

144. We are convinced that the farming community must take an active part in its own economic advancement, social progress, and cultural betterment. Those who live on the land can hardly fail to appreciate the nobility of the work they are called upon to do. They are living in close harmony with Nature — the majestic temple of Creation. Their work has to do with the life of plants and animals, a life that is inexhaustible in its expression, inflexible in its laws, rich in allusions to God the Creator and Provider. They produce food for the support of human life, and the raw materials of industry in ever richer supply.

145. Theirs is a work which carries with it a dignity all its own. It brings into its service many branches of engineering, chemistry and biology, and is itself a cause of the continued practical development of these sciences in view of the repercussions of scientific and technical progress on the business of farming. It is a work which demands a capacity for orientation and adaptation, patient waiting, a sense of responsibility, and a spirit of perseverance and enterprise.

146. It is important also to bear in mind that in agriculture, as in other sectors of production, association is a vital need today — especially in the case of family farms. Rural workers should feel a sense of solidarity with one another, and should unite to form co-operatives and professional associations. These are very necessary if farm workers are to benefit from scientific and technical methods of production and protect the prices of their products. They are necessary, too, if they are to attain an equal footing with other professional classes who, in most cases, have joined together in associations. They are necessary, finally, if farm workers are to have their proper voice in political circles and in public administration. The lone voice is not likely to command much of a hearing in times such as ours.

Social responsibility

147. In using their various organizations, agricultural workers — as indeed all other classes of workers — must always be guided by moral principles and respect for the civil law. They must try to reconcile their rights and interests with those of other classes of workers, and even subordinate the one to the other if the common good demands it. If they show themselves alive to the common good and contribute to its realization, they can legitimately demand that their efforts for the improvement of agricultural conditions be seconded and complemented by public authority.

148. We therefore desire here to express Our satisfaction with those sons of Ours the world over who are actively engaged in co-operatives, in professional groups, and in worker movements intent on raising the economic and social standards of the agricultural community.

149. In the work on the farm the human personality finds every incentive for self-expression, self-development, and spiritual growth. It is a work, therefore, which should be thought of as a vocation, a God-given mission, an answer to God's call to actuate His providential, saving plan in history. It should be thought of, finally, as a noble task, undertaken with a view to raising oneself and others to a higher degree of civilization.

JUST as the racial problem is more than an American domestic problem, since it has world-wide ramifications, so likewise the study of United States farm problems fittingly follows the treatment of international political, social, and economic issues. Farmers throughout the world face difficulties because of the impact of changing technology. Hungry people in many areas cast longing eyes upon the surpluses piled up in American granaries. Understandably, then, the great Catholic farm group of the United States, the National Catholic Rural Life Conference, has, as was noted in Chapter XIV, a world-wide perspective.[1]

The Church has shown an abiding interest in problems connected with the land. Numerous popes have testified to their special affection for the farmer. Moreover, in many countries, Catholic rural organizations are among the most flourishing forms of Catholic life. The United States is no exception in this regard. While the Church is not generally strong in rural areas, it is nonetheless disproportionately active in these regions. The National Catholic Rural Life Conference has shown a vigor and comprehensiveness in its programs unexcelled by any urban Catholic group. It has also worked out a thorough philosophy of rural life, as well as varied methods for putting this into practice.

---

[1] For a graphic description of world rural problems, see "Christianity and the Land" (Des Moines: NCRLC, 1951), pp. 9–12.

Some of the most carefully prepared literature on United States rural problems to appear anywhere has been published by the NCRLC. Its fundamental position was first stated in the 1939 *Manifesto on Rural Life*. These views have been amplified and kept up to date by frequent policy statements. The 1965 publication of the *New Manifesto on Rural Life* applies the traditional NCRLC principles to the newest realities of the agricultural revolution. Nor are the interests of the Conference confined to social and economic problems of the farm. It has helped in every phase of personal, family, and community living, including fostering an awareness of the liturgy and the preparation of a unique book of prayers and blessings for many occasions.[2]

MORAL VALUES IN RURAL LIFE

One of the main reasons for extensive Catholic interest in rural problems derives from the moral values inherent in farm life. Many phases of country living contribute to Christian culture. It fosters family life. It contributes to the character of those living on farms. There is a stability and sound conservatism about rural life which is favorable to religious ideals. For all these reasons, we can truly say that the farm is the cradle of many of the best elements in a nation's culture.

The Family. Farm life is family life. Practically every phase of rural activity tends to strengthen family bonds, whereas city living imposes many obstacles and difficulties in the way of the family. This can be seen from the nature of work on the farm. The whole family participates in the common task. As soon as children are old enough to work, they have their share of the chores. They may be given charge of some particular animal or allowed to cultivate their own plot of land. This gives them a sense of independence and self-reliance. But they also have a portion of common duties. They may milk the cows or turn them out to graze. They help bring in firewood or assist in the kitchen. Thus, their independence is tempered by a sense of social solidarity. This social sense is closely tied up with the family, thereby deepening and reinforcing the ties which bind all together. By contrast, city labor is often divisive. The

---

[2] An annotated selection of NCRLC literature is given at the end of this chapter. Unfortunately it will not be possible to give page and chapter references to the *New Manifesto on Rural Life*, since it is not in print at the time that these pages are being written. The author has examined some manuscript chapters and has seen extensive summaries of every chapter. It promises to be a major contribution to Catholic thinking on rural life.

family does not often have a natural interest in the work done by its various members, except insofar as it contributes to total family income. Children in the city are not normally integrated into a family productive unit. They may aid in small duties around the home, but most of their activity and recreation is done outside the home. Thus, one form of life is cohesive and centripetal, whereas the other is divisive and centrifugal.

The farm family is particularly well adapted for children's needs. They have space to live, to play, and to work. From the economic viewpoint, they are assets to the family, instead of liabilities as often happens in city life. Today they have practically all the advantages of city children — education, companionship, and recreation — without the disadvantages of crowded conditions, immoral influences, and excessive strain and tension. The country child faces more constructive challenges than is often the case with his city cousin. He must be resourceful and quick thinking, but he learns this constructively from meeting farm economic problems. The city child is also usually resourceful, but he often gains these qualities in contests with his fellows or by surmounting the hazards of the streets. It is this ingenuity which has so often distinguished Americans: both the positive and useful form of achieving marvels of production, and the less desirable form of mere cleverness sometimes associated with antisocial practices. The former quality is more likely to be derived from the farm, whereas the latter is more a product of urban living.

In the light of Church interest in the family, it is not surprising that Pope Pius XII said that "the tiller of the soil still reflects the natural order of things willed by God."[3] The Pontiff goes on to say:

> This, then, is the deep-seated cause of the modern conflict between city and country: each viewpoint produces altogether different men. The difference of viewpoints becomes all the more pronounced the more capital, having abdicated its noble mission to promote the good of all groups in society, penetrates the farmer's world or otherwise involves it in its evils. It glitters its gold and a life of pleasure before the dazzled eyes of the farmworker to lure him from his land to the city where he may squander his hard-won savings. The city usually holds nothing for him but disillusionment; often he loses his health, his strength, his happiness, his honor, and his very soul there.[4]

At the same time, there are disadvantages in rural living. They are not inherent or inevitable; indeed, they should be removed if families are to remain on farms. Farm families still suffer at times from isolation, scarcity

---

[3] Pope Pius XII *To Italian Farmers*, November 15, 1946, in *The Pope Speaks on Rural Life* (NCRLC), p. 10.
[4] *Ibid.*, pp. 10–11.

of social and cultural contacts, and lack of educational and religious facilities. Their health and hospital care is often inadequate. Sometimes, there is a cultural barrenness in the country, caused by overconservatism and excessive individualism. Too many farmers are blind traditionalists, unwilling to adopt new methods and processes. All this makes rural life less attractive, particularly for children who learn from motion pictures and radio some of the surface glamour and excitement of the city. This makes them less content with their way of living. Poor economic practices tend to lower living standards, thereby further accentuating the contrasts between farm and factory. Unless farmers living on the estimated two million marginal farms can get more land, capital, and better methods of operation, they are condemned to poverty and insecurity.

Farmers too often fail to realize the values inherent in education and cultural development. It is true that low per-capita incomes have frequently stifled the growth of rural schools, but even when income is available it is not always willingly used for such aims. The same is true in regard to beautifying the home and the use of laborsaving machinery. Thus, farm children today want electric lighting and inside plumbing. The lack of such comforts is sometimes caused by conservatism as much as by economic stringency. Church and other groups should take an interest in these matters, since they influence the choice of young farmers as to their future way of life. There is no inherent reason why the farm should not offer all the real advantages of city life, together with its own special attractions.[5]

Family Farms. Because the farm is the natural cradle of the family, it is understandable that the NCRLC should favor family farms instead of farm corporations. The ideal is a farm owned or securely held by its operator.

A formal definition of the family farm, offered by the NCRLC, is "a socioeconomic institution in which the capital, labor, and management of the family is organized toward the production of food and fiber for the benefit of the family and society."[6] Among the necessary characteristics are ownership or security of tenure, management by the family, the bulk of labor contributed by the family, a full-time occupation for

---

[5] For a recent expression of the advantages and problems of farm life, see the 1957 NCRLC policy statement, "A Program for the Rural Community," pp. 7–9, 16–17.

[6] "A Program for the Family Farm," 1956 NCRLC policy statement, p. 4. See also the statements issued in January and June, 1958, as well as "Christianity and the Land," cited earlier.

the family, and income fully adequate for the support of the family. Its size will vary according to the economics of the crop. It could be a ten-acre truck farm in Delaware or a five-thousand-acre ranch in Texas. The family farm is not to be confused with small farms, subsistence farms, or part-time farms.

In contrast to the family farm are the very large commercial farms, sometimes called "corporations in the fields." These latter depend upon large numbers of hired workers, often migrants. Many of these workers are poorly paid. Often they have been immigrants from Mexico, either illegal (wetbacks) or legal (braceros) who are willing to work for as little as 50 cents an hour. It is alleged that such farms profit disproportionately from government aid programs. On the other hand, family farms that meet the definition used above (adequate size, capital, and management) have been more efficient than corporation farms, either in terms of output per acre or return per dollar of investment. Understandably, the family farm is far superior in terms of noneconomic values. It is for this reason, and not because of fear of economic competition, that the NCRLC wants government policy to work in favor of family farms and against the oversized commercial farm.

The city dweller may be astonished to know of the capital investment in the average family farm. A sum of $100,000 is not unusual. This is the key problem in regard to the two million marginal farms in the United States. Their owners will need credit if they are to secure sufficient land and machinery to make productive use of their labor and management. The alternative, as will be noted later in this chapter, is (preferably) part-time industrial work for added income or (less desirable) programs to help farmers move to the city and obtain industrial work.

Even were family farms less efficient economically, there would be social reasons to encourage them. Pope Pius XII is very clear on this point: "During the last century and even at the present time, there have been discouraging examples of attempts to sacrifice farming to other ends. If one is looking for the highest and most rapidly increasing national economy, or for the cheapest possible provisioning of the nation with farm products, there will be in either case a temptation to sacrifice the farming enterprise."[7] In another section of the address, he attacks speculative ownership or unwise proposals for nationalization or collective farming. He concludes: "The Church teaches that the whole economy of a people is organic and that the productive capacities of a national

---

[7] *Ibid.*, p. 4.

territory should be developed in healthy proportion. The conflict between country and city would never have become so great if this fundamental truth had been observed."[8] Any program which subordinates agriculture, with its family values, to considerations of productive efficiency alone would be contrary to the common good and to the organic nature of economic life.

To facilitate family ownership of farms, the NCRLC favors private and governmental measures which definitely foster family farms. It would have tax and aid programs graduated in such a way that a differential exists in favor of the smaller group. In addition, it is considered most important to have fair arrangements for transferring title to the farm to a son, without the problems involved in the payment of estate taxes and the division of property among heirs. With this in mind, the NCRLC favors the "father-son agreement." The son who is to take title to the farm could build up an equity over the years by payments to compensate for his labor and managerial services. Moreover, under our tax laws, gifts of under $3,000 a year are not taxable. Thus, a timely program of purchase and gift would permit the orderly and intact transfer of the property, with no problems of estate taxes or buying out other heirs.

The NCRLC has many other programs to aid family farmers. It encourages land-placement service in rural parishes. In this way, Catholic farmers can learn about land for sale or rent. The Conference is especially concerned about developing the full potentialities of farm youth. It wishes to help those who belong on the farm to hold to this way of life. Conference priests also emphasize the integration of the liturgy with farm family life. By making the sacraments, family prayer, and special blessings a basic part of farm living, these priests bring a richness of life to farm families and thus encourage them in their chosen path.

While the Conference favors family farms, it also sees distinct benefits in what is sometimes called "rurban living." The factory worker who owns and tills an acre or two of land is raising his family in a more wholesome environment. He has added security in that his food needs are not dependent upon his factory job. He may even get some additional income from the sale of surplus farm products. But he is primarily an industrial worker living on the land, not a farmer.

Rural Culture. In addition to family values, rural life affects individual character. Indeed, it has produced its own definite psychological traits in farm dwellers. Thus, Emerson Hynes, in the June, 1948, issue

---

[8] *Ibid.*, pp. 10–11.

of the *American Catholic Sociological Review*, enumerates seven quantitative and five qualitative differences between farm and city life. Rural occupations are more diversified; they are influenced more directly by nature; population density is less; mobility is also less; fertility is higher; costs are lower; and social statistics vary sharply, sometimes in favor of the country (as with crime, divorce) and sometimes in favor of the city (standards of living, medical care). Qualitative differences include a different philosophy of life; distinct psychological traits, such as conservatism; self-contained family life; deeper but more limited social contacts; and varying types of arts and skills.

Rural attitudes differ clearly, although often intangibly, from those of most city dwellers. There is definite meaning to the phrase: close to nature. The farmer is constantly engrossed in such deep realities as birth, growth, and death. He lives in a world of biology. His environment is organic in the original sense of the term. By contrast, the city dweller often lives in a mechanical world. His work concerns machines and inanimate products, and often such abstractions as buying and selling, finance, statistics and calculations, and other impersonal things. Of course, urban residents deal with other human beings. They have their families, with the basic human problems and contacts implied in this. But this is often a different world from that in which they work. By contrast, the farmer is close to life in all his work. He is engrossed with elemental nature and hence may find it easier to think of nature's God. It may be more than a coincidence that the religious literature of the Old and New Testaments is full of references to various forms of living things and to nature in its elemental form of sea and sky. It is at least possible that the preoccupation with the mechanical and the works of man leads city people more easily into a humanistic and secularistic mentality, forgetting God and His works. At any rate, religion and religious values are held with greater tenacity by farm families than is often the case with urban families.[9]

The versatile nature of farm life tends to develop a well-rounded human being. A farmer's life is varied. Today he must have skills ranging from making simple repairs to a tractor to some knowledge of soil chemistry. He nurses injured animals and builds houses and barns. He must adapt his plans to the varied pattern of weather and season. Since he sells for a market, he must know something of business and economics. Thus,

---

[9] See "Christianity and the Land," pp. 8–9, and "A Program for the Rural Community," p. 14.

he has a chance to develop many aspects of his nature, much more than is the case with the assembly-line worker. This in turn affects personality and character. There is a stability and self-assurance which goes with the known possession of skill and the conquest of obstacles and difficulties. This is evident in the skilled city craftsman, and it is even more true with the versatile and competent farmer.

These qualities are further accentuated when the farmer owns his land. He then has the added stability which goes with ownership and relative independence. He has more control than is normally the case with urban workers of such essentials as food, clothing, and housing. For the essentials of life, at least, he is not so subject to the vagaries of an economic system. Moreover, he is his own boss. He does not get detailed orders in regard to every phase of his activity. This is why he becomes restive under government controls. It is noticeable that the tremendous extension of federal power in recent years softened its impact considerably when it reached farm areas. The administration of farm legislation is normally less bureaucratic and more decentralized than has been the case for most social legislation. In the past, rural independence had been carried too far. The farmer was too conservative in the matter of adopting new techniques, particularly in such matters as soil conservation and increasing soil fertility. But at least, this was an antidote to the pragmatism and experimentalism which too often prevailed among urban groups.

The self-reliance of the farmer has now extended into useful forms of social co-operation. Thus, in the United States there are over ten thousand organizations for co-operative marketing or purchasing. About one fifth of the farm products sold commercially are marketed through such groups. Farmers often buy such items as fertilizer, seed, cattle feed, and gasoline through their own purchasing groups. In addition, they have credit organizations, co-operative insurance, and irrigation, telephone, and elec-trification projects achieved through common action. As an illustration, over 90 per cent of farms are now electrified, whereas the use of electricity on farms was relatively rare three decades ago. Understandably, the NCRLC favors co-operative action:

> Farm co-operatives are necessary. Were it not for co-operative enterprise, the family-type farmer would be at the mercy of the economically powerful in society. Unorganized, he would find himself pitted as an individual against the organized forces of concentrated wealth. The farmer cannot allow himself to become a slave either of a domineering state or of the

economic dictatorship of the mighty of the earth. The farmer will be free only insofar as he is organized.[10]

Thus, the principle of self-help, stressed by Pope Pius XII, has been vital and fruitful in our farm life. The isolation fostered by scattered homesteads, in contrast to the village community where farmers live and drive to their outlying holdings, has been largely broken down both by new forms of transportation and by community projects. Today farm life is in many ways more social and more effectively organized than is the case with city life. The cities are intensively organized from one aspect, but the individual participates less in actual community work. He delegates such actions to civic or union officials and remains content to pay taxes or dues. Thus city dwellers are generally farther removed from an organic social life, whereas our rural population is now participating richly in such organic activities.

Farm Labor. Many of the social problems connected with rural life exist where the family-type farm is not the norm. Farm workers, for example, are often underpaid and insecure. This is particularly the case with migratory workers, although it also obtains for stable workers on large commercialized farms. The institutions of tenancy and share cropping are likewise fraught with social evils which could be removed by long-term plans for fostering ownership. In other cases, social ills can be traced to a long history of low income for farmers. This is especially true of educational and medical facilities. Since it happens that whole states are affected by low-average incomes this becomes a national rather than a local problem. As a result, there is considerable pressure for federal aid both in the educational and the medical fields.

Many crops require little care during the ripening season, but need a large labor force for harvesting when they are ripe. Such is obviously the case with cotton, sugar beets, fruit, vineyards, and even truck crops. Some of these crops are highly perishable, so that the farmers must have assistance for the short period of harvesting. Much of this help is furnished by migratory workers, who move north with the ripening of crops, particularly on the East and West coasts. Usually entire families move, living in shacks or barracks for the period of employment in a region. Often the whole family, including very small children, works. As a result of this migration, children do not receive much education and have little oppor-

---

[10] *Manifesto*, p. 56. For more specific pronouncements on the function of co-operatives, see "A Program for the Rural Community," p. 18; "The Land: God's Gift to Man," pp. 21–22; and "Christianity and the Land," pp. 18–20.

tunity for normal social contacts. Furthermore, employment methods are casual, so that at times families may travel to a region only to find all jobs filled. The same situation often obtains in canning industries, which are equally seasonal adjuncts to agricultural work.

The number of migratory farm workers is not known with certainty. The low figure cited for domestic workers, excluding *braceros* and non-working family members, is 300,000. Many church and civic groups, however, estimate that the total volume of migrants is over a million and may approach two million, counting families traveling with male workers. Average annual cash earnings, in 1962, were estimated as less than $1,105 for male workers and at $295 for women workers.[11] This includes a small amount of nonfarm earnings. As many as 15 per cent of the children never go to school, and education for the rest is often a hit-or-miss proposition. Families often live in shacks of unbelievable squalor. Some have social security but are covered by workmen's compensation in only five states. Because hiring practices are casual, Mexican labor is imported even where there is unemployment among American migrant workers.[12]

For the sake of clarity, it is necessary to distinguish among three different types of farm labor that should be classified in the problem group. These are: Mexican farm labor, native migratory workers, and seasonal farm workers. Mexicans may be admitted for temporary work at not less than 50 cents an hour, under suitable working conditions. About 300,000 such workers have entered in recent years. They are called *braceros*. Illegal Mexican workers, *wetbacks*, can be more easily exploited because they are subject to deportation. But even legal workers may get lower pay and poorer working conditions than specified in their contracts, partly because they are often not able to assert their rights, and partly because of poor enforcement. Low wages and poor conditions affecting the Mexicans tend to drive down standards for native migratory workers (including Puerto Ricans). Seasonal farm workers do not suffer the disabilities connected with being on the move, but their wages are quite low in many areas. About half of farm hired workers are employed in the South. Most of these (over 80 per cent) were seasonal, having less

---

[11] United States Department of Agriculture, "The Hired Farm Worker Force of 1962."

[12] For further data, see *Migratory Labor in American Agriculture* (Washington: Superintendent of Documents, 1951). See also "A Program for the Rural Community," pp. 18–19; "The Land: God's Gift to Man," pp. 25–26, and a "Program for Migratory Labor" (1961). The bracero program was scheduled to end December 31, 1964.

than one hundred and sixty days' work per year. Most hourly workers get less than eighty-five cents an hour. The average daily wage, for those paid by the day, was slightly over seven dollars. Those paid by the week or month might get around thirty dollars a week or one hundred and ten dollars a month. These figures are based upon the 1962 Census statistics.

It is easier to outline the problems of migratory workers than to offer a feasible solution for these problems. Unquestionably, many farm crops are such that temporary heavy labor demand is inevitable. These farms could not possibly support such a labor force during the entire year. Given this fact, three types of approach may be considered. First, the condition of migratory workers could be improved through public and private efforts to obtain suitable housing and a steady flow of employment. Enforcement of child labor regulations could prevent deprivation of schooling to children of migrants. Second, increased mechanization might lessen the labor needs for some crops and hence reduce the number of migrants. This has been done successfully for some field crops, such as wheat, where huge combines do the work of many men. It may also be found feasible for other crops, if suitable research were undertaken. Finally, it may be possible to recruit casual labor locally through the use of college students or even more mature high school students in their summer vacations. All this would assume adequate safeguards and more attractive conditions than are currently available.

Since the problem of migratory work is regional or even national, it is clear that the handling of it should be on a large scale. One possible approach is through unionization of workers to demand better wages and more regular conditions of employment. By this method, a labor union would act as a stabilizing force, just as it has been in the clothing industry. Another approach would be through action by the federal government, after a thorough study of the entire issue, including the agricultural economics involved. From the political viewpoint the union approach is preferable. If workers organized to demand better conditions, farmers would be forced to make the necessary adjustments or do without labor at a critical time. They might then welcome any help which the federal government might give. But if the government were to act first, there would be tremendous political opposition from the highly organized and effective farm lobby. A parallel case would be the condition of domestic servants. Evils in this field seemed impervious to legislative remedy, but when economic conditions gave workers more attractive alternate conditions of employment, the shortage of servants quickly led to raised standards. In many cities, this form of work is now on an organized basis, sometimes handled by teams working from a central office. Thus, necessity forced the overcoming of inertia and lethargy and led to greatly improved conditions. A similar approach may be the more feasible answer to the problem of migratory and casual labor.

It should not be assumed that farm labor is the only form of migratory labor. In addition to canneries previously mentioned, there are elements of casualness in logging, construction, shipping, and resort occupations. As a rule, however, these occupations do not pose the serious social problem associated with migratory farm labor, since techniques have been found for stabilizing employment and income. In all likelihood, similar gains can be made in connection with farm labor, provided sufficient incentives are present. Apathy and neglect tend to perpetuate the *status quo*. If government, labor, farm organizations, and various reform groups can keep up constant pressure for higher standards, it is likely that this most exploited group of workers in the United States can begin to move up the economic ladder.

ECONOMIC PROBLEMS OF AGRICULTURE

Few issues in public life are so complex and controversial as the so-called "farm problem." Actually, the title is a misnomer. There are many farm problems. If we approach the situation from the viewpoint of average farm income, we find that nearly three million farms are generally profitable, whereas two million or more are considered marginal. If the approach is in terms of product, again there are wide variations. Hogs may be very profitable one year and two years later they may cause a glut in the market. Cotton may be grown profitably in Texas and at a loss in Georgia. A region that is prosperous for five years may then face five years of drought. Because of this complexity, it is not easy to make generalizations about farm economics. Likewise, any single method of solution is likely to be uneven in result.

Some sources of farm difficulties are inherent in the very process of farming. Weather conditions, crop and animal diseases, and varying fertility of the soil primarily reflect natural conditions. Man is learning ever new techniques to control these conditions. but they still remain to some degree beyond prediction and control. Other problems spring from revolutionary improvements in agriculture. In almost every area of farming, there has been startling progress in the quality of seeds and animals, the use of machinery, and the general application of science to rural problems. The typical American farm today is a small or medium-sized business, involving very substantial amounts of capital and demanding specialized managerial ability. The result of these trends has been fewer but larger and more efficient farms. This in turn has meant a steady displacement of farm population. A century ago, the majority of Americans derived their living from farming. Today less than 10 per cent of our population is supported by farm income.

An important event in recent years has been the trend toward "vertical integration" in many crops. Here a processor or food dealer contracts for the entire output of a farm. Contracts vary, with some merely guaranteeing a price with the farmer furnishing his own resources, while others may involve the furnishing of capital, feed, and facilities. These guarantees help take some of the risk out of farming, and may furnish capital to some who could not otherwise obtain it, but they also pose the serious danger of lessening or destroying the independence of the farmer. Unless such farmers strengthen their economic position by collective bargaining with processors or other integrators, they may lose their freedom and become mere adjuncts to supermarkets and similar purchasers.

The market for farm products is constantly changing. On the plus side, population growth and higher living standards have expanded the domestic market. High-income conditions particularly favor meats, fruits, and vegetables. Proportionate direct consumption of cereals tends to go down. Foreign markets are more capricious. War periods tend to heighten demand. In times of peace, American products often lose out to competition from low-cost areas elsewhere. The expansion and contraction caused by this factor alone has been seriously disruptive for many farm areas. In addition, some crops, such as cotton, have felt the inroads of competition by synthetic fibers.

Surpluses. As production expanded more rapidly than markets, the problem of surpluses arose. A surplus is created when a crop cannot be sold at a price that will pay farmers' costs and give them a fair return on their investment, management, and labor. The federal government, through various laws, has tried to meet this problem by agreeing either to purchase and store certain crops at a support price, or to lend money to the farmer to perform this storage. Security for such loans is the stored crop; a farmer's capital is not subject to assessment should he default on this type of loan. Concomitant with price supports have been programs to retire land from production, either of the crop supported or of all crops. Such programs have not been very successful in reducing surpluses, since greater efficiency and intensive use of the remaining land kept total output at high levels.

Some farm problems are more easily solved than others. As was noted earlier, tremendous progress has been made in controlling the vagaries of nature. Irrigation, erosion control, better fertilizers, resistant strains of seeds, new insecticides, special breeds of animals — all these have lessened the element of risk attributable to natural causes. It is even feasible to insure certain crops against losses caused by weather. There are facilities for teaching most farmers the specialized knowledge needed by modern farming, although more aids are needed. Federal and private credit of various types is also available, yet many of the marginal farmers who need credit most cannot obtain the amounts they need.

The problem of price-depressing food surpluses is thornier. The NCRLC has repeatedly urged more imaginative disposal of surplus crops to needy persons abroad and at home. Such programs of shared abundance must be managed carefully, so as not to compete with normal markets and thus cause international or domestic tensions. But the piling up of unused surpluses, when millions are hungry, is a moral problem. It is also an economic problem both because of its direct cost and because of the impact that such surpluses have upon farm prices and income.

In recent years, Congress has authorized a "Food for Peace" program which dispenses several billion dollars' worth of surplus food and fibers to combat famine, malnutrition, and hunger in more than 100 developing nations outside the communist orbit. The foreign currencies received in payment are used to speed economic growth in the recipient nations, and also to pay for certain expenses of the United States government in these areas. These commodities move through private trade channels. Moreover there are provisions for disaster-relief operations, either on a government-to-government basis or through the services of voluntary relief agencies, including the Catholic Relief Services, N.C.W.C.

As these pages are being written, there is almost universal agreement among farm economists that a price-support program that leads to constantly increasing surpluses cannot be defended. It has received political support as a means of bolstering farm income, but even such support is waning. Current thinking is divided along many lines, but two lines of approach are frequently mentioned. One would guarantee farm incomes and let prices seek their free-market level. This might be less costly than storage and would mean lower prices to consumers. The second approach is to lower the level of support prices so that they, in effect, become a form of disaster insurance. Farmers would be freed of controls and left to produce the crop that they can produce most efficiently. It is maintained that efficient farmers could make good incomes under this system. Less efficient farmers would need to seek other forms of income. In effect, this would further cut down the number of American farms.

If this second program prevails, it is essential that Americans learn more about the Rural Areas Development Program of the federal government. This program is aimed at giving direct assistance to the marginal farmer who is the greatest sufferer from the present farm crisis and who contributes heavily to the class whose incomes are below two thousand dollars a year. It is estimated that over two million farmers belong in this class. Rural Development is a complex pilot program to stimulate local initiative in securing capital and knowledge for better farming, or aid in securing some other form of income. For example, a food-processing company might be persuaded to open a plant in an area where many farmers are underemployed. These farmers could continue to have the advantages of farm living, but they could supplement their incomes and thus achieve higher living standards. Some farmers even could be given training for full-time work in the cities or towns.

Much can be said in favor of a combined program of removing controls from more efficient farmers and aiding their marginal brothers. It is socially desirable to minimize the area of government control over farming. This should not mean a return to *laissez faire*, with farming as one of the few purely competitive groups in a highly organized economy. But government aid should involve a minimum interference with the normal function of the market in fixing prices and allocating resources. A controlled economy rarely, if ever, functions efficiently.

The farm is a bastion of family life and political stability. It should be maintained as a cradle of independence. Outside aid, when it is needed because of the complexities of farm economics, should be of a nature that contributes to, rather than weakens, this independence. Our entire society will be stronger as a result.

Pope John XXIII on Agriculture. The treatment of farm problems by Pope John XXIII is by far the most extensive and realistic in any papal document. Yet there are inherent difficulties in any presentation of a problem that manifests itself so differently in various parts of the world,

Indeed, within the borders of the United States there are diverse farm problems, depending on the crops under study, the regions of the country, and the size and quality of the farm involved.

Thus the generalization by the Pope that farmers are moving to the cities in sizable numbers is certainly valid here. The reasons given, the real or apparent advantages of city living as seen by underprivileged farmers, is also a correct description of our migration of farm dwellers.

But some of the remedies suggested by Pope John are lacking only for a minor part of our farm acreage. In general, basic public services are available in rural areas. Most of our farms, in terms of acreage, have taken advantage of technological gains in agriculture. We do offer some tax and credit advantages to our producers of food and fibers. Likewise we have price-support programs for most of our basic crops.

Our real problem, as noted earlier, is the two million or so marginal farms, often deficient in size, capital, and managerial talent. There is also the question of giving family farms a preferred position in existing price-support and related programs.

Hence it may be said of *Mater et Magistra* that it offers little in the way of concrete suggestions that are not, at least partially, in effect here. But it does offer a powerful stimulus to efforts to secure a better measure of justice for farmers and a more even balance in living standards for agriculture, as compared with industry and the services. Finally, its deep appreciation of the moral and spiritual values of farm living should be a source of inspiration and encouragement to all concerned with this vital aspect of American life.

READINGS*

New Manifesto on Rural Life
J. Y. Calvez, *Social Thought of John XXIII*, Chap. 5.
J. F. Cronin, *Christianity and Social Progress*, Chaps. 12–15.
B. L. Masse, *Justice for All*, Chap. 9.
Manifesto on Rural Life.
M. R. Benedict, *Can We Solve the Farm Problem?*
W. W. Cochrane, *Farm Prices: Myth and Reality.*
R. L. Mighell, *American Agriculture: Its Structure and Place in the Economy.*
T. W. Schultz, *Economic Organization of Agriculture.*
L. Soth, *Farm Trouble.*
Reports and Publications of the National Catholic Rural Life Conference.

---

* For further readings, consult List No. 13 in the Appendix.

The following are relatively recent and of special value in the fields indicated.
J. L. Vizzard, "Who Shall Own the Land?" A discussion of the right of private
property and also its limitations, in the context of rural problems.
"A Program for Migratory Labor," 1961 Policy Statement. Careful analysis of
the problem, remedies, and alternatives.
"Co-operative Bargaining for American Agriculture," 1961 Policy Statement.
This plea for co-operative bargaining was repeated in 1964, in connection
with efforts by the National Farmers' Organization to raise the prices of
meat products.
"Developing Rural Industry," 1960 Policy Statement. Suggests advantages of
having industrial growth in rural areas.
"Policy Statement, June 18, 1958." For statements on agricultural revolution,
vertical integration, and efficiency of family farms.
"Policy Statement, January, 1958." Vertical integration, large versus small
farms, low-income problems, migratory labor.
"A Program for the Rural Community," 1957 Policy Statement. Wide range
of issues, with excerpts from earlier statements; valuable as a brief but broad
presentation of NCRLC policies.
"Start Where You Are" (1957). Jocist-type brochure for young people, giving
them elements of Christian social action.
"A Program for the Family Farm" (1956). Defines the family farm, indicates
its importance, and notes how it may be strengthened.
"Our Thirty-Fourth Year" (1956). Brochure describing organization and work
of the Conference.
"A Program for Shared Abundance." Abundance for the farmer and for the
world.
"Conclusiones de Panama" (1955) and "Conclusiones de Manizales" (1953).
Primarily Latin-American problems, with principles that apply more widely
to world problems of population and food.
"The Land: God's Gift to Man" (1952). Another broad statement on farm
problems, with suitable reference material.
"Christianity and the Land" (1951). World conference report; excellent
primer on Catholic rural philosophy, as well as statements on international
food problems; contains papal address on farming, July 2, 1951.
Rural Life Prayer Book (1956). A 410-page prayer book, containing the Ordinary of the Mass, prayers for the country family, occasional prayers, blessings
from the Roman Ritual, prayers and devotions, liturgical devotions for country living, and selected psalms.

Chapter XVII

SOCIAL PRINCIPLES AND SOCIAL ACTION

SPIRITUAL NATURE OF MODERN CRISIS

Leo XIII, Graves de Communi

10. For it is the opinion of some, which is caught up by the masses, that the social question, as they call it, is merely economic. The precise opposite is the truth. It is first of all moral and religious, and for that reason its solution is to be expected mainly from the moral law and the pronouncements of religion.

Pius XI, Quadragesimo Anno

98. The first and most necessary remedy is a reform of morals.

127. Yet, if we look into the matter more carefully and more thoroughly, we shall clearly perceive that, preceding this ardently desired social restoration, there must be a renewal of the Christian spirit, from which so many immersed in economic life have, far and wide, unhappily fallen away, lest all our efforts be wasted and our house be built not on a rock but on shifting sand.

129. "Wherefore," to use the words of Our Predecessor, "if human society is to be healed, only a return to Christian life and institutions will heal it." For this alone can provide effective remedy for that excessive care for passing things that is the origin of all vices; and this alone can draw away men's eyes, fascinated by and wholly fixed on the changing things of the world, and raise them toward Heaven. Who would deny that human society is in most urgent need of this cure now?

136. No genuine cure can be furnished for this lamentable ruin of souls, which, so long as it continues, will frustrate all efforts to regenerate society, unless men return openly and sincerely to the teaching of the Gospel, to the precepts of Him who alone has the words of everlasting life, words which will never pass away, even if Heaven and earth will pass away. . . . We mean that perfect order which the Church with great force and power preaches and which right human reason itself demands, that all things be directed to God as the first and supreme end of all created activity, and that all created goods under God be considered as mere instruments to be used only insofar as they conduce to the attainment of the supreme end. . . . If these principles are observed by everyone, everywhere, and always, not only the production and acquisition of goods but also the use of wealth, which now is seen to be so often contrary to right order, will be brought back soon within the bounds of equity and just distribution. The sordid love of wealth, which is the shame and great sin of our age,

will be opposed in actual fact by the gentle yet effective law of Christian moderation which commands man to seek first the Kingdom of God and His Justice, with the assurance that by virtue of God's kindness and unfailing promise, temporal goods also, insofar as he has need of them, shall be given him besides.

143. But above all, let them hold in high esteem and assiduously employ for the good of their disciples that most valuable means of both personal and social restoration which, as We taught in Our Encyclical, *Mens*

Nostra, is to be found in the Spiritual Exercises for all the laity, but also the highly beneficial Workers' Retreats. For in that school of the spirit, not only are the best of Christians developed, but true apostles also are trained for every condition of life and are enkindled with the fire of the heart of Christ. From this school they will go forth as did the Apostles from the Upper Room of Jerusalem, strong in faith, endowed with an invincible steadfastness in persecution, burning with zeal, interested solely in spreading everywhere the Kingdom of Christ.

Pius XI, On Atheistic Communism

41. As in all the stormy periods of the history of the Church, the fundamental remedy today lies in a sincere renewal of private and public life according to the principles of the Gospel by all those who belong to the Fold of Christ, that they may be in truth the salt of the earth to preserve human society from total corruption.

44. And here We wish, Venerable Brethren, to insist more particularly on two teachings of our Lord which have special bearing on the present condition of the human race; detachment from earthly goods and the precept of charity. "Blessed are the poor in spirit" were the first words that fell from the lips of the divine Master in His sermon on the mount. This lesson is more than ever necessary in these days of materialism athirst for the goods and pleasures of this earth. All Christians, rich or poor, must keep their eyes fixed on heaven, remembering that "we have not here a lasting city, but we seek one that is to come." The rich should not place their happiness in things of earth nor spend their best efforts in the acquisition of them. Rather, considering themselves

only as stewards of their earthly goods, let them be mindful of the account they must render of them to their Lord and Master, and value them as precious means that God has put into their hands for doing good; let them not fail, besides, to distribute of their abundance to the poor, according to the evangelical precept.

45. But the poor, too, in their turn, while engaged, according to the laws of charity and justice, in acquiring the necessities of life and also in bettering their condition, should always remain "poor in spirit," and hold spiritual goods in higher esteem than earthly property and pleasures. Let them remember that the world will never be able to rid itself of misery, sorrow, and tribulation, which are the portion even of those who seem most prosperous. Patience, therefore, is the need of all, that Christian patience which comforts the heart with the divine assurance of eternal happiness.

77. Everywhere today there is an anxious appeal to moral and spiritual forces; and rightly so, for the evil we must combat is at its origin primarily an evil of the spiritual order.

Pius XI, Caritate Christi Compulsi, May 3, 1932

13. For God or against God — this once more is the alternative that shall decide the destinies of all mankind, in politics, in finance, in morals, in the sciences and arts, in the state, in civil and domestic society.

25. But to prayer we must also join penance, the spirit of penance and the practice of Christian penance.

27. Penance is of its very nature a recognition and re-establishment of the moral order in the world that is founded on the eternal law, that is, on the living God. He who makes satisfaction to God for sin recognizes thereby the sanctity of the highest principles of morality, their internal binding power, the need of a sanction against their violation.

29. It is a weapon that strikes right at the root of all evil, that is, at the lust for material wealth and the wanton pleasures of life. By means of voluntary sacrifices, by means of practical and even painful acts of self-denial, by means of various works of penance, the noblehearted Christian subdues the base passions that tend to make him violate the moral order.

30. No leader in public economy, no power of organization will ever be able to bring social conditions to a peaceful solution, unless first in the very field of economics there triumphs moral law based on God and conscience.

Pius XII, Summi Pontificatus, October 20, 1939

1437. For true though it is that the evils from which mankind suffers today come in part from economic instability and from the struggle of interests regarding a more equal distribution of the goods which God has given man as a means of sustenance and progress, it is not less true that their root is deeper and more intrinsic, belonging to the sphere of religious belief and moral convictions. . . . The re-education of mankind if it is to have any effect, must be, above all things, spiritual and religious. Hence it must proceed from Christ as from its indispensable foundation; must be actuated by justice and crowned by charity.

1444. There is no opposition between the laws that govern the life of faithful Christians and the postulates of a genuine brotherly humanitarianism, but rather unity and mutual support.

Pius XII, To Members of Pax Christi, September 13, 1952

A supernaturalism that withdraws itself from economic and political needs and duties as if they did not concern the Christian and Catholic is something unhealthy, something alien to the thinking of the Church.

Pius XII, To Italian Catholic Workers' Association, May 14, 1953

Certain Catholics, promoters of a new social order, are in error when they maintain that social reform must come first of all and that afterwards care will be taken of the religious and moral life of the individual and of society. The first cannot, in fact, be separated from the second, because this world cannot be disjoined from the other, nor can man, who is a living whole, be broken up into two parts.

John XXIII, Mater et Magistra

175. Scientific and technical progress, economic development and the betterment of living conditions, are certainly valuable elements in a civilization. But we must realize that they are essentially instrumental in character. They are not supreme values in themselves.

176. It pains Us, therefore, to observe the complete indifference to the true hierarchy of values shown by so many people in the economically developed countries. Spiritual values are ignored, forgotten or denied, while the progress of science, technology, and economics is pursued for its own sake, as though material well-being were the be-all and end-all of life. This attitude is contagious, especially when it infects the work that is being done for the less developed countries, which have often preserved in their ancient traditions an acute and vital awareness of the more important human values, on which the moral order rests.

177. To attempt to undermine this national integrity is clearly immoral. It must be respected and as far as possible clarified and developed, so that it may remain what it is: a foundation of true civilization.

210. The almost limitless horizons opened up by scientific research only go to confirm this truth. More and more men are beginning to realize that science has so far done little more than scratch the surface of nature and reality. There are vast hidden depths still to be explored and adequately explained. Such men are appalled when they consider how these gigantic forces for good can be turned by science into engines of destruction. They realize then the supreme importance of spiritual and moral values, if scientific and technical progress is to be used in the service of civilization, and not involve the whole human race in irremediable disaster.

211. Furthermore, the increasing sense of dissatisfaction with worldly goods which is making itself felt among citizens of the wealthier nations, is rapidly destroying the treasured illusion of an earthly paradise. Men, too, are becoming more and more conscious of their rights as human beings, rights which are universal and inviolable; and they are aspiring to more just and more human relations with their fellows. The effect of all this is to make the modern man more deeply aware of his own limitations, and to create in him a striving for spiritual values. All of this encourages Us in the hope that individuals and nations will one day learn to unite in a spirit of sincere understanding and profitable co-operation.

215. Let men make all the technical and economic progress they can, there will be no peace nor justice in the world until they return to a sense of their dignity as creatures and sons of God, who is the first and final cause of all created being. Separated from God a man is but a monster, in himself and toward others; for the right ordering of human society presupposes the right ordering of man's conscience with God, who is Himself the source of all justice, truth and love.

John XXIII, Pacem in Terris

151. In traditionally Christian states at the present time, civil institutions evince a high degree of scientific and technical progress and possess abundant machinery for the attainment of every kind of objective. And yet it

must be owned that these institutions are often but slightly affected by Christian motives and a Christian spirit.

152. One may well ask the reason for this, since the men who have largely contributed — and who are still contributing — to the creation of these institutions are men who are professed Christians, and who live their lives, at least in part, in accordance with the precepts of the gospels. In Our opinion the explanation lies in a certain cleavage between faith and practice. Their inner, spiritual unity must be restored, so that faith may be the light and love the motivating force of all their actions.

THE WORK OF THE CLERGY

Leo XIII, Letter to Italian Bishops, December 8, 1902

For this purpose We desire that the aspirants to the priesthood, while abstaining . . . from all participation in actual movements outside, should, toward the end of their seminary course, be duly instructed in the papal documents which have to do with the social question and Christian democracy. Later on, when advanced to the priesthood, let them employ themselves with the people who at every period have been the special object of the Church's most affectionate care. . . . To defend the principles of justice and Christian charity in which all the rights and duties of civil society find a fair and equitable balance, such in its outstanding characteristics is the grand duty and object of social activities.

Benedict XV, Letter to Bishop of Bergamo, March 11, 1920

Let no member of the clergy suppose that activity of this kind is something foreign to his priestly ministry because the field in which it is exercised is economic. *It is precisely in this field that the salvation of souls is imperiled. Therefore it is Our will that priests consider it as one of their duties to give as much of their life as possible to social science and social action*, by study, observation, and work, and to support in all ways those who, in this sphere, exercise a wholesome influence for the good of Catholics.*

Pius XI, Ad Catholici Sacerdotii

8. The priest contributes most effectively to the solution, or at least the mitigation, of social conflicts, since he preaches Christian brotherhood, declares to all their mutual obligations of justice and charity, brings peace to hearts embittered by moral and economic hardship, and alike to rich and poor points out the only true riches to which all men both can and should aspire.

---

* In this and the following sections of the quotations, many passages are italicized by the author. The purpose of this is to emphasize teachings which form the doctrinal basis of Catholic social action.

Pius XI, Quadragesimo Anno

27. Sacred ministers of the Church, thoroughly imbued with Leo's teaching, have, in fact, often proposed to the votes of the people's representatives the very social legislation that has been enacted in recent years and have resolutely demanded and promoted its enforcement.

142. A difficult task, certainly, is thus imposed on priests, and to meet it, all who are growing up as the hope of the Church, must be duly prepared by an intensive study of the social question. Especially is it necessary that those whom you intend to assign in particular to this work should demonstrate that they are men possessed of the keenest sense of justice, who will resist with truly manly courage the dishonest demands or the unjust acts of anyone, who will excel in the prudence and judgment which avoids every extreme, and, above all, who will be deeply permeated by the charity of Christ, which alone has the power to subdue firmly but gently the hearts and wills of men to the laws of justice and equity. Upon this road so often tried by happy experience, there is no reason why we should hesitate to go forward with all speed.

143. These Our Beloved Sons who are chosen for so great a work, We earnestly exhort in the Lord to give *themselves wholly to the training of the men committed to their care, and in the discharge of this eminently priestly and apostolic duty to make proper use of the resources of Christian education by teaching youth, forming Christian organizations, and founding study groups guided by principles in harmony with the Faith.*

Pius XI, On Atheistic Communism

61. To priests in a special way We recommend anew the oft-repeated counsel of Our Predecessor, Leo XIII, to go to the workingman. We make this advice Our own, and faithful to the teaching of Jesus Christ and His Church, We thus complete it: "Go to the workingman, especially where he is poor; and in general, go to the poor. . . ."

62. Indisputably much has been done in this direction, especially after the publication of the Encyclicals Rerum Novarum and Quadragesimo Anno. We are happy to voice Our paternal approval of the zealous pastoral activity manifested by so many bishops and priests who have with due prudence and caution been planning and applying new methods of apostolate more adapted to modern needs. But for the solution of our present problem all this effort is still inadequate. When our country is in danger, everything not strictly necessary, everything not bearing directly on the urgent matter of unified defense, takes second place. So we must act in today's crisis. Every other enterprise, however attractive and helpful, must yield before the vital need of protecting the very foundation of the Faith and of Christian civilization. Let our parish priests, therefore, while providing of course for the normal needs of the Faithful, dedicate the better part of their endeavors and their zeal to winning back the laboring masses to Christ and to His Church. Let them work to infuse the Christian spirit into quarters where it is least at home. The willing response of the masses, and results far exceeding their expectations, will not fail to reward them for their strenuous pioneer labor.

63. But the most efficacious means of apostolate among the poor and lowly is the priest's example, the practice of all those sacerdotal virtues which We have described in Our Encyclical *Ad Catholici Sacerdotii*. Especially needful, however, for the present situation is the shining example of a life which is humble, poor, and disinterested, in imitation of a divine Master who could say to the world with divine simplicity: "The foxes have holes and the birds of the air nests, but the Son of Man hath not where to lay His head." A priest who is really poor and disinterested in the Gospel sense may work among his flock marvels recalling a St. Vincent de Paul, a Curé of Ars, a Cottolengo, a Don Bosco, and so many others; while an avaricious and selfish priest, as We have noted in the above-mentioned Encyclical, even though he should not plunge with Judas to the abyss of treason, will never be more than empty "sounding brass" and useless "tinkling cymbal." Too often, indeed, he will be a hindrance rather than an instrument of grace in the midst of his people. *Furthermore, where a secular priest or religious is obliged by his office to administer temporal property, let him remember that he is not only to observe scrupulously all that charity and justice prescribe, but that he has a special obligation to conduct himself in very truth as a father of the poor.*

APOSTOLATE OF THE LAITY

St. Pius X, Il Fermo Proposito, June 11, 1905

Our Predecessor Leo XIII, of holy memory, fully perceived this, and pointed out, notably in the famous Encyclical *Rerum Novarum*, and in later documents, the object to which Catholic Action should be specially devoted, namely, the practical solution of the social question according to Christian principles.

Further, in order that Catholic Action may be effectual on all points, it is not enough that it be adapted to actual social needs only; it ought *also to be invigorated by all the practical methods furnished at the present day by progress in social and economic studies, by experience already* gained elsewhere, by the condition of civil society, and even by the public life of states. Otherwise there will be a risk of groping for a long time for new and hazardous things, while good and safe ones are ready to hand, and have been already well tried; or again, there will be the danger of proposing institutions and methods suitable, perhaps, in former times, but not understood by people of the present day; or finally, there will be the danger of stopping halfway by not using, in the measure in which they are granted, those rights of citizenship which modern constitutions offer to all, and therefore also to Catholics.

Pius XI, Quadragesimo Anno

141. For We are now confronted, as more than once before in the history of the Church, with a world that in large part has almost fallen back into paganism. That these whole classes of men may be brought back to Christ whom they have denied, we must recruit and train from among them, themselves, auxiliary soldiers of the Church who know them well and

their minds and wishes, and can reach their hearts with a tender brotherly love. The first and immediate apostles to the workers ought to be workers; the apostles to those who follow industry and trade ought to be from among them themselves.

142. *It is chiefly your duty, Venerable Brethren, and of your clergy, to search diligently for these lay apostles both of workers and of employers, to select them with prudence, and to train and instruct them properly.*

Pius XI, On Atheistic Communism

55. To give to this social activity a greater efficacy, it is necessary to promote a wider study of social problems in the light of the doctrine of the Church and under the aegis of her constituted authority. If the manner of acting of some Catholics in the social-economic field has left much to be desired, this has often come about because they have not known and pondered sufficiently the teachings of the Sovereign Pontiffs on these questions. *Therefore, it is of the utmost importance to foster in all classes of society an intensive program of social education adapted to the varying degrees of intellectual culture. . . . For there are some who, while exteriorly faithful to the practice of their religion, yet in the field of labor and industry, in the professions, trade, and business, permit a deplorable cleavage in their conscience, and live a life too little in conformity with the clear principles of justice and Christian charity. Such lives are a scandal to the weak, and to the malicious a pretext to discredit the Church.*

64. *Catholic Action is in effect a social apostolate also, inasmuch as its object is to spread the Kingdom of Jesus Christ not only among individuals, but also in families and in society. It must, therefore, make it a chief aim to train its members with*

special care and to prepare them to fight the battles of the Lord. This task of formation now more urgent and indispensable than ever, which must always precede direct action in the field, will assuredly be served by *study circles, conferences, lecture courses, and the various other activities undertaken with a view to making known the Christian solution of the social problem.*

66. In addition to this individual apostolate which, however useful and efficacious, often goes unheralded, *Catholic Action must organize propaganda, on a large scale, to disseminate knowledge of the fundamental principles on which, according to the pontifical documents, a Christian Social Order must build.*

68. We are thinking likewise of those associations of workmen, farmers, technicians, doctors, employers, students, and others of like character, groups of men and women who live in the same cultural atmosphere and share the same way of life. *Precisely these groups and organizations are destined to introduce into society that order which We have envisaged in our Encyclical Quadragesimo Anno, and thus to spread in the vast and various fields of culture and labor the recognition of the Kingdom of Christ.*

Pius XII, To World Union of Catholic Women's Organizations, September 29, 1957

Individual initiative has its place along with action that is organized

and applied through various associations. This initiative of the lay apostolate is perfectly justified even without a prior explicit "mission" from the hierarchy. The mother of a family who devotes herself to charitable

works, the one who shows courageous fidelity in guarding her dignity or the moral climate of her environment, all practice a real apostolate.

John XXIII, Mater et Magistra

182. It is a source of profound satisfaction to Us to see the prominent part which is being played by Catholic citizens of the less wealthy countries in the economic and social development of their own state.

183. Then, too, the Catholics of the wealthier states are doing all they can to increase the effectiveness of the social and economic work that is being done for the poorer nations. We would give Our special approval to the increasing assistance they are giving, in all sorts of ways, to African and Asian students scattered throughout the universities of Europe and America; and to the care that is being devoted to the training of those persons who are prepared to go to the less wealthy areas in order to engage in work of a technical and professional nature.

184. To these Our beloved sons in every land who, in promoting genuine progress and civilization, are a living proof of the Church's perennial vitality, We wish to extend Our kind and fatherly word of appreciation and encouragement.

222. *First, we must reaffirm most strongly that this Catholic social doctrine is an integral part of the Christian conception of life.*

223. It is therefore Our urgent desire that this doctrine be studied more and more. First of all it should be taught as part of the daily curriculum in Catholic schools of every kind, particularly seminaries, although We are not unaware that in some of these latter institutions this has been done for a long time now and in an outstanding way. We would also

like to see it added to the religious instruction programs of parishes and of associations of the lay apostolate. It must be spread by every modern means at our disposal: daily newspapers, periodicals, popular and scientific publications, radio and television.

224. Our beloved sons, the laity, can do much to help this diffusion of Catholic social doctrine by studying it themselves and putting it into practice, and by zealously striving to make others understand it.

225. They should be convinced that the best way of demonstrating the truth and efficacy of this teaching is to show that it can provide the solution to present-day difficulties. They will thus win those people who are opposed to it through ignorance of it. Who knows, but a ray of its light may one day enter their minds.

226. *It is not enough merely to formulate a social doctrine. It must be translated into reality. And this is particularly true of the Church's social doctrine, the light of which is Truth, Justice its objective, and Love its driving force.*

227. It is vitally important, therefore, that Our sons learn to understand this doctrine. They must be educated to it.

Theory and practice

228. No Christian education can be considered complete unless it covers every kind of obligation. It must therefore aim at implanting and fostering among the faithful an awareness of their duty to carry on their economic and social activities in a Christian manner.

229. The transition from theory to

practice is of its very nature difficult; and it is especially so when one tries to reduce to concrete terms a social doctrine such as that of the Church. There are several reasons why this is so; among them We can mention man's deep-rooted selfishness, the materialism in which modern society is steeped, and the difficulty of determining sometimes what precisely the demands of justice are in a given instance.

230. *Consequently, a purely theoretical instruction in man's social and economic obligations is inadequate. People must also be shown ways in which they can properly fulfill these obligations.*

231. In Our view, therefore, formal instruction, to be successful, must be supplemented by the students' active co-operation in their own training. They must gain an experimental knowledge of the subject, and that by their own positive action.

232. *It is practice which makes perfect, even in such matters as the right use of liberty. Thus one learns Christian behavior in social and economic matters by actual Christian action in those fields.*

233. The lay apostolate, therefore, has an important role to play in social education — especially those associations and organizations which have as their specific objective the christianization of contemporary society. The members of these associations, besides profiting personally from their own day-to-day experience in this field, can also help in the social education of the rising generation by giving it the benefit of the experience they have gained.

236. There are three stages which should normally be followed in the reduction of social principles into practice. First, one reviews the concrete situation; secondly, one forms a judgment on it in the light of these same principles; thirdly, one decides what in the circumstances can and should be done to implement these principles. These are the three stages that are usually expressed in the three terms: *look, judge, act.*

237. It is important for our young people to grasp this method and to practice it. Knowledge acquired in this way does not remain merely abstract, but is seen as something that must be translated into action.

238. Differences of opinion in the application of principles can sometimes arise even among sincere Catholics. When this happens, they should be careful not to lose their respect and esteem for each other. Instead, they should strive to find points of agreement for effective and suitable action, *and not wear themselves out in interminable arguments, and, under pretext of the better or the best, omit to do the good that is possible and therefore obligatory.*

The Christian in the world

254. We have only been able to touch lightly upon this matter, but Our sons, the laity especially, must not suppose that they would be acting prudently to lessen their personal Christian commitment in this passing world. On the contrary, We insist that they must intensify it and increase it continually.

255. In His solemn prayer for the Church's unity, Christ Our Lord did not ask His Father to remove His disciples from the world: "I pray not that thou shouldst take them out of the world, but that thou shouldst keep them from evil." *Let no man therefore imagine that a life of activity in the world is incompatible with spiritual perfection. The two can very well be harmonized. It is a gross error to suppose that a man cannot perfect himself except by putting aside all temporal activity, on the plea that such activity will inevitably lead*

him to compromise his personal dignity as a human being and as a Christian.

256. That a man should develop and perfect himself through his daily work — which in most cases is of a temporal character — is perfectly in keeping with the plan of divine Providence. *The Church today is faced with an immense task: to humanize and to Christianize this modern civilization of ours.* The continued development of this civilization, indeed its very survival, demand and insist that the Church do her part in the world. That is why, as We said before, she claims the co-operation of her laity. In conducting their human affairs to the best of their ability, they must recognize that they are doing a service to humanity, in intimate union with God through Christ, and to God's greater glory.

257. To search for spiritual perfection and eternal salvation in the conduct of human affairs and institutions is not to rob these of the power to achieve their immediate, specific ends, but to enhance this power.

Animated, too, by the charity of Christ, he finds it impossible not to love his fellow men. He makes his own their needs, their sufferings and their joys. There is a sureness of touch in all his activity in every field. It is energetic, generous, and considerate.

John XXIII, Pacem in Terris

147. And yet, if they are to imbue civilization with right ideals and Christian principles, it is not enough for Our sons to be illumined by the heavenly light of faith and to be fired with enthusiasm for a cause; they must involve themselves in the work of these institutions, and strive to influence them effectively from within.

148. But in a culture and civilization like our own, which is so remarkable for its scientific knowledge and its technical discoveries, clearly no one can insinuate himself into public life unless he be scientifically competent, technically capable, and skilled in the practice of his own profession.

150. If these policies are really to become operative, men must first of all take the utmost care to conduct their various temporal activities in accordance with the laws which govern each and every such activity, observing the principles which correspond to their respective natures. Secondly, men's actions must be made to conform with the precepts of the moral order. This means that their behavior must be such as to reflect their consciousness of exercising a personal right or performing a personal duty. Reason has a further demand to make. In obedience to the providential designs and commands of God respecting our salvation and not neglecting the dictates of conscience, men must conduct themselves in their temporal activity in such a way as to effect a thorough integration of the principal spiritual values with those of science, technology and the professions.

161. There are indeed some people who, in their generosity of spirit, burn with a desire to institute wholesale reforms whenever they come across situations which show scant regard for justice or are wholly out of keeping with its claims. They tackle the problem with such impetuosity that one would think they were embarking on some political revolution.

162. We would remind such people that it is the law of nature that all things must be of gradual growth. If there is to be any improvement in human institutions, the work must be done slowly and deliberately from

within. Pope Pius XII expressed it in these terms: "Salvation and justice consist not in the uprooting of an outdated system, but in a well designed policy of development. Hotheadedness was never constructive; it has always destroyed everything. It has inflamed passions, but never assuaged them. It sows no seeds but those of hatred and destruction. Far from bringing about the reconciliation of contending parties, it reduces men and political parties to the necessity of laboriously redoing the work of the past, building on the ruins that disharmony has left in its wake."

163. There is an immense task incumbent on all men of good will, namely, the task of restoring the relations of the human family in truth, in justice, in love, and in freedom: the relations between individual human beings; between citizens and their respective political communities; between political communities themselves; between individuals, families, intermediate associations, and political communities on the one hand, and the world community on the other. This is a most exalted task, for it is the task of bringing about true peace in the order established by God.

164. Admittedly, those who are endeavoring to restore the relations of social life according to the criteria mentioned above, are not many; to them We express Our paternal appreciation, and We earnestly invite them to persevere in their work with ever greater zeal. And We are comforted by the hope that their number will increase, especially among Christian believers. For it is an imperative of duty; it is a requirement of love. Every believer in this world of ours must be a spark of light, a center of love, a vivifying leaven amidst his fellow men: and he will be this all the more perfectly the more closely he lives in communion with God in the intimacy of his own soul.

Vatican Council II, On the Apostolate of the Laity

7. But lay people must take the renewal of the secular order as their own proper task. They must immerse themselves directly and decisively in it, guided by the light of the Gospel and the mind of the Church, and motivated by Christian love. They must work as citizens together with other citizens, each person with his own specific competence, and his own proper responsibility; and their goal must be to seek always and in all matters the justice of the kingdom of God. The secular order must be so renewed that, without violence to the integrity of its own laws, it is brought into harmony with the deepest principles of Christian living, and made to conform to the human needs of our varying localities, times, and peoples. Principal among the tasks of this apostolate is the social action of Christians, which this holy synod today desires to see extended to the whole range of temporal realities, and especially to the advancement of the intellectual order.

WORK WITH NON-CATHOLICS

Pius XI, On Atheistic Communism

72. But in this battle joined by the powers of darkness against the very idea of Divinity, *it is Our fond hope that, besides the host which glories*

in the name of Christ, all those —
and they comprise the overwhelming
majority of mankind — who still believe in God and pay Him homage
may take a decisive part.

Pius XII, To Sacred College of Cardinals, June 2, 1948

Only on the principles of Christianity and in accord with its spirit
can social reforms, called for impera-
tively by the necessities and aspirations of our times, be carried out.
They demand from some the spirit
of renunciation and sacrifice, from
others the sense of responsibility and
endurance, from everybody hard and
strenuous work.

Wherefore we turn to the Catholics of the whole world, exhorting
them not to be satisfied with good
intentions and fine projects, but to
proceed courageously to put them into
practice. *Neither should they hesitate
to join forces with those who, remaining outside their ranks, are nonetheless in agreement with the social
teaching of the Catholic Church and
are disposed to follow the road she
has marked out, which is not the
road of violent revolution but of experience that has stood the test, and
of energetic resolution.*

John XXIII, Mater et Magistra

239. In their economic and social
activities, Catholics often come into
contact with others who do not share
their view of life. In such circumstances, they must, of course, bear
themselves as Catholics and do nothing to compromise religion and morality. Yet at the same time they
should show themselves animated by
a spirit of understanding and un-
selfishness, ready to co-operate loyally
in achieving objects which are good
in themselves, or can be turned to
good. Needless to say, when the Hierarchy has made a decision on any
point Catholics are bound to obey
their directives. The Church has the
right and obligation not merely to
guard ethical and religious principles,
but also to declare its authoritative
judgment in the matter of putting
these principles into practice.

John XXIII, Pacem in Terris

157. The principles We have set
out in this document take their rise
from the very nature of things. They
derive, for the most part, from the
consideration of man's natural rights.
Thus the putting of these principles
into effect frequently involves extensive co-operation between Catholics
and those Christians who are separated from this Apostolic See. It even
involves the co-operation of Catholics
with men who may not be Christians
but who nevertheless are reasonable
men, and men of natural moral integrity. . . .

158. *It is always perfectly justifiable
to distinguish between error as such
and the person who falls into error —*
even in the case of men who err regarding the truth or are led astray as
a result of their inadequate knowledge, in matters either of religion or
of the highest ethical standards. A
man who has fallen into error does
not cease to be a man. He never for-
feits his personal dignity; and that is
something that must always be taken
into account. Besides, there exists in
man's very nature an undying capacity
to break through the barriers of error

and seek the road to truth. God, in His great providence, is ever present with His aid. Today, maybe, a man lacks faith and turns aside into error; tomorrow, perhaps, illumined by God's light, he may indeed embrace the truth.

Catholics who, in order to achieve some external good, collaborate with unbelievers or with those who through error lack the fullness of faith in Christ, may possibly provide the occasion or even the incentive for their conversion to the truth.

THIS concluding chapter is more than a summary of the chapters preceding. The purpose rather is to integrate Catholic social principles and Catholic social action. We seek to present our beliefs about the proper goals of society, and our views as to the proper steps to be taken toward these goals.

THE GOAL SOUGHT

Economic Society. In the most general terms, we seek an economic society which ministers to the needs of man. It should serve as the material basis for the protection of individual freedom and dignity, a sound family life, and properly organized civic society. Negatively, we should root out evils and abuses which threaten human values. Positively, we should strive for such economic balance that social institutions will of their own nature tend to promote the general welfare. These positive and negative aspects are rarely separated in practice, any more than moral reform is likely in the concrete to be distinct from institutional reform. We should remove evils by replacing them with healthy social institutions. We replace, not merely displace.

In a proper social order, the institutions of economic life should promote both the immediate interests of the affected parties and the common good of all. This means a society organized along lines of collaboration and co-operation, rather than conflict and strife. Against individualism, we bespeak the need for organization in labor, business, industry, finance, trades, professions, and farming. Well organized groups must, above all, seek the common interests of all concerned in the several occupations, subordinating such concerns, however, to the general welfare of the body public. In practice, this means labor-management co-operation in industry, organized action in business and the professions to place proper limits upon competition, and collaborative action by all economic groups to handle on the highest level common problems such as depressions and unemployment. In such a society, there will be a legitimate place for special-interest groups, such as labor unions or employer associations. But their activities will likewise be subject to the demands of the common good, and should be ultimately subordinate in importance to the common-interest groups.

As a foundation for a collaborative society, there should be diffusion of economic power. This is to be sought by three main methods: encouragement of widespread ownership of productive property; the development of a partnership atmosphere between labor and management; and the transference of many functions, now assumed by government as a result of default by private groups, into the hands of quasi-public common-interest groups in business, industry, finance, trade, the professions, and farming. Diffusion of power will check collectivist trends which threaten individual freedom. Collaborative action for the general welfare means exercise of social responsibility by free individuals and groups, thus avoiding the danger of individualism and selfish atomization of society. In this social order the first duty of government will be to promote the aims outlined above. Then the state, freed from complex problems of detailed regulation, will more efficiently perform those duties which belong to it alone, encouraging, directing, or restraining the actions of lesser groups in the interests of the community.

Through common action, the various economic groups will seek the most efficient use of natural resources and, as a result, a national standard of living adequate to meet human needs. Production will be organized in a rational fashion, so that labor productivity will be enhanced and workers can earn a family living wage. Sound methods of distribution and other devices should keep the level of production reasonably constant, with a long-range trend toward higher output, thus avoiding depressions and unemployment. Many men will then have the independence which comes with the ownership of productive wealth. Millions more, who are wage earners, will have security in employment and dignity in work. Such a well-organized society could gradually clear up social problems in regard to housing, medical care, unsuitable employment of women and children, and even the economic factors entering into racial and other forms of discrimination. With material needs thus taken care of, man would have the opportunity to devote more time to the cultural and spiritual side of his nature.

Means Used. The fundamental means for achieving this goal involve a combination of moral reform and institutional change. We use the phrase moral reform in the broader sense, including a replacement of secularism by the restoration of God to His proper place in society; by working against selfishness, greed, avarice, and unsound ambition for power, with the aim of making social justice and social charity dominant forces in economic life; and by using all the resources of the Church in raising man to God, so that thereby he may be truly human. But at the same time we seek to infuse the social virtues into the institutions of economic society, so that organized groups will collaborate for the common interests of their occupation and the general good of all. This means that men of good will should strive to influence their economic environment, even aspiring to positions of leadership, so that the truth of Christ will permeate these groups. "The kingdom of heaven is like unto a leaven."

In carrying out this program, the Church has a great duty of education and inspiration. In the first place, it must train and inspire its own sons to think clearly and soundly in social matters. More than this, they should be given the flaming zeal of apostles, so that they will influence others according to their stations in life. Nor should the Church overlook the opportunity of direct influence on those who do not accept its discipline. Men of good will are looking for the truth. They will not reject our message, if it is properly presented to them.

It may be necessary to distinguish between long-range and short-term objectives in working out a program of social reform. Once the desired goal is seen clearly, we must appraise the existing social order and evaluate it in terms of the ideal. Undoubtedly the result of such study will be mixed. Areas of injustice and selfish individualism will be found. Here stern measures must be taken to secure justice for workers, farmers, small businessmen, or others who are victims of economic aggression. In other regions we will find much good will and high aspiration. This must be encouraged, nurtured, guided, and integrated into a sound pattern of common welfare. Much of the economy will be found in an intermediate position — confused, uncertain, and groping. Here we can offer an outlook which some will eagerly accept and others will at least examine, sometimes skeptically, sometimes with a feeling of desperate hope. We will have enemies in our crusade. Some will be from the reactionary right, seeking to go back to nineteenth-century *laissez faire*. Others will be liberals or even radicals of the left, who seek a collectivist or at least an excessively centralized economy. Fortunately, the influence of extremists is usually slight, if only the great intermediate mass can be given a sense of unity and direction. The Church can meet this challenge, if we have the zeal and energy to put our own ideals into effect.

THE TASK OF THE CHURCH

Social Education Needs. The first task of the Church must include an intensified study of the social problem and the training of its members in sound Christian ideals in relation to economic life. In general, education must be the prelude to action. This does not of necessity involve chronological priority, in the sense that social action must remain dormant for twenty years until we have finished our task of education. There is such a thing as education through action. Again, we can use our present trained resources, while seeking a broader program of indoctrination. But, generally speaking, we will not have much influence until our own thinking is clarified, a large body of clergy trained in the social field, our laity in turn instructed in schools and through adult-education devices, and all groups inspired with the zeal to permeate social life with justice and charity.

We need more study in the social field. The goal should be a large corps of priests and laymen, trained to high scientific excellence in the fields of economics or sociology, and equally conversant with the social ethics of the Church. It would be tragic if the social encyclicals were misapplied through shoddy economic thinking. It would be equally calamitous, were our experts in social science to ignore the place of ethics and religion in setting goals and determining values in this field. There is need for further clarification in matters of social ethics. Obligations and objectives should be made as precise as possible in terms of modern conditions. But sound principles must be applied with exactitude and with full knowledge of the scientific and practical problems involved. We stultify ourselves if we give, as an application of Catholic social theory, a program based on unsound economic analysis. Nor is it a practical solution of this difficulty to say: Let the theologians and economists consult. Men trained exclusively in either discipline find it difficult to understand the problems of the other science. The only feasible approach is to have a sufficient number of men who are experts in both fields. Such men can write for theologians in their language and for economists or sociologists in terms which carry meaning and conviction.

The training of these experts should be primarily the duty of our colleges and universities and of the religious communities or other authorities who direct them. This is not an advocacy of inbreeding. On the contrary, it would be desirable that some priests get their Ph.D. in economics at a high-class secular university and then an S.T.D. at some Catholic university. But Catholic schools might well require for their degrees in the social sciences a knowledge of social ethics as well as technical competence in the specific discipline involved. The idea of theology courses for laymen, now happily taking root, might furnish an opportunity for our lay professors to acquire a high degree of competence in both fields. Our schools might subsidize such courses and consider this training in offering academic advancement in the social sciences. The Catholic Economic Association, the Catholic Theological Society, and the American Catholic Sociological Society could be important factors in stimulating these programs.

Training the Clergy. The next step, again logically rather than chronologically, is the training of the clergy. What is needed here, more than anything else, is to capture the sense of urgency contained in papal writings on the subject. It is difficult to reconcile the quotations given at the head of this chapter and elsewhere in this book with the uneven and haphazard courses offered in many seminaries. Too often the only training offered is in connection with the moral theology course in justice. The textbooks used are frequently antiquated in regard to social problems and, at times, the professors do not have the technical competence to supplement them. Regardless of this fact, it is doubtful that any incidental training in connection with the treatise on justice meets adequately the needs of the times and the commands of the popes.

For a priest to speak with even minimum assurance in this field, it would seem that at least four courses are necessary, dealing with economics, sociology, Catholic social principles, and Catholic social action. The first two could be offered in the philosophy section and the latter two given at the theology levels, with social action studied at the same time that pastoral theology is taken. Such a program would not interfere with adequate training in philosophy, dogmatic and moral theology, Sacred Scripture, canon law, and divine liturgy. Few seminaries confine their students only to these last-named courses. Most of them offer other subjects, suitable in another age, but less vital today than a careful training in social problems. Secondary studies of this nature might well yield place in these days to the social sciences. The need is equally great for religious as for diocesan priests. Even students for the foreign missions find that in most mission regions social problems are pressing concerns. If present professors are not trained to handle social subjects, there are abundant opportunities for summer courses in the field.

For the seminarian or priest who is somewhat diffident about his formal training, Pope John XXIII offers words of considerable encouragement. He puts great stress upon learning through experience to supplement formal training. Priests and laity alike can benefit from the Jocist approach of "look, judge, act." Thus knowledge does not remain abstract, but is seen as something that should be translated into action.

It is not usually difficult to establish contacts with social-action or racial-action organizations. Most of them are eager for new recruits. If a priest were to join the local branch of the National Association for the Advancement of Colored People or the National Urban League, he would soon find out a great deal about the actual problems of his area. He could also be active in a Catholic Interracial Council. Many cities have community associations concerned with such problems as slums, urban decay, poverty, and delinquency. Alert interest in such groups can be highly educational.

Approach to socioeconomic groups such as labor unions or employers' associations may be more difficult at first. But service clubs often offer good contacts with the business and professional community. Labor leaders may be invited to address parish groups or classes in the parochial high school. This can be the beginning of more extensive contacts and later of real influence.

Nor should a priest underestimate the social value of his more strictly religious functions. The liturgy, for example, should instill in the Christian people a sense of unity and community. Real worship in common can do much to lessen labor-management tensions or racial prejudices. Preaching can likewise be helpful. Without bringing controversial matters into the pulpit, a priest could concentrate on the topics contained in the excerpts at the head of this chapter. Emphasis on charity, justice, a spirit of poverty, penance, and special retreats for professional or worker groups can indeed be helpful in disposing Catholics toward the social apostolate.

Training the Laity. A trained clergy could give moral instructions to the laity in social matters. The task of social education of the laity must be carried out on many levels. In the first place, there should be a social emphasis in our schools. The task of preparing a curriculum for this purpose has been brilliantly achieved for elementary schools by the Commission on American Citizenship, at the Catholic University. The Commission is currently proceeding with the high school curriculum. Moreover, many of the more recent Catholic textbooks in social sciences and in religion bring the Church teaching on social questions to high school students. Indeed, the problem now is to train teachers to use the newer texts in an adequate manner. Social institutes for teachers as well as for the clergy are a pressing need.

On the other hand, our social program has been quite uneven in colleges, universities, and professional schools. Many Catholic colleges require all students to study ethics, but not all offer courses in social ethics and the papal encyclicals. The ideal would be a required course in Catholic social principles to be taken by all students in Catholic colleges. This should be supplemented in professional schools by a special course applying these principles to the needs of doctors, lawyers, businessmen, teachers, and even chemists and engineers. It often happens that engineers or similar technicians advance to managerial positions in industry. Accordingly, they should receive the same social training offered (if the ideal were realized) in schools of business and commerce. Quite apart from future business or professional opportunities, our Catholic college graduates normally attain to some position of leadership or civic responsibility. They need commensurate social training.

Once again, however, we cannot wait for a new generation to emerge from the schools. The social problem is with us today. Hence there is need for general and specialized adult social education. This involves use of all the media for adult education, such as lectures, forums, schools, discussion and study clubs, the radio, the press, sermons, and similar devices. Nearly all the techniques named have been mentioned explicitly in papal encyclicals in connection with the social training of the laity. Moreover, there is an important place for specialized forms of adult education. These would include labor schools and forums for employers. Likewise, farmers and all the various professions should be reached, preferably through Catholic organizations in each field. In this way, Catholic laymen would be trained and inspired to the work of the apostolate, so vitally needed if we are to permeate our society with justice and charity. This training could be given by parish priests, by diocesan social action groups, and by various specialized groups of Catholic action. Whether the work be done by older groups, such as the Confraternity of Christian Doctrine and various Catholic societies, or by newer groups such as the Young Christian Workers and similar Jocist-inspired movements or the Christopher movement, the important point is that it be done. Experience will determine which techniques insure the best results. In all likelihood, it will be found that any of several approaches may be equally successful. The main point is to keep the goal clear: the thorough training of the laity in the social teaching of the Church, so that they will be apostles in their respective fields of work.

As the work progresses, the need will be felt for various teaching aids, such as simple books, pamphlets, specialized studies, films, radio scripts, and the like. We have adequate resources in the way of trained personnel to meet these needs. Here the main problem will be one of co-ordination and direction of activity. This should be a challenge to national Catholic groups, such as learned societies in the social field and the various departments and affiliated organizations of the National Catholic Welfare Conference. These national groups could visualize needs and map out a suitable program. The execution of these writings and related projects could then be entrusted to teachers, specialists in religious orders, and lay experts in various walks of life. For current applications, Catholic periodicals and newspapers would be of service. Ultimately it would be desirable to set up a national research and information service, as has already been done in the social field by several Protestant groups. We would then be doing a full job of teaching and applying the social principles of the Church in the light of current problems.

Catholics should realize that social action can be sanctified and harmonized with a deeply spiritual life. Pope John XXIII insists that a life of activity in the world is compatible with spiritual perfection. Indeed, our task is "to humanize and Christianize this modern civilization of ours." Christians should serve their fellow man "in intimate union with God through Christ, and to God's greater glory."

The commitment urged by the Pope does not preclude the choice of some who seek lives of contemplation in the cloister. Their prayer and sacrifice, properly directed, can be truly apostolic. Indeed, there must be some element of the contemplative in every true apostle. This is the source of the charity of Christ that "makes it impossible not to love his fellow men. He makes his own their needs, their sufferings, and their joys. There is a sureness of touch in all his activity in every field. It is energetic, generous, and considerate." These remarks, certainly autobiographical, show how a saintly soul approaches social action.

With this type of approach, as the Pope remarks in *Pacem in Terris*, one does not lose control of one's emotions and become embittered by social injustice. There is not the temptation to use revolutionary means to achieve results. One realizes that in human institutions, "it is not possible to renovate for the better except by working from within them, gradually." Love gives us the insight to see good in everyone, so that we try to build on this good, and not destroy those who oppose us. Thus we face the immense task "of restoring the relations of the human family in truth, in justice, in love, and in freedom. . . . This is a most exalted task, for it is the task of bringing about true peace in the order established by God." This call to truly Christian social action is "an imperative of duty . . . a requirement of love." "Every believer in this world of ours must be a spark of light, a center of love, and vivifying leaven amidst his fellow men: and he will be all this the more perfectly the more closely he lives in communion with God in the intimacy of his own soul."

The above quotations are equally autobiographical and explain the extraordinary world influence of Pope John XXIII. He was active, but not an activist. He was close to God, but he looked out from the sanctuary and saw the needs of the entire world. He wrote from the heart when he penned these words, and reliable sources indicate that they went to the printer in his own handwriting. One does not comment upon such words of high inspiration; one reads, meditates, and prays that he may live up to the vocation they announce.

INFLUENCE ON AMERICAN ECONOMIC LIFE

Principles. Since Catholics are a minority in this country, the question might legitimately be asked: Could our social program affect American economic life? In reply to this query, there are solid reasons to feel that we may be influential. Some may be prejudiced against our ideas in view of their source, but those ideas, properly presented, should carry considerable appeal on the basis of intrinsic merit. Here is a middle ground between statism and individualism which should be acceptable to those who are groping for sound solutions. Moreover, Catholics are not seeking their own selfish interests in promoting these ideals. We would gain by their adoption only to the extent that we participate in the public economic good and share the common benefits accruing to everyone.

We approach social-action problems with a twofold sense of respect, as was indicated by Pope John XXIII. We must be loyal to the teachings of the Church and the directives of the hierarchy. At the same time we must show the utmost respect for the religious convictions of those who do not share our faith. Their belief may be incomplete and indeed may contain elements of error. Yet we hold that: "The person who errs is always and above all a human being, and he retains in every case his dignity as a human person; and he must always be regarded and treated in accordance with that lofty dignity."

We should not meet opposition from Jewish or Protestant religious groups, since we have often discussed social questions with such groups in a friendly and harmonious atmosphere. There will be, of course, objections to any Church organization's mingling in the economic field, but this type of prejudice is now lessening among businessmen. Many are more receptive than formerly to the notion that religion can offer a positive contribution to the world of affairs. Accordingly, there is no inherent reason why the Catholic social program would not be of service to the general American public. Our task is to present our views in the proper language and with arguments designed to convince those not of our faith. We ask them to accept our principles, not because they are Catholic, but because they are true.

Given the ecumenical climate of our day, there is a wide range of social-action programs that can be carried out, at least in part, on an interreligious plane. This is already being done in regard to racial justice. It should be fairly easy for religious groups to work together on such matters as poverty, peace, urban problems, delinquency, and public morality. Wherever there is widespread agreement on the basic moral principles underlying social problems, and wherever a community approach to these problems is likely to be most effective, we can assume that interreligious action will be fruitful.

In the action field, Catholic lay apostles and priests engaged in social action will be working side by side with businessmen, industrialists, workers, professional men, and farmers — all men of varying principles and religious convictions. Our task will be to use the diverse techniques of influence and persuasion, adapted to concrete situations, to bring about a more social attitude in particular environments. In doing this, it is necessary to have both a clear view of long-range aims and sound ideas as to immediate objectives. The latter will normally be controlled by the former. Short-range programs should lead to the ultimate goal, although at times the course may be indirect and devious. Thus, justice may call for social legislation as the means for meeting a particular problem, although in the long run we may aim to decentralize economic authority and remove many regulatory burdens from government. Prudence and good sense will dictate the answers in this field.

Concrete Steps. For the Catholic desirous of improving the social climate of farming, business, labor, the local community, the state, and the nation, the proper approach is to learn, join, and act. We can learn by reading, by listening, and by observing. Alert Catholic societies can bring in speakers to tell them of community, state, or national problems. A Negro leader can talk about the problems of racial discrimination. Perhaps a rural pastor can be the voice of the migrant workers. Social workers can speak with authority on the cruelty of slum living. We can often find out more about these problems by reading. And we can seek to observe them first-hand.

If we are to master the trend toward socialization, as Pope John asked, we cannot remain mere observers. We must join action organizations, or found them if necessary. We should be active in the union or professional organization connected with our work. Some of us should be in politics or in civic associations. Groups such as the National Urban League or the National Association for the Advancement of Colored People need alert and dedicated members. There are Catholic interracial councils and diocesan units for the alleviation of poverty.

Involvement is the need of our time and selfish isolation is the cardinal sin of our day. Workers in the Peace Corps, PAVLA, and Vista are the apostles of the modern world, sensitive to man's needs and to the corporal works of mercy. While fearful and narrow souls drift into hate groups or confine their concern to denunciation of the world's evils ("prophets of doom," in the words of Pope John XXIII), the true Christian seeks to be positive and active. He wants to heal, not to destroy. Confronted with evils, he looks for causes and solutions, and not merely occasions to criticize. If he is blocked in some avenue of reform, he explores others. He expects failures and still keeps trying. In the words of Vatican Council II (Constitution on the Church, No. 36):

The faithful, therefore, must recognize the inner nature of all creation, its value and its intended role in giving praise to God; they must help each other to greater holiness of life, even by means of temporal activities. In this way the world may be permeated by the spirit of Christ and may more effectively achieve its purpose in justice, charity, and peace. The laity have the principal role in the overall fulfillment of this duty. Through their competence in secular subjects and through their activity, which has been elevated from within by Christ's grace, they should work diligently so that created goods may be perfected by human labor, technical skill and civilization for the benefit of all men, in accordance with the will of the Creator and the light of His Word; so that they may be distributed more suitably among men and in their own way lead to universal progress in human and Christian liberty. Thus Christ, through the members of the Church, will illuminate human society more and more with his saving light.

*   *   *

By reason of the salvation-economy itself, the faithful should learn to distinguish carefully between rights and duties that rest upon them as members of the Church and those that they possess as members of human society. They must take pains to reconcile the two harmoniously, remembering that they ought to be guided by a Christian conscience in every temporal affair; for there is no human activity, even in temporal matters, which can be withdrawn from God's control.

Two Johns in our day might serve as models and inspiration for those who try to apply the social teaching of the Church and to Christianize this modern world. There was Pope John XXIII who in five short years began a transformation of the entire religious world. Pope John saw the good in every person. His very optimism served to bring about the better qualities in all who observed him. His greatness was not that of a theologian or administrator; it was greatness of soul.

Then there was Father John LaFarge, S.J., whose "manner was ordinary." He too was simple, optimistic, positive. His chosen fields of social action were the two most neglected in his day: race relations and peace. He was admired, yet too seldom imitated. Yet the foundations he laid were to prove invaluable when finally the bulk of the American Catholic world caught up with this mild but determined pioneer.

Of Our Lord it was said that "he went about doing good." This is the primary requisite for social action: the will to do good. Add to this information, consultation, organization, and action, and the work of Christianizing the world has another apostle. In the words of Pope John, our mission is to do the good that is possible and therefore obligatory.

READINGS*

J. Y. Calvez, Social Thought of John XXIII, Chap. 7.
J. F. Cronin, Christianity and Social Progress, Chaps. 24–29, 31.
J. Messner, Social Ethics (rev. ed.), pp. 364–378.
O. von Nell-Breuning, Christian Social Reorganization, Chap. 18.
P. Riga, Peace on Earth, Part V.
J. A. Ryan, Social Doctrine in Action.

---

* For further readings, consult List No. 14 in the Appendix.

Appendix

ANNOTATED READING LISTS

IN GENERAL, these reading lists aim to facilitate further study of the problems considered in the text. So far as possible, the sequence of treatment is the same as the chapter order in the book. Occasionally, as in List No. 3, a compilation will cover several chapters of the text. Most lists have subheadings, with authors usually presented in alphabetical order.

In compiling this bibliography, preference is given to more recent books. This means that factual material is more likely to be current and that there is less danger of finding that a book is out of print. Some books no longer in print are cited because of unique features, but the fact that the publisher's supply is exhausted is noted in the comment. Those with access to a good library can consult this type of publication. Students doing dissertation work are advised to check the lists in the 1959 edition also, since space limitations precluded the retaining of a large number of works available only in libraries.

So far as possible, each list contains a selection of worthwhile studies on the topic in question. The citation of any given book is not of necessity an endorsement of the views presented. Nor need the absence of a title have any significance. The author, confronted with the pressures of administrative duties, may well have overlooked some items of value.

A few select periodicals are given at the end of List No. 1. They can be helpful in supplementing and updating the compilations given here.

List No. 1. THE SOCIAL QUESTION

This list primarily covers material treated in Chapter I, with some general source material included at the end.

Social Problems: Historical Background

Cochran, T. C., *The American Business System: Historical Perspective, 1900–1955* (Cambridge: Harvard University Press, 1958). A well-written history of modern industrial America.

Fanfani, A., *Catholicism, Protestantism, and Capitalism* (New York: Sheed and Ward, 1955). Traces individualist spirit to the eleventh century and shows how it led to rise of modern capitalism.

Pirenne, H., *Economic and Social History of Medieval Europe* (New York: Harcourt, 1956). Balanced in treatment. Generally favorable picture of medieval society.

Tawney, R. H., *Religion and the Rise of Capitalism* (New York: Harcourt, 1926). Brilliant in style and incisive in thought. Studies breakdown of medieval ethical controls and the rise of individualism. Available in Mentor paperback.

The Social Problem in the United States

Allen, F. L., *Lords of Creation* (New York: Harper, 1935). Interesting study of business mispractice during the years of 1901–1935. Out of print.

——— *The Big Change* (New York: Harper, 1952). A survey of the radical transformation of American economic society since the time of the New Deal.

Goldman, E. F., *Rendezvous with Destiny: A History of Modern American Reform* (New York: Knopf, 1956). History of social reform in the United States, with analyses of the various "liberal" camps.

Josephson, M., *The Robber Barons* (New York: Harcourt, 1934). Studies the great American capitalists during the period of 1861–1901. An exposé of various evils which characterized this period.

Myers, G., *History of the Great American Fortunes* (New York: Modern Library, 1936). A reprint of a classic depiction of the greed and corruption attendant upon the rise of industrialism in the United States.

Schlesinger, A. M., *The Age of Roosevelt* (New York: Houghton Mifflin, 1958). Account of the background crisis that led to President Roosevelt and the New Deal.

Steffens, Lincoln, *The Autobiography of Lincoln Steffens* (New York: Harcourt, 1931). The period from Cleveland to Wilson, seen through the eyes of an acute reporter.

Current Social Issues

Burnham, J., *The Managerial Revolution* (Bloomington, Ind.: Indiana Univ. Press, 1960). Upholds the thesis that business and government administrators are main centers of power today, displacing stockholders, labor and voters.

Carskadon, T. R., and Soule, G., *U. S. A. in New Dimensions: The Measure and Promise of America's Resources* (New York: Macmillan, 1957). Digest of the Dewhurst study on the growth prospects of the American economy.

Clark, J. M., *Economic Institutions and Human Welfare* (New York: Knopf, 1957). In the fight for the allegiance of the uncommitted peoples of the world, we must introduce moral considerations rather than undiluted self-interest in governing our economic activities. Professor Clark's views seem to be harmonious with Catholic social teaching, although he does not always think through his ethical positions.

Dewhurst, J. F., *America's Needs and Resources: a New Survey* (New York: Twentieth Century Fund, 1955). A major study of the possibilities for raising our standards through full use of resources.

Drucker, P. F., *The New Society: The Anatomy of Industrial Order* (New

York: Harper, 1950). Advocates a collaborative industrial society based on recognition of workers' dignity. Similar to the teaching of the popes on vocational order.

Galbraith, J. K., *The Affluent Society* (Boston: Houghton Mifflin, 1958). A sharp challenge to the thesis that indefinite growth in wealth is an unmixed blessing. We need a new look at the real goals of our society. Much of this book reads like passages from Pope Pius XII.

Kirk, R., *A Program for Conservatives* (Chicago: Regnery, 1954). True conservatism should be based on spiritual values, with great respect for human rights and liberties. Centralized power may endanger these liberties.

——— *The Intelligent Woman's Guide to Conservatism* (New York: Devin-Adair, 1957). True conservatism, as distinguished from reaction, appealingly presented by one of its best apologists.

Lerner, M., *America as a Civilization* (New York: Simon & Schuster, 1958). Massive study of American culture, with a number of chapters devoted to economic and social problems.

Myrdal, G., *Challenge to Affluence* (New York: Random House, 1963). America's most noted "visiting scholar" calls upon us to use our resources to abolish poverty and want and to reach our full economic potential.

Packard, V., *The Status Seekers* (New York: McKay, 1959). Satire directed against Americans who glory in a classless society yet constantly seek status.

——— *The Waste Makers* (New York: McKay, 1960). Planned obsolescence is considered an essential feature of our economy as we try to keep our factories busy.

——— *The Pyramid Climbers* (New York: McGraw-Hill, 1962). Tensions and pressures toward conformity in our corporations.

Pieper, J., *Leisure: The Basis of Culture* (New York: Pantheon Books, 1952). Proper use of leisure can save man from being fettered to his work.

Polanyi, K., *The Great Transformation* (Boston: Beacon Press, 1957). An evaluation of modern capitalism in terms of its effect on human welfare. Extensive bibliographical note.

Riesman, D., *The Lonely Crowd* (New Haven: Yale, 1950). We have become a crowd rather than a society because we lack the stabilizing force of either tradition or deep inner convictions.

——— *Faces in the Crowd* (New Haven: Yale, 1952). Series of interviews aimed to determine influence of our political structure upon the average individual.

——— *Individualism Reconsidered* (Glencoe, Ill.: Free Press, 1954). Illuminating insights into the institutions and ideas of the American people, and the reasons why we so often flounder without any strong sense of direction.

Roepke, W., *Civitas Humana* (London: William Hodge, 1948). This book criticizes collectivism and extreme individualism, proposing instead a humanism based on proper ownership and use of property. Critics differ on "Catholic" nature of this work.

Rossiter, C., *Conservatism in America* (New York: Knopf, 1962). A plea for enlightened conservatism, combining the spiritual values of older traditions with liberal views on social reform.

Schumpeter, J. A., *Capitalism, Socialism, and Democracy* (New York: Harper, 1950). The author is pessimistic as to the possibility of capitalist survival.

Discusses various forms of socialism which may succeed present-day capitalism.

Whyte, W. H., Jr., *The Organization Man* (New York: Simon and Schuster, 1956). Conformity and consistency are the main values in our society, with discussion and group action the way to get things done. An angry protest against the stifling of individuality and initiative.

Church Reaction to the Social Problem

Broderick, F. L., *Right Reverend New Dealer: John A. Ryan* (New York: Macmillan, 1963). A sensitive biography of America's leading Catholic social thinker and reformer.

Carlyle, R. W. and A. J., *A History of Medieval Political Theory in the West* (New York: Barnes & Noble, 1903–1936). Two non-Catholic authors devote six volumes to a documented study of medieval institutions.

Fogarty, M. P., *Christian Democracy in Western Europe* (Notre Dame, Ind.: University of Notre Dame Press, 1957). The origins and development of a movement that has contributed so much to the stability of Europe after World War II.

Hales, E. E., *The Catholic Church in the Modern World: A Survey From the French Revolution to the Present* (New York: Doubleday, 1958). Background material on Church's reaction to modern problems, with emphasis upon the political.

Moody, J. N., ed., *Church and Society; Catholic Social and Political Thought and Movements, 1789–1950* (New York: Arts, Inc., 1953). A monumental study of the evolution of Catholic social and political thought in various countries. Treatment is divided according to country and region. No previous book in English has the scope and depth of this study.

Moon, P. T., *The Labor Problem and the Social Catholic Movement in France* (New York: Macmillan, 1926). Well-documented study of French social Catholicism, with reference to related movements elsewhere. Out of print.

O'Brien, G. A., *Essay on Mediaeval Economic Teaching* (New York: Longmans, 1920). The social ethics of great medieval theologians, applied to economic problems. Valuable, but out of print.

Troeltsch, E., *The Social Teaching of the Christian Churches* (New York: Macmillan, 1949). A monumental two-volume study covering the period from the Gospels to the nineteenth century.

Weber, M., *The Protestant Ethic and the Spirit of Capitalism* (New York: Scribner's, 1948). Holds that ethical teachings of Protestantism contributed to the rise of modern capitalism.

Social Ethics From Non-Catholic Sources

Boulding, K. E., *Principles of Economic Policy* (Englewood Cliffs, N. J.: Prentice-Hall, 1958). Economic policy involves moral and political as well as economic considerations. Seeks means to assure progress, stability, justice, and freedom.

Duff, E., S.J., *The Social Thought of the World Council of Churches* (New York: Association Press, 1956). Penetrating and sympathetic study by a Catholic priest of the development of social principles in various meetings of the World Council and its subordinate organs.

Munby, D. L., *Christianity and Economic Problems* (New York: St. Martin's

Press, 1958). An Anglican Scottish layman shows considerable skill in relating his religious principles to major economic problems.

National Council of Churches of Christ, series on "Ethics and Economics of Society." This series comprises ten volumes, issued from 1953 to 1958, dealing with various phases of American economic life, as seen from a religious aspect. More detailed information available from the National Council or from Harper & Brothers.

Vorspan, A., and Lipman, E. J., *Justice and Judaism* (New York: Union of American Hebrew Congregations, 1959). The authors cover a wide range of social problems, with special emphasis upon civil liberties.

Economic Source Material

Colm, G., and Geiger, T., *The Economy of the American People* (Washington: National Planning Association, 1958). A nontechnical and inexpensive study of the working of our economic system.

The Economic Report to the President (Washington: Government Printing Office, annually). These reports contain, in addition to the analyses of the Council of Economic Advisers, selected statistics on national production and income. Statistics kept current by monthly publication, *Economic Indicators*.

Harriss, C. L., *The American Economy* (Homewood, Ill.: Irwin, 1962). Economic principles and a description of the American economy, in a well-written textbook.

Samuelson, P. A., *Economics, An Introductory Analysis* (New York: McGraw-Hill, 1961). A readable text with full emphasis upon modern theories.

Shackle, G. L., *Economics for Pleasure* (New York: Cambridge University Press, 1959). Economics in simple English for those who do not relish charts and graphs.

Statistical Abstract of the United States (Washington: Government Printing Office, annually). Basic compilation of government statistics.

In addition to the books and periodicals listed above, *America, Commonweal, Ave Maria,* and *Sign* often have worthwhile material. General publications of value include *U. S. News and World Report, Business Week, Fortune, Annals of the American Academy of Political and Social Science,* and the *Industrial and Labor Relations Review. The Pope Speaks* is unique as a source of papal documents, although *The Catholic Mind* carries some addresses, in addition to other useful articles.

List No. 2.   THE CHURCH AND THE SOCIAL PROBLEM

This list consists of primary source material on Catholic Social Teaching.

Papal Social Teaching

Chinigo, M., *The Pope Speaks: the Teachings of Pope Pius XII* (New York: Pantheon, 1957). This compilation of the selected excerpts from the writings of Pope Pius XII is arranged in topical order. There is a good table of contents, but the index is only fair. Out of print.

Discorsi e Radiomessagi di sua Santità Pio XII (Rome: Tipographia Poliglotta Vaticana, 1939–1959). The best single source for the complete utterances of

Pope Pius XII. All documents are given in the language of the authentic original document.

Haigerty, L. J., *Pius XII and Technology* (Milwaukee: Bruce, 1962). Compilation of addresses of Pope Pius XII on problems arising from technology.

Harte, T. J., *Papal Social Principles* (Gloucester, Mass.: Peter Smith, 1960). Summary of major papal social pronouncements of the past seventy-five years.

Husslein, J., S.J., ed., *Social Wellsprings* (Milwaukee: Bruce, 1940–1942). These two volumes contain the main social encyclicals of Popes Leo XIII and Pius XI. Paragraph numbering differs from that used in many N.C.W.C. and Paulist Press pamphlet editions of the same encyclicals. Out of print.

Koenig, H. C., ed., *Principles for Peace* (Milwaukee: Bruce, 1943). Selections from papal documents dealing with peace, arranged chronologically from 1878 to 1942. Excerpts are generous and include many documents dealing with socioeconomic problems. Out of print. See H. Flannery, *Patterns for Peace,* in List No. 11.

Pollock, R. C., ed., *The Mind of Pius XII* (New York: Crown, 1955). Topically arranged excerpts from the writings of Pope Pius XII. Good selections, but sources are difficult to trace because of the method of editing. Out of print.

Powers, F. J., ed., *Papal Pronouncements on the Political Order* (Westminster, Md.: Newman, 1952). A well-organized collection of crucial passages from papal documents from Leo XIII to Pius XII, covering the nature and purpose of the state, relations of Church and state, liberty and law, war and peace. Out of print.

Werth, A., and Mihanovich, C., *Papal Pronouncements on Marriage and the Family from Leo XIII to Pius XII (1878–1954)* (Milwaukee: Bruce, 1955). This compilation gives valuable excerpts from papal writings on the important topic of marriage and the family. Useful for students seeking accurate information without the necessity of lengthy study of original papal sources. Out of print.

Wills, G., *Politics and Catholic Freedom* (Chicago: Regnery, 1964). A well-written and balanced study of the teaching authority involved in papal encyclicals, unfortunately flawed by intrusion of polemics.

List No. 3.   SOCIAL ETHICS

Included here are commentaries on Catholic social principles and books dealing with social ethics and special problems in this area. Pertinent to Chapters III, IV, and VII.

General Works

Calvez, J. Y., *Social Thought of John XXIII* (Chicago: Regnery, 1964). Supplements the following study, although the title is somewhat misleading. Only *Mater et Magistra,* of Pope John's writings, is studied in this text.

Calvez, J. Y., and Perrin, J., *The Church and Social Justice* (Chicago: Regnery, 1961). Scholarly and sophisticated study of papal social teaching, especially useful for historical background of major pronouncements.

Clune, G., *Christian Social Reorganization* (Dublin: Browne & Nolan, 1940). A careful study of Christian social ethics as applied to economic and political life. While written for Irish readers, it has a much broader field of usefulness. Out of print.

Cronin, J. F., *Christianity and Social Progress* (Baltimore: Helicon, 1965). This popularly written commentary on *Mater et Magistra* is adapted from a series that ran in *Our Sunday Visitor*. About one third of the treatment is completely rewritten.

Cronin, J. F., and Flannery, H. W., *The Church and the Workingman* (New York: Hawthorn, 1965). Father Cronin presents Catholic social teaching on labor problems and Mr. Flannery gives the reaction of Catholics to the industrial revolution in major nations of the world. A *Twentieth Century Encyclopedia of Catholicism* study.

Dempsey, B. W., *The Functional Economy* (Englewood Cliffs, N. J.: Prentice-Hall, 1958). An advanced and highly useful study of social order in the light of the American economy. The author has exceptional insight into both the social teaching of the Church and the workings of economic life.

Dirksen, C. R., *Catholic Social Principles* (St. Louis: Herder, 1961). Simple explanation of social philosophy.

Ford, J. C., S.J., and Kelly, G., S.J., *Contemporary Moral Theology* (Westminster, Md.: Newman, 1958). Essays on current problems in moral theology. Chapters 1–3 of Volume I deal with problems of social economics.

Garrett, T. M., *Ethics in Business* (New York: Sheed and Ward, 1963). Moral principles relevant to the businessman in determining company policy.

Guery, E., *The Social Doctrine of the Catholic Church* (New York: Alba House, 1961). The Archbishop of Cambrai outlines basic elements of Catholic social teaching.

Huber, R. M., O.F.M., ed., *Our Bishops Speak* (Milwaukee: Bruce, 1952). Pastorals, statements, and occasional messages of the national hierarchy of the United States, 1919–1951. Out of print.

International Union of Social Studies, *A Code of Social Principles* (Oxford, England: Catholic Social Guild, 1952). Latest edition of the well-known Malines Code, quoted freely in these pages.

Leclerq, J., *Christianity and Money* (New York: Hawthorn, 1959). Gospel attitudes toward wealth applied to modern conditions.

Lubac, H., ed., *Catholicism* (New York: Sheed, 1958). Dogmatic basis for social Catholicism. Profound doctrinal study of the solidarity of the Church.

Masse, B. J., *Justice for All* (Milwaukee: Bruce, 1964). Popularly written presentation of the Church's social teaching by a well-known associate editor of *America*.

Messner, J., *Social Ethics* (St. Louis: Herder, 1965). A learned study of social ethics with emphasis on political and economic problems. More profound than most English studies on the subject. Revised edition.

Moody, J. N., and Lawler, J. G., eds., *The Challenge of Mater et Magistra* (New York: Herder and Herder, 1963). Contains several good essays and also some that are thin and superficial. Worth using selectively.

Mulcahy, R. E., *Readings in Economics* (Westminster, Md.: Newman, 1959). Father Mulcahy has compiled a set of readings which reflect, or are compatible with, the social teachings of the Church. Stresses Scholastic economic doctrine and the vocational order.

Nell-Breuning, O., *Reorganization of Social Economy* (Milwaukee: Bruce, 1936). A careful commentary on the general principles of *Quadragesimo Anno*. The translator, Rev. Bernard Dempsey, S.J., has given an English bibliography. Out of print.

Riga, P., *Peace on Earth* (New York: Herder and Herder, 1964). Brief but useful commentary on *Pacem in Terris.*

Sheed, F. J., *Society and Sanity* (New York: Sheed and Ward, 1953). Principles of human behavior in terms of the individual, the family, and the state. Reverence and respect for man's dignity are leading ideas in this book.

Welty, E., *Handbook of Christian Social Ethics* (New York: Herder and Herder, 1960 ff.). Social principles explained in catechism-type treatment, with ample citations from encyclicals and other authoritative sources.

Special Problems

Drummond, W. F., S.J., *Social Justice* (Milwaukee: Bruce, 1955). An effort to expand the concept of social justice as distinct from legal justice. Emphasis upon proper use of material goods. Out of print.

Ferree, W., *The Act of Social Justice* (Dayton, Ohio: Marianist Publications, 1951). An excellent doctoral study on the nature of social justice.

Gearty, P. W., *The Economic Thought of Monsignor John A. Ryan* (Washington: Catholic University Press, 1953). Msgr. Ryan, a pioneer in American Catholic social thought, holds eclectic economic views considered most suitable for implementing ethical ideals.

Johnston, H., *Business Ethics* (New York: Pitman, 1961). Quite valuable for its insight into current social problems and their ethical implications. Case histories are stimulating.

Mihanovich, C. S., and Schuyler, J. B., S.J., *Current Social Problems* (Milwaukee: Bruce, 1956). Economic and social problems, carefully selected, factually treated, and clearly analyzed.

Rommen, H. A., *The Natural Law* (St. Louis: Herder, 1947). The history of natural-law ethics.

Ryan, J. A., *A Living Wage; Distributive Justice; A Better Economic Order;* and *Social Doctrine in Action.* Principal works of Monsignor Ryan. All out of print.

List No. 4.   INDIVIDUALISM, CAPITALISM, SOCIALISM, AND STATISM

A selected list of materials pertinent to Chapter V.

Individualism

Auerbach, M. M., *The Conservative Illusion* (New York: Columbia University Press, 1959). Sharp attack on various types of conservatism in present-day America.

Chamberlin, W. H., *The Evolution of a Conservative* (Chicago: Regnery, 1959). Thoughtful defense of moderate conservatism.

Cheit, E. F., ed., *The Business Establishment* (New York: Wiley, 1964). Distinguished American and European scholars debate social responsibility of business in very realistic terms.

Hayek, F. A., *The Constitution of Liberty* (Chicago: University of Chicago Press, 1960). A careful argument for political individualism based on the theory that social controls ultimately destroy freedom.

Meyer, F. S., ed., *What Is Conservatism* (New York: Holt, Rinehart, and Winston, 1964). Twelve leading conservative thinkers explain and defend their positions.

Roepke, W., *A Humane Economy* (Chicago: Regnery, 1960). Strong advocacy of complete freedom for the economy, with an absolute minimum of social controls.

Sennholz, M., *On Freedom and Free Enterprise* (Princeton, N. J.: Van Nostrand, 1956). The extreme right, economic liberalism as condemned by the popes, presented in a collection of essays.

Von Mises, L., *Human Action* (New Haven: Yale, 1962). A plea for a free economy in contrast to a controlled system.

Capitalism

Chamberlain, J., *The Roots of Capitalism* (New York: Van Nostrand, 1959). Lively and solid defense of the American variety of capitalism.

Kelso, L. O. and Adler, M. J., *The Capitalist Manifesto* (New York: Random House, 1958). Striking defense of capitalism, with emphasis upon wide distribution of wealth. Somewhat impractical in suggesting means toward this end.

Miller, R. W., *Can Capitalism Compete?* (New York: Ronald Press, 1959). An explanation of American capitalism directed particularly to foreign readers who misunderstand its social spirit.

Salvadori, M., *The Economics of Freedom: American Capitalism Today* (Garden City, N. Y.: Doubleday, 1959). Persuasive advocacy of our economic system as dynamic and creative.

Schonfield, A., *Modern Capitalism* (New York: Oxford, 1965). This study ranges over the entire industrialized world and shows how modern states control the economic system.

Wallich, H. C., *The Cost of Freedom: A New Look at Capitalism* (New York: Harper, 1960). While freedom under capitalism may lead to loss of efficiency, it more than compensates for this in terms of enduring satisfaction produced.

Socialism

Eastman, M., *Reflections on the Failure of Socialism* (New York: Devin-Adair, 1955). An account of how a leading American socialist gave up Marxism and embraced a conservative point of view.

Egbert, D. D., and Persons, S., eds.; Bassett, T. D. S., bibliographer, *Socialism and American Life* (Princeton, N. J.: Princeton University Press, 1952). An encyclopedia of American socialism, with various competent authors, plus a volume of bibliographical study of the movement.

Thomas, N., *Socialism Re-examined* (New York: Norton, 1963). Our leading socialist re-examines theory and the state of the Socialist Party here.

Statism

Florence, P. S., *Industry and the State* (New York: Hillary House, 1957). British experience of state controls, showing dangers of government interference in areas best left to private initiative.

Friedrich, C. J., and Brzezinski, Z. K., *Totalitarian Dictatorship and Autocracy* (New York: Praeger, 1957). Penetrating study of dictatorship based primarily upon communist techniques.

Metz, H. W., and Thomson, C. A. H., *Authoritarianism and the Individual* (Washington: Brookings Institution, 1950). The impact of authority upon the freedom of the individual is studied, with special reference to historical background as well as modern statism.

List No. 5.   COMMUNISM

Reading list for Chapter VI.

General Works

Almond, G., et al., *The Appeals of Communism* (Princeton, N. J.: Princeton University Press, 1954). Sociological study of 221 former communists from four countries. Suggests emotional problems as important factors in adherence to this movement.

Chambre, H., *Christianity and Communism* (New York: Hawthorn, 1960). Valuable Catholic statement from a leading French author.

Cronin, J. F., *Communism: Threat to Freedom* (New York: Paulist Press, 1962). Popularly written booklet on domestic and world communism.

Daniels, R. V., *The Nature of Communism* (New York: Random House, 1962). One of the best one-volume studies of communist theory and practice.

Djilas, M., *Anatomy of a Moral* (New York: Praeger, 1959). Criticism of totalitarianism based on inside knowledge.

———— *The New Class* (New York: Praeger, 1957). Masterful dissection of communism, showing that its failures are inherent in the system.

Ferkiss, V., *Communism Today: Belief and Practice* (New York: Paulist Press, 1962). Well-written and balanced study of every aspect of communism.

Hoover, J. E., *A Study of Communism* (New York: Holt, Rinehart, and Winston, 1962). Communist theory and practice studied on a world scale, with sound recommendations for American policy.

Hunt, R. N. C., *The Theory and Practice of Communism* (New York: Macmillan, 1961). A well-written and orderly study of communist theory and its practical working.

Meyer, F. S., *The Moulding of Communists* (New York: Harcourt, 1961). Formation of hard-core communists and their central role in the party.

Orwell, G., *Animal Farm* (New York: Harcourt, 1954). Satire describing the transformation of communism into an exploitive system, in terms of a fable of animal life. A highly superior treatment.

———— *Nineteen Eighty-Four* (New York: Harcourt, 1949). The impact of statism on human personality is discussed in novel form.

Overstreet, H., and Overstreet, B., *What We Must Know About Communism* (New York: Norton, 1958). Written primarily for the liberal who is sceptical about the agitation against communism. Shows the menace of this system both in its international and domestic aspects.

Rossiter, C. L., *Marxism: The View from America* (New York: Harcourt, 1960). An able American political scientist examines Marxist teachings about man, society, government, and history.

Selznick, P., *The Organizational Weapon* (New York: Free Press of Glencoe, 1959). Emphasizes seizure of power at all levels as a basic tactic of communism. An unusually valuable work.

Problems of Communism (Washington, D. C.: Superintendent of Documents, $2.50 per year). Bimonthly publication of the U. S. Information Agency. Contains high-quality articles and book reviews on communist problems. One of the best single sources in the English language for appraisal of trends in the communist world.

World Communism

Kirkpatrick, J. J., ed., *The Strategy of Deception: A Study in World-Wide Communist Tactics* (New York: Farrar, Straus, and Co., 1963). Valuable essays on the tactics used by communist parties throughout the world. The authors are competent and perceptive.

Kissinger, H. A., *The Necessity for Choice* (New York: Harper, 1961). This book had considerable influence on American policy under President Kennedy. It offers a Cold War strategy.

Petersen, W., ed., *The Realities of World Communism* (Englewood Cliffs, N. J.: Prentice-Hall, 1963). Eight scholars summarize world communist developments since 1945. General bibliography included.

Seton-Watson, H., *Neither War Nor Peace: The Struggle for Power in the Postwar World* (New York: Praeger, 1960). A study by continents of revolution, totalitarianism, and imperialism, with emphasis upon communist expansion.

Strausz-Hupé, R., and others, *Protracted Conflict* (New York: Harper, 1959) and *A Forward Strategy for America* (New York: Harper, 1961). Techniques and stratagems of the Cold War are analyzed in the earlier study. The later book calls for a hard and aggressive American reaction.

Soviet Union — Internal Conditions

Bauer, R. A., Inkeles, A., and Kluckhohn, C., *How the Soviet System Works: Cultural, Psychological, and Social Themes* (Cambridge: Harvard University Press, 1956). Social relationships in a communist society, as told by hundreds of refugees interviewed. Especially enlightening in classifying causes of unrest.

Bereday, G., and others, *The Changing Soviet School* (Boston: Houghton Mifflin, 1960). Relatively recent study of Soviet school system based on an extensive survey in the U.S.S.R. by a group of seventy American educators.

Berman, H. J., *Justice in the USSR* (Cambridge: Harvard University Press, 1963). This updated version of an earlier work gives a balanced account of the Soviet legal system.

Brumberg, A., ed., *Russia Under Khrushchev* (New York: Praeger, 1962). Leading specialists examine every phase of Khrushchev's Russia.

Fainsod, M., *How Russia is Ruled* (Cambridge: Harvard University Press, 1963). Sociological-historical study of the power system in the Soviet Union. Explains necessity for centralization and the glorification of rulers.

Hazard, J. N., *The Soviet System of Government* (Chicago: University of Chicago Press, 1960). Discussion of Soviet government as it actually operates, with due recognition of possible instability because of army or intelligentsia dissatisfaction.

King, E. A., ed., *Communist Education* (New York: Bobbs-Merrill, 1963). A series of essays by experts in comparative education, explaining the educational systems of four of the largest communist nations.

Korol, A., *Soviet Education for Science and Technology* (New York: Wiley, 1957). Balanced and critical examination of Soviet educational system, noting its narrow aims as well as its impressive gains.

Kulski, W. W., *The Soviet Regime: Communism in Practice* (Syracuse: Syracuse University Press, 1959). This monumental study can serve as a one-volume encyclopedia of communist practice in the Soviet Union.

Mehnert, K., *Soviet Man and His World* (New York: Praeger, 1962). Examines the attitudes and thoughts of Soviet citizens and concludes that any change in the direction of freedom will be slow.

Meissner, B., *The Communist Party of the Soviet Union: Party Leadership, Organization and Ideology* (New York: Praeger, 1956). Since the Communist Party rules the Soviet Union, under the control of its leaders, it is important to have this careful study of its functioning.

Nove, A., *The Soviet Economy* (New York: Praeger, 1961). Broad but simply written study of Soviet planning and economic life.

Nutter, G. W., *Growth of Industrial Production in the Soviet Union* (Princeton, N. J.: Princeton University Press, 1962). The reality of economic growth in the U.S.S.R. and the factors contributing to this advance.

Spulber, N., *The Soviet Economy* (New York: Norton, 1962). Working principles, institutional structure, and problems of the Soviet economic system.

Ulam, A. B., *The New Face of Soviet Totalitarianism* (Cambridge: Harvard University Press, 1963). Outlines the conflict faced by a government when it attempts to rule by Marxist principles. It needs freedom and education for efficient production, yet its dogma cannot tolerate dissent.

Soviet Union — Foreign Policy

Allen, R. L., *Soviet Economic Warfare* (Washington, D. C.: Public Affairs Press, 1960). This warfare takes two forms: competition with industrialized countries and penetration of selected developing nations. An often overlooked phase of the Cold War.

Barghoorn, F. C., *Soviet Foreign Propaganda* (Princeton, N. J.: Princeton University Press, 1964). Successes and failures in the use of propaganda as a weapon in the Cold War.

Berliner, J. S., *Soviet Economic Aid to Underdeveloped Countries* (New York: Praeger, 1958). Factual information on a vital aspect of Soviet foreign policy.

Brzezinski, Z., *The Soviet Bloc: Unity and Conflict* (Cambridge, Mass.: Harvard University Press, 1960). Interaction of ideology and power politics in nations allied to the Soviet Union.

Dallin, A., *The Soviet Union at the United Nations* (New York: Praeger, 1962). Variations in Soviet UN policy, leading to the conclusion that the U.S.S.R. is becoming more willing to act within the UN framework.

Kulski, W. W., *Peaceful Coexistence: An Analysis of Soviet Foreign Policy* (Chicago: Regnery, 1959). Basic patterns, objectives, and means of Soviet foreign policy.

Laqueur, W. Z., *The Soviet Union and the Middle East* (New York: Praeger, 1959). Analysis of Soviet policy in this troubled but vital area.

Mehnert, K., *Peking and Moscow* (New York: Putnam, 1963). Scholarly research into the background factors leading to the Sino-Soviet split.

Zagoria, D. S., *The Sino-Soviet Conflict* (Princeton, N. J.: Princeton University Press, 1962). A readable analysis of the main factors in this titanic dispute.

Communism in Europe, Africa, and Asia

Barnett, A. D., *Communist China and Asia* (New York: Harper, 1960). Survey of China's foreign policies and problems confronting U. S. policy.

Brimmell, J. H., *Communism in Southeast Asia: A Political Analysis* (New

York: Oxford University Press, 1959). An able study for the Royal Institute
of International Affairs.

Brzezinski, Z., ed., *Africa and the Communist World* (Stanford, Calif.: Stanford University Press, 1963). Polycentrism may aid rather than hinder
communist penetration in Africa, since it removes the fear of the Soviet
monolith.

Burks, R. V., *The Dynamics of Communism in Eastern Europe* (Princeton,
N. J.: Princeton University Press, 1961). Origins of Communist Party
membership in Eastern European nations and ethnic tensions in this area.

Hoffman, G. W., and Neal, F. W., *Yugoslavia and the New Communism*
(New York: Twentieth Century Fund, 1962). Internal and foreign policy
of Yugoslav communists since break with Stalin in 1948.

Mao Tse-tung on Guerrilla Warfare (New York: Praeger, 1961) and *Che
Guevara on Guerrilla Warfare* (New York: Praeger, 1961). Since guerrilla
warfare is now one of the major weapons of communist strategy, these source
books are most useful for the serious student of communism.

Scalapino, R. A., ed. *The Communist Revolution in Asia* (Englewood Cliffs,
N. J.: Prentice-Hall, 1965). Superb study of entire area.

Taborsky, E., *Communism in Czechoslovakia, 1949–1960* (Princeton, N. J.:
Princeton University Press, 1961). History and evaluation of Czech communism.

Biographical and Autobiographical Material

Chambers, W., *Witness* (New York: Random House, 1952). Widely considered as the greatest American work on the communist movement. It is
written with great feeling and deep insight.

Dodd, B., *School of Darkness* (New York: Devin-Adair, 1963). Dr. Dodd was
a top educational leader for the Communist Party. Her autobiography is
powerfully written and quite revealing.

Leonhard, W., *Child of the Revolution* (Chicago: Regnery, 1958). Clinical
autobiography of a German communist who reached high levels in the
East German Party and defected in 1949. He studied in the Soviet Union
and hence can give a forceful picture of how communism affected his
generation.

Communism and Religion

Galter, A., *The Red Book of the Persecuted Church* (Westminster, Md.:
Newman, 1957). A complete study, country by country, of the communist
war on religion. Essential documentation for any extended discussion of
this persecution. Out of print.

Goldberg, B. Z., *The Jewish Problem in the Soviet Union* (New York: Crown
Publishers, 1961). Factual study of persecution of Jewish minority in the
Soviet Union.

Kolarz, W., *Religion in the Soviet Union* (New York: St. Martin's Press,
1961). Comprehensive, balanced, and scholarly treatment of religious life
in the U.S.S.R.

Roy, R. L., *Communism and Churches* (New York: Harcourt, 1960). Largely
discounts the charge that communism has seriously infiltrated religious
bodies in the United States.

Communism in America

Alexander, R. J., *Communism in Latin America* (New Brunswick, N. J.: Rutgers University Press, 1957). Excellent study of trends of communism in the nations of Latin America.

Bouscaren, A. F., *A Guide to Anti-Communist Action* (Chicago: Regnery, 1958). Suggested techniques for handling both external and internal communist threats. Seven chapters were written by well-known experts other than the author.

Brzezinski, Z., and Huntington, S. P., *Political Power: USA/USSR* (New York: Viking, 1964). Similarities and differences, strength and weaknesses, and trends in the two systems are studied by the authors. They hold that economic growth need not lead to political liberalization in the Soviet Union.

Budenz, L. F., *The Techniques of Communism* (Chicago: Regnery, 1954). An analytical study of the aims and methods of the Communist Party, suitable for general reading or classroom use.

Draper, T., *Castro's Revolution: Myths and Realities* (New York: Praeger, 1962). Factors leading to Cuban revolt and communist take-over of the revolution.

Glaser, N., *The Social Basis of American Communism* (New York: Harcourt, 1961). Analysis of social groups that make up bulk of Communist Party membership in United States.

Hoover, J. E., *Masters of Deceit* (New York: Holt, 1958). Complete and accurate study of the communist movement in the United States in the late 1950's.

Howe, I., and Coser, L., *The American Communist Party: A Critical History, 1919–1957* (New York: Praeger, 1958). Balanced and judicious study of the workings of the Communist Party in the United States.

Iverson, R. W., *The Communists and the Schools* (New York: Harcourt, 1959). Examines evidence of communist infiltration into our school system and into teachers' unions.

Saposs, D., *Communism in American Unions* (New York: McGraw-Hill, 1960). Communist infiltration in the A. F. of L. and the C.I.O. in the united front period.

Shannon, D. A., *The Decline of American Communism: A History of the Communist Party of the United States Since 1945* (New York: Harcourt, 1959). Chronicles and explains decline in communist fortunes here after World War II.

List No. 6 CAPITAL AND FREE ENTERPRISE

Reading list for Chapter VIII.

Special Problems

Kaplan, A. D. H., *et al.*, *Pricing in Big Business* (Washington: Brookings Institution, 1958). The authors conclude that a variety of factors influence so-called administered prices. Attitudes range from sensitivity to competition to virtual disregard of market considerations.

Moore, W. E., *Industrial Relations and the Social Order* (New York: Macmillan, 1951). Social organization of industry and relationship of industry to society. Labor relations also discussed.

Noonan, J. T., Jr., *The Scholastic Analysis of Usury* (Cambridge: Harvard University Press, 1957). Well-written and challenging analysis of the attitudes of the medieval Churchmen. Author upsets, with proof, many theories that have become part of the literature on interest-taking.

Business Leadership

Barnard, C. I., *The Function of the Executive* (Cambridge: Harvard University Press, 1938). Studies the techniques of business organization, with stress on the ability to develop co-operation.

Roethlisberger, F. J., *Management and Morale* (Cambridge: Harvard University Press, 1941). One of the pioneer studies in human relations, calling for co-operation between management and workers.

Ross, M. G., and Hendry, C. E., *New Understanding of Leadership* (New York: Association Press, 1957). Summary of recent research on the nature and meaning of leadership. Useful for all organizations, as well as business groups.

Tead, O., *The Art of Leadership* (New York: McGraw-Hill, 1935). Still considered a classic in its field of defining the functions of a leader.

Terry, G. R., *Principles of Management* (Homewood, Ill.: Irwin, 1960). Well-written suggestions on industrial management, with emphasis upon the human-relations approach.

Industrial Psychology and Sociology

Blum, M. L., *Industrial Psychology and Its Social Foundations* (New York Harper, 1956). The human dignity of workers and method of co-operation studied from a psychological aspect.

Heron, A. R., *Sharing Information with Employees* (Stanford, Calif.: Stanford University Press, 1942). First volume of a valuable trilogy on making workers effective partners in industry.

Yoder, D., *Handbook of Personnel Management and Labor Relations* (New York: McGraw-Hill, 1958). An experienced writer condenses the main problems and offers constructive solutions.

Human Relations

Barnard, C. I., *Organization and Management* (Cambridge: Harvard University Press, 1948). A selection of papers dealing with good human relationships in industry.

Bursk, E. C., ed., *Human Relations for Management, the Newer Perspective* (New York: Harper, 1956). A selection of articles having religious implications. One was written from a Catholic viewpoint.

Davis, K., *Human Relations at Work* (New York: McGraw-Hill, 1962). Excellent study of the main approaches to the human problems of industrial relations.

Gardner, B. B., and Moore, D. C., *Human Relations in Industry* (Homewood, Ill.: Irwin, 1955). New edition of a management-oriented study of the human factor in industry. The place of unions is fairly presented.

Profit Sharing

Lesieur, F. G., ed., *The Scanlon Plan* (New York: Wiley, 1958). Brief but competent study of group incentives as developed by Joseph Scanlon.

Meier, J. B., ed., *Profit Sharing Manual* (Chicago: Council of Profit Sharing

Industries, 1957). Up-to-date information on profit sharing presented in a balanced and comprehensive fashion.

Mentzger, B. L., *Profit Sharing in Perspective* (Chicago: Profit Sharing Research Foundation, 1964). Directed primarily toward medium-sized and small business firms interested in learning techniques of profit-sharing.

Nunn, H. L., *Partners in Production* (Englewood Cliffs, N. J.: Prentice-Hall, 1962). Firsthand account of one of the famous experiments in industrial democracy and profit sharing.

Codetermination

Blumenthal, W. M., *Codetermination in the German Steel Industry* (Princeton: Industrial Relations Section, Princeton University, 1956). Excellent study based on intensive field investigation of this important experiment in labor-management partnership enforced by law. Out of print.

Newman, J., *Co-responsibility in Industry* (Westminster, Md.: Newman, 1956). The problems of labor-management relations as seen by an eminent Irish scholar. Emphasis is largely European, with special stress upon the German experiment in codetermination.

Shuchman, A., *Codetermination: Labor's Middle Way in Germany* (Washington: Public Affairs Press, 1957). History and present trends in the German experiment. Author's sympathies lie with union demands for extension of comanagement. Out of print.

List No. 7. LABOR PROBLEMS

Material herein contained refers mainly to matters covered in Chapters IX and X.

General Works

Chamberlain, N. W., *Labor* (New York: McGraw-Hill, 1958). How business and labor organize for collective bargaining, and the impact of union policies upon the general economy.

Rayback, J. G., *A History of American Labor* (New York: Macmillan, 1959). Realistic, lively, and often critical portrayal of the American labor movement from its beginning until recent times.

Reder, M. W., *Labor in a Growing Economy* (New York: Wiley, 1957). Sound, well-written, and interesting textbook on labor problems.

Reynolds, L. G., *Labor Economics and Labor Relations* (New York: Prentice-Hall, 1959). A textbook in labor economics, with considerable emphasis upon the history of the labor movement.

Taft, P., *Organized Labor in American History* (New York: Harper, 1964). Monumental history of American unionism, with emphasis upon problems confronted.

Tannenbaum, F., *A Philosophy of Labor* (New York: Knopf, 1950). A non-Catholic Columbia University professor elaborates a philosophy of labor which is quite similar to that of the encyclicals.

Union Structure and Policy

Bakke, E. W., and others, *Unions, Management and the Public* (New York: Harcourt, 1960). Uses many sources to show impact of trade unionism on workers, management, and the public.

Barbash, J., *Labor's Grass Roots* (New York: Harper, 1961). The place of the local union in the labor movement told in an interesting and authoritative fashion.

———— ed., *Unions and Union Leadership* (New York: Harper, 1959). A broad view of the labor movement in the United States, based on 43 essays selected by a knowledgeable editor.

Beirne, J. A., *New Horizons for American Labor* (Washington, D. C.: Public Affairs Press, 1962). A top union official calls for a sweeping re-examination of policy to meet new problems and needs.

Jacobs, P., *The State of the Unions* (New York: Atheneum, 1963). Argues that American unions have lost their fire and idealism.

Kuhn, J. W., *Bargaining in Grievance Settlement: The Power of Industrial Work Groups* (New York: Columbia University Press, 1961). Relationships built up in grievance negotiations are of vital importance in labor-management conduct.

LeRoy, A., *The Dignity of Labor* (Westminster, Md.: Newman, 1957). Part played by Catholics in the International Labor Organization, written by a priest long associated with this important organization.

Mire, J., *Labor Education: A Study on Needs, Programs, and Approaches* (Madison: Inter-University Labor Education Committee, 1956). An effort to make workers' education more effective by studying gaps in the present system and making recommendations for expansion and improvement.

Pound, R., *Legal Immunities of Trade Unions* (Washington: American Enterprise Association, 1957). One of our greatest jurists contends that labor enjoys exemption from laws enacted to prevent monopoly and exploitation.

Richberg, D. R., *Labor Union Monopoly: A Clear and Present Danger* (Chicago: Regnery, 1957). A sample of the most extreme and all-out attacks upon the labor movement and its economic policies.

Seidman, J., *The Worker Views His Union* (Chicago: University of Chicago Press, 1958). Documents the thesis of rank-and-file apathy.

Collective Bargaining

Bernstein, I., *Arbitration of Wages* (Berkeley: University of California Press, 1954). Problems faced in wage arbitration. Author holds that such processes should be considered as extensions of collective bargaining.

Braun, K., *Labor Disputes and Their Settlement* (Baltimore: Johns Hopkins Press, 1955). Methods used here and abroad to achieve peaceful rather than forced settlements of labor-management disputes.

Chamberlain, N. W., *Collective Bargaining* (New York: McGraw-Hill, 1951). The author does not hesitate to express strong viewpoints, thus producing a valuable and provocative study of this basic problem.

Davey, H. W., *Contemporary Collective Bargaining* (New York: Prentice-Hall, 1959). Unusually realistic and comprehensive study of the realities of labor-management relations. Emphasizes the value of free collective bargaining.

Davey, H. W., and others, eds., *New Dimensions in Collective Bargaining* (New York, 1959). Reflects dramatic changes in collective bargaining since World War II, with both new problems and techniques.

Kornhauser, A., Dubin, R., and Ross, A. M., eds., *Industrial Conflict* (New York: McGraw-Hill, 1954). Forty authors contribute to this symposium,

exploring every phase of industrial strife. Moderate and realistic in approach.
Peters, E., *Strategy and Tactics in Labor Negotiations* (New London: National Foremen's Institute, 1955). A primer in labor negotiations, interestingly written, for executives and others concerned with collective bargaining.
Selekman, B. M., *Labor Relations and Human Relations* (New York: McGraw-Hill, 1947). Social changes enforced by collective bargaining analyzed, with special stress on need for leadership on both sides. Excellent.
Slichter, S. H., and others, *The Impact of Collective Bargaining on Management* (Washington, D. C.: Brookings, 1960). This thorough rewrite of Professor Slichter's 1941 study affords a comprehensive picture of modern industrial relations.
Weber, A. R., ed., *The Structure of Collective Bargaining* (New York: Free Press of Glencoe, 1961). Objectives of labor and management in collective bargaining, with important case studies analyzed.

Automation

Einzig, P., *The Economic Consequences of Automation* (New York: Norton, 1957). The author is a facile popularizer of difficult economic problems. In this volume he explains well the implications of automation.
Phillips, A., *Automation, Its Impact on Economic Growth and Stability* (Washington: American Enterprise Association, 1957). Argues that automation will bring undreamed-of prosperity, without causing economic dislocations.
Shils, E. B., *Automation and Industrial Relations* (New York: Holt, Rinehart, and Winston, 1963). Survey of the problem of automation and summary of the major disputes as to its impact and trends.

Wage Determination and Employment Problems

Burns, A. F., *Prosperity Without Inflation* (New York: Fordham University Press, 1957). One of America's best known economists holds that inflation is a major threat to our economic welfare. Especially valuable because of the author's government experience.
Denison, A. F., *The Sources of Economic Growth in the United States and the Alternatives Before Us* (New York: Committee for Economic Development, 1962). Expert appraisal of factors affecting economic growth in the United States.
Dunlop, J. T., ed., *The Theory of Wage Determination* (New York: St. Martin's Press, 1957). A 1954 symposium of the International Economic Association. A mine of information on the forces behind wages.
Maddison, A., *Economic Growth in the West* (New York: Twentieth Century Fund, 1964). While this study is not light bedside reading, it is useful as a comparative analysis of the divergent factors in northern Europe and North America, which led to strikingly different growth rates.
Ross, A. M., *Trade Union Wage Policy* (Berkeley: University of California Press, 1956). Stimulating study of collective bargaining considered as a political activity.
Taylor, G. W., and Pierson, F. C., eds., *New Concepts in Wage Determination* (New York: McGraw-Hill, 1957). Descriptive approach to wage theory. Not entirely successful in developing new concepts as promised by the title.

Labor Law

Gregory, C. O., *Labor and the Law* (New York: Norton, 1958). Gives both the basic laws and the most important judicial decisions affecting labor.

Millis, H. A., and Brown, E. C., *From the Wagner Act to Taft-Hartley: A Study of National Labor Policy and Labor Relations* (Chicago: University of Chicago Press, 1950). A thorough study of our basic labor laws and their administration.

List No. 8. FAMILY ECONOMIC PROBLEMS

Material for Chapter XI.

The Family and Its Economic Problems

Clemens, A. H., *Marriage and the Family* (Englewood Cliffs, N. J.: Prentice-Hall, 1957). Textbook with useful hints on family economic problems.

Kyrk, H., *The Family in the American Economy* (Chicago: Chicago University Press, 1953). Economic position of the family in our nation. Notes changes both in the family and its economic status.

Mihanovich, C. S., et al., *Marriage and the Family* (Milwaukee: Bruce, 1952). Brother Schnepp has a chapter, with bibliography, on family economics.

Ogburn, W. F., and Nimkoff, M. F., *Technology and the Changing Family* (Boston: Houghton Mifflin, 1955). Modern technology has changed the family from a productive unit to a loosely knit society, more likely to fall apart. Useful, but somewhat oversimplified.

Smuts, R. W., *Women and Work in America* (New York: Columbia University Press, 1959). Well-rounded study of women in the work force in the United States.

Thomas, J. L., *The American Catholic Family* (New York: Prentice-Hall, 1956). One of our best sociologists studies the Catholic family in an environment which often poses problems of adjustment and conflict. Excellent treatment of the cultural differences which this situation exposes.

Troelstrup, A., *Consumer Problems* (New York: McGraw-Hill, 1957). One of the better texts in treating economic problems as they affect family life.

Vadakin, J. C., *Family Allowances* (Miami, Fla.: University of Miami Press, 1959). One of the strongest pleas in English for a family-allowance system here.

Whalen, W. J., *Christian Family Finance* (Milwaukee: Bruce, 1960). Aids to married couples concerned with the problem of making ends meet when confronted with family obligations.

Health, Housing, and Social Security

Beyer, G. H., *Housing, a Factual Analysis* (New York: Macmillan, 1958). Represents the result of a seminar and hence reflects many viewpoints regarding the housing problem.

Burns, E. M., *Social Security and Public Policy* (New York: McGraw-Hill, 1956). Policy and practice of social security, with its impact on individuals and families assessed.

Clark, D., *Cities in Crisis: The Christian Response* (New York: Sheed, 1960). The problems that our cities confront are a real challenge to social action.

Haber, W., and Cohen, W., eds., *Social Security Programs, Problems, and Policies* (Homewood, Ill.: Irwin, 1960). Selected articles dealing with problems connected with our social-security system.

Harris, S. E., *The Economics of American Medicine* (New York: Macmillan, 1964). Comprehensive survey of every aspect of medical costs and systems for payment.

Somers, H. M., and Somers, A. R., *Doctors, Patients, and Health Insurance* (Washington, D. C.: Brookings, 1961). Thorough study of medical economics, particularly good in evaluation of private health-insurance plans.

Spiegelman, M., *Enduring Medical Care for the Aged* (Homewood, Ill.: Irwin, 1960). Factual study of medical problems of the aged and various types of solution available or proposed.

Poverty

Bagdikian, B. H., *In the Midst of Plenty: The Poor in America* (Boston: Beacon Press, 1964). Descriptive treatment of both urban and rural poverty in terms of the human tragedy involved.

Harrington, M., *The Other America: Poverty in the United States* (New York: Macmillan, 1962). Graphic portrayal of the impact and extent of poverty here.

Humphrey, H. H., *War on Poverty* (New York: McGraw-Hill, 1964). Calls for a broad attack on the problem, with co-operation and partnership between government and industry particularly stressed.

Miller, H. P., *Rich Man, Poor Man: The Distribution of Income in America* (New York: Crowell, 1964). Figures on poverty presented in a clear and interesting manner.

List No. 9.   PROPERTY

Selected works for Chapter XII.

Berle, A. A., *The Twentieth Century Capitalist Revolution* (New York: Harcourt, 1954). Big business is developing a higher code of morality and concern for the public interest.

Berle, A. A., and Means, G. C., *The Modern Corporation and Private Property* (New York: Macmillan, 1933). The authors study the social implications of power concentration through narrow control of corporate wealth. A masterly treatment.

Harbrecht, P., *Pension Funds and Economic Power* (New York: Twentieth Century Fund, 1959). Documentation of points raised in Chapter XII, on concentration of power involved in our growing pension funds.

Kaplan, A. D. H., *Big Enterprise in a Competitive System* (Washington: Brookings Institution, 1954). Another favorable study that gives the nod to big business in terms of dynamic growth and vigorous competition.

Kolko, G., *Wealth and Power in America* (New York: Praeger, 1962). Income statistics prove the prevalence of poverty and the concentration of wealth.

Lilienthal, D. E., *Big Business: a New Era* (New York: Harper, 1952). A New Deal liberal defends modern big business as growing in social responsibility. Available in pocket-book paperback.

Mason, E. S., *Economic Concentration and the Monopoly Problem* (Cambridge: Harvard University Press, 1957). Collection of essays by one of the nation's foremost experts in antitrust problems. Authoritative and inspiring.

List No. 10.   THE STATE

Readings for Chapter XIII.

General Works on Government

De Jouvenel, B., *Sovereignty: An Inquiry into the Political Good* (Chicago: University of Chicago Press, 1957). Qualities of political leadership and moral requirements for just rule.

Evans, J. W., and Ward, L. R., eds., *The Social and Political Philosophy of Maritain* (New York: Scribner's, 1955). A compilation of the writings of Jacques Maritain in the field of social and political philosophy. Many important modern problems are covered in these selections.

Gilby, T., O.P., *Between Community and Society; a Philosophy and Theology of the State* (New York: Longmans, 1953). A thorough study of the political writings of St. Thomas Aquinas, presented brilliantly in terms of current problems. The author's knowledge of history adds richness to his presentation.

Hayes, C. J., *Nationalism: A Religion* (New York: Macmillan, 1960). The rise of modern nationalism and its various forms in contemporary society.

Hoover, C. B., *The Economy, Liberty, and the State* (New York: Twentieth Century Fund, 1959). After showing how excessive state control hurt the economies of Soviet Russia and Hitler Germany, the author seeks a method which would permit needed guidance without crippling domination.

Keller, J., M.M., *Government Is Your Business* (Garden City, N. Y.: Doubleday, 1951). A primer on the workings of government and suggestions for infusing Christian principles into this important field. Inspiring and practical.

Kerwin, J. G., *Catholic Viewpoint of Church and State* (Garden City, N. Y.: Hanover House, 1960). Theory of Church-State relations and practical problems faced in the United States, with suggestions for improvement.

———— *Politics, Government, Catholics* (New York: Paulist Press, 1961). Emphasizes moral duty to participate in political life and the task of our schools in preparing students adequately for this function.

Lippmann, W., *Essays in the Public Philosophy* (Boston: Little, Brown, 1955). The tradition of natural law is considered essential for the proper working of a democracy. Unless people adhere to standards, they cannot hold firm principles when confronting the difficult issues of our time.

Maritain, J., *Man and the State* (Chicago: University of Chicago Press, 1951). An eloquent defense of the moral character of politics and political theory, with excellent chapters on the rights of man, the natural law, and the *jus gentium*.

Democracy

Blaisdell, D. C., *American Democracy Under Pressure* (New York: Ronald Press, 1957). A thorough study of pressure groups as important factors in our governmental process.

Dahl, R. A., *A Preface to Democratic Theory* (Chicago: University of Chicago Press, 1956). Unusual insight into the underlying philosophy of our democracy and its unanswered problems.

Eby, K., and Greenlief, J., *The Paradoxes of Democracy* (New York: Association Press, 1956). Shortcomings of democracy which must be overcome if we are to realize our full potential.

Hallowell, J. H., *The Moral Foundation of Democracy* (Chicago: University of Chicago Press, 1954). Emphasizes need for a philosophy of life underlying democratic institutions. Considers democracy a means, not an end.

McCarthy, E. J., *Frontiers in American Democracy* (Cleveland: World, 1960). The purpose and ideals of democracy, portrayed by a well-known United States senator.

Maritain, J., *Christianity and Democracy* (New York: Hillary, 1944). A study of the close interrelationship between the two.

Murray, J. C., *We hold These Truths* (New York: Sheed, 1960). Brilliant analysis of basic ideas underlying American democracy.

Shields, C., *Democracy and Catholicism in America* (New York: McGraw-Hill, 1963). The author examines classic liberalism, democracy, and Catholicism. Holds that Catholicism is compatible with democracy, but that liberalism is incompatible.

Simon, Y. R., *Philosophy of Democratic Government* (Chicago: University of Chicago Press, 1951). A consideration of the advantages, difficulties, and characteristic features of democracy, which does not make the usual mistake of falling into vague generalities and wishful thinking.

Stamps, N. L., *Why Democracies Fail* (Notre Dame, Ind.: University of Notre Dame Press, 1957). The author holds that dictatorship does not arise merely because of the personality of its leaders. There is also a failure on the part of previous democratic regimes.

Stumpf, S. E., *A Democratic Manifesto* (Nashville: Vanderbilt University Press, 1954). Democracy will survive if we keep our faith in the dignity of man. Religious principles should be applied to public life.

Ward, B., *Faith and Freedom* (New York: Norton, 1954). Freedom as developed through the centuries is the main theme of this book. The author concentrates upon the Western world as the finest embodiment of human liberty.

Civil Rights and Liberties

Bell, D., ed., *The Radical Right* (New York: Doubleday, 1963). Right-wing extremism in the United States studied by eight distinguished authors.

Cushman, R. E., *Civil Liberties in the United States: A Guide to Current Problems and Experience* (Ithaca, N. Y.: Cornell University Press, 1956). Orderly summary of the main challenges to American civil liberties today.

Forster, A., and Epstein, B. R., *Danger on the Right* (New York: Random House, 1964). Operations of the radical right and principal sources of funds.

Gardiner, H. C., S.J., *Catholic Viewpoint on Censorship* (Garden City: Hanover House, 1958). Realistic defense of Catholic views and programs in the area of censorship.

Hand, L., *The Bill of Rights* (Cambridge: Harvard University Press, 1958). One of America's greatest jurists takes issue with the thesis that the Supreme Court has the right to overrule the legislature.

Hook, S., *Common Sense and the Fifth Amendment* (Chicago: Regnery, 1963). Dr. Hook holds that the public is right in making reasonable inferences when a witness or defendant uses the Fifth Amendment. He claims that arguments to the contrary are based on fanciful suppositions.

Kirk, R., *Academic Freedom: An Essay in Definition* (Chicago: Regnery,

1955). Strong defense of the thesis that we have freedom to teach the truth, but not license to propogate error.

Konvitz, M. R., and Rossiter, C., *Aspects of Liberty* (Ithaca, N. Y.: Cornell University Press, 1958). Basic philosophy of human rights and civil rights.

Overstreet, H., and Overstreet, B., *The Strange Tactics of Extremism* (New York: Norton, 1964). Carefully documented study of extremist groups in the United States and their potential danger.

Sherwin, M., *The Extremists* (New York: St. Martin's Press, 1963). Popular description of left and right, with major emphasis upon the latter.

Taylor, T., *Grand Inquest: the Story of Congressional Investigations* (New York: Simon and Schuster, 1955). Congressional investigations have a long and honored history. Here is the legal and historical background of this important congressional function. Available in Ballentine paperback.

Special Problems

Dimock, M. E., *Business and Government* (New York: Holt, 1957). The mixed economy of private enterprise under some government control analyzed from economic and political aspects.

Douglas, P., *Ethics in Government* (Cambridge: Harvard University Press, 1952). Senator Douglas discusses a much publicized problem of our day. He puts the issue into perspective and offers some sound remedies for corruption in government.

MacIver, R. M., *The Web of Government* (New York: Macmillan, 1947). A sociopolitical study of government. Warns against excessive concentration of power in the state.

Myrdal, G., *Beyond the Welfare State* (New Haven: Yale University Press, 1960). Problems faced by modern nations in economic planning both on a domestic and on an international scale.

List No. 11. INTERNATIONAL ECONOMIC AND POLITICAL PROBLEMS

Selected works for Chapter XIV.

General Works

Asher, R. E., Kotschnig, W. M., Brown, W. A., Jr., and associates, *The United Nations and Economic and Social Cooperation* (Washington: Brookings Institution, 1957). Case study of the Economic Commission for Europe, as an example of the broad economic work of the United Nations.

De Soras, A., *International Morality* (New York: Hawthorne, 1963). Broad but brief study of Catholic principles as applied to relationships between nations.

Eppstein, J., *The Catholic Tradition and the Law of Nations* (London: Burns, Oates, 1935). Christian principles on peace. Out of print.

——— ed., *Code of International Ethics* (Westminster, Md.: Newman, 1953). The latest revision of the Malines code, with commentary by a distinguished specialist on international problems. Discusses among other things the morality of atomic bombing.

Flannery, H. W., ed., *Patterns for Peace* (Westminster, Md.: Newman, 1962). Selections from papal and other authoritative writings on world problems.

Leclerq, J., *The Christian and World Integration* (New York: Hawthorne,

1963). Christian principles applied to concept of the unity of the human race.
Pamphlet studies by the Catholic Association for International Peace, 1312 Massachusetts Avenue, N.W., Washington, D. C. 20005. A series of timely studies on both ethical principles and current problems.

Economic and Social Problems

Bauer, P. T., *Economic Analysis and Policy in Underdeveloped Countries* (Durham, N. C.: Duke University Press, 1957). A strong plea for private, as contrasted with statist, development in newly growing economies. Many suggestions closely parallel the warnings of Pope Pius XII.

Cepede, M., and others, *Population and Food* (New York: Sheed, 1964). Distinguished Catholic authors examine the population and food problem on a world scale.

Clark, C., *The Conditions of Economic Progress* (London: Macmillan, 1957). Comparative study of national economies and their ability to provide economic welfare. Author is an internationally known expert

Coffin, F. M., *Witness for Aid* (Boston: Houghton Mifflin, 1964). Cites positive advantages of our foreign-aid programs and also areas for improvement.

Divine, R. A., *American Immigration Policy, 1924–1952* (New Haven: Yale, 1957). Background material on our immigration policy, explaining not only the major laws, but the pressures that influenced legislation and policy.

Enke, S. S., and Salera, V., *International Economics* (Englewood Cliffs, N. J.: Prentice-Hall, 1957). Stresses interrelationship of economic policy and international relations.

Heilbroner, R. L., *The Great Ascent: The Struggle for Economic Development in Our Time* (New York: Harper, 1963). Political, cultural, and social factors that influence the growth of developing nations.

McCormack, A., *World Poverty and the Christian* (New York: Hawthorn, 1963). The problem of poverty and hunger throughout the world and the Christian approach to the solution of this problem.

———— ed., *Christian Responsibility and World Poverty* (Westminster, Md.: Newman Press, 1963). Observations on population and world poverty by a group of distinguished Catholic authors.

Millikan, M. F., and Rostow, W. W., *A Proposal: Key to an Effective Foreign Policy* (New York: Harper, 1957). Emphasizes the necessity for a long-range program for aiding developing nations.

Shonfield, A., *The Attack on World Poverty* (New York: Random House, 1960). Calls for a more flexible and selective approach to problems of aiding developing nations.

Ward, B., *The Rich Nations and the Poor Nations* (New York: Norton, 1962). Problems confronting developing nations and the fear that they may fall further behind wealthier countries.

List No. 12.   THE RACE QUESTION

Books for Chapter XV.

General Works

Brink, W., and Harris, L., *The Negro Revolution in America* (New York: Simon and Schuster, 1964). Survey of attitudes on racial problems, first reported in *Newsweek* in 1963.

Frazier, E. F., *Black Bourgeoisie* (Glencoe, Ill.: Free Press and Falcon's Wing Press, 1956). Analysis, possibly exaggerated at times, of the Negro middle class and its alleged weakness.

———— *The Negro in the United States* (New York: Macmillan, 1957). Standard text on Negro problems.

Myrdal, G., *An American Dilemma* (New York: Harper, 1962). One of the basic works on Negro problems, based on an extensive survey by a Swedish sociologist.

Rose, A., *The Negro in America* (Boston: Beacon, 1958). A summary of Myrdal's two-volume work.

Warren, R. P., *Segregation* (New York: Random House, 1956). Report on attitudes of Southerners regarding segregation. Finds them uneasy over their prejudices.

Woodward, C. V., *The Strange Career of Jim Crow* (New York: Oxford University Press, 1957). Development of racial segregation in the South from 1877 to the present. Many will be surprised to know that restrictions are often relatively recent.

Religion and Race

Ahmann, M. H., *Race: Challenge to Religion* (Chicago: Regnery, 1963). Papers from the historic National Conference on Religion and Race.

Cantwell, D. M., ed., *The Challenge of Interracial Justice* (Techny, Ill.: Divine Word Publications, 1959). Collection of statements from popes, bishops, and theologians on race relations.

Considine, J. D., *Fundamental Catholic Teaching on the Human Race* (Maryknoll, N. Y.: Maryknoll Publications, 1961). A philosophy built on God's all-embracing love for the totality of mankind.

Leonard, J. T., *Theology and Race Relations* (Milwaukee: Bruce, 1963). Extensive study of moral issues involved in race relations. Not only treats of discrimination, but also examines protest and reform techniques.

McManus, E. P., *Studies in Race Relations* (Baltimore: Josephite Press, 1961). Discusses nature of prejudice and morality of discrimination and segregation.

O'Neill, J. E., *Catholic Case Against Segregation* (New York: Macmillan, 1961). Effect of segregation in both North and South.

Senser, R., *A Primer on Interracial Justice* (Baltimore: Helicon, 1962). Basic problems treated succinctly and well by Catholic specialist.

Washington, J. R., *Black Religion: The Negro and Christianity in the United States* (Boston: Beacon Press, 1964). Critical both of the conduct of Negro Christianity and white Christianity in the current struggle. The author holds that neither is really an adequate example of true Christian faith.

Special Problems

Abrams, C., *Forbidden Neighbors: A Study of Prejudice in Housing* (New York: Harper, 1955). The broad pattern of xenophobic discrimination, including religion, national origin, and race as reasons for rejection.

Ginzberg, E., *The Negro Potential* (New York: Columbia University Press, 1956). Emphasizes the tremendous possibilities of Negro advances, given the proper opportunities.

King, M. L., *Stride Toward Freedom. The Montgomery Story* (New York:

Harper, 1958). Rev. Martin Luther King tells how the example of Gandhi influenced him in his inspired leadership of his people.

Laurenti, L., *Property Values and Race* (Berkeley and Los Angeles: University of California Press, 1960). Extensive surveys show the complexity of the problem of racial in-migration and property values, with indications that they tend to remain stable under these conditions.

McEntire, D., *Residence and Race* (Berkeley and Los Angeles: University of California Press, 1960). Report of Commission on Race and Housing, prepared by its research director.

Norgren, P. H., and Hill, S. E., *Toward Fair Employment* (New York: Columbia University Press, 1964). History of fair-employment laws and a plea for federal action in this area.

Record, W., *Race and Radicalism* (Ithaca, N. Y.: Cornell University Press, 1964). Documents the almost total failure of the Communist Party to influence the policies of the NAACP.

Wilner, D. M., and others, *Human Relations in Interracial Housing* (Minneapolis: University of Minnesota Press, 1955). Study of effects of various patterns of interracial housing.

Liberal Southern Viewpoint

Ashmore, H. S., *An Epitaph For Dixie* (New York: Norton, 1958). Little Rock editor discusses problems of integration.

Cash, W. J., *The Mind of the South* (New York: Knopf, 1941). Classic analysis of basic Southern attitudes on race matters.

Norris, H., ed., *We Dissent* (New York: St. Martin's Press, 1962). Prominent Southern spokesmen dissent from racism and segregation.

Rowan, C., *Go South to Sorrow* (New York: Random House, 1957). A Northern Negro reporter visits the South and learns how his people are treated there.

Sources of Tension

Booker, S., *Black Man's America* (Englewood Cliffs, N. J.: Prentice-Hall, 1964). A strong voice of dissent in the Negro community, claiming that the real leadership is generally not known to the white public. Hence we are in danger of misjudging problems and solutions.

Hentoff, N., *The New Equality* (New York: Viking, 1964). Strong presentation of deep-seated Negro resentments and the need for immediate and basic reforms.

Lincoln, C. E., *The Black Muslims in America* (Boston: Beacon Press, 1961). Description of Negro radicalism and its origin and probable trends.

Silberman, C. E., *Crisis in Black and White* (New York: Random House, 1964). Wide-ranging and hard-hitting study of the racial crisis.

Westin, A. F., ed., *Freedom Now! The Civil Rights Struggle in America* (New York: Basic Books, 1964). Sources of the civil-rights struggle and its morality, moods, reasoning, and strategy, with top names in the Negro and white community as contributors to the symposium.

Young, W. M., *To Be Equal* (New York: McGraw-Hill, 1964). The Negro seeks opportunity to get better jobs, education, and housing. The author is executive director of the National Urban League.

List No. 13. FARM PROBLEMS

Selected works for Chapter XVI.

Baer, U. J., *Letters to an American Farmer* (Des Moines, Iowa: National Catholic Rural Life Conference, 1956). A rural pastor writes to a friend on the problems of the day. Emphasis upon secularism.

Benedict, M. R., *Can We Solve the Farm Problem?* (New York: Twentieth Century Fund, 1955). Historical study of farm problems and policies, with some recommendations for future handling of surpluses.

Bowen, E. R., *The Cooperative Road to Abundance* (New York: Abelard, 1953). Balanced treatment of the co-operative movement by an author with more than twenty-five years of experience in this area.

Cochrane, W. W., *Farm Prices: Myth and Reality* (Minneapolis: University of Minnesota Press, 1958). Cogent analysis of the core of the farm problem.

Higbee, F., *Farms and Farmers in an Urban Age* (New York: Twentieth Century Fund, 1963). Description of the farm problem in the United States and the major lines of solutions proposed.

Mighell, R. L., *American Agriculture: Its Structure and Place in the Economy* (New York: Wiley, 1955). Strong plea for family farms, arguing that they are economically efficient as well as socially desirable.

Schultz, T. W., *Economic Organization of Agriculture* (New York: McGraw-Hill, 1953). Factual and comprehensive survey of new problems and developments in American farming.

Shotwell, L., *The Harvesters: The Story of the Migrant* (Garden City, N. Y.: Doubleday, 1961). Graphic description of the plight of migrant workers in the U. S.

Soth, L., *Farm Trouble* (Princeton, N. J.: Princeton University Press, 1957). Considers an excess number of marginal farms as the root of the farm problem. Would solve this problem by government aids to get marginal farmers off the land.

List No. 14. Social Principles in Action

Material for Chapter XVII.

Abell, A. I., *American Catholicism and Social Action* (Garden City, N. Y.: Hanover House, 1960). Begins with the conclusion of the Civil War and ends in 1950. A carefully documented study on the beginnings of Catholic social action here and its flourishing under Monsignor John A. Ryan.

Cardijn, J., *Laymen Into Action* (London: Chapman, 1964). Compact observations on lay apostolate by the founder of Jocism.

Geaney, D. J., O.S.A., *You Are Not Your Own* (London: Chapman, 1958). The lay apostolate of the YCW variety, with emphasis upon penetration of environment with Christian principles.

Houtart, F., *The Challenge to Change* (New York: Sheed, 1964). Noted Belgian priest sociologist examines problems confronting the twentieth-century Church.

Marx, P. B., *Life and Work of Virgil Michel* (Washington, D. C.: Catholic

University Press, 1957). Biography of a leader in a still too little understood aspect of social action. Emphasizes religious motivation that must underlie the full practice of justice and charity.

Meyer, B. F., M.M., *Lend Me Your Hands* (Chicago: Fides, 1955). The Christian Family Movement as a means of exercising the social apostolate. Appeal for new techniques to meet modern problems.

Montcheuil, Y. De, *A Guide for Social Action* (Chicago: Fides, 1954). Emphasizes the need for spiritual motivation for any program of social renovation.

Priest and Worker: the Autobiography of Henri Perrin (New York: Holt, Rinehart, and Winston, 1964). Valuable for its insights into the priest-worker movement, and the problems faced by the French clergy in seeking to win over the workers.

Quigley, M., and Connors, E. M., *Catholic Action in Practice* (New York: Random House, 1963). Catholic action in the youth, education, family-life, and international areas of the apostolate.

Retif, L., and Retif, A., *The Church's Mission in the World* (New York: Hawthorn, 1962). Although written from a French viewpoint, the book offers a mature and sophisticated study of the relevance of Christian teaching to the changed modern world.

Thorman, D. J., *The Emerging Layman* (Garden City, N. Y.: Doubleday, 1962). The dynamic role of the laity in the Catholic Church, U.S.A., as they confront the major social problems of our time.

Ward, L. R., *Catholic Life, U.S.A.* (St. Louis: Herder, 1959). Description of a dozen or so of the most active and promising lay movements in the United States.

Wilmes, A. F., and Martin, C. J., eds., *Liturgy and the Social Order* (Elsberry, Mo.: National Liturgical Conference, 1956). These papers represent a major step forward in the efforts to bind the liturgical and social-action movements.

INDEX OF AUTHORITATIVE STATEMENTS

Quebec Hierarchy, on labor unions, 167; on living wage, 198; on strikes, 169

Racial problems, 313 ff
Religion, and economic life, 21 ff; and race, 313 ff; and social reform, 42, 358 ff
Resources, sharing of, 299 ff
Retreats, spiritual, 359
Revolution, rejected, 368
Right to work, 164, 167 f
Right-to-work laws, 168
Rights, to association, 43; basic, 315, 317 f; basis of, 38; enumerated, 38; to living wage, 194 ff; in society, 45; under communism, 101, 104; to work, 163
Rural, see Agriculture

St. Pius X, on lay apostolate, 364
St. Thomas Aquinas, on the common good, 68; see also General Index
Science and spiritual values, 361
Security, conditions of, 222 f; and property, 243, 249
Segregation, effects of, 317; morality of, 316 f
Self-financing, corporate, 146
Seminarians, and social problems, 363
Slums, effect of, 221 f
Small business, value of, 249 f
Social action, by clergy, 362 f; by laity, 364 ff; need for, 368 f
Social charity, 68 ff
Social education, 365 ff
Social insurance, 198, 222 f; for farmers, 339
Socialism, 87 ff, 277; and religion, 89
Socialization, 43 ff
Social justice, 64 ff; and the Church, 221; defined, 67; demands of, 64 f; and housing, 221; and income distribution, 143 f; and living wage, 195 f; practice of, 66 f; and social order, 125; and the state, 66; and union security, 168; and wages, 65, 200 f; and wealth distribution, 248
Social legislation, 275 ff
Social order, 24; explained, 124 ff
Social problem, see Social question
Social progress, and human relations, 147 f; need for, 46 f
Social question, 3 ff; and the clergy, 362 ff; current status, 7 f; and the laity, 364 ff; moral aspects of, 23 f; nature of, 23 f; and religion, 23 f, 358 ff
Social reform, and the Church, 358 ff; and the clergy, 362 ff; and the laity, 364 ff
Social responsibility, of farmers, 340

Social security, 223 f; see also Social Insurance
Society, civil, 269 ff; differences in, 40; fundamental institutions of, 8; and the individual, 42; and growth in social relationships, 43 ff; and man, 41, 43, 66 f; private, 43; purpose of, 38 f, 66 f; and slums, 222; under communism, 101; under socialism, 88; unity of, 39; world, 293 f, 296; see also State
Sovereignty, 294
Spiritual values, in economic life, 358 ff; on farms, 340, 341
State, 269 ff; abuses affecting, 4 f, 84 f; authority in, 269 f; and the Church, 269 f; and common good, 66 f; duties in, 273 ff; and economic life, 43 f, 270 f; and employment, 245; excessive authority of, 89 f; and family needs, 218; function of, 4 f, 41, 84, 269 ff; and housing, 221 f; and human rights, 272 f; and labor unions, 165 f; and living wage, 196 ff; and nationalization, 275; nature of, 269 ff; and private enterprise, 87, 275; and private societies, 43; and property, 245; purpose of, 42; rights of, 293; and rural needs, 338; and social legislation, 275 f; and social order, 125, 129; and society, 41; and strikes, 168; subsidiary function of, 130; and taxes, 245 f; under communism, 101
Statism, 89 f
Strikes, 166, 168; conditions for, 169
Subsidiarity, 130
Supernaturalism, misguided, 360

Taxation, 245 ff; and farmers, 338 f
Technical assistance, 300 f, 366
Technology, 199 f; approved, 45 f, 47; effects of, 8 f; limitations of, 45 f; see also Automation
Totalitarianism, condemned, 89 f

Underdeveloped countries, 298 ff
Unemployment, 200 ff; and automation, 199 f
United Nations, 297
Unions, see Labor unions
United States, segregation in, 315 ff
Usury, and the Church, 3

Vatican Council II, on Church social teaching, 26; on citizens' duties, 273 f; on human dignity, 40; on labor unions, 167; on lay apostolate, 369; on man's social nature, 41; on property, 244; on public authority, 269; on public owner-

GENERAL INDEX

Abell, A. I., on Catholic social action, 409
Abrams, C., on housing prejudice, 407
Adler, M. J., on capitalism, 391
Advertising, fraudulent, 74
Age, of workers, 173
Aged, medical problems of, 231 f
Agriculture, 341 ff; child labor in, 236; and the Church, 341 ff; and cultural values, 346 ff; economic problems of, 352 ff; and the family, 342 ff; federal aid for, 353 f; and human values, 347 f; John XXIII on, 355 f; labor problems in, 349 ff; markets in, 353 f; migratory labor in, 349 ff; moral values in, 342 ff; prices in, 344 f; social problems of, 343 ff; Soviet, 113 f; surpluses in, 353 ff; see also Farms
Ahmann, M. H., on National Conference on Religion and Race, 407
Alexander, R. J., on Latin American communism, 396
Allen, F. L., on business abuses, 384; on New Deal, 384
Allen, R. L., on Soviet Economic Warfare, 394
Almond, G., on communist appeals, 392
Almsgiving, 82, 259
America, recommended, 387
A.F.L.-C.I.O., 77
Annals of the American Academy of Political and Social Science, recommended, 387
Antitrust, 266
Apathy, political, 283
Apostolate, of clergy, 375 f; lay, 376 ff
Aquinas, St. Thomas, see St. Thomas Aquinas
Arbitration, compulsory, 186
Asher, R. E., on UN in Europe, 405
Ashmore, H. S., on integration, 408
Association, right of, 52, 56 f
Auerbach, M. M., on conservatism, 390
Autarky, 311
Authoritarianism, 98 f
Automation, effects of, 19, 209 f; and living wage, 209
Avarice, 61
Ave Maria, recommended, 387

Baer, U. J., on farm life, 409
Bagdikian, B. H., on poverty, 402

Bakke, E. W., and others, on unions, 398
Barbash, J., on local unions, 399; on labor movement, U.S.A., 399
Barghoorn, F. C., on propaganda, 394
Barnard, C. I., on executive leadership, 397; on human relations, 397
Barnett, A. D., on China's foreign policy, 394
Bauer, P. T., on economic development, 406
Bauer, R. A., on Soviet life, 393
Beirne, J. A., on policy for American labor, 399
Bell, D., ed., on extremism in U. S., 404
Bellarmine, R., on consent of governed, 279
Benedict, M. R., on farm problems, 409
Bereday, G., and others, on Soviet school system, 393
Berle, A. A., on capitalist revolution, 402; on modern corporation, 402
Berliner, J. S., on Soviet economic aid, 394
Berman, H. J., on Soviet legal system, 393
Bernstein, I., on labor arbitration, 399
Beyer, G. H., on housing, 401
Big business, need for, 266; and social justice, 161; trends toward, 261 f; see also Business
Birth control, 307
Black Death, 13
Blaisdell, D. C., on pressure groups, 403
Blum, M. L., on industrial psychology, 397
Blumenthal, W. M., on codetermination, 398
Booker, S., on leadership in Negro community, 408
Boulding, K. E., on economic policy, 386
Bouscaren, A., on communist techniques, 396
Bowen, E. R., on co-operatives, 409
Boycott, 187
Braun, K., on collective bargaining, 399
Brimmell, J. H., on communism in Southeast Asia, 394 f
Brink, W., on racial problems, 406
Broderick, F. L., biography of Monsignor Ryan, 386
Brown, E. C., on labor law, 401